EGYPTIAN MYSTERIES Vol. 3:
Shetaut Hemu
The Priests and Priestesses of Ancient Egypt

"House of God (Temple) Priests and Priestesses"
A Guidebook for Priests and Priestesses of Shetaut Neter
and the Organization of the Modern Neterian Temple

Cruzian Mystic Books
P.O. Box 570459
Miami, Florida, 33257
(305) 378-5432 Fax: (305) 378-6253

©2004 By Reginald Muata Ashby

All rights reserved. No part of this book may be used or reproduced in any manner whatsoever without written permission (address above) except in the case of brief quotations embodied in critical articles and reviews. All inquiries may be addressed to the address above.

The author is available for group lectures and individual counseling. For further information contact the publisher.

Ashby, Muata
EGYPTIAN MYSTERIES Vol. 3: Shetaut Hemu, The Priests and Priestesses of Ancient Egypt.
ISBN: 1-884564-53-4

Library of Congress Cataloging in Publication Data

1- Ancient Egyptian Religion, 2- African Philosophy, 3- Mysticism .

Sema Institute of Yoga
Cruzian Mystic Books and Music

www.Egyptianyoga.com

Table of Contents

DEDICATION 8

Preface: Where is Ancient Egypt, When did it Exist and Who Were the Ancient Egyptians? 9

Where is Egypt? 9
The Term Kamit and the Origins of the Ancient Egyptians 10
When Was Neterian Religion Practiced in Ancient Times? 11
Early Beginnings: The First Religion in Human History 11
The Far Reaching Implications of the New Evidence Concerning the Sphinx and Other New Archeological Evidence in Egypt and the Rest of Africa 12

Foreword: The Importance of Ancient Egyptian Religion and Philosophy to the World 18

Impact of Ancient Egyptian Religion on present day religions, philosophies and world culture 20
Originators of Culture and Civilization abroad and the Study of the Stars 23

Overture: Who Was the Founder of Neterianism and What is the Lineage of the Neterian Teaching? 28

Khepri and the Creation Myth 29

Introduction: Who is Qualified to be an Initiate of Shetaut Neter and be taught the Spiritual Philosophy of Shetaut Neter and Who is Qualified to Become a Priest or Priestess of Shetaut Neter? 33

What does it mean to live by truth? What does it mean to face the truth? 35
Fitness to Join the Neterian Clergy 39

Chapter 1: The Power of the Priesthood in the Old Kingdom Era and the Downfall of Ancient Egyptian Culture due to the Deterioration of the Clergy, Caused by Attacks from Asiatic and European Countries and Western Religions 45

Respect and Support of the Priests and Priestesses in the Ancient Period 46
Egypt in the Early Late Period: A Nation in Decline 48
The Government Organizational Structure in Kamit During The New Kingdom Period 50
The Sixth Century B.C.E. Social and Political Upheaval in Ancient Egypt 51
Minimization of the clergy and the Decline of Society: A Nation in Decline 53
The Neterian clergy and the control over the Pharaoh (King or Queen) and the Governance of society 57
Early Christian and Roman-Christian Conquest Periods and the Closing of Egyptian Temples 63
The Muslim Movement and the Closing of the Ancient Egyptian Temples 67
Islamic Views on the Polytheists Including the Ancient Egyptian and Hindu religions 69

Chapter 2: The Fundamental Principles of Ancient Egyptian Religion for the Hemu Neter (Clergy of Shetaut Neter) 74

Neterianism (Ancient Egyptian Religion) may be condensed into four teachings. 74
Neterian Great Truths 74

The Spiritual Culture and the Purpose of Life: Shetaut Neter 76
Who is Neter in Kamitan Religion? 77
Neter and the Neteru 77
The Neteru 77
   The Neteru and Their Temples 78
   The Anunian Tradition 80
   The Memphite Tradition 81
   The Memphite Tradition 82
   The Theban Tradition 83
   The Goddess Tradition 84
   The Aton Tradition 86
The General Principles of Shetaut Neter 87

Introduction to Egyptian Yoga 88

Choosing a Sema Spiritual discipline as a Support for the Spiritual Tradition and Culture 92
   Tjef Neteru Sema Paut Ritual Postures of Enlightenment 95
   Summary of The Great Truths and the Shedy Paths to their Realization 95
   Summary of The Great Truths and the Shedy Paths to their Realization 96
Chapter 3- The Ancient Neterian Temple 97
The Purpose of the Neterian Temple 97
   The Stages of African Religion 99
   The Tutelary Deity 101
   Ancient Egyptian (Neterian Temple) Flag 101
Chapter 4: The Benefits and Immeasurable Joys of Being the Priests and Priestesses ... 104
Chapter 5: The Designations of the Clergy of Shetaut Neter, Their Functions and Spiritual Disciplines 109
   The Specialized Disciplines and Education of the Hm and Hmt 110
   Specialization of the Hm and Hmt in Ancient times 111
   Choosing a Spiritual Tradition 112
Clergy Choosing an Area for Selfless Service as a Support for the Spiritual Tradition and Society, and Choosing a Tutelary Divinity 112
   The Organizational Structure of a Typical Ancient Egyptian Temple Clergy 114
   The Hmt Neter - High Priestess – Tends to the needs of the Divinity – Oversees Temple 122
   Male and Female Service in the Temple 123
   The Sma - Takes care of the Clothing, ornaments and offerings at the Altar 126
   The Urshy – Watches over the Image and those who Meditate upon it 126
   Shmai Neter - Divine Musicians - The Music Discipline 126
   Dua Neter – Divine Adorers 126
   Above: a priest offers Incense and Libations The Sbai – Spiritual Preceptor and the Unra ... 127
Chapter 6: Duties of the Servants of God 130
   Left: Egyptian man and woman-(tomb of Papyri) 18th Dynasty displaying the naturalistic style (as people really appeared) in ancient times. 130
What Does a Servant of God Actually Do? 131
   Mysteries of the Gods and Goddesses and the Work of the Neterian Clergy 134
   Myth and Dreams and the Work of the Neterian Clergy 135
   Basic Duties of the Priests and Priestesses 136
   Opening the Mouth 136

Daily, Monthly and Annual Disciplines, Festivals, Rituals of Shetaut Neter 141
The Main Temple Mystery Rituals 142
The Main Temple Mystery Rituals 143
Opening the Temple and the Daily Worship Program 143
Ritual of the Carrying of The Divine Boat 147
Ritual of the Dawn of the New Year at the Temple of Hetheru 149
The Wisdom Discipline 151
Maintaining The Neterian Library 152
Below: Relief of an Ancient Egyptian Scribe Sacred Scriptures of Ancient Egypt and the Duty of the Clergy 152
Sacred Scriptures of Ancient Egypt and the Duty of the Clergy 153
The Medu Neter Of Neterian Culture 154
Hekau, Medu Neter and Shetitu 156
Ancient Egyptian Theater and Music 160
What do the Priests and Priestesses Teach and How do They Teach It? 167
What do the Priests and Priestesses Teach and How do They Teach It? 168
The Glorious Duty 170
Special Meditation Discipline of the Priests and Priestesses of Shetaut Neter 171

Chapter 7: Qualifications of the Clergy and Admonition to Priests and Priestesses for Righteous Conduct 175

Chapter 7: Qualifications of the Clergy and Admonition to Priests and Priestesses for Righteous Conduct 176

Admonition to Priests and Priestesses from the Ptolemaic Period 177
Admonition to part-time Priests and Priestesses (Unut) from the Ptolemaic Period 178
Guarding Against Impatience, Self Willed Nature and Irreverent Attitude 179
What is the Role of the King or Queen? 183
The Concept of Maat as the Foundation of the Neterian Priesthood 183
The Lifestyle of Priests and Priestesses and their Service to God and Society 188
Shaved Hair, Baldness and the Philosophy of Nothingness of the Ancient Egyptian Priests and Priestesses 188
Marriage, Sexuality and Celibacy for Neterian Priests and Priestesses 191
Neterianism and Sexual Misconduct. 194
Vegetarianism, Celibacy and Self-Control of the Neterian Clergy 196
Faithfulness to the Tradition 200

Chapter 8: The Sebait Curriculum- Education For the Clergy in Ancient Egypt 204
Mentoring System 205
The Higher and the Lower Mysteries 206
Levels of Initiation of the Neterian Priests and Priestesses 212

Chapter 9: Cultural, Historical, Political and Social Concerns for the Neterian Clergy in the 21st Century 214
Shetaut Neter and other Spiritual Traditions 215
Identity, Race, and the Neterian Clergy 216

    The Struggle for Survival 217
    Culture, the Spiritual Practice and the Name 218
    Interactions Between Neterians and Orthodox Religions Practitioners 219
    Forced Conversion 222
    Social and Political Perspectives for the 21st Century 224
    Challenges for Neterian Priests and Priestesses in the 21st Century 226
    CONCLUSION 227
Chapter 10: Pledging One's Life to The Temple 230
    Pledging One's Life to The Temple: The Creed of the Rekhyt 231
    The Concept of Guru and The Concept of Seba 233
    Priestess is Mother, Priest is Father 235
    The Ritual of Initiation 236
INDEX 243
Other Books by Sebai Muata Ashby 252
Other Books Sebai Muata Ashby 253
Music Based on the Prt M Hru and other Kemetic Texts 260

Who is Sebai Muata Abhaya Ashby D.D. Ph. D.?

Priest, Author, lecturer, poet, philosopher, musician, publisher, counselor and spiritual preceptor and founder of the Sema Institute-Temple of Aset, Muata Ashby was born in Brooklyn, New York City, and grew up in the Caribbean. His family is from Puerto Rico and Barbados. Displaying an interest in ancient civilizations and the Humanities, Sebai Maa began studies in the area of religion and philosophy and achieved doctorates in these areas while at the same time he began to collect his research into what would later become several books on the subject of the origins of Yoga Philosophy and practice in ancient Africa (Ancient Egypt) and also the origins of Christian Mysticism in Ancient Egypt.

Sebai Maa (Muata Abhaya Ashby) holds a Doctor of Philosophy Degree in Religion, and a Doctor of Divinity Degree in Holistic Health. He is also a Pastoral Counselor and Teacher of Yoga Philosophy and Discipline. Dr. Ashby received his Doctor of Divinity Degree from and is an adjunct faculty member of the American Institute of Holistic Theology. Dr. Ashby is a certified as a PREP Relationship Counselor. Dr. Ashby has been an independent researcher and practitioner of Egyptian Yoga, Indian Yoga, Chinese Yoga, Buddhism and mystical psychology as well as Christian Mysticism. Dr. Ashby has engaged in Post Graduate research in advanced Jnana, Bhakti and Kundalini Yogas at the Yoga Research Foundation. He has extensively studied mystical religious traditions from around the world and is an accomplished lecturer, musician, artist, poet, screenwriter, playwright and author of over 25 books on Kamitan yoga and spiritual philosophy. He is an Ordained Minister and Spiritual Counselor and also the founder the Sema Institute, a non-profit organization dedicated to spreading the wisdom of Yoga and the Ancient Egyptian mystical traditions. Further, he is the spiritual leader and head priest of the Per Aset or Temple of Aset, based in Miami, Florida. Thus, as a scholar, Dr. Muata Ashby is a teacher, lecturer and researcher. However, as a spiritual leader, his title is *Sebai*, which means Spiritual Preceptor. Sebai Dr. Ashby began his research into the spiritual philosophy of Ancient Africa (Egypt) and India and noticed correlations in the culture and arts of the two countries. This was the catalyst for a successful book series on the subject called "Egyptian Yoga". Now he has created a series of musical compositions which explore this unique area of music from ancient Egypt and its connection to world music.

Who is Hemt Neter Dr. Karen Vijaya Clarke-Ashby(Dja)?

Karen Clarke-Ashby (Seba Dja) is a Kamitan (Kamitan) priestess, and an independent researcher, practitioner and teacher of Sema (Smai) Tawi (Kamitan) and Indian Integral Yoga Systems, a Doctor of Veterinary Medicine, a Pastoral Spiritual Counselor, a Pastoral Health and Nutrition Counselor, and a Sema (Smai) Tawi Life-style Consultant." Dr. Ashby has engaged in post-graduate research in advanced Jnana, Bhakti, Karma, Raja and Kundalini Yogas at the Sema Institute of Yoga and Yoga Research Foundation, and has also worked extensively with her husband and spiritual partner, Dr. Muata Ashby, author of the Egyptian Yoga Book Series, editing many of these books, as well as studying, writing and lecturing in the area of Kamitan Yoga and Spirituality. She is a certified Tjef Neteru Sema Paut (Kamitan Yoga Exercise system) and Indian Hatha Yoga Exercise instructor, the Coordinator and Instructor for the Level 1 Teacher Certification Tjef Neteru Sema Training programs, and a teacher of health and stress management applications of the Yoga / Sema Tawi systems for modern society, based on the Kamitan and/or Indian yogic principles. Also, she is the co-author of "The Egyptian Yoga Exercise Workout Book," a contributing author for "The Kamitan Diet, Food for Body, Mind and Soul," author of the soon to be released, "Yoga Mystic Metaphors for Enlightenment."

Hotep -Peace be with you! Seba Muata Ashby & Karen Ashby

DEDICATION

To the *Hemu of Kamit*

"How happy are they {priests & priestesses} who celebrate Your Majesty, oh great God, and who do not cease serving Your Temple! Those {priests & priestesses} who elevate Your power, exalt Your grandeur, and fill their heart with You.... Those {priests & priestesses} who go on Your path, and come on Your water, and are concerned with Your Majesty's plans! Those {priests & priestesses} who adore Your spirit with paeans[1] intended for deities, and who pronounce Your ritual.... Those {priests & priestesses} who conduct the regular service and the festival service, free of ignorance.... You who tread the path of Ra in his Temple; who keep watch in His home, conducting His festivals and presenting offerings, without cease: enter in peace, leave in peace, go happily! For life is in His hand, health is in His grip, and all goodly things are there where He is: there are the dishes that lie on His table, there is the food of those who eat His offerings! There is no ill or misfortune for those {priests & priestesses} who live on His goods; there is no damnation for those {priests & priestesses} who serve Him, for His care extends to the sky and His security to the earth: His protection is greater than that of all (other) deities."

-Inscription at the Temple of Edfu

Preface: Where is Ancient Egypt, When did it Exist and Who Were the Ancient Egyptians?

Where is Egypt?

Below: Egypt is located in the northeastern corner of the African Continent.

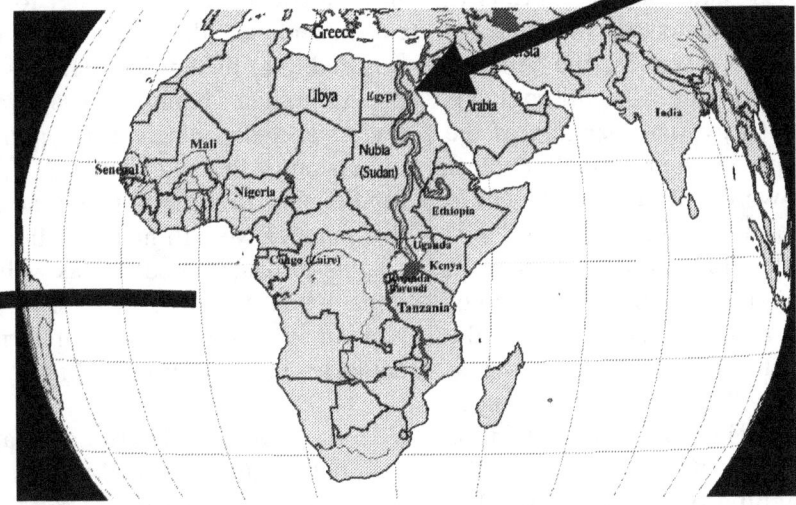

Below left: A map of North East Africa showing the location of the land of Ta-Meri or Kamit, also known as Ancient Egypt and South of it is located the land which in modern times is called Sudan.

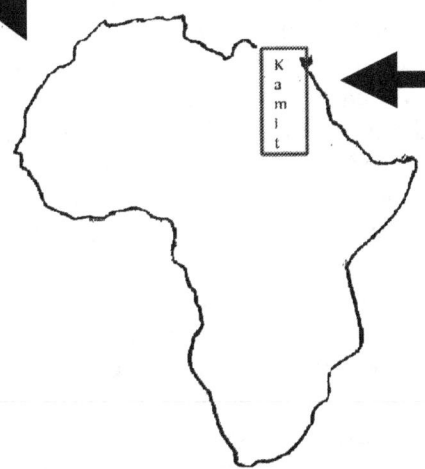

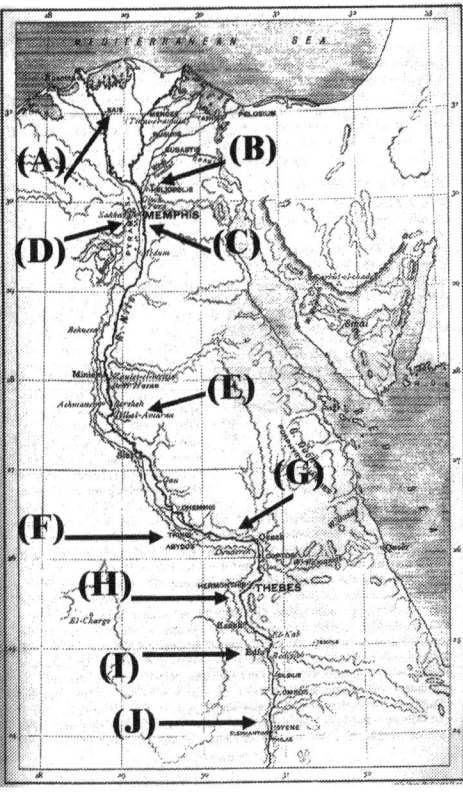

Figure: right- The Land of Ancient Egypt-Nile Valley

The main ancient cities wherein the theology of the Ancient Egyptian Religion was developed were: A- Sais (Temple of Net), B- Anu (Heliopolis- Temple of Ra), C-Men-nefer or Hetkaptah (Memphis, Temple of Ptah), and D- Sakkara (Pyramid Texts), E- Akhet-Aton (City of Akhnaton, Temple of Aton), F- Abdu (Temple of Asar), G- Iunet (Denderah) (Temple of Hetheru), H- Waset (Thebes, Temple of Amun), I- Djebu (Edfu) (Temple of Heru), J- Pilak (Philae) (Temple of Aset). The cities wherein the theology of the Trinity of Asar-Aset-Heru was developed were Anu, Abydos, Pilak (Philae), Iunet (Denderah) and Djebu (Edfu).

The Term Kamit and the Origins of the Ancient Egyptians

The Ancient Egyptians were the inhabitants of the land located in the northeastern corner of the continent of Africa they called Qamit. They came there from the south, the land later known as Kash or Kush. The terms "Kush" and "Sudan" all refer to "black land." In the same manner we find that the name of Egypt which was used by the Ancient Egyptians also means "black land." The hieroglyphs below reveal the Ancient Egyptian meaning of the words related to the name of their land. It is clear that the meaning of the word Qamit is equivalent to the word Kush as far as they relate to "black land" and that they also refer to a differentiation in geographical location, i.e. Kush is the "black land of the south" and Qamit is the "black land of the north." Both terms denote the primary quality that defines Africa, "black" or "Blackness" (referring to the land and its people). The quality of blackness and the consonantal sound of K or Q as well as the reference to the land are all aspects of commonality between the Ancient Kushitic and Kamitan terms.

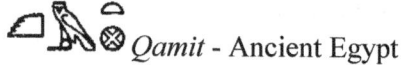*Qamit* - Ancient Egypt

*Qamit* - blackness – black

*Qamit* - literature of Ancient Egypt – scriptures

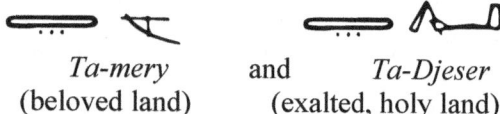*Qamiu* or variant, - Ancient Egyptians-people of the black land. Qamit is also referred to as:

Ta-mery   and   *Ta-Djeser*
(beloved land)   (exalted, holy land)

The Two Lands of Egypt

In Chapter 4[2] and Chapter 17[3] of the Ancient Egyptian mystical text, the *Prt m Hru, The Ancient Egyptian Book of Enlightenment*, more commonly known as the *Book of the Dead*, the term "Sema (Smai) Tawi" is used. It means "Union of the two lands of Egypt." The two lands refers to the two main districts of the country, North and South, and in a mystical sense they refer to the gods Heru (the north) and Set (the south land), who are elsewhere referred to as the spiritual Higher Self and lower self of a human being, respectively. In order to understand the Ancient Egyptians, we must also understand their origins in Nubia and their relationship to the Nubians (ancient Ethiopians). In this manner we will have a full grasp of the African origins of Kamitan culture as well as fathom the full impact that it had on the rest of Africa through the Nubian kingdoms, which in turn influenced other countries in the interior of Africa.

> "Our people originated at the base
> of the mountain of the Moon, at the origin of the
> Nile river where the god Hapi dwells."
> -The Ancient Egyptian tradition.

The Ancient Egyptians themselves said that their ancestors originated in the interior of Africa, the place known as the source of the Nile. The land they were referring to is up-river, in the area of modern day Africa that is today occupied by the countries Uganda and southern Sudan. The Nile River, which flows down to the Mediterranean Sea, originates in a mountainous region from which several tributary rivers flow to make one main watercourse known as the Nile River. The mountains in this region have such an elevation that even though they are located close to the equator, one may experience not only extremely low temperatures, but extreme weather conditions as well. This topography is ideal for promoting rains at particular times of the year. The interaction between the mountains and the winds, and the attendant atmospheric conditions which develop annually, are the key to what causes the production of snow. Then the snow melts forming streams, which then coalesce into rivers, which in turn nourish the entire region. Thus it is not surprising that this region, which includes Tanzania, would have been the place where the remains of the oldest known human being were discovered.

---

[2] Commonly referred to as Chapter 17
[3] Commonly referred to as Chapter 176

When Was Neterian Religion Practiced in Ancient Times?

Chronology of Ancient Egyptian Religion
Based on Confirmed Archeological Dating of artifacts and Monuments[4]

Major Cultural-Theological Developments

c. 10,000 B.C.E. Neolithic – period
c. 10,500 B.C.E.-7,000 B.C.E. Creation of the Great Sphinx Modern archeological accepted dates – Sphinx means Hor-m-akhet or Heru (Horus) in the horizon. This means that the King is one with the Spirit, Ra as an enlightened person possessing an animal aspect (lion) and illuminated intellect. Anunian Theology – Ra
c. 10,000 B.C.E.-5,500 B.C.E. The Sky GOD- Realm of Light-Day – NETER Androgynous – All-encompassing –Absolute, Nameless Being, later identified with Ra-Herakhti (Sphinx)
>7,000 B.C.E. Kamitan Myth and Theology present in architecture
5500+ B.C.E. to 600 A.C.E. Amun -Ra - Ptah (Horus) – Amenit - Rai – Sekhmet (male and female Trinity-Complementary Opposites)
5500+ B.C.E. Memphite Theology – Ptah
5500+ B.C.E. Hermopolitan Theology- Djehuti
5500+ B.C.E. The Asarian Resurrection Theology - Asar[RA2]
5500+B.C.E. The Goddess Principle- Theology, Isis-Hathor-Net-Mut-Sekhmet-Buto
5500 B.C.E. (Dynasty 1) Beginning of the Dynastic Period (Unification of Upper and Lower Egypt)
5000 B.C.E. (5th Dynasty) Pyramid Texts - Egyptian Book of Coming Forth By Day - 42 Precepts of MAAT and codification of the Pre-Dynastic theologies (Pre-Dynastic period: 10,000 B.C.E.-5,500 B.C.E.)
4950 B.C.E. Neolithic – Fayum
4241 B.C.E. The Pharaonic (royal) calendar based on the Sothic system (star Sirius) was in use.
3000 B.C.E. Wisdom Texts-Precepts of Ptahotep, Instructions of Ani, Instructions of Amenemope, Etc.
2040 B.C.E.-1786 B.C.E. Coffin Texts
1800 B.C.E.-Theban Theology - Amun
1570 B.C.E.-Books of Coming Forth By Day (Book of the Dead)
1353 B.C.E. Non-dualist Philosophy from the Pre-Dynastic period was redefined by Akhenaton.
712-657 B.C.E. The Nubian Dynasty

Early Beginnings: The First Religion in Human History

Shetaut Neter[5] is the Ancient Egyptian Religion and Philosophy. Ancient Egypt was the first and most ancient civilization to create a religious system that was complete with all three stages of religion, as well as an advanced spiritual philosophy of righteousness for social and spiritual order, called Maat Philosophy, that also had secular dimensions. Several Temple systems were developed in Kamit; they were all related. The later Jewish, Christian and Muslim religions drew from Ancient Egyptian religion in order to create their religions, ironically enough, only to later repudiate the source from whence they originated. In any case, the Great Sphinx remains the oldest known religious monument in history that denotes high culture and civilization as well. Ancient Egypt and Kash (Kush) produced the oldest religious systems and their contact with the rest of the world led to the proliferation of advanced religion and spiritual philosophy. People who were practicing simple animism, shamanism, nature based religions and witchcraft were elevated through Ancient Egyptian religion to the level of not only understanding the

---

[4] For more details see the Book *African Origins of Civilization, Religion and Yoga Spirituality and Ethics Philosophy* by Sebai Muata Ashby
[5] For more details see the Book *Egyptian Mysteries Volume 1.* by Sebai Muata Ashby

nature of the Supreme Being, but also attaining salvation from the miseries of life through the effective discovery of that Transcendental Being, not as an untouchable aloof Spirit, but as the very essence of all that exists.

The Far Reaching Implications of the New Evidence Concerning the Sphinx and Other New Archeological Evidence in Egypt and the Rest of Africa

In the last 20 years of the 20th century, traditional Egyptologists, non-traditional Egyptologists, archeologists and others have been taking note of recent studies performed on the Ancient Egyptian Sphinx and Pyramids which sit at Giza, in Egypt. Beginning with such students of Ancient Egyptian culture and architecture as R. A. Schwaller de Lubicz in the 1950's, and most recently, John Anthony West, with his book *Serpent In the Sky*, many researchers have used modern technology to study the ancient Sphinx monument and their discoveries have startled the world....to the extent it has be promulgated, which has been limited, due to the far reaching implications for rewriting the entire history of humanity. They now understand that the erosion damage on the Sphinx could not have occurred after the period 10,000 B.C.E. - 7,000 B.C.E. because this was the last period in which there would have been enough rainfall in the area to cause such damage. This means that most of the damage which the Sphinx displays, which would have taken thousands of years to occur, would have happened prior to that time (10,000 B.C.E.).

Below: Sphinx rump and Sphinx enclosure show detail of the water damage (vertical damage).

The following evidences must also be taken into account when examining the geology of the Sphinx and the Giza plateau.

> - The surrounding Sphinx Temple architecture is similarly affected.
> - Astronomical evidence agrees with the geological findings.
> - Ancient Egyptian historical documents concur with the new evidence.
> - The Sphinx Temple Architecture matches the architecture of other buildings in other parts of the country.

It is important to understand that what we have in the Sphinx is not just a monument now dated as the earliest monument in history (based on irrefutable geological evidence). Its existence signifies the earliest practice not only of high-art and architecture, but it is also the first monumental statue in history dedicated to religion. This massive project including the Sphinx and its attendant Temple required intensive planning and engineering skill. Despite its deteriorated state, the Sphinx stands not only as the most ancient mystical symbol in known human history, but also as the most ancient architectural monument, and a testament to the presence of Ancient African (Egyptian) culture in the earliest period of antiquity. Further, this means that while the two other emerging civilizations of antiquity (Sumer and Indus) were in their Neolithic period (characterized by the development of agriculture, pottery and the making of polished stone implements), Ancient Egypt had already achieved mastery over monumental art, architecture and religion as an adjunct to social order philosophy, as the Sphinx is a symbol of the Pharaoh (leader and upholder of Maat-order, justice and truth) as the god Heru. The iconography of the Sphinx is typical of that which is seen throughout Ancient Egyptian history and signals the achievement of a culture of high morals, which governs the entire civilization up until the Persian and Greek conquest.

> "The water erosion of the Sphinx is to history what the convertibility of matter into energy is to physics."
> -John Anthony West *Serpent In the Sky*

The findings related to the Sphinx have been confirmed by seismographic tests[6] as well as examination of the water damage on the structures related to the Sphinx and the Sphinx Temple, as compared to the rest of the structures surrounding it which display the typical decay due to wind and sand. It has been conclusively found that the Sphinx and its adjacent structures (Sphinx Temple) were built in a different era and that the surrounding structures do not display the water damage. Therefore, the wind and sand damaged structures belong to the Dynastic Era and the Sphinx belongs to the Pre-Dynastic Era. Therefore, the evidence supporting the older dating of the Sphinx is well founded and confirmed.

These new evidences constitute a momentous discovery on the order of the discernment of the Ancient Egyptian Hieroglyphic text. It requires an opening up of the closely held chronologies and timelines of ancient cultures for revision, thereby allowing for the deeper study of the human experience on this earth and making the discovery of our collective past glory possible. Thus, it is clear to see that the problem in assigning dates to events in Ancient Egypt arises when there is an unwillingness to let go of closely held notions based on biblical based assumptions, and biased information that is accepted as truth and passed on from one generation of orthodox Egyptologists to the next generation, rather than on authentic scholarship (constant search for truth). This deficiency led to the exclusion of the ancient historical writings of Ancient Egypt (*Palermo Stone, Royal Tablets*

---

[6] *Traveler's Key to Ancient Egypt*, John Anthony West

at Abydos, Royal Papyrus of Turin, the *Dynastic List* of Merndjehuti- Manetho). However, now, with the irrefutable evidence of the antiquity of the Sphinx, the carbon dating of the Great Pyramid and the excavations at Abdu (Greek-Abydos) and Nekhen (Greek-Hierakonpolis), the mounting archeological evidence and the loosening grip of Western scholars in the field of Egyptology, it is no longer possible to ignore the far reaching implications of the Ancient Egyptian historical documents.

A Long History

For a period spanning over 10,000 years the Neterian religion served the society of ancient Kamit. It is hard to comprehend the vastness of time that is encompassed by Ancient Egyptian culture, religion and philosophy. Yet the evidence is there to be seen by all. It has been collected and presented in the book *African Origins of Civilization, Religion and Yoga Philosophy.* That volume will serve as the historical record for the Neterian religion and as record of its legacy to all humanity. It serves as the basis or foundation for the work contained in all the other books in this series that have been created to elucidate on the teachings and traditions, as well as the disciplines of the varied Neterian religious traditions.

The book *African Origins of Civilization, Religion and Yoga Philosophy,* and the other volumes on the specific traditions detail the philosophies and disciplines that should be practiced by those who want to follow the path of Hm or Hmt, to be practitioners of the Shetaut Neter religion and builders of the Neterian faith worldwide.

Above: The Giza Pyramid Complex-with Great Pyramid.

New Evidence from the Great Pyramid

Newly refined radio carbon tests on organic material found in recent years in the Great Pyramid have shown that it "was built at least 374 years earlier" than previously thought (*Egypt: Child of Africa,* Ivan Van Sertima 1994). The oldest radiocarbon dating of the organic material in the Great Pyramid yielded a date of 3,809 B.C.E. Further, there is evidence that the lower section of the Great Pyramid is older than the upper parts.

While the date when the stone to create the Great Pyramid was originally cut apparently cannot as yet be dated with available instruments, tests performed on 16 samples of organic materials such as charcoal, discovered in the Great Pyramid in Giza, Egypt, by a prominent orthodox Egyptologist (Mark Lehner), showed that the Pyramid was in use as early as 3,809 B.C.E. So on this evidence alone the chronologies given for the age of the Great Pyramid by traditional Egyptology as belonging to the reign of Pharaoh Khephren (Cheops) of 2551 B.C.E.- 2528 B.C.E. are simply untenable and must be revised forthwith. While momentous in and of itself, the evidence of the Sphinx fits into the larger scheme of scientific evidences which are unraveling the mysteries of history, and leads us to the understanding of life in ancient Northeast Africa as a high point in human cultural achievement, which was attained in Ancient Egypt and later spread out to the rest of the world.

Below: The Great Pyramid-new radio-carbon dating: older than 3,809 B.C.E. A-older section, B-newer section

Who Were the Ancient Egyptians?

The Kamitan people (Ancient Egyptians) left records of their own origins and their relationships to other peoples; they also left pictorial renditions of themselves. All of those records allow us to see and understand where they came from, what they looked like and what they thought about other peoples from other countries and cultures.

Pictorial Evidence of the African Origins of Ancient Egyptian Culture and Civilization from Ancient Egyptian Records.

From the Tomb of Rameses III: The four branches of mankind, according to the Ancient Egyptians: A- Egyptian as seen by himself, B- Indo-European, C- Other Africans, D- Semites (Middle Easterners) (1194-1163 B.C.E.). [7]

In ancient times Ethiopia and Egypt were strongly related. In fact, Ethiopia was the birthplace of the early Egyptians and also, according to Herodotus, the Indians as well. They appeared the same to him at the time of his travels through those countries. Thus, the picture shows that the Ancient Egyptians looked no different from other Africans.

The followings texts from Greek classical writers who visited Egypt support the pictorial evidences presented above and also support the Ancient Egyptian legend of being originally Ethiopians who migrated to North-East Africa from further south.

Historical evidence proves that Ethiopia-Nubia already had Kingdoms at least 300 years before the first Kingdom-Pharaoh of Egypt.

> "Ancient Egypt was a colony of Nubia - Ethiopia. ...Asar having been the leader of the colony..."

> "And upon his return to Greece, they gathered around and asked, "tell us about this great land of the Blacks called Ethiopia." And Herodotus said, "There are two great Ethiopian nations, one in Sind (India) and the other in Egypt."
> **-Recorded by** Diodorus **(Greek historian 100 B.C.)**

---

[7] *Photo: From Cheikh Anta Diop's "Civilisation ou Barbarie", Courtesy of Présence Africaine.*

Diodorus Siculus (Greek Historian) writes in the time of Augustus (first century B.C.):

"Now the Ethiopians, as historians relate, were the first of all men and the proofs of this statement, they say, are manifest. For that they did not come into their land as immigrants from abroad but were the natives of it and so justly bear the name of autochthones **(sprung from the soil itself)**, is, they maintain, conceded by practically all men..."

"They also say that the Egyptians are colonists sent out by the Ethiopians, Asar having been the leader of the colony. For, speaking generally, what is now Egypt, they maintain, was not land, but sea, when in the beginning the universe was being formed; afterwards, however, as the Nile during the times of its inundation carried down the mud from Ethiopia, land was gradually built up from the deposit...And the larger parts of the customs of the Egyptians are, they hold, Ethiopian, the colonists still preserving their ancient manners. For instance, the belief that their kings are Gods, the very special attention which they pay to their burials, and many other matters of a similar nature, are Ethiopian practices, while the shapes of their statues and the forms of their letters are Ethiopian; for of the two kinds of writing which the Egyptians have, that which is known as popular **(demotic)** is learned by everyone, while that which is called sacred **(hieratic)**, is understood only by the priests of the Egyptians, who learnt it from their Fathers as one of the things which are not divulged, but among the Ethiopians, everyone uses these forms of letters. Furthermore, the orders of the priests, they maintain, have much the same position among both peoples; for all are clean who are engaged in the service of the gods, keeping themselves shaven, like the Ethiopian priests, and having the same dress and form of staff, which is shaped like a plough and is carried by their kings who wear high felt hats which end in a knob in the top and are circled by the serpents which they call asps; and this symbol appears to carry the thought that it will be the lot who shall dare to attack the king to encounter death-carrying stings. Many other things are told by them concerning their own antiquity and the colony which they sent out that became the Egyptians, but about this there is no special need of our writing anything."

The Ancient Egyptian texts state:

"Our people originated at the base of the mountain of the Moon, at the origin of the Nile river."

"KMT""Egypt", "Burnt", "Land of Blackness", "Land of the Burnt People."

Foreword: The Importance of Ancient Egyptian Religion and Philosophy to the World

Much has been written about Ancient Egyptian religion and history. In the latter half of the 20th century, several scholars showed two important and momentous historical human events, conclusively. First, it is now known and accepted that all human beings alive today are descendants of people who originated in Africa and who migrated to other parts of the world.[8] So all human beings are Africans! The second discovery is that Ancient Egyptian culture and civilization was created by native African people.[9] However, the implications of this fact have scarcely been explored. Since Ancient Egyptian culture and civilization is known to have influenced later cultures, coming down to the present day, there is a great possibility for gaining insight into the present day religions and philosophies through the study of Ancient Egyptian culture and civilization. This is important not only for understanding the deeper meaning of the present day religious traditions, but it is also important because studying Ancient Egypt really means studying Africa, and Ancient Egypt can lead humanity to both its common origins and spiritual roots, opening the opportunity to bring about unity, peace and spiritual Enlightenment for all human beings.

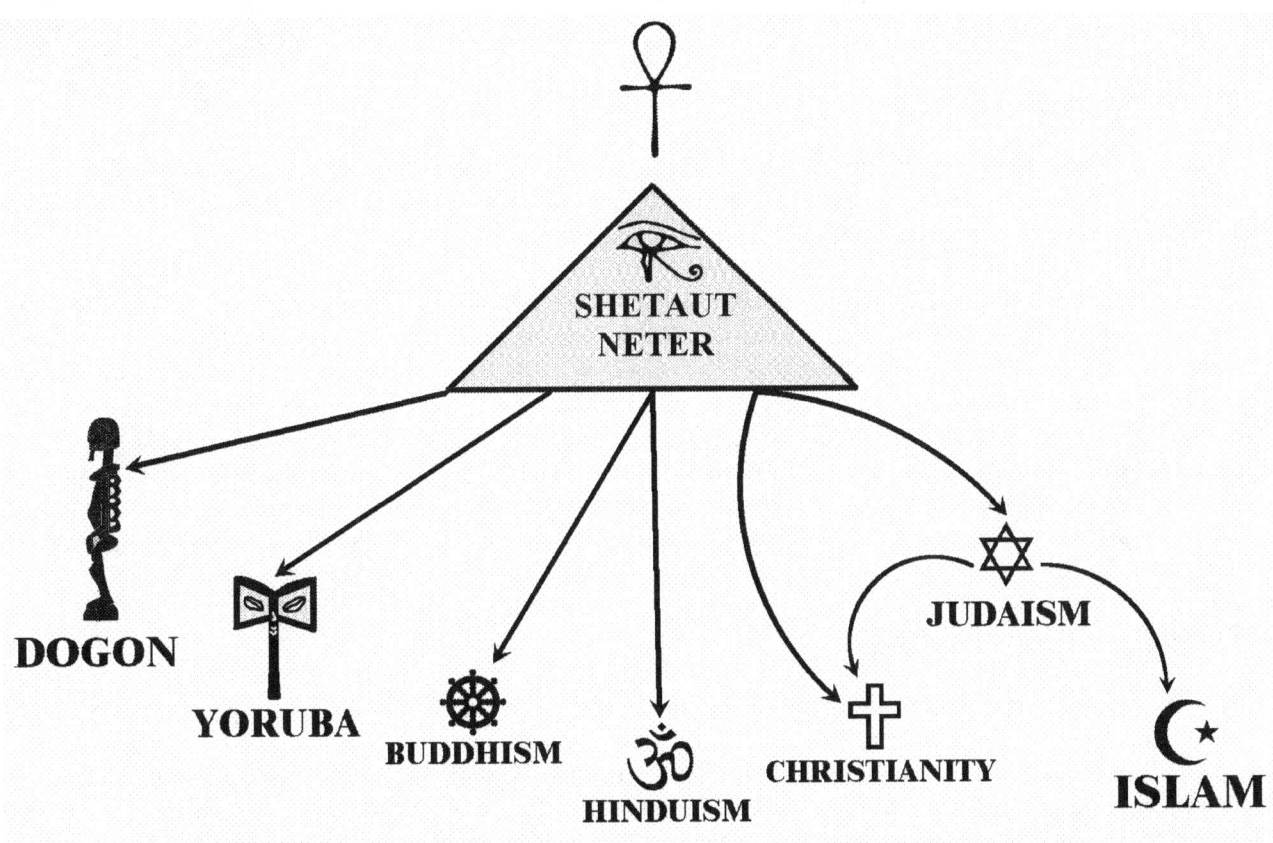

Why is it important to study Neterian Spirituality and Kamitan Culture? This section has been included to show the important contributions of Neterianism to the world. However, this also signifies an important responsibility for those who want to carry on the Neterian Tradition. The world has deviated from the original teaching. Those who tread the path of Hem (Ancient Egyptian clergy) must do so with the purpose of attaining Self-knowledge first and foremost, and secondly to elevate humanity by their example, teaching and good works.

---

[8] See the book *African Origins of Civilization*, Muata Ashby
[9] ibid

Impact of Ancient Egyptian Religion on present day religions, philosophies and world culture

Ancient Kamitan (Ancient Egyptian) culture and Philosophy were the most influential forces that helped to shape culture, philosophy and religion in ancient Africa; the effects of this influence are still evident in the present day African religions, world religions as well as in world philosophies. The ancient Egyptians created two main social factors that guided their culture. These were Maat philosophy to promote social order and justice, and Shetaut Neter religious philosophy, rituals and traditions. The ancient Egyptians had contact with the early Greeks, Hindus, Buddhists, Jews and Christians.[10] This contact influenced the development of the concept of the Hindu Trinity, Buddhist Iconography, Philosophy, and the Judeo-Christian-Islamic concepts of monotheism, salvation and resurrection.[11]

Influences on Greek Culture

Culture may be defined as all aspects of a group of people that denote their unique expression of their life. The most important factors of culture are philosophy and religion. These in turn influence other factors of culture, including architecture, laws, and general social values.

Ancient Egyptian culture spanned from 10,000 B.C.E. to 450 A.C.E. Through trade and social contact with Knossos (2,000-1,400 B.C.E.), the archaic Greek culture, and later contacts with Greek philosophers of the Greek classical period (700 B.C.E.-300 B.C.E.) such as Plato, Pythagoras and Thales, the Greeks adopted the framework of Ancient Egyptian religion, music, myth, medical science, law and other cultural factors as attested by classical Greek writers such as Herodotus and Plutarch. Western scholars regard classical Greek culture as the dawn of Western culture. Therefore, Western culture is based in part on ancient African culture. That influence is still evident today in the adoption of Greek architecture, which has been shown to be based on Ancient Egyptian models and some direct adoptions from Ancient Egyptian culture.

Influences on Western Culture

Most western scholars claim Greek culture as the origin of Western culture. Throughout history, many organizations in western culture have sought to associate themselves with ancient Egyptian culture, especially the *Shetaut Neter* (*Egyptian Mysteries*), to establish their legitimacy by showing a link to the ancient tradition. It is important to understand that the Egyptian Mysteries (Shetaut Neter) are not teachings originated by or controlled by organizations which in modern times refer to themselves as *fraternal orders, lodges, masons, freemasons, illuminati, Odd Fellows, Shriners, new world orders, Satanists, occultists,* or *psychics*. In fact, the organizations just mentioned have their origins in Western countries, and not in Africa, although they were influenced by the original Grand Temples of the Mystery teachings of Kamit (Ancient Egypt).

For example, the use of the pyramid on the reverse of the seal of the United States would seem to mean that the founding fathers of the United States had the idea of invoking the principles of the Kamitan (Ancient Egyptian) tradition in the founding of the new country (United States). However, upon close examination, the original philosophies associated with the symbols have been altered in many cases, leaving only the external idea of the symbol, sometimes with completely new and different ideologies

---

[10] For documented proofs see the book *African Origins of Civilization* by Sebai Muata Ashby
[11] ibid

attached to them. It was explained by the occultist and reputed expert in Masonic lore, Manly Hall, that many of the U.S. founding fathers were masons, and that they received assistance from masons in Europe to establish the United States for *"a peculiar and particular purpose known only to the initiated few."* Hall said that the seal was the signature of the masons, and that the unfinished pyramid symbolizes the task that the government has to accomplish. The Eagle is a representation of the Phoenix, which is the ancient Greek reinterpretation of the Kamitan (ancient African) Bennu bird, which is a symbol of the Kamitan god Ra and rebirth.

Other Kamitan symbols evident in the iconography of the United States include the Washington Monument, which is a reproduction of the Ancient Egyptian Obelisk, the Lincoln memorial, and Mount Rushmore. The latter two, which are important icons of the United States, were admittedly (by their creators) inspired by the Temple of Rameses II at Abu Simbel. Another important symbol is the pyramid on the face of the dollar bill, complete with capstone and All-Seeing Eye.

Some of the organizations mentioned above that profess to be the originators, descendants or authentic custodians of the Kamitan Mysteries have much to prove, since it is well established that those organizations have a recent origin by comparison. This is demonstrated easily by the records of modern encyclopedias, which are themselves produced by the same culture (Western) in question. Also, the regulations against the admittance of women that are endemic in most of the organizations mentioned above are a modern convention instituted by the impetus within the male dominated Western culture to exclude females from the pursuit of spiritual Enlightenment and social empowerment. These injunctions were foreign to the Mystery Systems of Ancient Africa in which women participated as equal partners, sometimes even holding positions that would today be referred to as "Grand Masters," or "Pontiffs."

> The Order of the Hospital of St. John of Jerusalem, or the Knights of Malta, for instance, originated as a crusading order in 1070. The first Grand Lodge of Freemasonry, probably the best known of the secret orders, was founded in London in 1717.
>
> Lodges and other secret orders are primarily men's organizations. Women may not join the Masons, Odd Fellows, or Shriners. There are, nevertheless, a number of women's societies associated with individual lodges. Perhaps the best known is the Order of the Eastern Star, founded in 1876. Its rituals are devised by Masons, and the organization is presided over by Masons. Men are allowed to join the Eastern Star.
>
> The secret orders have a great deal of ritual at their meetings. It is used to initiate members and to promote fellowship and religious and moral values. One may not simply join a society such as the Masons but must be elected to membership. Once initiated, a member may advance within the society in a series of stages called degrees. In one rite of Freemasonry, there are 32 degrees. Some lodges have eased their rules.
>
> The Sons of Norway, for instance, was founded in 1895 as a fraternal society to provide aid to members who were ill or who had lost someone through death. Like the secret orders, the Sons of Norway had membership requirements and secret rituals.
>
> A similar society, the Aid Association for Lutherans, was founded by Germans at Appleton, Wis., in 1899. [1]

Influences on Judeo-Christian Culture[12]

In the Jewish Holy Scriptures, the Old Testament, it is stated that the Jewish people (people who follow Judaism) emerged from Egypt with Moses as their leader and that "Moses was skilled in all the magic of the Egyptians." There are varied correlations that can be made between Ancient Egyptian religious

---

[12] See books *Mystical Journey from Jesus to Christ* and *African Origins of Civilization, Religion, Yoga and Ethics Philosophy* by Muata Ashby

traditions and rituals and those of the Jews. For example, the Jewish tradition originally describes God as the "Elohim" which is a general Hebrew term that is used in the Old Testament meaning any divine being, but more importantly, it is used frequently in reference to The God of the Israelites. Actually the term means Gods and Goddesses (plural), implying that divinity is multifaceted. The Jewish term Elohim is correlated to the Neterian (Ancient Egyptian Religion) term "Neter" which means "The God" or "Divinity" in general. Neter manifests as "neteru" or the "Gods and Goddesses."

The Jews developed a philosophy of a devil or a Satan as rival to God Almighty. Prior to that development there was no such model in ancient religions. Christianity later adopted that concept of a devil as they adopted the Old Testament as the starting point of their religion. The Ancient Egyptian God Set represents egoism, lower desires, chaos and negativity. Set is the Divinity that many scholars, including myself, believe that the early Jews confused, and used to develop their concept of Satan. Actually one of the names of Set is Setek or Sutek. "Setek" and "Satan" are very similar. This (Satan) was a new concept in spirituality that emerged with Judaism and a few other traditions, such as Zoroastrianism. Other Jewish traditions adopted from Ancient Egyptian culture include the tradition of three-fold daily worship from Anunian Theology of Ancient Egypt, the tradition of bathing the body of the deceased before burial, the idea of monotheism, and the Ten Commandments as well as several passages in the Bible that have been correlated to Ancient Egyptian sages such as the Wisdom of Amenemope.

In Christianity, there are several direct correlations to the Ancient Egyptian traditions. These adoptions are attested to by the early Christian writers and scholars, who admit the cooptation of the Ancient Egyptian and Greek symbols, traditions, and some philosophies, in order to attract the followers of Pagan traditions to the new religion, Christianity. While the correlations between Ancient Egyptian religion and Christianity are too numerous to include here, the most prominent ones will be briefly described. The Christians adopted the Ancient Egyptian winter solstice celebration of the birth of the Neterian god Heru on December 25th as the birthday of the Christian savior, Jesus. Other adoptions include the concept of the resurrection, the Eucharist, the cross, the Trinity, the Mother (Madonna) and Child iconography, the concept of anointing the Christ, the persecution of Jesus upon his birth, and the concept of Baptism. These are all fundamental Christian concepts and symbols still in use today, which were in existence previously in Ancient Egyptian/African religion; some still contain the original African-Neterian values.

Influences on other African Cultures[13]

Ancient Egyptian culture has also influenced other African cultures. In ancient times, the Ancient Egyptians were in contact with the Nubians, their southern neighbors, who carried on the Neterian traditions after the Christians had taken over the land of Egypt and stopped the practice of the Neterian religion. There was direct contact with the ancestors of the Nuba peoples, the Dogon and the Yoruba, who even today acknowledge the contributions of Ancient Egyptian culture and spirituality to their traditions. Most notably perhaps is the influence of Maat Philosophy. Maat philosophy is a system of beliefs, values and regulations that promote social order and justice for all members of society. Its modern expression in Africa is called "Ubuntu."

Influences on Eastern Culture[14]

Ancient Egyptian culture has also influenced the Eastern traditions. In ancient times, the empire of Ancient Egypt stretched from Northeast Africa to China and southern Europe. Some classical writers such as Herodotus state that the Ancient Egyptians, Nubians and Indians formed one whole group as opposed

---

[13] See book *African Origins of Civilization, Religion, Yoga and Ethics Philosophy* by Muata Ashby
[14] ibid

to separate cultures. Even today there are many Indians in India who revere the land of Africa as the source of their religion and divinities. While the correlations between Ancient Egyptian religion and Hinduism-Buddhism are too numerous to include here, the most prominent ones will be briefly described. The Hindus adopted the Ancient Egyptian theme of the persecution of the Divine incarnation upon his birth (Krishna in India, Heru in Kamit). The concept of the Hindu Trinity follows the Neterian Trinity almost exactly. There are several iconographies of the Hindu divinities that can be directly correlated to Kamitan divinities, along with their symbolic meaning and philosophical teaching. The practice of Yoga in India can be correlated to the practice of Yoga in ancient Egypt. Other correlations include the concept of Divine incarnation (avatarism), the primeval ocean, the divine lotus, and the sacred celestial river.

In ancient times (500 B.C.E.) there was direct contact between Buddhist priests and the priests of the Ancient Egyptian city known as Menefer (Memphis). Some Buddhist teachings can be correlated to Memphite (Menefer) Theology. Some of the most important teachings that developed in Buddhism which were already present in Memphite Theology or Neterianism in general include: The concepts of Enlightenment, nirvana, the divine lotus and the philosophy of Sakshin Buddhi. These fundamental Hindu and Buddhist concepts and symbols still in use today contain some of the original African-Neterian values.

Originators of Culture and Civilization abroad and the Study of the Stars

The Ancient Egyptian Priesthood as Originators of Greek Religion and Philosophy[15]

Ancient Greek culture and philosophy drew heavily from Ancient Egypt. The Greek classical writers such as Plutarch affirm the relationship. (Highlighted texts by Ashby)

> "This is also confirmed by the most learned of Greeks such as Solon, Thales, Plato, Eudoxus, Pythagoras, and as some say, even Lycurgus going to Egypt and conversing with the priests; of whom they say Euxodus was a hearer of **Chonuphis of Memphis (city in Ancient Egypt)**, Solon of **Sonchis of Sais (city in Ancient Egypt)**, and Pythagoras of **Oenuphis of Heliopolis (city in Ancient Egypt)**. Wherefore the last named, being, as is probable, more than ordinarily admired by the men, and they also by him imitated their symbolic and mysterious way of talking; obscuring his sentiments with dark riddles. For the greatest part of Pythagoric precepts fall nothing short of those sacred writings they call hieroglyphical..."[16]
> –Plutarch (Greek historian c. 46-120 A.C.E.) (Plutarch, Morals, 10)

"Democritus, on his part, visited the priest (in Egypt) five years to learn things related to astronomy." [Il Diogenes Laerce, Democritus, 3]

"..,for Eudoxus accompanied Plato this far: arrived at Heliopolis (Egypt), they established themselves here and both resided there thirteen years in the society of the priests: the fact is affirmed by several authors" [Strabo (XVII,1,29)]

Thales is recognized as the first Greek philosopher of ancient Greek history. His important association with the Ancient Egyptian priests fomented a movement among early Greeks to travel to Egypt to "complete their training" in matters of philosophy and culture.

---

[15] See the books *From Egypt to Greece* and *African Origins of Civilization, Religion, Yoga and Ethics Philosophy* by Muata Ashby
[16] Ancient Egyptian and Greek or Arabic: Djebu (Greek or Arabic= Edfu), Pilak (Greek or Arabic= Philae), Iunet (Greek or Arabic= Denderah), Abdu (Greek or Arabic= Abydos), Anu (Greek or Arabic= Heliopolis), Waset (Greek or Arabic= Diospolis (i.e., Thebes), Menefer (Greek or Arabic= Memphis), Zau (Greek or Arabic= Sais).

> "He (Thales) had no instructor, except when he went to Egypt and spent some time with the priests there...," [Diogenes Laertius, I. 2-29]
>
> ". . . **Thales of Milet made voyage to the priests and the astronomers of Egypt**, and according to his biographers, he seems to have **learned geometry from the Egyptians**. . ."
>
> [Diogenes Lierce, Thales, 43 and 24]

Greek Philosophy has been equated with the origin of Western civilization. Ancient Greek philosophers such as Thales (c. 634-546 B.C.E.) and Pythagoras (582?-500? B.C.E.) are thought by many to have originated and innovated the sciences of mathematics, medicine, astronomy, philosophy of metaphysics, etc. These disciplines of the early Greek philosophers had a major impact on the development of Western culture and religion. The version of Christianity (primary western religion) which was practiced in the Western and Eastern empires was developed primarily in Alexandria (Greek city in late period Egypt) and Greece, alongside Greek culture and the Greek language. However, upon closer review, the ancient writings of contemporary historians (during the time of the development of early Christianity) point to different sources of Greek Philosophy and Christianity, hence we are led to discover correlations in the earlier philosophy by tracing their origins to a common source in Ancient Egyptian religion.

There is evidence that shows how Ancient Egypt supported not only the education of the early Greek philosophers, who came to study in Egypt itself, but Egypt also supported the Egyptian Mystery Temples that were established in Greece. Some Egyptian pharaohs even sponsored or financed Temples abroad that taught mystical philosophy as well as other disciplines. One such effort was put forth by the Ancient Egyptian King, Amasis, who is known to have financed the reconstruction of the famous Temple of Delphi in Greece, which was burnt down in 548 B.C.E. The Greek oracle of Zeus at Dodona was the oldest and the one at Delphi, the most famous with the teaching of "Know Thyself." Herodotus records a Greek tradition that held that Dodona was founded from the Priesthood in Egyptian Thebes. Further, he asserts that an Egyptian who became king of Athens in 1558 B.C.E founded the oracle at Delos. This would be one of the earliest suggested dates for the existence of civilization in Greece, and it is being attributed here to an Ancient Egyptian origin by the Greeks themselves in their own myth and folklore. The connection to and dependence on Ancient Egypt for the creation of Greek culture is unmistakable and undeniable.

Thales was the first Greek philosopher of whom there is any mention in Greek history and therefore, he is sometimes called the "Father of Greek philosophy." Thales was known to have traveled to and studied the wisdom of Ancient Egypt. After studying in Egypt with the Sages of the Ancient Egyptian Temples he founded the Ionian school of natural philosophy which held that a single elementary matter, water, is the basis of all the transformations of nature. The similarity to the Ancient Egyptian Primeval Waters should be noted here. The ancient writings state that Thales visited Egypt and was initiated by the Egyptian priests into the Egyptian Mystery System and that during his time in Egypt he learned astronomy, surveying, engineering, and Egyptian Theology which would have certainly included the mystery teachings related to Asar (Osiris), Amun (Zeus) and Ptah (Hephaestus). Pythagoras was a native of Samos who traveled often to Egypt on the advice of Thales and received education there. He was introduced to each of the Egyptian priests of the major theologies which comprised the whole of the Egyptian religious system based on the Trinity principle (*Amen-Ra-Ptah*). Each of these legs of the Trinity were based in three Egyptian cities. These were *Anu* (Heliopolis of the Greeks) -Priesthood of Ra, *Menefer* (Memphis of the Greeks) -Priesthood of Ptah and in *Waset* (Thebes of the Greeks) -Priesthood of Amen (Amun) in Egypt.

The Priests and Priestesses of Ancient Egypt

Due to the immense impact that Pythagoras had on the whole of Ancient Greek religion and philosophy, it is important to examine the writings about him. Iamblichus, in the *Life of Pythagoras*, writes <u>*"Pythagoras met all the priests (Egyptian), learning from each what they knew ...and it is in these conditions that he passed twenty-two years in the Temples of Egypt... He returned to Greece to teach in a way perfectly similar to the documents by which he had been instructed in Egypt."*</u> Plutarch confirms this by saying: <u>*"Most of the precepts he taught he copied from the Egyptian hieroglyphic texts."*</u> Again, Plutarch also reports that not only did Thales and Pythagoras study under the Egyptian philosophers, but that Plato, Eudoxus, and Lycurgus did as well. Thales was instrumental in the early education of Pythagoras and also he encouraged Pythagoras to travel to Egypt for more training. Later Pythagoras became perhaps the most important philosopher of Greece; his achievements were attributed to his training in Egypt.

> "...Thales increased the reputation Pythagoras had already acquired, by communicating to him such disciplines as he was able to impart: and, apologizing for his old age, and the imbecility of his body, he **exhorted him to sail into Egypt, and associate with the Memphian and Diospolitan priests. For he confessed that his own reputation for wisdom, was derived from the instructions of these priests;** but that he was neither naturally, nor by exercise, endued with those excellent prerogatives, which were so visibly displayed in the person of Pythagoras. Thales, therefore, gladly announced to him, from all these circumstances, that he would become the wisest and most divine of all men, if he associated with these Egyptian priests." (Iamblichus, Life of Pythagoras, Chapter II)

In the late period of Ancient Egyptian history there were several Greeks who obtained entry into the Ancient Egyptian schools of philosophy. Their interaction with those schools and their priests and priestesses offers us valuable insight into how foreigners were treated by the Ancient Egyptian clergy. When the writings of Antiphon are consulted, the true fortitude and determination of Pythagoras come into focus.

> "He [Pythagoras] had three silver flagons[17] made and took them as **presents to each of the priests of Egypt**...While still young, so eager was he for knowledge, he left his own country and had himself initiated into all the mysteries and rites not only of Greece but also of foreign countries. Now he was in Egypt when Polycrates sent him a letter of introduction to Amasis; **he learnt the Egyptian language,** so we learn from Antiphon in his book *On Men of Outstanding Merit*""

Prior to being received by the Ancient Egyptians, Pythagoras studied other mystery systems and obtained references that led him to Amasis, and from Amasis to the priests. He did not go to them empty handed but with gifts, in the tradition of giving in order to receive. Porphyry (233-304 C.E.) records Pythagoras' journey in these terms:

> "Having been received by Amasis (king of Egypt, 568-526 B.C.E.), he obtained from him letters (of recommendation) to the priests of Heliopolis, who sent him to those of Memphis since they were older-which was, at heart, only a pretext. Then, for the same reasons, he was again sent from Memphis to the priests of Diospolis (i.e., Thebes). The latter, fearing the king and not daring to find false excuses (to exclude the newcomer from their sanctuary), thought they would rid themselves of him by forcing him to undergo very bad treatment and to carry out very difficult orders quite foreign to a Hellenic education. All that was calculated to drive him to despair so that he would give up his mission. But since he zealously executed all that was demanded of him, the priests ended by conceiving a great admiration for him, treating him respectfully and even

---

[17] **flag·on** (flăg/ən) *n.* **1.** A large vessel, usually of metal or pottery, with a handle and spout and often a lid, used for holding wine or other liquors.

allowing him to sacrifice to their deities, which until then had never been permitted to a foreigner."[18]

Another biographer and Egyptian initiate, Iamblichus, describes Pythagoras's time in Egypt as follows:

"[He] visited every holy place, full of great zeal.... admired and cherished by the priests and prophets with whom he associated. He learned everything most attentively, and neglected neither any oral instruction commended in his own time, nor anyone known for sagacity, nor any rite anywhere and at anytime honored. He also left no place unvisited where he thought he would find something exceptional. Hence, he visited all the priests, and benefited from the special wisdom of each. So he spent twenty-two years in the sanctuaries of Egypt."[19]

According to Diodorus, Plato visited Egypt in search of knowledge regarding "geometry and theology" and "priestly knowledge in general."[20] The geographer Strabo describes the pilgrimage of Plato and Eudoxus to Anu (Heliopolis) as follows:

"...at Heliopolis (sic) the houses of the priests and the schools of Plato and Eudoxus were pointed out to us; for Eudoxus went up to that place with Plato, and they both passed thirteen years with the priests, as is stated by some writers; for since these priests excelled in their knowledge of the heavenly bodies, albeit secretive and slow to impart it, Plato and Eudoxus prevailed upon them in time and by courting their favour to let them learn some of the principles of their doctrines; but the barbarians concealed most things. However, these men did teach them the fractions of the day and the night which, running over and above the three hundred and sixty-five days, fill out the time of the true year. But at that time the true year was unknown among the Greeks, as also many other things, until the later astrologers (i.e., astronomers) learned them from the men who had translated into Greek the records of the priests; and even to this day they learn their teachings, and likewise those of the Chaldaeans." [21]

These encounters confirm that the Ancient Egyptian priesthood was "slow" to accept students. The candidates were required to show persistence, diligence and patience in being admitted to the higher knowledge. Sometimes they were asked to remain for long periods of time without receiving any teaching, to see if they desire it truly or if they are just searching for a passing fancy. Seriousness, maturity and patience are essential qualities of a true aspirant that the priests and priestesses of Ancient Egypt demanded. However, purity was most important. An aspirant must exhibit purity of heart and virtuous nature, brightness of mind and full dedication to the teaching. That is the only way to succeed in understanding the advanced teaching.

Much is made of the people known as the Chaldaeans. The following passage provides insight into their identity and relationship to the Ancient Egyptian clergy.

According to the Egyptians, Diodorus reports, the Chaldaeans were *"a colony of their priests that Belus had transported on the Euphrates and organized on the model of the mother-caste, and this colony continues to cultivate the knowledge of the stars, knowledge that it brought from the homeland."* So it is that "Chaldean" formed the root of the Greek word for astrologer.[22]

---

[18] Porphyry, *Life of Pythagoras*, chap. 7.
[19] J. Dillon and J. Hershbell, trans., *Iamblichus, On the Pythagorean Way of Life: Text, Translation, and Notes,* Texts and Translation, Graeco-Roman Series II (Atlanta, 1991), 45 *(= De Vita Pythagorica,* chap. 4, §§ 18-ig)
[20] Murphy, *Diodorus,* 130 *(= Historical Library, 1,* chap. 98)..; and on geometry, see Hicks, *Diogenes Laertius, Vol. II* (Cambridge, Mass., 1950), 445 *(= Lives of Eminent Philosophers, IX,* chap. 34).
[21] H. L. Jones, trans., *The Geography of Strabo, Vol. VIII* (London and New York, 1932), 85 *(Geography, XVII,* chap. I), § 29).
[22] <u>*The African Origins of Civilization*</u>, Cheikh Anta Diop, 1974

Thus we are to understand that the Chaldaeans are just Egyptians. Ancient Greek theater had its origin in the mysteries of Dionysus. Upon investigation it is discovered that Dionysus is the Greek's name for the Ancient Egyptian god Asar (Osiris). The Greek writings attest to the fact the Dionysus was the same Osiris, brought into Greece from Egypt. The dates of the prominence of Dionysus coincide with the association of the first Greek philosophers of the Greek classical period with the Ancient Egyptian priests. The qualities of Dionysus are the same as those of the Egyptian Asar and the Temple mysteries including vegetation, death and resurrection, were also the same. The enactment of those mysteries constitutes the Egyptian "Theater" which was adopted by the Greeks and which was later developed by the Greek playwrights into other themes.[23]

> Born of the union of Zeus and a mortal, Semele, **Dionysos rose to prominence around the 6th century B.C. under many names and forms.** The principles of life and generation, as well as the cyclical life of vegetation (death and rebirth), are central to the worship of Dionysos: lord of the vine, but also god of the tree. He is often considered in reference to the fig tree, ivy (undying life), and all blossoming things -- symbols of life and vitality. His celebration is marked by the joy of his epiphany in the Spring, and the sorrow of his death or descent in the Winter. Dionysos also appears as a bull god, long considered an important symbol of fertility in the Ancient World. Other symbols that are associated with him include snakes, goats, lightening bolts, as well as moistness, madness and the phallus. Dionysos is typically followed by satyrs and maenads who participate in the music, wine, and dancing which make up an integral aspect of his mystery. Satyrs, or primitive, goat-like men, usually lurk in the shadows of the more primary maenads, or mad women, which typified Dionysian worship. These maenads, "the frenzied sanctified women who are devoted to the worship of Dionysos."(Harrison -401), are 'nurses' who look after and follow the infant Dionysos-- likely referring to the largely female following he inspired and the great Mother goddess he came from.[24]

The concepts of: life and generation, the bull, the cyclical life of vegetation (death and rebirth), vine, the tree, ivy (undying life), all blossoming things, life and vitality, celebration marked by the joy of his epiphany in the Spring, the sorrow of his death or descent in the Winter, moistness, madness and the phallus, music, wine, and dancing are all prominent aspects of the Ancient Egyptian Asarian (Osirian) mysteries.

Bibliography for Foreword

Cheikh Anta Diop, *Civilization or Barbarism*, Brooklyn, New York:
    Laurence Hill Books, 1991
Martin Bernal, *Black Athena: The Afroasiatic Roots of Classical Civilization,* New Brunswick, New Jersey:
    Rutgers University Press, 1987
Muata Ashby, *African Origins of Civilization, Religion, Yoga Mysticism and Ethics Philosophy.* Miami, Florida:
    Sema Publishing, 2002
Muata Ashby, *Egyptian Yoga: The Philosophy of Enlightenment.* Miami, Florida:
    Sema Publishing, 1995
Muata Ashby, *From Egypt To Greece.* Miami, Florida:
    Sema Publishing, 1998-2002
Muata Ashby, *Mystical Journey From Jesus to Christ.* Miami, Florida:
    Sema Publishing, 1998
Greek Mythology Link, created and maintained by Carlos Parada. Since 1997© 1993-2004
    http://homepage.mac.com/cparada/GML/index.html

---

[23] Origin of the Greek Theater by B. H. Stricker, Journal of Egyptian Archeology
[24] *Greek Mythology Link*, created and maintained by Carlos Parada. Since 1997© 1993-2004
http://homepage.mac.com/cparada/GML/index.html

Overture: Who Was the Founder of Neterianism and What is the Lineage of the Neterian Teaching?

One of the most important questions in life for followers of any religion is who started it? The next important question is what is the lineage of the spiritual teaching, that is, how was it transmitted down through history? In order to understand who founded Neterianism, the teaching of Shetaut Neter, we must also understand the origins of creation. In the sacred scriptures of Shetaut Neter we are told that Creation is a cycle. That is, that Creation occurs cyclically. God brings creation into existence and then dissolves it again.

ABOVE: LORD KHEPRI, FOUNDER OF NETERIANISM

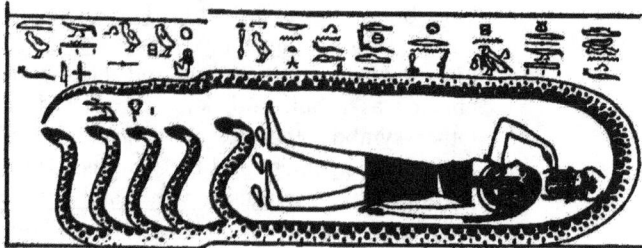

The Sun-god of night surrounded by the five-headed serpent of 'Many Faces'. On his head is the beetle of Khepri the rising sun of the following day.

The current cycle of Creation began around the year 36,000 B.C.E. In the beginning there was nothing more than a watery mass, a primeval ocean, called Nun. Nun is the body of Khepri. Prior to the creation, Khepri remained in a recumbent posture. He rested on the back of the great serpent *Asha-hrau* ("many faces"). From that Nun the Divine Spirit arose by stimulating Asha-hrau to move and churn the ocean. Then he named himself Khepri, Creator. Khepri called out his own name and *dchn* – vibrations were infused in the ocean and waves were formed. Just as there are many waves in the ocean with many shapes and sizes, the objects of the world came into being in the form of elements, Ra (fire), Shu (air-space), Tefnut (water), Geb (earth), Nut (ether). Everything in creation emanates from the Nun or primordial ocean, and expresses in the form of elements in succeeding levels of denseness. These elements also manifest in the form of the opposites of Creation (man-woman, up-down, white-black) which appear to be exclusive and separate from each other, but which are in reality complements to each other.

Khepri and the Creation Myth

Having created Creation, Khepri now sails the ocean, which has now become Creation itself, with his divinities, on the divine boat. Khepri-Ra and the *pauti,* Company of gods and goddesses, travels in the Boat of Millions of Years, which traverses the heavens, and thereby sustains creation through the wake of the boat that sends ripples (vibrations) throughout Creation.

Khepri congealed the Nun, his own body, into all the forms of Creation. The first spot that was congealed from the Nun is called *Benben*, the first place, the Ben-Ben dot, •, of Creation. That dot is the center point in the symbol of Khepr-Ra ☉. That dot is the very point at the top of the Pyramid *mr-* Obelisk, *tekhnu*. The pyramid-obelisk symbolizes the mound that formed from that initial spot. Khepri sat atop the hill of Creation and all solid ground took form underneath him.

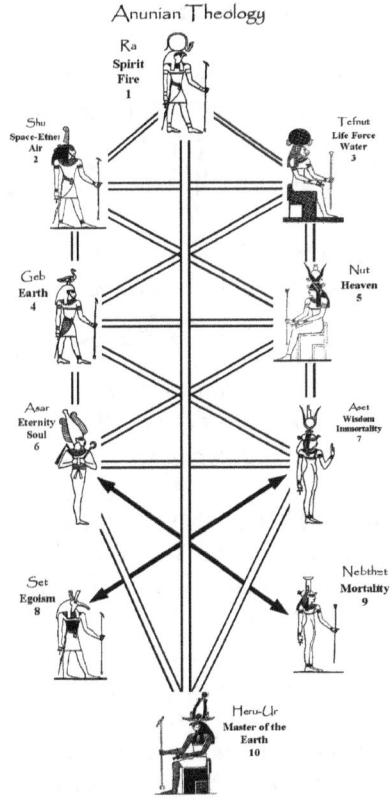

Khepri then bought forth Creation by emerging in a boat. The Nun waters lifted him and his boat up with his great arms. He brought nine divinities with him in that boat, lesser gods and goddesses, to help him sustain the Creation and lead human beings on the righteous path to life and spiritual enlightenment.

The act of "Sailing" signifies the motion in creation. Motion implies that events occur in the realm of time and space relative to each other, thus, the phenomenal universe comes into existence as a mass of moving essence we call the elements. Prior to this motion, there was the primeval state of being without any form and without existence in time or space. The gods and goddesses of the boat form the court of Kheper-Ra. As Ra, the Supreme Being governed the earth for many thousands of years. He created the world, the planets, the stars and the galaxies; he also created animals, as well as men and women. In the beginning, men and women revered the Divine, but after living for a very long time, they began to take Ra for granted. They became arrogant and vain. Ra sent his daughter, Hetheru, to punish them, but she forgot her way and became lost in the world. Then He left for his abode in heaven and gave the earthly throne to his son Shu, and daughter, Tefnut. After a long period of time, they turned over the throne to their children, Geb and Nut. After some time again, Geb and Nut gave the throne to their children, Asar and Aset, and so on in a line of succession throughout history, down to the Pharaohs of Kamit.

Lord Khepri manifests as Neberdjer, "All-encompassing Divinity." Aspirants are to say:

tu-a m shems n Neberdjer[26]
"I am a follower of Neberdjer

er sesh n Kheperu
in accordance with the writings of Lord Kheperu"

The Shetaut Neter "Mystery teachings" were originally given by the Creator, Khepri in his capacity as Creator, he is known as *Shetaut Kheperu,* "hidden Creator of forms." Lord Djehuti codified these Mystery teachings into the hieroglyphic texts. The teachings of Shetaut Neter or the Mysteries, given by Lord Khepri and codified by Lord Djehuti, was taken by Lord Asar who developed the *Shedy* or means to penetrate the mysteries. The disciplines of Shedy (study of philosophy, Divine Worship, Maat-right action and Meditation) were taught to Lady (goddess) Hetheru, Lady (goddess) Aset, and other divinities by Lord Djehuti. Djehuti, Asar, Aset, Hetheru taught the priests and priestesses the mysteries. Those teachings of Shetaut Neter and Shedy have come down through history in varied forms, sometimes openly and at others, in secrecy through initiates who have kept the teachings alive, and in latent form through traditions kept alive in varied spiritual traditions that have developed based on the Neterian teachings.

So Lord Khepri imparted his knowledge to the divinities, and especially to his son Djehuti. Thus, Lord Khepri, the Self Created Divinity, is the founder of Shetaut Neter. The codifier was his first main disciple, Djehuti. Djehuti has the body of a man and the head of an Ibis bird. He also has another form as a baboon. The teaching that Lord Khepri gave to Djehuti became known as *Shetitu* and it was conveyed through the *Medu Neter* (hieroglyphic texts).

"𝕸𝖊𝖉𝖚 𝖓𝖊𝖙𝖊𝖗"

The teachings of the Neterian Traditions are conveyed in the scriptures of the Neterian Traditions.

Above: Lord Djehuti imparted the teaching he learned from Khepri to goddess Hetheru (here in the form of a cow goddess). She became lost in the world and forgot her true identity. He showed her how to discover her true Self, how

---
[25] i am follower of Neberdjer... *Pert M Heru* Chap 4 (commonly 17)
[26] The Supreme Being, all-encompassing Divinity

to know herself and how to find her way back to heaven, to her father Ra. Here Djehuti is shown presenting to Hetheru, the healed right eye of Ra, her true essence.

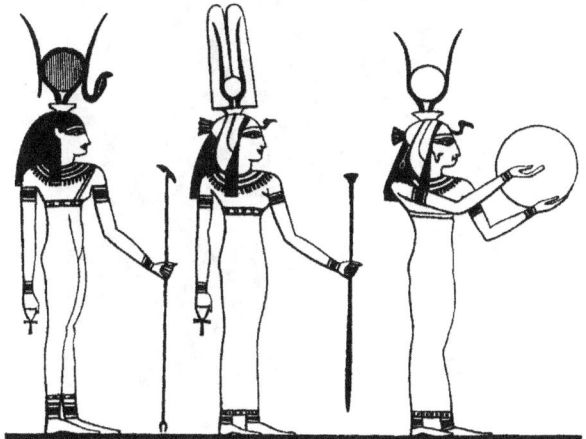

Above: Hetheru as Queen

Lord Khep-Ra knew that human beings needed guidance, so he sent his great grandchildren, Asar and Aset, to be teachers and role models for human beings on earth. Lord Djehuti also imparted the hidden knowledge of life to Aset and Asar, so that they would lead people on earth in a righteous manner, showing them the path of peace, prosperity and spiritual enlightenment. Asar and Aset established the Shetaut Neter, "Divine Mysteries," ritual worship and Ancient Egyptian religion. When human beings become too involved in the world they forget their true nature, and so the Temple,

Het Neter {House of the Divinity {God(dess)}-Temple}, was created, where the pressure of the world can be relieved, and an association with something other than the worldly perspective (i.e., with Divinity) can occur.

Temple of Aset, Egypt, Africa

Such a place and its teaching are needed so that the mind can become aware of higher possibilities and turn away from *umt-ab-* "mental dullness" due to *Khemn,* "ignorance," and be led to *Nehast* –"Resurrection, spiritual awakening," *Akhu,* "enlightenment" and so that human beings may become *Sheps-* "nobility, honor, venerableness, honored ancestors."

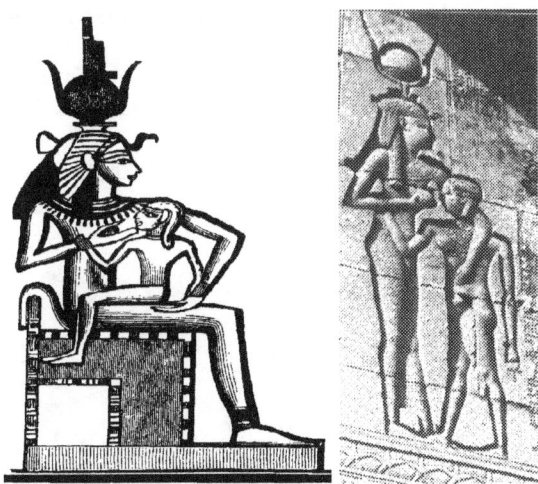

Above: *Aset nurses baby Heru*

So, Aset learned the Mystery teachings from Lord Djehuti. Aset is the ancient African prototype of the mother and child which is popular all over Africa, and also in Christian and Indian iconography with the birth of Jesus and Krishna, respectively. The mother is the first teacher. Aset not only raised Heru, but also initiated him into the mysteries of life and creation, with the teaching she learned from Djehuti and Khepri, in order to enlighten him and make him strong for the battle of life. Heru became a powerful initiate and became the model for all human beings who strive to master the lower forces of nature and to discover their higher essential nature.

Heru is the redeemer, the challenger, the one who stands up for his father, Asar, and liberates him from the imprisonment of death. Heru represents spiritual aspiration and success in the spiritual path. Heru reestablishes order after defeating the evil Set, and takes the throne of Kamit. In his form as Heru Behdet, Heru is a warrior. He fights for truth, justice and freedom for all.

Heru, the redeemer, the warrior, the greatest advocate of Asar (the soul) and triumphant aspirant is the one who leads the aspirant to the initiation hall. As seen above, Heru is often the one shown leading the aspirant by the hand, into the inner shrine. In rituals, the priest wears a Heru mask in the context of a ritual theatrical ceremony of the temple that is meant to awaken the glory of the Neterian teaching.

Introduction: Who is Qualified to be an Initiate of Shetaut Neter and be taught the Spiritual Philosophy of Shetaut Neter and Who is Qualified to Become a Priest or Priestess of Shetaut Neter?

The Priests and Priestesses of Ancient Egypt

Who is qualified to be taught the teaching?

People who are reasonably well adjusted in life (who can cope with reality without undue stress) are ready to and should face new challenges to their closely held notions. In that way a person grows, ultimately to leave behind all notions of worldly existence and eventually adopt the highest form of self-knowledge and spiritual enlightenment. That is the ideal of natural development. Spiritual teachers strive to find those who are mature and well adjusted since they are better equipped to tread the path of authentic spiritual life.

- A person who is mildly neurotic (prone to excessive anxiety and emotional upset) should also face challenges, but not beyond a level of stress that will incapacitate their basic level of cognitive function. Forcing a person to face realities they cannot agree with or adopt in such a way that they stop rational thought reflection about the subject will be a useless and possibly damaging process.
- A person who is borderline psychotic[27] or severely mentally afflicted will not be able to make good use of higher knowledge (particularly knowledge that relates to self-identity and spiritual evolution) and will likely develop more severe psychosis.[28]

In order to have learning and evolution, an ordinary person must experience some cognitive dissonance. When the dissonance is experienced there needs to be reflection on the new information; then there needs to be assimilation of that information. Then there must be accommodation of that information. This process constitutes adjusting and adapting to the challenges of life, but more importantly it is the process by which the spiritual teaching is adopted and through which the spiritual teaching is assimilated in a way that renders it "integrated" into the personality. Integration, from a spiritual perspective, means developing a higher vision, being transformed by the new knowledge and changed psychologically so as to in fact become a different personality.

Those people who are not fully committed to the path of new learning because it conflicts with their previously held knowledge are not good candidates for mystical spiritual philosophy and the priesthood in particular. They should be admonished to continue reflecting on their notions and continuously challenge them until they no longer hold sway over the personality. Their level of practice is historical study, study and practice of virtue, mental and physical purification, as well as devotional exercises. They should not be introduced to the higher spiritual philosophy. Their intellectual incapacity, irreverence and egoistic notions will preclude them from understanding the teaching and consequently they will distort it, denigrate it or otherwise excuse themselves for their failure to realize its true meaning and potential. They will neither transcend their egoistic notions nor overcome their mental complexes, and may even blame their failure on the teaching. Only when the error of previous knowledge is admitted can there be the hope to counteract it with new knowledge. If the willingness to admit insufficiencies or fallacies in previous knowledge is not present, the foundations of the new teaching (in this case Neterian spiritual philosophy) will not be fully adopted, and there will only be partial success in its adoption and practice. Consequently, since its practice and acceptance is partial, its full benefits and goal will not be achieved. People who are accustomed to following truth based on evidences are more qualified to tread the path of authentic spirituality. However, truth is not dependent on empirical evidences alone. Some forms of reality are perceived in the mind; they transcend ordinary physical reality. This is not faith, imagination or delusion. It comes from experiencing a higher reality. Only those with strong minds can accomplish that goal. Delusion, imagination and error occur in those whose minds are weak or beset with ignorant notions of spiritual reality (fanatics, those who hold son to egoistic previously held knowledge). An example of this are ideas such as *"When I die I will go to heaven or hell."* Such notions will color any transcendental experience and will thus render it contaminated with egoistic misunderstandings that reinforce the previously held knowledge. Keep in mind that in ancient

---

[27] **psy·chot·ic** (sī-kŏt′ĭk) *adj.* **1.** Of, relating to, or affected by psychosis. **--psy·chot·ic** *n.* A person affected by psychosis. [psych(osis) + -otic.] **--psy·chot/i·cal·ly** *adv.* American Heritage Dictionary
[28] **psy·cho·sis** (sī-kō′sĭs) *n., pl.* **psy·cho·ses** (-sēz). A severe mental disorder, with or without organic damage, characterized by derangement of personality and loss of contact with reality and causing deterioration of normal social functioning. American Heritage Dictionary

times the sages scarcely dealt with this issue in the magnitude of the present day. Most people in modern culture are besieged with the notions of the dominant cultures including secularism, theism (especially orthodox theism: Judaism, Christianity and Islam). Ordinary secular notions of life (pursuit of happiness, pleasure-seeking, wealth-building, etc.) require remedial work in the area of developing dispassion and detachment towards the objects and desires of the world in order to render the mind lucid to the fact that there is no ultimate and abiding happiness to be found in the world. Those notions of orthodox dogmatic religion force the necessity to implement extensive remedial work on history, right reasoning and psychological healing (from the damage done by guilt and fear) in order to qualify as an aspirant of mystical spiritual philosophy.

Those who think that true spiritual teaching is listening to a fire and brimstone sermon from a preacher are following a deluded notion of spirituality and will not succeed in the Mysteries. Those who feel that they must always be in a large group of people to worship the Divine in order to get a "spiritual feeling" are also deluded.

It should be clearly understood that all difficulties in listening and following truth stem from the presence of egoism, the dualistic way of seeing life through the personality and its desires caused by ignorance of the true Self which is in reality non-dual, immortal and transcendental. If that affliction (egoism) is alleviated, the capacity to adopt and integrate truth increases. Therefore, an egoistic person should be guided to practice the mystical disciplines of selfless service and divine worship. Service allows one to see the world beyond the little me (ego-self), to see the world is not about the little me, and that some day the little me will end. Divine worship allows one to feel love for something more than the little me, to love Spirit and to love the universe and all its contents (including all peoples, animals, planets, stars, etc.). That expansion purifies the heart and allows one to open the doors to truly engage the spiritual disciplines in an effective and successful manner, free from self-doubt, self-sabotage, feelings of inadequacy or other mental complexes.

What does it mean to live by truth? What does it mean to face the truth?

"I have not stopped my ears against the words of right and wrong (Maat)."
(From the 42 Precepts of Maat in the Prt M Hru (Ancient Egyptian Book of Coming Forth by Day)

A successful Neterian aspirant must learn the art of living by truth. This is one of the most important injunctions of Maat philosophy. Those who cannot face higher truth in order to leave behind their ignorant notions about life cannot attain spiritual enlightenment or function as reasonably well adjusted human beings in the ordinary sense of society or civilization. In order to become caught up in the illusions, desires and fears of human life, a person must overlook the truth. An example of this is the attitude towards death. Most people do not acknowledge their mortality even though they see others around them dying. So people live as if they are not going to die and consequently they do not take care to seek the deeper meaning of life and the afterlife. However, even if truth is acknowledged that does not mean that one can be immediately free from fear, anxiety or desire and their attendant entanglements and sufferings. That condition developed over lifetimes so it cannot be cured overnight. However it can be cured. A Neterian priest/priestess does not overlook the truth about life. He/She undergoes a specific training to face the truth. The ultimate reality of life is death, and after death there is potentially immortality, and in that realization there is supreme peace, power and freedom. In order to realize that highest of truths the practitioner must undergo a radical change in the attitude towards the world and their own existence. That is accomplished by living in accordance with greater and greater insights into the truth – of Self. There are two truths (Maati). There is the truth of time and space and the truth that transcends time and space. In order to realize the truth that transcends time and space (mortality) it is necessary to adopt a lifestyle governed by the precepts of Maat and the initiatic way of life of the Hemu (Priests and Priestesses).

Living by truth simply means adopting a way of live that is predicated upon the idea that reality is good and delusion is not. Most people live by their own deluded notions. They see the world through their own egoistic desires and convictions that they have acquired on their own throughout their life, have learned as children or through experiences in previous lives. When a person lives by their own ideals and desires it is called *Shems-ab* – "those who follow the desire of their egoistic heart-desire, greed, lust, personal wishes." This is explained in the ancient Egyptian proverb: *"There are two roads traveled by humankind, those who seek to live MAAT and those who seek to satisfy their animal passions."* The followers of the gods and goddesses go after the spiritual teaching and virtue. The followers of their own hearts go after their own desires, conceptions, and passions and support these through their own rationalizations and by shielding themselves from the words of truth. This in direct contradiction with the precept of Maat *"I have not stopped-up my ears against the words of right and wrong {Maat}."* The *shemsu-ab* are self-willed people who lack the capacity to *sedjm* {heed-listen and obey} the teaching because they have allowed their intellect to become dull, atrophied- *umet-ab* - "dull, dense, dull of heart."

The main obstacle to *shems-maat* (following the teachings, the truth) is *suga* – {"foolishness, helplessness, miserable, half-witted, immature nature"}. This word, *suga,* is derived from *sug-mes* – which means "suckling, baby, helpless child, etc.," and *sug-mit* – which means "foolish silly." Childishness prevents a person from giving up desires for worldly pleasures and worldly attainments, but also the egoistic childish notions are lingering complexes in the mind. Some examples are: lingering desire for worldly pleasures (relationships) or objects (cars, stereos, etc.) or lingering desires to experience worldly enjoyments (parties, travel, shows, physical ecstasies, etc.). Other complexes may be deeply held notions about how others will view them, if other will like or dislike them, how their physical appearance is accepted by others or their own self-concept or ideal about themselves, etc. There may be fear of embarrassment and also there may be the desire to be the one who is looked up to, revered, etc.

Following truth means letting go of childish, immature notions. Most people are unable to let closely held notions or sentimental ideas go in favor of higher truths, and yet that is what a child does when they leave toys behind in order to move into adulthood. However, as human beings go, most people who have become physically "adult" remain mentally childish in their ideas, prejudices and aspirations. Sometimes this occurs because they have been traumatized by their experiences and thus, they are unwilling to grow up and face the world since they see it as painful and stressful. Perhaps it is because they have no better way to follow; they have not been helped to maturate since their elders are also ignorant and worldly. That can happen when a society loses its way, when worldly values and desires become the goal of life. In those cases society itself shields itself from the truth of its incapacity, failures and disease. Such a society uses material wealth, cultural achievements (having a militarily or economically strong country) and social status symbols as smokescreens to hide the disappointment of life, the failure society and the bankruptcy of spiritual-moral development. In such a society money becomes the religion, greed becomes virtue, and pleasure seeking becomes the measure of success; but with every success the individual becomes more and more frustrated and empty, and this promotes the degradation of society as a whole.

In order to follow truth, there must be a mature willingness to face the errors of society and those of one's own life, as well as the will to recognize and follow a better way. Glossing over the truth with jokes, entertainments, rhetoric or other forms of self-delusion will ultimately delay or even stunt a person's ability to cognize the truth.

What the ancients were referring to as *stopping-up the ears against the words of right and wrong* is the same concept that present day psychologists call cognitive dissonance. *"Cognitive dissonance"* is when a person is unable to face the truth that conflicts with a previously held notion. Cognitive dissonance is a psychological phenomenon which refers to the discomfort felt at a discrepancy between what you already know or believe, and new information or interpretation. It therefore occurs when there is a need to accommodate new ideas, and it may be necessary for it to develop so that we become "open" to them.[29]

Cognitive dissonance is a necessary feature in life. Sometimes life offers shocking situations, the purpose of which is to show us that there is another way to look at life. Otherwise human beings would be forever stuck, and never grow and evolve. However, many people, unable to face the dissonance, seek to resist it or reinterpret it in a way that is favorable to the previous knowledge so that the previous knowledge does not have to be consciously abandoned. The immature or mentally atrophied reactions to cognitive dissonance will cause resistance to learning.

Resistance to learning can occur for many reasons. Resistance to learning can occur due to unwillingness to adopt something that conflicts with prior knowledge to which a person is committed. In such cases, those persons will hold on to the prior knowledge no matter how many empirical evidences are presented. This is usually prevalent in those who follow irrational forms of faith in religious settings, but also it occurs in cultural settings. An example of insurmountable cognitive dissonance in the spiritual setting is the inability of a fanatical follower of orthodox Christianity to adapt to the idea that there is no evidence that a single person called "Jesus" ever existed historically, and that the basic notions of Christianity (eucharist, death and resurrection, the cross, etc.) were already present in ancient religion; Christianity, therefore, is not a revelation, but a degraded transposition of ancient (mostly Egyptian) teachings which existed previously. Such people would have even more difficulty in accepting that the early church fathers admitted taking teachings and rituals of ancient religion and changing its name to Christianity-even if the evidence (writings of the early church fathers) is presented to them. Many orthodox religions such as the Judaism, Christianity and Islam indoctrinate their youth with absolutist notions about spiritual realities. They promote suspension of critical thinking and blind faith in dogma, reinforced by fear, and guilt; there is fear of going to hell if the teaching is not accepted and guilt if there is straying form the dogma or even consideration of any ideas outside the prescribed dogma. Those impressions of fear and guilt are extremely powerful preventatives to the successful learning of new teachings and their subsequent adoption and integration. An example of a socio-cultural setting is racism. A person who has been reared in an environment of racism will have much difficulty adjusting to the notion that there is no such thing as racial groups as far as human beings are concerned or the knowledge that all human beings came from the same ancestors in Africa, etc.

- If someone is called upon to learn something that contradicts what they already think they know — particularly if they are committed to that prior knowledge — they are likely to resist the new learning.
- For most people accommodation (integration) of new knowledge is more difficult than assimilation. Some people can hear and even intellectually agree with the new knowledge and still be unable to integrate it.

---

[29] NEIGHBOUR R (1992) *The Inner Apprentice* Plymouth UK; Petroc Press

- If learning something has been difficult, uncomfortable, or even humiliating enough, people are not likely to admit that the content of what has been learned is not valuable. To do so would be to admit that one has been "had," or "conned."
- Sometimes learning may be acknowledged but not accepted. Such personalities "know" the teaching but do not practice it as that would require them to change their actions and they may lose status in society by doing so.
- Sometimes people refuse to face a new reality because they feel they are losing something of self. They have invested their hopes and dreams on certain notions that now they are asked to leave behind.
- Sometimes people refuse to face a new reality because they feel fatigued. Mental fatigue arises due to the strain of diffidence, the struggle between the reality to be accepted and its suppression or conscious exclusion of unacceptable desires, thoughts, or memories from the mind. Such a person cannot "handle" the difficult situations of life and may even descend into depression, irritation or even mania and physical illness.
- Others may refuse the new information because they have been degraded and seeking acceptance by some group that upholds the knowledge they have previously learned. Their denigration has rendered them weak to the extent of seeking approval and depending on the group in question for their self-worth, direction and purpose in life.

In reality, the higher learning experience is indeed a loss of something; that something is ignorance, and its ensuing capacity to lead human beings to suffering. In its place there is a gain of higher understanding, and with that comes peace and insight into the secrets of the universe including the discovery of immortality and infinity. Of course, this highest of human attainments requires the highest of efforts and the highest form of letting go of previously held notions about self, creation and God (Higher Self). Therefore, it is understandable that very few people have the capacity to make the necessary adjustments to achieve the highest ideal of personality integration.

Closely held notions over a period of time accumulate mental impressions in the unconscious mind. So even if a person "desires" sincerely to adopt a new teaching they may be unable to for some time until they are able to neutralize their contrary unconscious impressions. Many have attempted to adopt the practice and philosophy of Shetaut Neter spirituality just as others have adopted other religions after they have lived their early lives in another culture and religion. This presents special challenges, as it means that those people who have "converted" recently actually have the conscious and unconscious "mental baggage," the *ariu*- {actions, deeds, unconscious mental impressions that impel the desires of the mind [Indian term is *karma*]} accumulated over previous years and lifetimes, to overcome in their adoption of the new tradition. Try as they might to integrate the new teaching, there is inevitably a struggle between the new ideas and the old, which will not be resolved until there is sufficient maturity and mental stability to allow for thoughtful reflection on the central questions of life, unfettered by knowledge that one previously committed to.

People who have invested much time and energy in holding on to notions are psychologically weak and have done so to bolster their self-concept (ego). Therefore, they have entered into a condition of needing dogmas to support their concept of reality; if that crutch of dogma is removed, the personality will collapse since its intellect is atrophied and incapable of cognizing a new and better reality for itself. This is the notion that "you can't teach old dogs new tricks." Of course that adage does not apply to human beings who are evolving spiritually since they have a special capacity that other forms of life do not have. Humans have the capacity to intellectualize. But that capacity exists to the extent that egoism does not cloud (dull) the intellect. If egoism, desires, childishness, etc., hold sway over the personality, that personality will exist in a manner not unlike animals, at the level of instinct, and those persons cannot be considered fully human, even though they may appear to live as other human beings. In actuality, if those people with diminished capacity are challenged beyond a certain limit they will descend into personal base thought processes (instinct based) and a society populated by such people will degenerate to anarchy. Therefore it is said in the Kamitan Wisdom Texts: "The lips of Wisdom are closed, Except to the ears of Understanding." Wisdom cannot help those who are unable to understand it (reflect upon it, assimilate it and accommodate it-adjust and adapt to it- and finally integrate it in the mind-transforming oneself by it into a new personality). Those who do not want to change will resist new knowledge and cannot be transformed. Also, this is why it is also said in the Kamitan Wisdom Texts: *"When the student is ready, the master will appear."* The teachings are always there, and teachers are always there in the world, but people are unable to recognize the teaching or the teachers due to their cognitive blinders as it were; they "choose" to see the world they are comfortable with, and so they "prevent" any notions that contradict that illusion from consideration.

Fitness to Join the Neterian Clergy.

"Morals are judged by deeds"

-Ancient Egyptian Proverb

Who is a proper candidate to be inducted into the ranks of the priesthood? What makes a person fit or unfit to practice the teachings in an effective manner? In order to be effective, the personality must be mature, virtuous and centered on the goal of spiritual Enlightenment. If that goal is mixed with worldly ideas or deluded notions, a person's capacity to advance in spiritual life will be diminished, because the energy necessarily will be diffused between conflicting agendas. The conflicting notions also affect the mind. The delusions and agitated actions in life stir up the thought vibrational structure of the mind, and thereby it tends towards movement and ignorance, and away from stillness and insight. The avid aspirant must learn to counteract the ego driven movements of the mind, the thoughts, by first controlling the physical actions of the body, and then controlling the mind, in order to turn the vital forces of life towards that which is true, righteous and pure. That is the path to success in spiritual life, and only those who are ready to tread the path in such a manner are capable of succeeding in the advancing disciplines of the clergy.

Those people who are fond of loud music, sexual dances, racy parties, theater or movies to feel "happy" or to "enjoy life" are not fit to pursue the path of the clergy. Those who pursue dangerous lifestyles for the sake of "thrill-seeking" because they want to experience the "fullness" of life are misguided and will not "enjoy life" beyond the next act of thrill-seeking, and so will fail in their quest and will not be fit to practice the teaching. Those who cannot control their eating habits, preferring to "enjoy" foods that are known by them to be health hazards, are unfit for higher spiritual advancement. Those who are boisterous, rowdy, always needing to talk, caught up fanatically in sports or the lives of celebrities, or need to constantly watch television in order to occupy the mind so as to not think about serious issues in life, are unfit for advanced spiritual life. Those who straight away go out to purchase what they have seen on television or heard on the radio or were told by a friend, or who believe what they hear in the news without reflection or seeking alternative points of view in order to make an informed decision are weak personalities, and are not fit to be more than consumers who are herded like cattle to the store and then to the slaughterhouse of life (the miseries, suffering, and frustrations of life, born of a person's own delusions, unrighteousness and weakness "kill" a person's ability to discover peace, true happiness and abiding peace). Those whose minds are weak and get caught up in dramas (real or imagined) of the world such as soap operas, Hollywood gossip or sports are unfit for the priesthood. Those who produce their own drama, violence, strife, domestic disturbances, frequently find themselves in trouble with the authorities, get into fights frequently, have frequent car accidents and blame others, or even believe they were wronged by being put in jail after committing a crime, are also unfit. Those people who are fond of detailing their cars or having pets, and see those kinds of things as ways to impress others or feel better about themselves are also not fit to be admitted to the Neterian clergy. An aspirant may own a car or a pet, but they are not to be used as extensions of the ego personality. A person who has the most vicious animal in the neighborhood and through that feels important, feared or admired is a deluded personality and is not fit for higher spiritual practice. Those who like to be seen with members of the opposite sex because that makes them feel wanted and important, or who do not feel "whole" unless they are in a relationship with someone else are deluded and unfit also. Equally unfit are those who live through their job and see their worth through their career or occupation, to the extent that are crushed if they lose their job. Such personalities are unfit for advanced spiritual practice. Those who live vicariously through their children or others or who look for approval from family members or society are also not fit. Those who do not understand why those things (listed above) are not compatible with spiritual maturity are not fit for the clergy.

Those people who have severe mental aberrations and abnormalities like schizophrenia are not qualified to become priests and priestesses. In order to be effective, the teachings need to be approached by a person who is reasonably well adjusted and highly virtuous by worldly standards. Those people who search for tranquility and sanity through spirituality in a fanatical way or as a means of escape from the world because they cannot handle the stresses of life will also not handle the pressures of authentic spiritual life. Those people with mental complexes, insecurities, self-doubt, defeatist nature, faultfinding nature, etc. will not succeed either because they are complexing their own mind, making their own mind insecure, sabotaging themselves, and finding fault in themselves. Those who cannot restrain the emotions or feel justified in hurting others or take pleasure in causing distress in others cannot succeed in the teachings because they are causing distress in themselves through these actions. Likewise, those who put down others in order to feel important and those who enslave others for personal gain or other unrighteous reasons are also unfit to practice the teachings effectively. Those who are covetous, vain or prideful are caught in the web of worldly delusion and will surely lead themselves to worldly entanglements, frustrations and disappointments and will not succeed in the teachings. Those who are easily frazzled by life, who cannot adjust and adapt to life's changes, will not succeed. Those who are agitated easily by the words of others, their beliefs, demands, criticism or ideas lack the character and stamina to pursue the path. Those who are bothered by changes in the weather or by their own moods will not succeed in the teaching. Those who believe they are on earth to suffer will not succeed. Those who value sentimental egoistic attachments and relationships above righteousness, order and truth (the teaching) will not succeed. Those who attempt to manipulate others with emotionality, drama or sexuality are very degraded personalities and are not fit to practice the teaching effectively. Those who want to "enjoy life" by practicing the teachings and also "eat, drink and be merry" in order to have "the best of both worlds" will not succeed. Those who want to believe that sexuality is a God given right and should be pursued without restriction are wasting their time pursuing the teaching; they would better spend their time pursuing sexual liaisons without the burden of guilt from the regulations imposed by the teaching. Those who believe in pursuing wealth as a means to obtain pleasure, power or "happiness" or who believe that they can pursue the capitalist agenda and also be "spiritual" are following a deluded notion and will not succeed in the teaching. Those who do not trust in the teaching or think that somehow life should become easier for them without effort, just by professing to believe in the teaching will not succeed. Those who hold on to resentments, grudges or animosities against others for any reason will remain at the level of animal instinct, combating with others like waves in the ocean that crash into each other. The aforementioned deficiencies disqualify a person from succeeding as a practitioner of the teaching and more so from the clergy.

Those who do not accept their imperfections and the imperfections of others or rationalize their own mediocrity and failures in life are also not fit to advance in the teaching. Those who obsess over being perfect or over the miseries of life will be ill prepared to practice the teachings and their movements will counteract their stated goals in life. Those who do not accept the opinion of others, but rather, become angry with them for not agreeing with their own opinion are dogmatists who will surely develop strife and agitation in life. Self-examination and following the path of truth require discipline with the personality and forgiveness of its foibles and failings as well as those of others. Even though a mistake may be made even without realizing it at first, once the error is discovered, it cannot be swept under the rug, so to speak, or overlooked; it must be acknowledged and an aspirant must take responsibility and resolve to discover the source of the error and improve in the future.

The first responsibility of an aspirant is to learn and practice Maat Philosophy. In Maat philosophy, the most important injunction of the 42 precepts of Maat is *Not Lying*. That practice begins with not lying to oneself. Those who allow themselves to live deluded worldly lives will also lead deluded priestly lives as well. So this is why the personality must be purified through Maat first before proceeding on the spiritual path of Neterianism, or any spiritual tradition for that matter. Otherwise the person should remain in the secular world and pursue their desires until they have reached a level of maturity sufficient to recognize the illusion of physical worldly pleasures and distractions. Those who propose to take up the advanced lifestyle of the

Neterian clergy should strive to implement the injunctions of Maat and also the admonition of the sages, to steer clear of the unfit, immature personalities and to keep company with the wise, the sages, and the virtuous aspirants who are sincerely making an effort to succeed on the spiritual path.

The teaching recognizes that there is no perfection in human existence. Even sages have negative aspects. However, sages do not have negative tendencies. The Higher Self is in control in them. Virtue is the tendency towards righteousness, to make the righteous choice and not the choice based on egoistic desires, prejudices or greed. Thus, in order to become sagely, the aspirant needs to tend towards truth and order instead of desire and chaos. This is more important for those who aspire to qualify for the priesthood. They need to exercise more control and more vigilance over the personality and work harder to purify the mind so as to eradicate the power of the negative tendencies within. Then the movement towards righteousness will be effortless and the path to Enlightenment will be clear.

Q & A - IMPORTANT CONSIDERATIONS FOR DISCUSSION AND REFLECTION FOR THOSE WHO WANT TO BECOME NETERIAN PRIESTS AND PRIESTESSES

Question: The question has been asked "Do Neterian priests and priestesses need to give up their religion of birth or one which they have adopted previously in life?"

Answer

YES! This would be like asking a Christian priest if he could be a Muslim Imam or a Jewish Rabbi at the same time! Of course you must give up your previous affiliations if you want to concentrate on a chosen path. It is an adorable idea that we should all be able to be universal, to practice universal religion and minister to all people. Yet in reality it cannot work that way. Most people are conditioned to follow a particular path and they have come to believe in dogmatic teachings that preclude their capacity to follow or even acknowledge multiple spiritual paths. Even if that were not true, the average human intellectual capacity would not support that kind of spiritual outlook. That is for a more advanced personality. In any case, it would take a lifetime to study the Neterian path and become proficient at it, let alone study it and other paths at the same time. If you are one of those people who are dabbling, undecided, or if you are reluctant to give yourself fully to the path because you feel guilty about leaving your previous religion or because your family members will repudiate you or some other such reason, then you have no business even inquiring about the priesthood. That is not a path for you. You are not mature or ready to tread that path. Better you should stay in your world than becoming a haphazard Neterian priest, caught up in mental complexes, regrets, anxieties and guilt. If you follow this path do so in freedom and with the deepest conviction; only then will you be of true service to yourself and to humanity. Leave behind the childish notions of holding on to your illusions and nostalgic notions and also attaining the high mysteries at the same time; that will never work. Yes, you must give up your allegiance with other religions; withdraw your financial support and your volunteer efforts. Those should be employed towards THIS path. You may remain friends with people of other religions and collaborate on projects of common good. But consider, would a Muslim, a Jew or a Christian come to your temple services, donate to your temple, participate in your rituals? Do not fool yourself into remaining in a one sided relationship with those who promote narrow-minded ideals and orthodox teachings about spirituality. They will in the end always repudiate anything that is not in accordance with their dogma, and they will curse that which they consider as "pagan," namely you. If you do not like that designation (pagan), then you should go with them and stay with them. At least in that manner you will expend your *Ariu* (karmic) entanglement with that path and someday return to authentic religion in freedom and empowered. That will only happen when you are ready to leave the kindergarten religions (orthodox) that are practiced by the masses of ignorant people in the world and go to high school and college for mature spiritual aspirants (mystical religion).

Furthermore, you should also change your name as well. When you are initiated on the path you receive your spiritual name. That is your true name. Why do Christians have Christian names? Why do Muslims have Arabic Islamic names? Why do Jews have Hebrew names? How would it be if a Muslim Imam had a name like St. Paul Christian or Bishop James? How would it be if a Christian priest had a name like Muhammad? Such names would denote incongruent intentions and crossed ideologies in the personality and in the teachings.

There are many common tenets in religions. However, the fundamental teachings differ widely even in the western orthodox religions. So while practitioners of different religions can meet to confer on those points of commonality, the prospect of melding religious path extensively or completely is quite a misapprehension that must be abandoned by all who are serious practitioners in any path. Only those who have attained the heights of spiritual evolution can comprehend and experience the ultimate commonality of all spiritual traditions. That is not an attainment that can be expected from the masses or even advanced practitioners of religion. Religions are like paths or roads. Many roads can lead to one destination (if they are authentic paths), but if they come from the east, south, north and west how can they all be coming together, in the same way? How can a person coming from the east see and experience the same things that a person who is coming from the west will see and experience? At the end of the road they may see the same destination, but the way to get there was different. Of course this analogy is predicated upon the idea that the roads lead to the same destination. Childish, dogmatic religions based on faith alone DO NOT lead to the same destination as authentic advanced mystical religions. Hypocrisy, illusion, arrogance, demagoguery, fear, guilt, disrespect, lackadaisicalness, hubris, patriotism, nepotism, tyranny, disease, and depending on the world for happiness have no place on the authentic spiritual path. An avid aspirant must understand the difference between talking the talk and walking the talk. Therefore, your choice should be clear. If it is not, then you are not ready and should study more, pursue the truth more, reflect and meditate more on the truth of these statements until there is full conviction. If that is not possible then the aspirant should act as outlined above until it is.

We do recommend and emphasize that an aspirant should strive to focus on/immerse her/himself in the Kamitan studies to promote her/his understanding of the teachings, and capacity to practice the teachings, and experience of the Neterian tradition/religion. Only by this concentrated focus will an aspirant be able to tell if this is the path they want to pursue. However, at the level of student or general aspirant, there is no contradiction with respect to the person continuing to privately practice and study the disciplines or philosophy of another tradition, especially one in which they are already engaged prior to beginning their Kamitan studies, if it has an ethical basis. To a certain degree, it is important to study about and understand other traditions, as those researches will contribute to your understanding of spirituality in general. However, if an aspirant chooses to fully commit to the Neterian path as a priestess or priest, that aspirant will need to refrain from teaching the philosophies or practicing the disciplines of other paths in the Neterian temple setting and gatherings with other Neterian aspirants. It is not even so much that an aspirant will be "forced" to refrain…but if the aspirant is evolving in a balanced manner (and maturity) in this tradition, such an aspirant will likely develop a desire, to focus solely on the Neterian path, which is in itself is extensive, both in terms of research and practices (disciplines).

With respect to programs/seminars associated with the Temple of Shetaut Neter, programs (music, dance, exercises, rituals, etc.) from other spiritual traditions/religions will not be featured, unless we are specifically promoting or participating in an interfaith type of seminar/program. This is standard among the different religious traditions. Christian churches do not promote yoga mysticism during their church programs. Buddhist monks do not promote Sufism during their programs, etc.

So, if you choose to commit to the full and advanced practice of Shetaut Neter you will find that your previous experiences will contribute to great inner discovery but you will need to apply yourself fully to the Neterian path. On any spiritual path it is necessary to concentrate in order to have success. Many aspirants are mistaken about the idea that since all is one and God is one that they can practice "salad-bar" spirituality, picking and choosing elements from different traditions. What would an Indian curry dish mixed with Turkish hummus mixed with Mexican tacos mixed with Spanish paella mixed with American steak and potatoes taste like? If the dish tastes bad how would you know which ingredient is the culprit? Which condiment would you take out? Most likely you would get indigestion anyway and throw the whole thing up! That is failure in religious practice often experienced by those in New Age circles and self-willed aspirants who refuse to humble themselves to a particular path and a particular teacher. This promotes and sustains a lack of commitment and denotes the lack of understanding that as time-space disciplines, religions, yoga philosophies, etc., though leading to the same goal, do so in differing ways. So mixing them will lead to confusion and eventual stagnation. This is the path taken by those who want to maintain their independence in a bid to "be spiritual" and at the same time live by their own rules and desires or those who are lost, without guidance, or those who are strong-willed, independent or those who are frustrated with or jaded by religion. A path is more than its philosophy; it is the feeling of its iconography, its tradition, the feeling of its sacred spaces and places, its sounds and rituals and of course, its philosophy, which is espoused uniquely by its sages and cannot be learned from books or discourses by intellectuals or charlatans, those who wear the garb and speak the words but do not walk the walk or produce extensive written commentaries displaying their absolute command of the teaching. Such practitioners of religion are not truly following any path but have created their own. Since their creation lack the insight of enlightened sages it is deficient and ultimately leads them to failure on the spiritual path. Those who are wise and mature aspirants will realize the fallacy of self-created religions and will seek out authentic spiritual traditions and their genuine representatives. Until such time as an aspirant is ready to commit in this way she or he will not be fit for advanced spiritual evolution and this form of deficient practice will act as an obstruction. The obstruction in fact originates with the aspirant's own inability to settle on one spiritual path due to ignorance in the form of intellectual pride or deluded understanding.

Question: Many times people from other spiritual traditions come to listen to introductory lectures on Shetaut Neter and Sema Tawi and afterwards they express comments like: "well this is the same thing that I learned in the church" or "that sounds a lot like what our teacher taught us in the Moorish temple."

Answer

Sometimes those same people even want to acknowledge that their teachings come from Ancient Egypt, with the idea of validating their own religion, so as to allow themselves to feel secure in the fact they are receiving the same teaching or even something greater already (so they do not have to change). The important aspect is that they never stay to listen to the high philosophy beyond the fundamental teachings which may appear to be similar, for example, the Ten Commandments are similar to the 42 Precepts of Maat. This is because beyond those teachings there is a high culture of mysticism that is quite at odds with the orthodox phenomenological concepts of western religions; it is that aspect of the western religions that sets them apart. It is a point of view of western fundamentalist religionists[30]. The mysticism of non-western religions is one of the aspects that is repudiated and which cannot be accepted, and is overlooked by them so that they do not need to acknowledge it or reconsider their own beliefs through comparative religion studies. If this were done, they might find that their viewpoint needs revision, but since the orthodox western view precludes such actions, the effort is preemptively obstructed by dogmas claiming the historicity, infallibility and or direct reception of their teaching from God.

Question: Many times followers of religions that are closely associated with Shetaut Neter such as *Yoruba* religion or the *Moorish Science Temple of America* communicate their fascination with the books written by Sebai Muata Ashby at the discovery of the fact that the Neterian teachings offer insights into the traditions they have been following, sometimes for many years.

Answer

Few ever bother to ask "why is it that I never received this insight from my own tradition?" or "why did I need to read a book about Ancient Egyptian philosophy in order to gain insight into my own religion?" Most are content to read the Neterian books and continue practicing their religion without realizing that if they

---

[30] **re·lig·ion·ism** (rĭ-lĭj'ə-nĭz'əm) *n.* Excessive or affected religious zeal. --**re·lig'ion·ist** *n.*

have not gained the deeper insight it might mean that their practice or their teaching is limited. When one is traveling on a road and the road is blocked due to debris or maybe there is construction, sometimes it is necessary to take another rout. When water flows, if it is obstructed it will find another path, or else it becomes stagnant; it flows nowhere. An avid aspirant will follow the truth even if they need to leave their religion and follow another one that has proven to convey a higher truth. So it is not correct to say that since they are gaining insight into their religion they are practicing the same thing, even if the lineage of their teachers claims to be of Ancient Egyptian descent. As the saying goes, "the proof of the pudding is in the eating." Just because a person says they follow a tradition or are trained in it does not mean that they are qualified to espouse its teachings or that they have attained proficiency in it. If they have to look outside of their tradition to achieve progress in it, they should reflect deeply on the viability of their path. The true mark of attainment in spiritual realization is the level of peace, philosophical insight and prolificness of their espousal of the teachings in the form of spoken explanation and in writings, especially in commentaries on the teachings handed down by the sages of ancient times. In order to truly learn the mysteries of life, a path must be taught by a person who has had this kind of attainment. The scriptures must be authentic and the student must be qualified. Otherwise the spiritual process will not work. Such people who approach the teaching in this way are not worthy to be taught the deeper mysteries and the Neterian clergy would do better to spend more time with sincere Neterian aspirants.

Question: Is it proper for priests and priestesses to go to parties, go to the beach, travel and enjoy themselves?

Answer

That question is predicated on the idea that a priest or priestess is not fulfilled through their clergy work. Frankly, those who are ready to tread the path of the priesthood have realized that the illusory pleasures of the world are ultimately unfulfilling and so they spend most of their time in spiritual work, delving into the mysteries of life, and that is the source of unimaginable pleasure and satisfaction. They may for varied reasons find themselves on a beach, traveling, or attending functions. But they do not do so pursuing illusory pleasures. They may enjoy a day at the beach but they will not suffer if they never go. If you are looking for that kind of pleasure then you are not ready for the priesthood. Better you should live as an ordinary person and study more of the teaching. As you pursue the desires of life, one day you will realize the folly of worldly pursuits and then you will be ready.

Personal Considerations for Priests/Priestesses with Respect to Working Aspirants:

Learning the spiritual teaching does not mean that you lose your individual expression and your experience, following the teaching blindly. Rather that personal insight is to be purified and integrated into the practice of the priesthood. Consider the following reflections as part of your evaluation: Is this a person I want to work with? Is this a person I want to welcome into my family? Do I need dysfunctional people around me? Would that be good for the future of the tradition? Remember we are looking for quality of Aspirants and not Quantity. However, realize that it would be unrighteous to reject someone because they irritate you, or they have a high-pitched voice, or because they tell you things about yourself you know are true but do not want to hear, or other personal reasons. Look for non-egoistic factors (outside of your own personal likes and dislikes). Look for objective factors. Is the teaching being followed properly or not? You are part of a small group that has embarked on a quest for spiritual enlightenment and this opportunity has been opened to you because of your work and dedication. Others who have not put in work and dedication should not be allowed to join such a group. The Neterian priesthood is an art, based on the structure of Neterian philosophy. It is your task to learn the academic knowledge and then learn to apply that in the world of practical realities. That part of your education does not come from books, but from communion with your teachers, your inner reflections through your own practice of the disciplines and through your experiences of applying the teaching in the practical situations such as teaching the Sebait Curriculum.

Chapter 1: The Power of the Priesthood in the Old Kingdom Era and the Downfall of Ancient Egyptian Culture due to the Deterioration of the Clergy, Caused by Attacks from Asiatic and European Countries and Western Religions

War scene from Karnak Temple

Respect and Support of the Priests and Priestesses in the Ancient Period

Egyptologists usually divide ancient Egyptian history into several sections and dynastic periods from the Predynastic era, Old Kingdom Era, Middle Kingdom Era, New Kingdom Era, Late Period era, Greek Period, Roman Period, Christian Period and Islamic Period. The Government of Ancient Egypt was a Humanist Theocracy. It was ruled by priests and priestesses based on Maatian principles. More about this system will be discussed later. In the most ancient times the priests and priestesses were accorded great respect and they exercised great power not only over spiritual affairs of the Temple, but also over political and economic affairs of the state. The priests and priestesses presided over an unprecedented and unparalleled culture of spirituality, material wealth and political strength that has not been duplicated even to this day. Thus, every aspect of the society was benefited with spiritual wisdom and oversight. However, that respect accorded to the clergy changed over time and so too the strength and stability of the society also changed. The marginalization of the clergy and wars against invading forces led to the denigration of ancient values and the weakening of the society. The panel of Inty provides an example of the status of the clergy in the Old Kingdom Era.[31]

Section 1 (name)

Inty
Name= *Inty*

Section 2 (mirror image texts)

Su-hetep di Anpu Hetep di khenti Neter sh-kher-yat Sem amakhyt kher Neter aah
Royal offering given to Anpu, offering given to foremost divinity of the shrine in the cemetery region, the Sem Priestess in the presence of the God Great

Section 3 (center texts - title)

Suten rekh Hetheru Neter Hemt Nebt n het
Royal counselor (minister) of the Temple of Hetheru Priestess Mistress of the Temple

Section 4 (mirror image texts)

Su-hetep di Asar per kheru n Sem heb neb ra neb
Royal offering is given to Asar spoken offering of Sem Priestess of festivals and every day

This Panel from the tomb of Inty of the Old Kingdom period shows that at a very early date, in fact at the beginning of Kamitan civilization, women and the priesthood held important positions of power in social and political areas. The term *rech (rekh)* in particular, denotes "wise," "counselor," "advisor," etc., i.e. royal counselor, member of the royal court.

---

[31] translation by M. Ashby Copyright 2004

Decree of Neferirkara about priests in the old Kingdom Dyn 5 -limestone.

The decree above was written in reign of Neferirkara Kakai in the 5th Dynasty. In one section it frees the priesthood of the city of Abdu from compulsory labor in the district. So the priesthood's only responsibility was then to maintain the Temples and of course, the rituals, festivals and other services to the people including counseling and healing services. Anyone who did not obey the edict met with harsh penalties including, loss of property. This important Decree shows that at a very early date the office of clergy was accorded special status and dispensation by Kamitan society. This is because it was recognized that while it is possible to have priests and priestesses working at the Temple and also performing other duties, the value of the clergy is most effective to society when those individuals are able to exercise the practice of spirituality on a full-time basis. For additional and seasonal services there are Unut priests and priestesses. This point cannot be understated. It is the same principle accorded in the present day through exemptions of clergy from paying taxes. However, the difference between the present day and ancient times is that in ancient times the state and the culture actually supported the Temple through grants of land, labor, food offerings, etc. This was seen as divine offerings so that there might be reciprocation in the form of spiritual uplift to society and spiritual guidance. So the Temple and the clergy perform a service and the society supports them in the clergy work. The later Greek aspirants recognized the importance of the freeing up of the priesthood. The following statement shows how the ancient Egyptian clergy were able to freely engage in secular and non-secular researches in order to advance culture and civilization as well as the spiritual evolution of Kamitan society.

> "Hence when all the discoveries of this kind (practical) were fully developed, the sciences which relate neither to pleasure nor yet to the necessities of life were invented, and first in those places where men had leisure. **Thus the mathematical sciences originated in the neighborhood of Egypt**, because there the priestly class was allowed leisure."
> (Aristotle, Metaphysics I. I. 15, 1, trans. by H. Tredennick)

Egypt in the Early Late Period: A Nation in Decline

The Government Organizational Structure in Kamit Prior to The New Kingdom Period (beginning c.1,580 B.C.E.):

In the Old and Middle Kingdom Periods (5,500 B.C.E.- 1,730 B.C.E.) the Ancient Egyptian government was set up in such a way that the Pharaoh (king and/or queen) was the political leader and religious figure head of the country. They were advised by the clergy, who in turn oversaw a group of overseers who supervised the workers, farmers and trades.

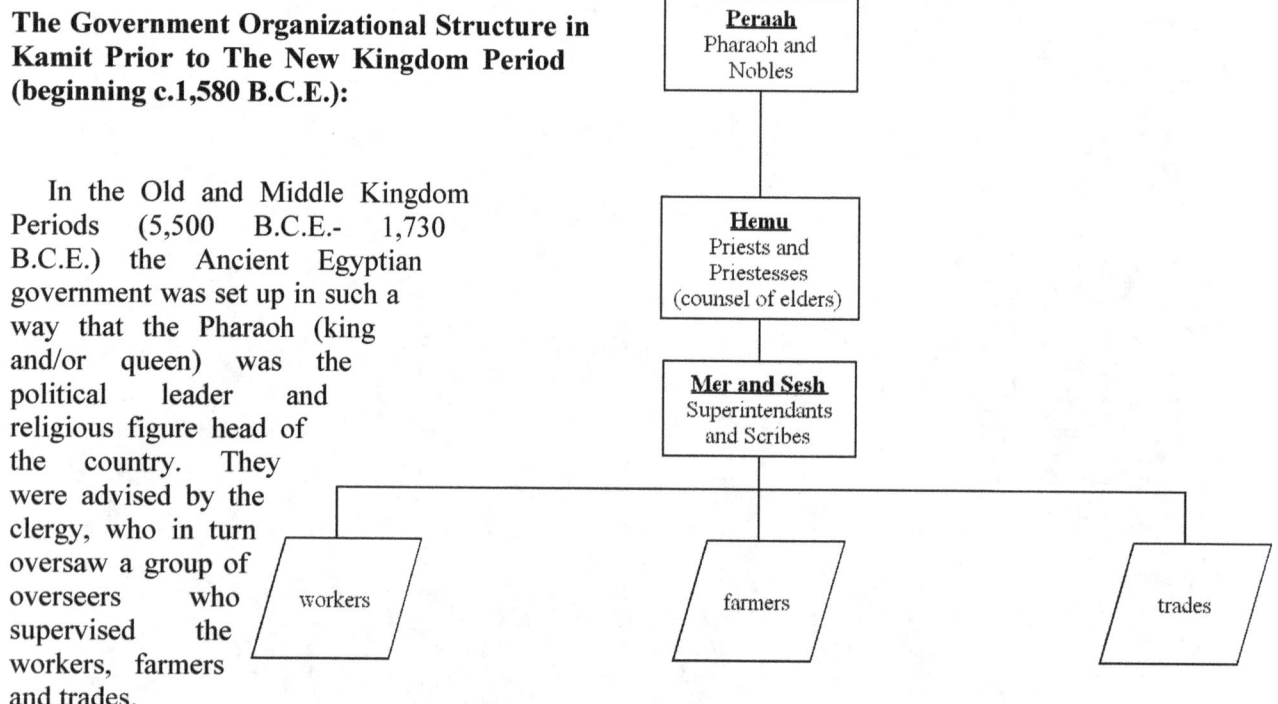

Sometimes the Peraah would not only be the political leader and religious figurehead, but the Pontiff as well, i.e. Political and Religious leader, spiritual Sage and Philosopher. The turning away from the previous system of government in Egypt coincided with the initial rise in power of the military, a revival of the arts, and Temple construction. This led to the eventual downfall of the nation.

Above: Decree of King Pepi II (Dyn. 6) It grants the temple of Min exemption from taxes.

The Government Organizational Structure in Kamit During The New Kingdom Period

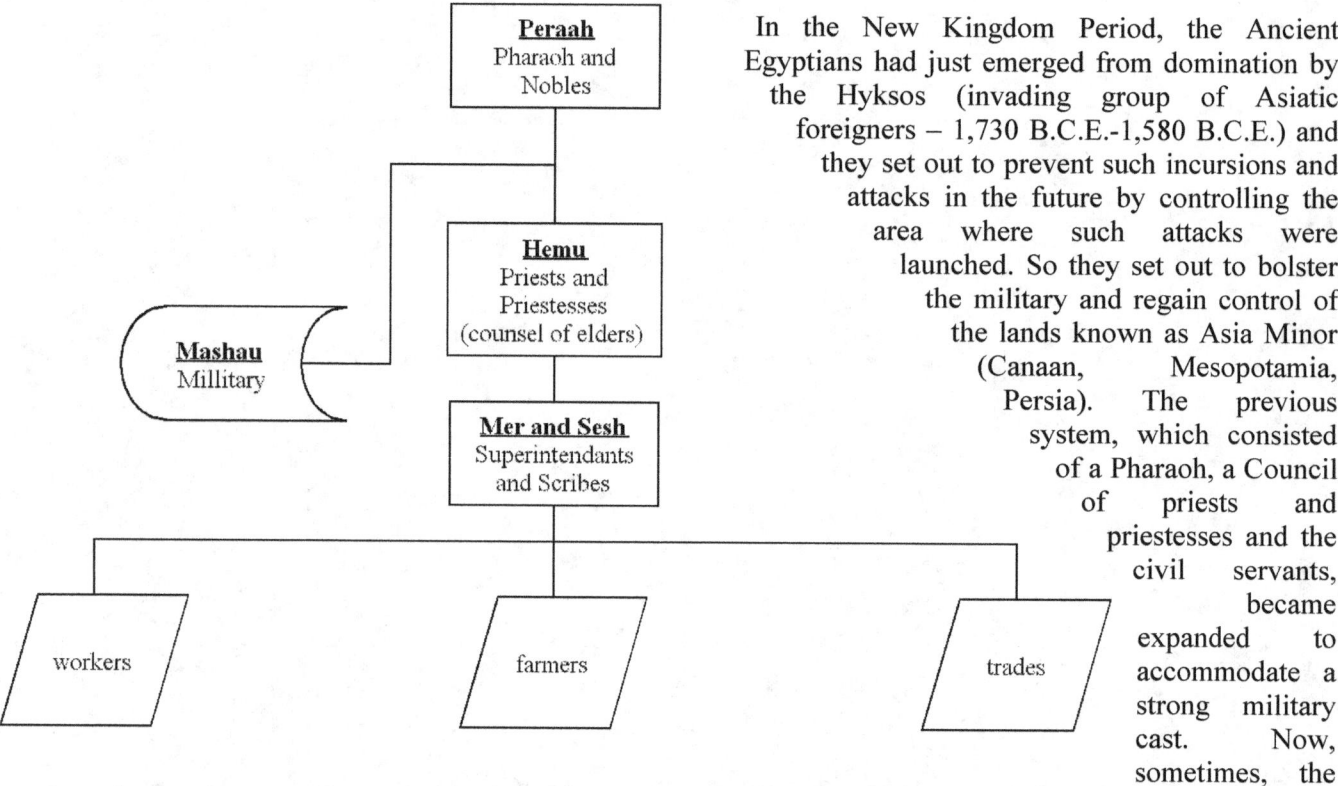

In the New Kingdom Period, the Ancient Egyptians had just emerged from domination by the Hyksos (invading group of Asiatic foreigners – 1,730 B.C.E.-1,580 B.C.E.) and they set out to prevent such incursions and attacks in the future by controlling the area where such attacks were launched. So they set out to bolster the military and regain control of the lands known as Asia Minor (Canaan, Mesopotamia, Persia). The previous system, which consisted of a Pharaoh, a Council of priests and priestesses and the civil servants, became expanded to accommodate a strong military cast. Now, sometimes, the Peraah was not so much a political and religious leader but a political and military leader. The balance that had been established between the secular and non-secular aspects of the society became disrupted and began to shift towards the secular, and with this turn, more emphasis was placed on worldly concerns, endeavors, desires and pursuits. The contact with the barbarians of Asia Minor required a closer relationship between people and many customs from Asia Minor were introduced to Egypt at that time. It is at this time that Love Poetry, the custom of kissing on the mouth, lavish parties among the nobles, explicit sexual imagery outside of the tantric iconography and other elements of a degraded society later seen in the extreme during the Greek and Roman Periods, begin to emerge. A critical factor, contributing to the weakening of culture in Ancient Egypt was the minimization of the clergy and of women in general.

One of the most important duties of the Peraah is to protect righteousness and order (Maat) in society. That duty includes protecting the country from invading forces. In the New Kingdom era, the concern with outside invasions became paramount and thus the New Kingdom era Temples display many examples of the Peraah as a fighter on a chariot defeating the invading forces. This also symbolizes control of the forces of entropy and disorder (an-Maat). An example of such an image is presented on the following page which depicts Rameses on a chariot (from the Abu Simbel Temple of Amun.) The following passage is presented to give an idea of what the Ancient Egyptians were facing. During the ninth dynasty, 3,000 B.C.E., before the first Eurasian invasion of Egypt by the Hyksos, a Pharaoh passed on to his heir the following wisdom: *"Lo the miserable Asiatic, he is wretched because of the place he's in, short of water, bare of wood. Its paths are many and painful because of mountains. He does not dwell in one place. Food propels his legs. He fights since the time of Horus."*

The Sixth Century B.C.E. Social and Political Upheaval in Ancient Egypt

The events in Ancient Egypt leading up to the sixth century B.C.E. offer an interesting prospect for answering the intriguing question with respect to the upsurge in spiritual culture in the ancient world during that time and thereafter. The circumstantial evidence linking Ancient Egypt to the unprecedented upsurge in world spiritual culture, is compelling testimony of the impact of Ancient Egypt on the ancient world, including Greece, the Middle East (Asia Minor) and especially India. The relationship of Ancient Egypt to Europe and Asia and its influence on ancient European and Asian culture and religion as well as the dire conditions in Ancient Egypt in the sixth century B.C.E. suggest a plausible explanation for the sudden development of spiritual cultures around the ancient world that are essentially alike.

There was an important development in the 6th century B.C.E. that occurred in Egypt at the time when Buddhism emerged. Cambyses II (reigned 529-522 BC), the king of Persia, led an expedition to conquer Egypt, which at the time was the sole independent kingdom in the aftermath the conquests of Asia by his father. Cambyses defeated Psamtik III, king of Egypt, and succeeded in conquering Egypt as far south as Nubia, but he failed in later attacks on the Egyptian oasis of Ammonium (now Siwa) and in campaigns in Ethiopia.

The attacks and conquest of Egypt by the Persians caused an extensive displacements of the Egyptian population. It was at this time that some of the Priests and Priestesses were forced out of the Temples due to fires set by the armies of the Persians. Also, many Egyptians were forcibly taken as slave workers to Persia and other parts of Asia Minor to build monuments and Temples for the Persians in those areas.[32][33] It is during this time that the most powerful and influential philosophies of ancient Eurasia (Europe), Asia Minor (Middle East) and East Asia (India and China) came into being. The philosophies and world religions that emerged for the first time during that period included:

- Buddhism   6th century B.C.E.
- Pythagoreanism   6th century B.C.E.
- Taoism   6th century B.C.E.
- Confucianism   6th century B.C.E.
- Zoroastrianism   6th century B.C.E.
- Jainism   6th century B.C.E.

The Ancient Egyptians had been attacked and the country taken over by foreigners twice before. The first time was the Hyksos invasion, which precipitated the "Second Intermediate Period," and the second time was the invasion of the Assyrians which was put down by the Nubians. However, the records indicate[34] that the viciousness of the attack and conquest by the Persians was so severe that it prompted a migration of Ancient Egyptians not only to Asia Minor, but also to India, Europe and other parts of Africa, including Nubia to the south, and West Africa also. Therefore, a causal connection can be drawn between the events in Egypt and the events in other parts of the ancient world. The surviving culture of Egypt was severely weakened after the Persian conquest, so much so that after a brief reestablishment of Egyptian rule by Egyptians, they were conquered again by the Greeks, who themselves had conquered the Persians. This period brought some stability to Egypt as the Greeks allowed the Ancient Egyptian religion to continue under their auspices, and the connection that had been established between other countries and Egypt through the Egyptians that had migrated out of Egypt 200 years earlier[35] during the invasion of Cambyses

---

[32] Cambyses II (d. 522 BC), son of Cyrus the Great and King of Persia (529-522 BC), his main achievement was the conquest of Egypt. His other campaigns failed and turned him from a benevolent to a harsh ruler. He died in battle in Syria. (Random House Encyclopedia Copyright (C) 1983,1990)
[33] *The African Origins of Civilization*, Cheikh Anta Diop, 1974
[34] *History of Herodotus*, Reliefs on the palace of Ashurbanipal
[35] Review section entitled **Paleoanthropology shows a connection between Ancient Egypt, Ancient Persia and Ancient India**

and the open relations fostered by the Ptolemaic rulers continued into a new phase. Now Egypt was fully opened to the spiritual seekers of the ancient world, and they flocked to the land of the Pyramids.

In this respect some researchers have noted the similarities between the Ancient Egyptian and Buddhist iconographies and point to these, and the evidences of philosophical correlations and evidences of contact along with the images of Buddha himself, as sufficient proof to show that Buddha was an African-Egyptian priest.[36] Indeed, even when we consider that no images of Buddha were allowed until the 1st century B.C.E. with the advent of Mahayana Buddhism, the images that appear even at that time, and later, up to the present day, bear a resemblance to the Kamitan-Kushitic forms of imagery and human appearance. There is a resemblance especially in the depiction of the hair and certain aspects of the physiognomy, in particular the nose and eye region of the face. It is curly or in locks, a form that was originated in ancient Kamit. This view was also expressed earlier by the German physician and traveler, Engelbert Kaempfer (1651-1716) who spent ten years, 1683-1693, traveling through Persia and Southeast Asia, including two years in Japan, 1690-92.[37]

When the Roman Emperor Theodocius decreed that there should be no other religion in the Roman Empire other than Christianity, a systematic effort was begun to stop the practice of all other religions except Roman Catholicism. So even other forms of Christianity were outlawed, their leaders and followers were persecuted or killed and their churches were closed just as those of other religions whom they referred to as "heathens." During this second time of the persecution in Egypt, other spiritual upsurges occurred again in religions in India and Asia Minor. Those included:

Events in Egypt	Developments in World Religion
1,800 B.C.E Ancient Egypt – New Kingdom Era Discipline of Sema Paut-Egyptian Yoga Postures, Arat Shetaut Neter (Goddess Mysteries), Arat Sekhem (Serpent Power), Hekau ("Magic) Pert m Hru (Book of the Dead) Tantrism All-already ancient	No Judaism exists yet No Hinduism exists yet (800-500 B.C.E.) No Buddhism exists yet No Christianity exists yet No Islam exists yet No Pythagoreanism exists yet No Taoism exists yet No Confucianism exists yet No Zoroastrianism exists yet No Jainism exists yet
550 B.C.E. (6th Century B.C.E.) Cambyses invades Egypt. Some priests and priestesses are killed and taken as slaves to Asia Minor	Buddhism Comes into existence Pythagoreanism Comes into existence Taoism Comes into existence Confucianism Comes into existence Zoroastrianism Comes into existence Jainism Comes into existence
356-323 B.C.E. Alexander the Great conquers Greece, Egypt, Asia Minor, India.	
250 B.C.E. Buddhist colony known to have existed in Memphis Egypt.	**261 B.C.E.** Indian Emperor Ashoka convenes Buddhist Council
	c. 100 ACE – Tantrism – Emerges as a Distinct culture of Spirituality in Hinduism, Buddhism and Jainism Emphasizing Shaktism (Goddess female energy and

---

[36] *Buddhism and Africa* by M. Clasquin and J.S. Kruger
[37] **The History of Japan by Engelbert Kaempfer (1651-1716) Reprint published in 1906**

	Goddess as female aspect of the Absolute), Occultism, Magic, Kundalini
394-450 A.C.E. Theodosius I, the Great (346?-395), decrees that all Mystery Temples be closed. Last Hieroglyphic writing discovered at the Temple of Aset (Isis) –Last Temple of Ancient Egyptian Mysteries was closed by the Roman Christians.	**c. 460-490 A.C.E.** Shakta and Tantra Spirituality emerge in India. Writings elaborating on Tantric spirituality and mysticism of the Chakras appear.
	c. 550-650 A.C.E. Tantric Buddhism arrives in Tibet, later developments include a *Tibetan Book of the Dead*.
	c. 1000 A.C.E. Goraksha – Develops Hatha Yoga to "Force" the movement of Kundalini- based on Tantric Buddhism

Minimization of the clergy and the Decline of Society: A Nation in Decline

"When a king has good counselors, his reign will be peaceful."[38]

-African Proverb

That the clergy of Ancient Egypt served as counselors to the ruler is evident in the following passage from Ancient Egyptian history. The Egyptian clergy would accompany the Pharaoh on trips to foreign countries. An example of this is the following surviving text of a message that was circulated that summoned one priest from each Temple to form a council that would accompany the ruler to ceremonies or on journeys. The different Temples would send representatives to answer the call. The following message was circulated in year 4 of Psammetichus II:

> "they sent to the great Temples of Upper and Lower Egypt, saying: "Pharaoh L. P. H., is going to the Land of Palestine.... Let the priests come with the bouquets of the gods of Egypt to take them to the Land of Palestine with Pharaoh, L. P. H." And they sent to Teudjoy saying: "Let a priest come with the bouquet of Amun, in order to go to the Land of Palestine with Pharaoh, L. P. H ." And the priests agreed and said to Pediese… "you are the one who, it is agreed, ought to go to the Land of Palestine with Pharaoh. There is no one here in the town who is able to go to the Land of Palestine except you. Behold, you must (do it), you, a scribe of the House of Life; there is nothing they can ask you and you not be able to answer it, for you are a priest of Amun. It is (only) the priests of the great gods of Egypt that are going to the Land of Palestine with Pharaoh, L. P. H."[39]

In the book "Life in Ancient Egypt," the author Adolf Erman noted the composition of two courts in different periods of Ancient Egyptian history. The composition was listed as follows:

---

[38] *African Proverbs* compiled by Charlotte and Wolf Leslau
[39] K. S. Freedy and D. B. Redford, "The Dates in Ezekiel in Relation to Biblical, Babylonian and Egyptian Sources," *Journal of the American Oriental Society go (1970): 479.* "L. P. H." stands for "may he live, prosper, and be healthy," a wish often added to mentions of the king.

The Priests and Priestesses of Ancient Egypt

On 21st of Athyr in the 16th year of Rameses IX, the court of justice sitting in judgment on the princes of the town consisted of:

"The governor Cha'emuese, the superintendent of the town.
Amenhotep, the first prophet of Amon Re, king of the gods.
Nesamun, of the Temple of Rameses IX. enduring for millions of years, the prophet of Amon Ra, king of the gods.
The royal vassal Nesamun, the scribe of the Pharaoh, and chief of the house of the high priestess of Amon Ra, king of the gods.
The royal vassal Neferkere-em-per-Amun, the speaker of the Pharaoh.
Hor'e, the deputy of . . .
The fan-bearer of the household of Hor'e.
Paser, the prince of the town."

In this case the lay element preponderated, but on the 14th of Phaophi in the 46th year of Rameses II, we find the members of the court consisted of:

Bekenchons, the first prophet of Amon.
Ueser-mont, the prophet of Amon.
Ram, the prophet of Amon.
The prophet Uennofre of the Temple of Mut.
The prophet Amen-em-'en of the Temple of Chons.
The (holy father?) Amen-em-opet of the Temple of Amon.
Amenhôtep, the priest and reader of Amon.
Ani, the priest and reader of Amon.
The priest Huy of the Temple of Amon.
The accountant Huy of the court of justice of the town."

In the case therefore we find nine priests and but one layman, *i.e.*, the permanent scribe of the court who reported the lawsuit.

In the court of Rameses IX (c. 1131-1112 – 20th Dynasty) we observe the predominance of laypersons presiding. There are two clergy out of eight total attendants. In the earlier court (Rameses II, c.1290-1224 – 19th Dynasty) there was a preponderance of clergy. There are nine clergy out of ten total attendants. The term "Prophet," means priest or priestess. One of the functions of the priesthood is to provide clear insight into the pressing issues of life. Therefore, it is natural to seek the Council of priests and priestesses since they have spent a lifetime studying and meditating on Maat Philosophy and the mysteries of life. The priesthood related to the court proceedings were initiated into the religion and philosophy of Maat, the philosophy of ethics, justice, righteousness, order and cosmic (spiritual) harmony. In larger terms the composition of these two courts suggests a movement away from clergy and towards laity. It also happened that the turn away from the clergy coincided with a period in Egyptian history that historians often refer to as being led by "weak rulers," which led to a decline in Ancient Egyptian culture and power. There is an Ancient Egyptian proverb that goes *"The lips of wisdom are closed, except to the ears of understanding."* This means that when society becomes imbalanced, and when worldly concerns are lifted above spiritual concerns, then society is in for a period (cycle) of unrighteous leadership. This will lead to universal suffering of the populace due to corruption and greed. The wisdom texts are replete with admonitions in reference to righteous conduct of leaders, clergy and laity. Thus there are other Ancient Egyptian Proverbs that express the wisdom with which the priests and priestesses guided the country: *"If the social order judges success by material gain, the most successful will be the most corruptible and selfish."* This wisdom came not from concept but from experience.

In the long history of Kamit, careful records had been kept in reference to the previous periods of social breakdown that the country had briefly experienced. There are several sources of breakdown in the social order that were observed at varied periods. Paramount among these was greed. Greed led to internal disputes over power and control of the country, unrighteous behavior, stealing, burglary, misappropriation of property by individuals, etc. When the leaders in government become corrupted by greed, the entire society becomes poisoned with avarice, as well as resentment and hatred due to injustice. Therefore, the administration of justice firmly and in a timely manner is essential to the survival of any culture, and those working in the courts should be well trained in law, but more importantly, in truth and righteousness.

The philosophy of righteousness can have far-reaching implications in economics and trying to establish a government based on righteousness, service and the public good. This is exactly the ideal that was achieved in Ancient Egypt. It must be borne in mind that when authentic spiritual teachers are leading a spiritual tradition this form of degradation cannot occur. As was the case in Ancient Egypt during the final period of the New Kingdom Era, the degraded management of religion led to the temporary downfall of culture. When people choose to turn towards worldliness and vice, spiritual preceptors cannot and should not force them to a rule or standard that is beyond their capacity to follow. People can be controlled to some extent through laws, and violence as well as other degrading acts should be outlawed, but opinions, desires and passions cannot be legislated. Rather, by example and subtle influence, authentic teachers around the world work in concert, even though they may never meet in person, to promote the good of humanity by helping people realize the true nature of life and the way to real and abiding peace and prosperity. Even though the politics and social order of the country may become degraded, there were always those individuals who maintained the tradition of universal mystical spirituality; they are constantly being joined by honest seekers (aspirants). They wait quietly until called upon to espouse the teachings and for the time when the cycle of negative *ari* (karmic) expression in society turns towards a more spiritual consciousness, and then culture experiences a renaissance wherein the authentic spiritual tradition is revered and spiritual teachers are respected. Then they can assume their place as shepherds of society, leading it to prosperity and glory.

From the time of the Old to the Middle Kingdom, the roles of the clergy were mixed with regard to gender. There were priests and priestesses in the service of male and female divinities alike. The clergy also formed an integral part of the governance of the country. However, the New Kingdom Period saw a change in the importance of the priesthood in general as well as the role of the priestess. This downgrade was part of the general decline of the culture even though it saw great heights in building, political expansion and economic power. Thus, the weakening of the spiritual infrastructure of the country eventually led to internal corruption and a minimization of spiritual values in society, precipitating the weakening of the society as a whole and making it susceptible to outside conquests.

Before the New Kingdom era, the Ancient Egyptian priests and priestesses actively and diligently maintained a strict control over immigrants. Trade with foreign countries existed, but immigration was controlled. Few immigrants were allowed until the Late Period (after 1000 B.C.E.), But during the New Kingdom Period, the military and royalty felt the necessity to conquer and subdue Asia Minor in order to prevent any further attack from that region, the most severe of which was that of the Hyksos, whose ousting allowed the Ancient Egyptians to establish a new Egyptian Dynasty (the 18th) and to build up the army in order to protect the country from being overrun again in the future. Between the time of the beginning of the New Kingdom and the commencement of the Late Period with the decline of the power of the Ancient Egyptian government and the attacks from the Persians and Assyrians, the Ancient Egyptians had already begun to accept many foreign customs. This manifested in their eating habits, sexuality (love poetry, lip kissing and sexual imagery appear during this period). This precipitated a move away from control by the priests and priestesses and a move towards rule by the secular and military elite. This represents a turning away from the traditions of the ancient culture and a decline of cultural values with a concomitant turn towards foreign culture, traditions and morals.

On the next page: Priest Akhtihotep (Dynasty 4) Saqqara

The Neterian clergy and the control over the Pharaoh (King or Queen) and the Governance of society

In the following passages from Diodorus (History of Egypt BOOK 1. 69-71, 73), there are important descriptions of the Kamitan system of government, the system of priestly council, as well as the system of laws that governed the Kings and Queens who ruled Egypt (Kamit). This provides special insights into the manner in which the spiritual philosophy should be applied to government and the rulers of society, and how they in turn should apply the laws in order to best serve their country.

From Diodorus (History of Egypt BOOK 1. 69-71, 73)	*Commentary by Sebai Maa*

69. Now that we have discussed sufficiently the deeds of the kings of Egypt from the very earliest times down to the death of Amasis, we shall record the other events in their proper chronological setting; but at this point we shall give a summary account of the customs of Egypt, both those which are especially strange and those which can be of most value to our readers. For many of the customs that obtained in ancient days among the Egyptians have not only been accepted by the present inhabitants but have aroused no little admiration among the Greeks; and for that reason those men who have won the greatest repute in intellectual things have been eager to visit Egypt in order to acquaint themselves with its laws and institutions, which they considered to be worthy of note. For despite the fact that for the reasons mentioned above strangers found it difficult in early times to enter the country, it was nevertheless eagerly visited by Orpheus and the poet Homer in the earliest times and in later times by many others, such as Pythagoras of Samos and Solon the lawgiver. Now it is maintained by the Egyptians that it was they who first discovered writing and the observation of the stars, who also discovered the basic principles of geometry and most of the arts, and established the best laws. And the best proof of all this, they say, lies in the fact that Egypt for more than four thousand seven hundred years was ruled over by kings of whom the majority were native Egyptians, and that the land was the most prosperous of the whole inhabited world; for these things could never have been true of any people which did not enjoy most excellent customs and laws and the institutions which promote culture of every kind.
70. In the first place, then, the life which the kings of the Egyptians lived was not like that of other men who enjoy autocratic power and do in all matters exactly as they please without being held to account,
    70.1.   but all their acts were regulated by
	69. This important passage that reveals the high esteem in which Kamitan culture was held in ancient times. The government of Kamitan culture is what set it apart from other nations, and this is what allowed it to persist in harmony and peace for thousands of years. Aside from the Temple mystery teachings, this is why so many illustrious personalities went to Kamit to study its system of government and the reasons for its success, in order to replicate them in their own country.
	
	70. Kings were not allowed to have autocratic power.
	    70.1. their acts were controlled by established laws.
	    70.2. their personal servants and confidants and counselors were priests.
	
	    70.3. Particular importance is placed on the ministers of the king. It is recognized that people become corrupt through bad associations, and those

prescriptions set forth in laws, not only their administrative acts, but also those that had to do with the way in which they spent their time from day to day, and with the food which they ate.

70.2. In the matter of their servants, for instance, not one was a slave, such as had been acquired by purchase or born in the home, but all were sons of the most distinguished Priests, over twenty years old and the best educated of their fellow-countrymen, in order that the king, by virtue of his having the noblest men to care for his person and to attend him throughout both day and night, might follow no low practices; for

70.3. no ruler advances far along the road of evil unless he has those about him who will minister to his passions. And the hours of both the day and night were laid out according to a plan, and at the specified hours it was absolutely required of the king that he should do what the laws stipulated and not what he thought best. For instance, in the morning, as soon as he was awake, he first of all had to receive the letters which had been sent from all sides, the purpose being that he might be able to dispatch all administrative business and perform every act properly, being thus accurately informed about everything that was being done throughout his kingdom. Then, after he had bathed and bedecked his body with rich garments and the insignia of his office, he had to sacrifice to the gods…For there was a set time not only for his holding audiences or rendering judgments, but even for his taking a walk, bathing, and sleeping with his wife, and, in a word, for every act of his life. And it was the custom for the kings to partake of delicate food, eating no other meat than veal and duck, and drinking only a prescribed amount of wine, which was not enough to make them unreasonably surfeited or drunken. And, speaking generally, their whole diet was ordered with such continence that it had the appearance of having been drawn up, not by a lawgiver, but by the most skilled of their physicians, with only their health in view.

71. Strange as it may appear that the king did not have the entire control of his daily fare, far more remarkable still was the fact that (Ancient Egyptian) kings were not allowed to render any legal decision or transact any business at random or to punish anyone through malice or in anger or for any other unjust reason, but only in accordance with the established laws, relative to each offence. And in following the dictates of custom in these matters, so far were they from being indignant or taking offence in their souls, that, on the contrary, they actually

who encourage ("minister to") and reinforce their negative tendencies. The priests, who are trained to control their passions, help the king to control his and make sure that he or she (Queen) follows the prescribed course of action based on truth and righteousness as opposed to personal passions and desires. (Notice the importance placed here on control of passions). Note that even if nepotism and hereditary rulership was allowed, the counsel of priests and priestesses would maintain control over the ruler and the judgments.

70.3 The king did not control his own daily schedule nor to a great extent the day-to-day activities, diet, time spent with family etc. The royal schedule was prescribed to promote health and well-being, alertness and fitness of body and mind.

71. The king did not control his own daily schedule and could not render legal decisions based on whims, personal vendettas, anger, hatred, greed, jealousy or any unfair reason. He or she could not act with personal excesses such as those seen in the later Roman culture, or the dictatorships, aristocracies, etc., of modern times

71.1. It was

held that they led a most happy life;

71.1. for they believed that all other men, in thoughtlessly following their natural passions, commit many acts which bring them injuries and perils, and that oftentimes some who realize that they are about to commit a sin nevertheless do base acts when overpowered by love or hatred or some other passion, while they, on the other hand, by virtue of their having cultivated a manner of life which had been chosen before all others by the most prudent of all men (priests), fell into the fewest mistakes.

71.2. And since the kings followed so righteous a course in dealing with their subjects, the people manifested a goodwill towards their rulers which surpassed even the affection they had for their own kinsmen; for not only the order of the Priests but, in short, all the inhabitants of Egypt were less concerned for their wives and children and their other cherished possessions than for the safety of their kings.

71.3. Consequently, during most of the time covered by the reigns of the kings of whom we have a record, they maintained an orderly civil government and continued to enjoy a most felicitous life, so long as the system of laws described was in force; and, more than that, they conquered more nations and achieved greater wealth than any other people, and adorned their lands with monuments and buildings never to be surpassed, and their cities with costly dedications of every description.

73. And since Egypt as a whole is divided into several parts which in Greek are called nomes, over each of these a nomarch is appointed who is charged with both the oversight and care of all its affairs. Furthermore, the entire country is divided into three parts, the first of which is held by the order of the Priests,

73.1. which is accorded the greatest veneration by the inhabitants both because these men have charge of the worship of the gods and because by virtue of their education they bring to bear a higher intelligence than others.

73.2. With the income from these holdings of land they perform all the sacrifices throughout Egypt, maintain their assistants, and minister to their own needs;

73.3. for it has always been held that the honours paid to the gods should never be changed, but should ever be per formed by the same men and in the same manner, and that those who

understood from early times that when a person follows their "natural passions," they are led to suffering and ruin; if a ruler should act in that way, the country and its people will suffer greatly.

71.2. The prudent form of government leads to the fewest mistakes and the greatest goodwill between ruler (Heka) and ruled (Hekat)

71.3. Orderly civil government is maintained when society is governed by righteous laws, when the government leaders are accountable for their actions, and when they are guided by wise counsel instead of ego driven passions.

73. At one time Egypt was divided into three parts.

73.1. Due to their education and piety, the clergy were venerated and were thought to bring a special acumen to society.

73.2. The clergy caste owned 1/3 of the land, and through its income they sustained themselves and the work of the Temples.

73.3. The tradition is that the worship of the Divine should be performed by the same caste, and in the same manner as has been done thought-out history. This is a service performed on behalf of all citizens. And those

deliberate on behalf of all should not lack the necessities of life. 73.4. For, speaking generally, the Priests are the first to deliberate upon the most important matters and are always at the king's side, sometimes as his assistants, sometimes to propose measures and give instructions, and they also, by their knowledge of astrology and of divination, forecast future events, and read to the king, out of the record of acts preserved in their sacred books, those which can be of assistance. 73.5. For it is not the case with the Egyptians as it is with the Greeks, that a single man or a single woman takes over the priesthood, but many are engaged in the sacrifices and honours paid the gods and pass on to their descendants the same rule of life. They also pay no taxes of any kind, and in repute and in power are second after the king. 73.6. The second part of the country has been taken over by the kings for their revenues, out of which they pay the cost of their wars, support the splendour of their court, and reward with fitting gifts any who have distinguished themselves; and they do not swamp the private citizens by taxation, since their income from these revenues gives them a great plenty. 73.7. The last part is held by the warriors, as they are called, who are subject to call for all military duties, the purpose being that those who hazard their lives may be most loyal to the country because of such allotment of land and thus may eagerly face the perils of war. For it would be absurd to entrust the safety of the entire nation to these men and yet have them possess in the country no property to fight for valuable enough to arouse their ardour.	who those who "deliberate on the behalf of all" should not be destitute, and also notice that they are not being put in a position to be begging either. They provide for themselves with the land. 73.5 Again the priests are counselors to the ruler. In Neterian religion, there is no overall Pontiff such as in the case of the Catholic Church. The priesthood does have a hierarchy based on years of service, education and spiritual attainment. However, the ruling body of the clergy operates as a board of priests and priestesses who may have a leader of the council (*udjatnu* - Chief of Council of priests.).

CONCLUSION

It must be clearly understood from the above that the Neterian clergy discovered long ago that personality issues cloud the judgment of leaders and people generally. Therefore, great effort was made to create precedent law so that when issues came up they could be dealt with dispassionately and impartially, regardless of the tempers and emotions of the present. In this manner decisions could be made from the perspective of truth instead of personal desire or emotion. This concept is a hallmark of Neterian spirituality, which found expression later in Buddhist culture. Realize that the famous Buddhist term signifying the highest spiritual achievement, "Nirvana," means "without desire." In any case we must also acknowledge that any law, no matter how well constructed, can be distorted, or ignored. This is why laws are not enough. Ordinary individuals cannot sustain the law due to pressures of their own internal desires and those of society. A body elevated people, schooled in philosophy and trained in the disciplines of self-mastery (Shetaut Neter-Egyptian Mysteries, Shedy (Egyptian Yoga)) are necessary to interpret the law and enforce it with moral conviction. They are the conscience of society, and their task is not just to uphold laws, but also to explain why they are necessary and relevant, and to appeal to the better nature of the people. So along with moral laws, there must be moral people to enforce and follow them, being an example for others. Those people should be in leadership roles for the purpose of guiding society, so that it may have a tone of righteousness and truth and not a tone of selfishness and greed, which becomes accepted as a fact of life. Such a society acquiesces to the lower base culture, and it becomes corrupted thereby. This is the important and noble role of the priests and priestesses in reference to their role as leaders of society.

Thus, the outline above provides an impression of the clergy of Ancient Egypt, and an idea as to the changes that contributed to the degradation of society directly through a less spiritual and more lay management of the country, and indirectly through the minimization of the female gender and the clergy. These periods coincide with increasing social pressures due to internal corruption and greed, as well as external pressures due to attacks from other countries (especially the Asiatics and later the Greeks). The rule of Egypt by Asiatics introduced social aspects that had not been part of the Kamitan culture, including male dominance and a predilection for pleasure seeking as opposed to spiritual aspiration. The New Kingdom Period saw the beginning of poetry and prose writings exclusively dedicated to romance and love interests. The Ptolemaic period saw the introduction of sexual imagery in sculpture and on papyrus, that transcended the normal bounds of tantric iconography, and might be considered pornographic, as well as the custom of kissing on the lips. Customs like kissing on the lips was and continues to be characteristic of western culture. The Ancient Egyptian custom was to touch noses and share the Sekhem "Life Force."

Therefore, the lessons from the history of Ancient Egypt with respect to the long-term survival of a culture that is established upon the spiritual pillars of society, the priests and priestesses, and their particular disciplines and religious practices, need to be an important aspect of any historical study relating to Ancient Egypt. There are salient points here for every modern day practitioner of the Neterian faith. Further, degradation occurred when the Christian zealots and the later Muslim fanatics came to Egypt and set about destroying monuments, razing the Temples which had stood for thousands of years, and at the same time murdering those Neterian priests and priestesses who they could find, while forcing the general populace to follow the new religions.

Stela of Hetepsi, Priestess of Hetheru at the temple of Denderah. (Dynasty 6-8)

Early Christian and Roman-Christian Conquest Periods and the Closing of Egyptian Temples

The Roman Period lasted from c.30 B.C.E.-395 A.C.E., when Rome disintegrated due to internal corruption and foreign wars. The early Christians (300-450 A.C.E.) who came into Egypt from Rome and the Byzantine realm were not disposed to live side by side with the native people who continued to worship the Ancient Egyptian gods and goddesses. There was a tenuous harmony between the Christians and the Muslims (650-1000) who came into Egypt in the later part of the 1st millennium, because they were seen to be worshipping essentially the same God. In the case of the Ancient Egyptian gods and goddesses, the already dogmatic and fanatical early orthodox Christians (not the Gnostic Christians), who had themselves been persecuted for over 300 years, now began to persecute people of all other religions and even other Christian sects that did not agree with the particular form of Christianity approved by the Roman Church. Therefore, even the Gnostic Christians, who had developed mystical Christianity in Egypt over 300 years earlier, were also persecuted. The orthodox Christian misunderstanding about the symbolism and especially the sexual imagery in Ancient Egyptian iconography, and the instigation by the Roman government, coupled with the force of the Roman army, were all instrumental to the development of a particular hatred and ensuing violence against the Ancient Egyptian Temples, that were already spread across the Roman empire. The Temples of Isis (Ancient Egyptian goddess Aset) and Serapis (Ancient Egyptian Asar-Hapi) were especially favored in the Roman Empire up to that time. If anyone wonders why the Ancient Egyptian Temple system persisted through the Persian conquest, the Assyrian conquest, the Greek conquest, and the Roman conquest but came to a close during the emergence of the Roman Catholic Church, they have no further to look than the following statements by the leaders of the early orthodox Christian Church.

> *"What is now called the Christian religion has existed among the Ancients and was not absent from the beginning of the human race until Christ came in the flesh from which time the true religion which was already in existence began to be called Christian."*
>
> -St. Augustine

The Founder of Christian monasticism, Saint Anthony, led his followers in active attacks on the Ancient Egyptian Temples. The ignorance, intolerance and denigration of the Kamitan Temples and their images are readily evident in the following quote.

> *"Which is better, to confess the cross or to attribute adulteries and pederastys to these so called gods, beasts, reptiles and the images of men? The Christians, by their faith in God prove that the demons whom the Egyptians consider gods are no gods! The Christians trample them underfoot and drive them out for what they are, deceivers and corruptors of men. Through Jesus-Christ our lord, Amen"*

The statement above displays a disregard for the professed Christian values of peace, compassion and neighborly love (Bible book of Matthew 5:7, 22:39). While those Christian values are professed, they are often ignored when political and economic interests or where issues of living with others are concerned. The Crusades are a salient example. The acts and writings of Christians in ancient and modern times shows that the doctrines of love, forgiveness and compassion are applied to others of the same faith, to the extent that economic competition is not an issue, but not others of other faiths. They are considered as pagans and unworthy of respect – "since they are going to hell anyway."

Matthew 5

    7 Blessed [are] the merciful: for they shall obtain mercy.

Matthew 22

    39 And the second [is] like it, Thou shalt love thy neighbor as thyself.

It is ironic that the admonition of Jesus in Matthew 7:6, *Give not that which is holy to dogs, neither cast ye your pearls before swine, lest they trample them under their feet, and turn again and rend you,* can be applied to the Christian faith itself, as its zealotry and intolerance deem it as the very same degraded culture it itself speaks of, as it has not shown the ability to receive any wisdom since its followers have been led to believe that the Bible is the "true" and "only" and "perfect" "word of God" and that no other truth exists. Also ironically, Christians, once the persecuted in the late Roman times when the Roman emperors adopted Christianity as the state religion, became the persecutors and murdered "pagan" priests, priestesses and led a persecution against all non-Christians, forcing new symbols on the populace. The term "Fundamentalism" is a modern interpretation of orthodox Christianity but as we have seen its roots are deeply embedded in the fabric of the Roman Catholic Church and the Christian Bible. This was later expressed in the form of the Crusades, the destruction of Native American culture, the African slave trade and the African missionary movements as well as other efforts to convert peoples around the world to Christianity, and at the same time eradicate all other religions, something which has angered many nations around the world including China and the Muslim countries. The persecution and wonton destruction of the Ancient Egyptian scriptures along with the murder of those who were knowledgeable about the symbolism was lost to Western orthodox culture from that time on. All those who would study, practice or profess the teachings of Neterian spirituality or any other mystical traditions should maintain keen awareness of the dangers posed by followers of orthodox religions or those who profess dogmatic teachings or fanatical, fundamentalist forms of religion.

The wisdom related to the Ancient Egyptian symbolism such as that displayed by Dionysius the Areopagite was misunderstood and misrepresented by the orthodox Church leaders in favor of the simple but limited symbolism of orthodox Christianity. Gnostic Christianity followed more closely the Ancient Egyptian teachings.[40]

> *"If anyone suggests that it is disgraceful to fashion base images of the Divine and most Holy orders, it is sufficient to answer that the most holy Mysteries are set forth in two modes: one by means of similar and sacred representations akin to their nature, and the other to unlike forms designed with every possible discordance ... Discordant symbols are more appropriate representations of the Divine because the human mind tends to cling to the physical form of representation believing for example that the Divine are "golden beings or shining men flashing like lightning." But lest this error befall us, the wisdom of the venerable sages leads us through disharmonious dissimilitudes, not allowing our irrational nature to become attached to those unseemly images ... Divine things may not be easily accessible to the unworthy, nor may those who earnestly contemplate the Divine symbols dwell upon the forms themselves as final truth."*
>
> – Dionysius the Areopagite

Even mysticism did not escape the process of co-optation. The same Dionysius the Areopagite who wrote the statement above, which is in direct contradiction with that of Saint Anthony (above), was accepted into the Christian Church. Some in the traditional Christian literature and scholarship have recognized St. Paul as the first great Christian mystic. The New Testament writings best known for their deeply mystical emphasis are Paul's letters and the Gospel of John (John 10:30-34). Christian mysticism, as a philosophical system, is derived from Neo-Platonism through the writings of Dionysius the Areopagite, or Pseudo-Dionysius. The original Dionysius the Areopagite lived in the 1st century A.C.E. and became first bishop of Athens. Dionysius was martyred about 95 A.C.E. He is often confused with the Pseudo-Dionysius (c. 500) who created mystical writings using the name of Dionysius the Areopagite. He was later canonized as a Catholic Saint. Dionysius was converted to Christianity when he heard Paul preach the sermon concerning the nature of "the unknown God" on the Hill of Mars or Areopagus in Athens, as described in Acts 17:15-34. However, while some aspects of mysticism can still be found in the Christian church they are heavily veiled and

---

[40] See the book *The Mystical Journey From Jesus to Christ* by Sebai Muata Ashby

misunderstood. They are also de-emphasized by the church leadership as anomalies and thus, negated and consequently nullified in the course of Church activities.[41]

Most often in Western culture, the term fundamentalism is used to describe non-Christian religions, especially militant Islamic groups. However, the term fundamentalism refers to a movement within the Protestant churches in the United States of America which attempts to maintain what its believers consider to be traditional interpretations of the Christian faith. Fundamentalism arose in reaction to what was seen as modernist or liberal trends within Protestantism, which began in the later 19th century. The conservatives began to create conferences and schools, which emphasize literal interpretations of the Bible as opposed to mythological, metaphorical and mystical interpretations. The Fundamentalist movement received the name from "The Fundamentals," a series of small books produced by conservative scholars that were widely distributed in 1910-12, which supposedly contained the basic issues defining the Christian faith. The doctrines most emphasized by fundamentalists are:

1- The divinely inspired and infallible nature of the Bible.
2- The Trinity.
3- The immediate creation by the command of God.
4- Man's fall into depravity.
5- The necessity for salvation of being "Born Again" by faith in Christ.
6- Christ's deity, virgin birth, miracle-working power and substitutionary atonement for man, and his physical resurrection, ascension, and imminent pre-millennial Second Coming
7- The physical resurrection of man for Heaven or Hell.
8- Fundamentalism also stresses domestic and foreign evangelism and is strongly opposed to evolution, Communism, and ecumenism.[42]

The oversimplified ideal of having faith and worshipping God the Father in Judaism, God the Father and Jesus and Christianity, or Allah in Islam, as opposed to the seemingly elaborate system of Ancient Egyptian gods and goddesses, was palatable to the masses of people who had no capacity to enter into the practice of religion led by an Egyptian priest or priestess. When society is in a state of strife, fundamentalism gains more adherents. Under those conditions people tend to seek simple answers to the troubles of life and fundamentalist or cultish forms of spirituality that do not require, and even discourage, critical thinking, become more seductive to the weak or degraded mind. Those people also become more susceptible to demagoguery and the simple philosophy of zealots or those who advocate the destruction of those who they see as the source of the social strife. Evil tyrants throughout history have used many scapegoats; Ex, Africans persecuted by Europeans, Americans, Australians, and missionaries, etc. of European descent and the Jews in Europe persecuted by the Germans and the gentile community. Orthodox religion may be seen as a fanatical, dogmatic (extreme fundamentalist) reaction to tyrannical government and or debauched (morally wrong), depraved, decadent society. It is no coincidence that Judaism, Christianity and Islam originated and developed in periods of great social degradation and tyrannical governments. Christianity in particular, was a reaction to the cruelty, violence and moral depravity of Roman culture. As extreme reactions to the degraded social order, they promoted the opposite extreme to the prevailing degraded culture, thus becoming alternate forms of tyranny, enforcing their own philosophy of morality and destroying those who opposed them. The term zealot originates in the name of a Jewish sect that formed a movement in the first century A.C.E. that fought against Roman rule in Palestine, seeing Roman occupation incompatible with strict monotheism. In the year 394 A.C.E., the Temple of Aset at *Philae,* where Egyptologists discovered the latest hieroglyphic inscriptions, was closed by Christian Zealots who had taken over Egypt and Ethiopia by violence (as described above). Further, since the time of the Islamic takeover of Egypt there has been a systematic dismantling and destruction of Ancient Egyptian monuments and iconographies as being incompatible with Islam. The idea of incompatibility with other spiritual traditions or opinions is a hallmark of religious and social fundamentalism. Fundamentalism gives rise to zealotry, which is a form of fanaticism. In simple terms, it is the inability to coexist with those who

---

[41] See the book *The Mystical Journey From Jesus to Christ* by Sebai Muata Ashby
[42] Random House Encyclopedia.

disagree with one's point of view. This is why zealots feel not only the need to control, but also the need to convert. Fundamentalism and military/economic power engender social/cultural hubris and that in turn gives rise to the superiority complex that gives them the "right" to destroy others who do not submit to the "higher" moral authority. This is also why true spiritualists should work to promote authentic practice of religion and the universal philosophy of caring for all humanity. That is the best way to promote peace and harmony, and peace and harmony are the means to promote the mental capacity to feel free, to advance on the spiritual path and allow others to coexist in freedom and peace.

Further, the Christian exclusion of women from the priesthood and from a prominent position in the religion was agreeable to the Roman leaders whose culture, coupled with that of the Greeks, professed male dominance, unlike the Ancient Egyptian culture and religion. The fundamentalist concept of religion is necessarily in contradiction with mysticism and religions that make use of polytheistic monotheism (many deities to represent aspects of the one Supreme Being) such as the Ancient Egyptian, Yoruba and Hindu religions. This is because the fundamentalist model of religion is *idolatrous*. Orthodox religion is idolatrous because it espouses the belief that there is one God, one religion, one form or iconography, etc. Mystical religions do not hold that concept. They see divinity as universal and un-circumscribable by any image or form and therefore there can be many, while they all are understood to be expressions of the same Supreme Being operating everywhere and through all religions. The Christian missionary movement has followed the *Religious Conquest Pattern* of:

1st -Peaceful introduction of the religion,
2nd -Where conversion is slow they begin to denigrate the other religions,
3rd -The denigration turns to hatred and statements inciting violence and the illegitimacy of other religions,
4th -There is an active move to violently persecute the leaders (priest and priestesses) of the rival religions and prevent them from conducting their religions.
5th -close the Temples of their religious rivals and finally,
6th -If people do not convert after their Temple is destroyed, co-opt their symbols, rituals and traditions, forcing them to gradually believe they are worshipping the new divinity in some of the same ways they venerated the old (ancient) "pagan" one. Over a period of 1-3 generations of being deprived the opportunity to worship in the old fashion, in the old language and with the old understanding, the younger generation is cut off from their ancestry and those knowledgeable about their culture and traditions, so the old religion is forgotten. Some of the rituals, symbols and traditions remain, but the original meaning has been forgotten and whatever prestige was due to the old religion is now ascribed to the new.

Where outright destruction of Temples and murdering of priests and priestesses failed to convert people who persisted in carrying on the ancient religious traditions even when the priests and priestesses had been killed or forced to leave the Temple, the Christians had a separate plan – cooptation. The evidence given by the Christian tradition itself and its own documents suggests that images such as the cross (Ancient Egyptian Ankh), the dove (Ancient Egyptian sundisk), that of the Black Mary (Ancient Egyptian Aset), and the concepts of the resurrection, the eucharist, the birthday of the savior Jesus (Ancient Egyptian Heru), and many others[43] were taken directly from Ancient Egyptian religion and renamed (rededicated as it were) and used in Christian worship. This practice was consistent with the practice of inculturation, also known as co-optation,[44] the process of adopting symbols and rituals from other religions and calling them Christian, which were officially confirmed and endorsed as church policy by Pope St Gregory the Great in a letter given to priests written in 601 A.C.E.:

"It is said that the men of this nation are accustomed to sacrificing oxen. *It is necessary that this custom be converted into a Christian rite*. On the day of the dedication of the

---

[43] See the book *The Mystical Journey From Jesus to Christ* by Sebai Muata Ashby
[44] To neutralize or win over (an independent minority, for example) through assimilation into an established group or culture.

[pagan] Temples thus changed into churches, and similarly for the festivals of the saints, whose relics will be placed there, you should allow them, as in the past, to build structures of foliage around these same churches. They shall bring to the churches their animals, and kill them, no longer as offerings to the devil, but for Christian banquets in name and honor of God, to whom after satiating themselves, they will give thanks. Only thus, by preserving for men some of the worldly joys, will you lead them thus more easily to relish the joys of the spirit."

Here we have in the year 601 A.C.E., something like one of those memos that you find where the smoking industry knew all along that smoking was addictive and harmful or the memo of the Ford car company detailing how they knew all along that the Pinto car could blow up in an accident, but chose to proceed anyway. This is what is called the ***"smoking gun"*** kind of evidence, when people are caught incriminating themselves. This displays the premeditated plan of the early Christian church; they are saying the policy to convert the people is not working well enough. People still continued to visit their holy centers and practice their traditions. So now the Christians needed to destroy the Temples, the sacred sites, and or convert them by placing Christian churches on the previously "pagan" sites. This is what the Christians also did to the Native Americans, destroyed their sacred sites and built churches over them, and convinced the people that they are going to hell if they did not follow the new tradition. At the same time they killed or cut off those who spoke about or espoused other traditions.

The Muslim Movement and the Closing of the Ancient Egyptian Temples

The Islamic culture acted and continues to act in the same way. There were many converts to Christianity, but few who wanted to completely accept Christianity, and give up their mysticism of ancient times, even with its similarities to the Asarian Tradition. So then if a person wanted to go to the sacred site in some countries they had to go to the Christian Church or Muslim Mosque. While orthodox Islam professes a disbelief in symbols and idols as pagan and irreligious, the actual history of Islam even up to the present day contradicts this view in practice. For many hundreds of years, and especially during the occupation of India, the Muslims systematically dismantled or tore down Hindu Temples and on the same spots erected Mosques. The same thing was done in Kamit and elsewhere in Africa. One example which has caused much consternation to Egyptologists is the Mosque that was build on the site of the Temple to Amun in Waset (Luxor), Egypt which was constructed right on top of one of the most important Temples of Ancient Egypt.[45 \ 46] The picture below shows the location of the Mosque. The structure in the foreground is the Temple of Amun. The structures rising up from within the court of the Temple are the minarets of the Mosque. Since the dawn of Egyptology in the early 19th century, Egyptologists have repeatedly asked for permission to move the Mosque at their own expense. The Muslims in charge of the Mosque have refused, stating that it is located on "sacred ground."

The Priests and Priestesses of Ancient Egypt

Like the Christians, the Muslims used stones from the Temple to construct their Mosques. The following is A1- a line drawing showing the layout of the Temple floor plan and A2- a drawing showing the layout of the Temple floor plan with the Mosque, B- a grayscale woodcut drawing reconstruction of the Luxor Temple of Amun in the city of Waset (modern Luxor) to show how the Temple looked in ancient times before its dismantling and the location of the Mosque within it.

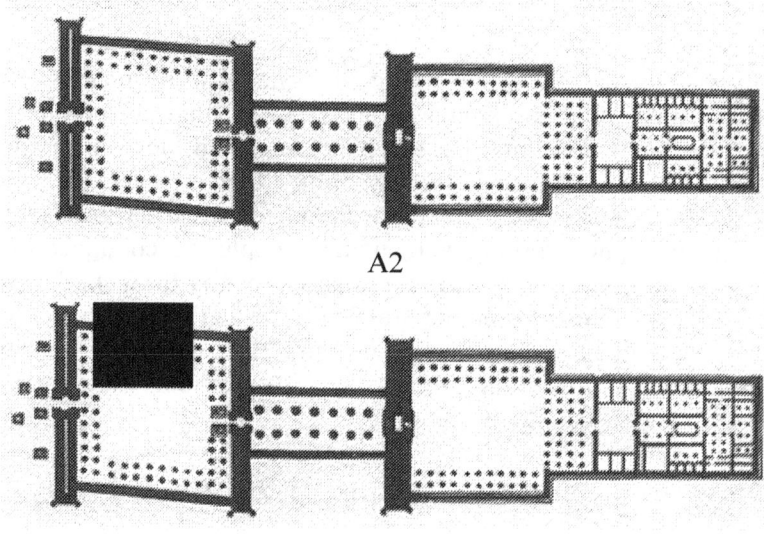

A2

B

The Moslems acted similarly when they invaded India. They told Hindus that they shouldn't have any symbols, and should abandon the primitive religion with many gods and goddesses; the Muslims considered the Hindu system as polytheism. But then they put mosques over thousands of the previously Hindu sites. They put the mosque right on top of where the Hindu Temple used to be with all of the Islamic iconography and the calligraphy. Islam claims that it does not have symbols, and yet it has the star and the crescent moon. Cooptation and violent conversion were the only way that they could convert people. In modern times financial and political coercion are still used by dominant cultures. If a person does not convert they are cut off from the economy and the capacity to join the government, and make laws to protect themselves.

This socio-political-psycho-spiritual study is important because the Neterian clergy must learn from the mistakes of the past, and how to cope with the ignorance of the masses and the forces of fanaticism and cooptation, which continues in Africa even today, and in other indigenous areas of the world as well, leading to strife, intolerance, and ignorance, because that is how those co-opting religions are practiced.

The violence, cruelty and intolerance of the western orthodox religions is more evident when it is realized that the Koran and Bible both appear to condone the killing of people, even though one of the Ten Commandments of God to Moses prohibits such an act. Therefore, it is not surprising to see people of the Judeo-Christian faith fighting in wars while professing non-violence, or engaging in acts of psychological violence, criminal behavior, etc. In this area the early Muslims thought they were superior in that they exhorted a strict moral code. However, they too inflicted great pain and suffering to many people while at the same time converting them to Islam. In Judaism and Christianity, the book of Exodus, Verses 32 25:28 provides insight into one of the examples that may be found, that promote violence and even killing (murder) of those who do not submit to the religion. Moses went to commune with God and when he returned from the conference in which he received the tablets with the Ten Commandments he found the people turning towards the Idols of Ancient Egypt. He instructed that all who wanted to follow him should get on one side and others on the other and then he ordered, "on God's instruction," the children of Levi to kill the unbelievers.

Exodus 32 25:28 (Jewish-Christian Bible)

25 And when Moses saw that the people were naked; (for Aaron had made them naked unto their shame among their enemies:)
26 Then Moses stood in the gate of the camp, and said, Who is on the LORD'S side? let him come unto me. And all the sons of Levi gathered themselves together unto him.
27 And he said unto them, Thus saith the LORD God of Israel, Put every man his sword by his side, and go in and out from gate to gate throughout the camp, and slay every man his brother, and every man his companion, and every man his neighbor.
28 And the children of Levi did according to the word of Moses: and there fell of the people that day about three thousand men.

Islamic Views on the Polytheists Including the Ancient Egyptian and Hindu religions

As for the Islamic views on the followers of the Ancient Egyptian religion, they are indirectly mentioned as polytheists and they are group together with the Jews and Christians as well as other groups, i.e. any groups who do not believe "the truth." The polytheists as well as the Jews and Christians will be "judged by Allah" (22:17) and since they have an "evil opinion of Allah" (48:6), and they "reject truth" (true faith) (98:5-6) they will go to hell (48:6).

22:17 (Koran) Those who believe (in the Koran), those who follow the Jewish (scriptures), and the Sabians, Christians, Megians, and Polytheists, -- Allah will judge between them on the Day of Judgment: For Allah is witness of all things.

48:6 (Koran) And that He may punish the Hypocrites, men and women, and the Polytheists, men and women, who imagine an evil opinion of Allah. On them is a round of Evil: The Wrath of Allah is on them: He has cursed them and got Hell ready for them: and evil is it for a destination.

98:5 (Koran) And they have been commanded no more than this: To worship Allah, offering Him sincere devotion, being True (in faith); to establish regular Prayer; and to practice regular Charity; and that is the Religion Right and Straight.

98:6 (Koran) Those who reject (Truth), among the People of the Book and among the Polytheists, will be in Hellfire, to dwell therein (for aye). They are the worst of creatures.

The Koran seems to accord special status to Jews and Christians, but only as earlier and imperfect followers of the same tradition that Islam emerges from, i.e. the tradition of Abraham. The following verse from the Koran is significant because it states in no uncertain language that the teaching brought to the world by the "holy Apostle" (Muhammad) supercedes that of the Jews because the Muslims have the truth and the Christians have a lie. Verse 9:30 Section 5 specifically takes issue with the Christian idea that *"Christ is the son of Allah"* and that in this they *"imitate what the Unbelievers of old used to say."* The Christian statement occurs previously in the Ancient Egyptian religion, as Heru, the savior and prototype for the Christian Christ figure, was also stated to be the *son of God* (Asar {Osiris}). The Muslims see this concept as a great *"delusion"* coming from *"their mouth"* i.e. not from revelation. Thus, the Islamic faith seeks to put down and invalidate the Jewish and Christian as well as the "polytheistic" faiths. The Christian faith also seeks to put down and invalidate any religion other than their own since those who are not saved by Jesus (who is the only way) will go to hell. In this way the seeds of dissention and disharmony with any religion other than their own have been embedded into the holy scriptures of the western religions themselves, and thus despite the attempts to promote harmony and peace between the religions there will ultimately be an incompatibility that will lead to conflict at some point (because those passages are unequivocally accepted by their respective followers to be God's "true" words. This conflict is even more pronounced when the views of these three religions, Judaism, Christianity and Islam, which consider themselves to be "monotheistic," are considered in so far as their relations with what they consider to be "polytheistic" religions, such as the Kamitan and the Hindu religions. There is more denigration, more invalidation, and hence more rejection and violence directed at those religions. So while many people claim that Islam is a religion of "peace" because the word "Islam" which means "submission to God" is related to the Arabic word for peace, in reality there can be no peace when such statements are included in the religious faith, because they inevitably lead to a separation and a competition between faiths as long as there are people who believe in the infallibility of the scriptures themselves. Since there is no way that these religions will continue without their "holy scriptures," and the prospect of amending them is nil, then it follows that there can be no resolution to this problem unless these aspects of the scriptures are ignored. If that occurs, there will be a contradiction since the "whole scripture" is regarded as a "divine revelation," and to most people this implies "true" and "perfect" teachings that must ALL be obeyed.

Koran 9:30 Section 5 The Jews call Uzair (Ezra) a son of Allah, and the Christians call Christ the Son of Allah. That is a saying from their mouth; (In this) they imitate what the Unbelievers of old used to say. Allah's curse be on them: How they are deluded away from the Truth!

Egypt is in the present day populated by a culture that is classified as "Arab." The Arabs are members of an Asiatic[47] people inhabiting Arabia, whose language and Islamic religion spread widely throughout Asia Minor (the Middle East) and northern Africa from the seventh century onward. Having conquered Egypt since the 7th century A.C.E., the Arabs in Egypt, who now refer to themselves as "Egyptians," have adopted the fame but not the legacy or heritage of Ancient Egypt. That is, the government and schools espouse the idea that Ancient Egyptian culture and civilization is part of the past history of the modern Arab Egyptian

---

[47] A group of people who originally lived in Asia Minor (Middle East), especially Arabia with mixed North (Aryan?) and East (European) Asian and African ethnicity.

people. Many present day secular Arabs of Egypt claim the heritage for themselves, but most of the population admittedly care little about Ancient Egypt except to the extent that is a magnet for tourists and is therefore a tourism financial boon. The government trains "guides" to lead tourists around the Temples and other sites of the country; they are taught to espouse the deficient chronology of Ancient Egypt and many distorted renditions of the myths. Further, one can hear in the speech of many guides a disdain and sometimes even disgust for the images presented in the iconography of the Temples. Interviews[48] of some present day Arab Muslims living in Egypt led to the discovery that the general view of those who are brought up in orthodox Islamic culture is that Ancient Egyptian religion was not religion at all, but rather feeble attempts at theorizing about spiritual matters. In fact, the underlying view, confirmed in many interviews of Arabs born in Egypt, is that they view "Islam as the only true" religion and religions such as the Ancient Egyptian as "idolatry." Consequently, the philosophy, art and spirituality of Ancient Egypt are perceived as nothing more than commodities to attract foreign dollars into the ailing economy as well as to support the military government there and at another level, they are means by which some Arabs attain higher status in the society by becoming "Egyptologists." They constitute some of the most vehement opponents to any view that suggests an older chronology for Ancient Egypt and anything that might suggest that there is a form of spirituality as correct and or valid as Islam. Consequently, they are some of the most ardent supporters of the orthodox Egyptological views, just as western scholars also profess the idea that while splendorous and vast, the Ancient Egyptian religion is a primitive system of spirituality and that Christianity is an advanced and civilized religion, superior to any Ancient Egyptian concepts.

Cooptation as a Strategy to Elevate a New Religion

What were the Ancient Egyptian priests and priestesses doing? What was it that the co-opting forces had to stop them from doing? The practice of Ancient Egyptian religion had to be stopped or neutralized in order to provide the new religions (Judaism, Christianity and Islam) a prominent place and not be overshadowed and considered as a new and/or minor religion. The idea is an old one, to elevate one by lowering and denigrating the other. The Jewish Bible itself states that the people following Judaism were originally Egyptians (Africans) who left the country to wander in order to find their own homeland. Egypt was so permeated by the ancient Shetaut Neter (Ancient Egyptian Religion and its gods and goddesses and their philosophy), that Judaism would not have survived there beyond cult status; hence, the need for an exodus. Further, although the Jewish religion has been erroneously linked with the idea of race or ethnicity, the term "Jew"[49] does not connote a racial, ethnic or genetic relationship, but rather it refers to religion. The term "Hebrew" means "those who pass from place to place." Judaism is a religion that was developed among some in the Hebrew culture. The Hebrews shared the same history of wandering in ancient times with other Semitic[50] nomads, and not all Hebrews who were living in Palestine, were Jews.

Many times in the emergence of new mythologies, the founders or followers of the new system will create stories (myths) to show how the new system surpasses the old. The story of Exodus is such an example. Moses went to Mount Sinai to talk to God and brought back Ten Commandments. At the time that Moses was supposed to have lived (1200?-1000? B.C.E.), Ancient Egypt was still the most powerful culture in the ancient world. However, it was also on a social and cultural decline from its previous height as the foremost culture in religious practice, art, science, social order, etc. So it became necessary for a small group who left Egypt, that were themselves Egyptians, to legitimize the inception of the new theology by claiming to have triumphed over the mighty Egyptians with the help of their new "true" God who defeated the "weak" God(s) of Egypt. This triumphant story would surely bring people to convert to the new faith since up to that time the Ancient Egyptian gods and goddesses had been seen not only as the most powerful divinities, but also as the source of all other deities in other religions. So in effect, by saying that the Jewish God is different (has a different origin) and "defeated" the Ancient Egyptian God by freeing the Jews, it is

---

[48] Conducted by Sebai Muata Ashby while traveling throughout Egypt 2000 – speaking to northern Arab-Egyptians (in Cairo) and one Nubian-Egyptian in Aswan

[49] **Jew** (jōō) *n.* **1.** An adherent of Judaism as a religion or culture.[115]

[50] Of or pertaining to the Semites, especially Jewish or Arabic. 2. Pertaining to a subfamily of the Afro-Asiatic language family that includes Arabic and Hebrew.[115]

the same as saying that a new, more powerful religion is to be followed. This form of commencement for a spiritual tradition is not uncommon.

In India, the emergence of Hinduism saw a similar situation as the one that occurred between the Jewish and Ancient Egyptian Religion. In the period c. 800 B.C.E., the earlier Vedic-Aryan religious teachings related to the God, Indra (c. 1,000 B.C.E.), were supplanted by the teachings related to the Upanishadic and Vaishnava tradition of Vishnu worship which includes the devotion to God in the form of the Vishnu avatars, Rama and Krishna. The Vaishnava tradition was developed by the indigenous Indian peoples to counter the religion imposed on them by the Vedic Aryans. In the epic stories known as the Ramayana and the Mahabharata, Vishnu incarnates as Rama and Krishna, respectively, and throughout their stories it is related how Vishnu's incarnations are more powerful than Indra, who is portrayed as being feeble and weak. Some of the writings of the Upanishadic Tradition[51] (from the non-Aryan Hindu tradition) contain specific verses stating that they supersede the Vedas. One such statement can be found in the Mundaka Upanishad and another in the Brihadaranyaka Upanishad.

A similar situation occurred with the emergence of Buddhism. The story of Buddha's struggle to attain Enlightenment is described in the inceptive and most influential work of Buddhist mythology. It relates how in the beginning of his spiritual quest he strived to practice the austere paths of Hinduism. He practiced renunciation of the world and all sorts of penances and asceticism, even to the point of almost starving to death as supposedly espoused by the austere disciplines of Hinduism. Then he discovered a "new" path, *The Middle Path*, which was and still is held to be superior to Hinduism by many Buddhist followers. In the beginning Buddhism spread widely throughout India, where it emerged originally, but later it declined and Hinduism reemerged again. It found a great and sustained following in China and Tibet, as well as the countries of Indo-China. The Indochinese peninsula includes a small part of Bangladesh, most of Myanmar (Burma), Thailand, Cambodia, and parts of Malaysia, Laos, and Vietnam. Currently in the west, Buddhism is rarely related to its roots in Hinduism and Yoga philosophy. Upon close examination, the roots of the teaching of the middle path along with the other major tenets of Buddhism can be found in the Upanishadic Tradition,[52] especially in the Isha Upanishad.

What allowed the attacks on Neterian Culture to Succeed?

The question is essentially what was it that brought on these attacks and this attempt at the destruction of Neterian culture. We have previously discussed how there was a turning away from the order, the Maatian order, which was kept for the society. There is a tradition that speaks of the karmic protection that one incurs when acting by righteousness. So if a person acts by righteousness, they are protected by the same righteousness. It is a very mystical understanding. If a person practices non-violence according to the teaching of non-violence as expressed in Maat philosophy, and is totally nonviolent and wished no one any wrong at all, there is no possible violence that can occur to them… but that person has to be perfect in nonviolence. Now consider, how many people are perfect in their nonviolence, including even at their unconscious level of mind. It means one cannot have even an inkling of negative thought about someone and can't have any kind of animosity– for example, one could not say, think or feel things like "O, why is this person doing that; they are not doing what they should be doing" –there must be perfect establishment in nonviolence. If that were possible, there would be a protective aura around that person or group of people, and it was said that there was an aura that protected Kamit for those thousands of years and that turning away allowed them to be vulnerable. Also consider that for most of Ancient Egyptian history, when Ancient Egyptian civilization was at its height, the other countries of the world were still living in the stone age or just coming into their Neolithic periods, just beginning to institute farming and pottery. So they were mostly uncivilized barbarians. When those barbarians organized sufficiently to achieve military power, but without civilized culture and spirituality, they posed a great threat to their neighbors (including the Ancient

---

[51] Any of a group of philosophical treatises contributing to the theology of ancient Hinduism-Vedanta Philosophy, elaborating on and superseding the earlier Vedas.
[52] Spiritual tradition in India based on the scriptures known as the Upanishads. It is also referred to as Vedanta Philosophy, the culmination or summary of the Vedic Tradition whish is itself based on the scriptures known as the Vedas.

Egyptians). There are many countries in the present day that are militarily powerful, but culturally immature, uncivilized and dangerous. They achieve great heights of technological advancement but emphasize greed, lust and violence against those who oppose their will or way of thinking, sometimes even professing a spiritual basis for their actions.

Any great society is susceptible to failure due to complacency caused by lack of challenge. Kamit had a history of thousands of years. What would happen if you had a society that was not challenged? Remember that if you are not challenged by the dis-order, by the forces contradicting society, what is going to strengthen you? If all you know is the society as it is going, as it has always been and you don't have any conception of what you need to be doing differently for the future, in order to survive and progress, there is going to be a failure, even if sages tell you what to do. People need to have experiences to test them, so they can have an opportunity to see the folly of egoism and the value of the wisdom teaching. Kamitan culture got into a groove, as it were. They were the only thing going on in the world essentially for thousands of years without worrying about any major attacks, any major breakdowns or any problems in the society. In that kind of environment there is the danger of complacency. However, in the spiritual field there was no complacency but rather expansion. But in other areas there was not the same kind of expansion and development. Others came (Hyksos-Asiatics) in and conquered the country, and then there was a backlash as we discussed. The royalty of Kamit said, we are going to takeover, and they did.

At the beginning of the New Kingdom Era the Kamitan royalty re-conquered the country and took over all the way from Nubia in the south to Asia Minor again; that lasted for a several hundreds of years coming down to the late period when the Assyrians finally were able to overcome them. In that period also, another important thing that happened was that in the conquering of those lands, Sumer, Persia, the Syrians and all those kingdoms, the Kamitans had to establish relations with those countries. They had to make political alliances and treaties. In those times, the usual way of accomplishing this was to arrange marriages between the royalties of the countries. So now you have a mixing of different cultures within the Kamitan society, which means the introduction of other cultural ways. Here we start seeing a lighter skin hue on the culture, since lighter skinned Asiatics are intermarrying with the darker skinned African-Egyptians. This mixing was always occurring, but here you have it happening at the highest levels of society with the power of influencing the whole culture. So there was an influx of foreign culture, and foreign ideas, some that were positive and some that were degrading, at that time. In this New Kingdom Period is where you start to see sentimental love poetry in Kamit, which you don't see in the prior years. That occurs in the Late Period. Mouth to mouth kissing is primarily a custom of Asia Minor and Europe, not an African custom. What was there in Kamit is the Eskimo kind of kissing where you touch the nose. You put the nose together and you breathe each other's breath. You breathe each other's life force. So if people of African descent desire those things it is because of western cultural influence.

So the Kamitan culture became weak, but the spiritual tradition remained strong. However, the culture could not protect the spiritual tradition. The ancient Egyptians held on fiercely to the gods and goddesses and what happened was that the early Christians saw that they were not going to convert them all, so they then turned to co-opting them. Co-optation means that you take the symbols and the traditions already there and then you start calling them yours. And so the Ancient Egyptian birth of Heru, which occurs on the 25th of December, now becomes Jesus' birth. That is co-optation. The Ancient Egyptian Ankh symbol becomes the cross; it now becomes a Christian symbol. The resurrection of Asar becomes the resurrection of Jesus. The Arit offering, eating the gods and goddesses, which symbolizes uniting with their cosmic energies or principles, becomes the Eucharist, the mass ritual. But that was not enough to stop the practice of Kamitan religion, and so they had to force it on them. It had to be done by the force of arms, by the sword.

For more details see the book *African Origins of Civilization, Religion, Yoga and Ethics*
by Sebai Muata Ashby

Chapter 2: The Fundamental Principles of Ancient Egyptian Religion for the Hemu Neter (Clergy of Shetaut Neter)

Shetaut Neter

Neterianism (Ancient Egyptian Religion) may be condensed into four teachings.
Neterian Great Truths

The Ancient Egyptian religion (Shetaut Neter), and its language and symbols provide the first "historical" record of mystical religion and Yoga Philosophy and Religious literature in this human history. Egyptian Yoga (*smai-tawy* ) is what has been commonly referred to by Egyptologists as Egyptian "Religion" or "Mythology," but to think of it as just another set of stories or allegories about a long lost civilization is to completely miss the greatest secret of human existence. This unique perspective from the highest philosophical system which developed in Africa over thousands of years ago provides an advanced way to look at life, religion, the discipline of psychology and the way to spiritual development leading to spiritual Enlightenment. Egyptian mythology, when understood, gives every individual insight into their own divine nature and also a deeper insight into all religions and Yoga systems.

The Ancient Egyptian Religion may be condensed into four statements. These statements may be thought of as summaries or formulas, which if understood, can provide a basic understanding of Neterian faith, but on a deeper level, they can also lead to a mystical understanding when their ramifications are fully explored. The four statements may be considered as great utterances or truths. They are to be known by all students of Neterianism and memorized. Their deeper mystical teaching is to be studied by all who propose to enter into the order of the priesthood.

Maa Ur n Shetaut Neter
"Great Truths of The Shetaut Neter Religion"

1

Pa Neter ua ua Neberdjer m Neteru

"The Neter, the Supreme Being, is One and alone and as Neberdjer,
manifesting everywhere and in all things in the form of Gods and Goddesses."

Neberdjer means "all-encompassing divinity," the all-inclusive, all-embracing Spirit which pervades all and who is the ultimate essence of all. This first truth unifies all the expressions of Kamitan religion.

2

an-Maat swy Saui Set s-Khemn

"Lack of righteousness brings fetters to the personality
and these fetters cause ignorance of the Divine."

When a human being acts in ways that contradict the natural order of nature, negative qualities of the mind will develop within that person's personality. These are the afflictions of Set. Set is the neteru of egoism and selfishness. The afflictions of Set include: anger, hatred, greed, lust, jealousy, envy, gluttony, dishonesty, hypocrisy, etc. So to be free from the fetters of Set, one must be free from the afflictions of Set.

3

s-Uashu s-Nafu n saiu Set

"Devotion to the Divine leads to freedom from the fetters of Set."

Uashu means devotion, and the classic pose of adoring the Divine is called "Dua," standing or sitting with upraised hands facing outwards towards the image of the divinity. To be liberated (Nafu - freedom - to breathe) from the afflictions of Set, one must be devoted to the Divine. Being devoted to the Divine means living by Maat. Maat is a way of life that is purifying to the heart and beneficial for society as it promotes virtue and order. Living by Maat means practicing Shedy (spiritual practices and disciplines) as follows.

4

ari Shedy Rekh ab m Maakheru

"The practice of the Shedy disciplines leads to knowing oneself and the Divine.
This is called being True of Speech"

Doing Shedy means to study profoundly, to penetrate the mysteries (Shetaut) and discover the nature of the Divine. There have been several practices designed by the sages of Ancient Kamit to facilitate the process of self-knowledge. These are the religious (Shetaut) traditions and the Sema (Smai) Tawi (yogic) disciplines related to them that augment the spiritual practices.

The Spiritual Culture and the Purpose of Life: Shetaut Neter

"Men and women are to become God-like through a life of virtue and the cultivation of the spirit through scientific knowledge, practice and bodily discipline."

-Ancient Egyptian Proverb

The highest forms of Joy, Peace and Contentment are obtained when the meaning and purpose of life are discovered. When the human being is in harmony with life, then it is possible to reflect and meditate upon the human condition and realize the limitations of worldly pursuits. When there is peace and harmony in life, a human being can practice any of the varied disciplines designated as Shetaut Neter to promote {his/her} evolution towards the ultimate goal of life, which is Spiritual Enlightenment. Spiritual Enlightenment is the awakening of a human being to the awareness of the Transcendental Essence which binds the universe and which is eternal and immutable. In this discovery is also the sobering and ecstatic realization that the human being is one with that Transcendental Essence. With this realization comes great joy, peace and power to experience the fullness of life and to realize the purpose of life during the time on earth. The lotus is a symbol of Shetaut Neter, meaning the turning towards the light of truth, peace and transcendental harmony.

It has been established that the Ancient Egyptians were African peoples who lived in the north-eastern quadrant of the continent of Africa. They were descendants of the Nubians, who had themselves originated from farther south into the heart of Africa at the Great Lakes region, the sources of the Nile River. They created a vast civilization and culture earlier than any other society in known history and organized a nation that was based on the concepts of balance and order, as well as spiritual Enlightenment. These ancient African people called their land Kamit, and soon after developing a well-ordered society, they began to realize that the world is full of wonders, order, regularity in life as well as entropy, stagnation, disorder and death, but also that life is fleeting, and that there must be something more to human existence. They developed spiritual systems that were designed to allow human beings to understand the nature of this secret being who is the essence of all Creation. They called this spiritual system "Shtaut Ntr (Shetaut Neter)."

The term "Neterianism" is derived from the name "Shetaut Neter." Shetaut Neter means the "Hidden Divinity." It is the ancient philosophy and mythic spiritual culture that gave rise to the Ancient Egyptian civilization. Those who follow the spiritual path of Shetaut Neter are therefore referred to as "Neterians." The fundamental principles common to all denominations of Ancient Egyptian Religion are summed up in the four "Great Truths" that are common to all the traditions of Ancient Egyptian Religion.

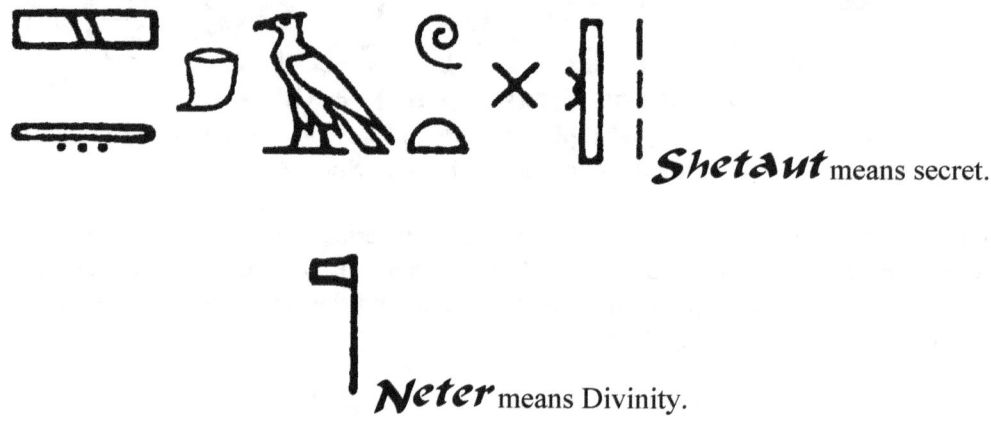

Who is Neter in Kamitan Religion?

Ntr

The symbol of Neter was described by an Ancient Kamitan priest as:
"That which is placed in the coffin"

The term Ntr , or Ntjr, comes from the Ancient Egyptian hieroglyphic language which did not record most of its vowels. However, the term survives in the Coptic language as *"Nutar."* The same Coptic meaning (divine force or sustaining power) applies in the present as it did in ancient times. It is a symbol composed of a wooden staff that was wrapped with strips of fabric, like a mummy. The strips alternate in color with yellow, green and blue. The mummy in Kamitan spirituality is understood to be the dead but resurrected Divinity. So the Nutar (Ntr) is actually every human being who does die physically, whose soul goes to live on in a different form. Further, the resurrected spirit of every human being is that same Divinity. Phonetically, the term Nutar is related to other terms having the same meaning, such as the Latin "Natura," the Spanish "Naturaleza," the English "Nature" and "Nutriment," etc. In a real sense, Ntr means power manifesting as Neteru and the Neteru are the objects of creation, i.e. "nature."

Neterianism is an aggregate of several related Kamitan mythic and philosophical traditions based on Gods and Goddesses who are all related. All the traditions relate the teachings of the sages by means of myths related to particular gods or goddesses. It is understood that all of these neteru are related, like brothers and sisters, having all emanated from the same source, the same Supremely Divine parent, who is neither male nor female, but encompasses the totality of the two.

Neter and the Neteru

**The Neteru (Gods and Goddesses)
proceed from
The Neter
(Supreme Being)**

The concept of Neter and Neteru binds and ties all of the varied forms of Kamitan spirituality into one vision of the gods and goddesses all emerging from the same Supreme Being. Therefore, ultimately, Kamitan spirituality is not polytheistic, nor is it monotheistic, for it holds that the Supreme Being is more than a God or Goddess. The Supreme Being is an all-encompassing Absolute Divinity.
The Neteru

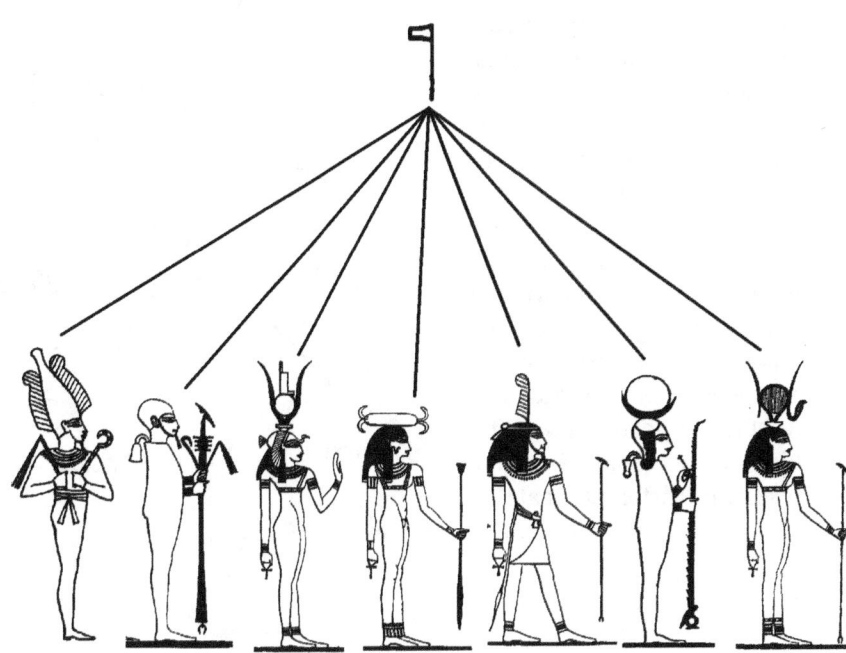

"Neteru"

The term "Neteru" means "gods and goddesses." This means that from the ultimate and transcendental Supreme Being, "Neter," come the Neteru. There are countless Neteru. So from the one come the many. These Neteru are cosmic forces that pervade the universe. They are the means by which Neter sustains Creation and manifests through it. So Neterianism is a monotheistic polytheism. The one Supreme Being expresses as many gods and goddesses. At the end of time, after their work of sustaining Creation is finished, these gods and goddesses are again absorbed back into the Supreme Being.

All of the spiritual systems of Ancient Egypt (Kamit) have one essential aspect that is common to all; they all hold that there is a Supreme Being (Neter) who manifests in a multiplicity of ways through nature, the Neteru. Like sunrays, the Neteru emanate from the Divine; they are its manifestations. So by studying the Neteru we learn about and are led to discover their source, the Neter, and with this discovery we are enlightened. The Neteru may be depicted anthropomorphically or zoomorphically in accordance with the teaching about Neter that is being conveyed through them.

The Neteru and Their Temples

Diagram 1: The Ancient Egyptian Temple Network

The sages of Kamit instituted a system by which the teachings of spirituality were espoused through an organization of Temples. The major divinities were assigned to a particular city. That divinity or group of divinities became the "patron" divinity (tutelary) or divinities of that city. Also, the Priests and Priestesses of that Temple were in charge of seeing to the welfare of the people in that district as well as maintaining the traditions and disciplines of the traditions based on the particular divinity being worshipped. So the original concept of "Neter" became elaborated through the "theologies" of the various traditions. A dynamic expression of the teachings emerged, which though maintaining the integrity of the teachings, expressed nuances of variation in perspective on the teachings to suit the needs of varying kinds of personalities of the people of different locales.

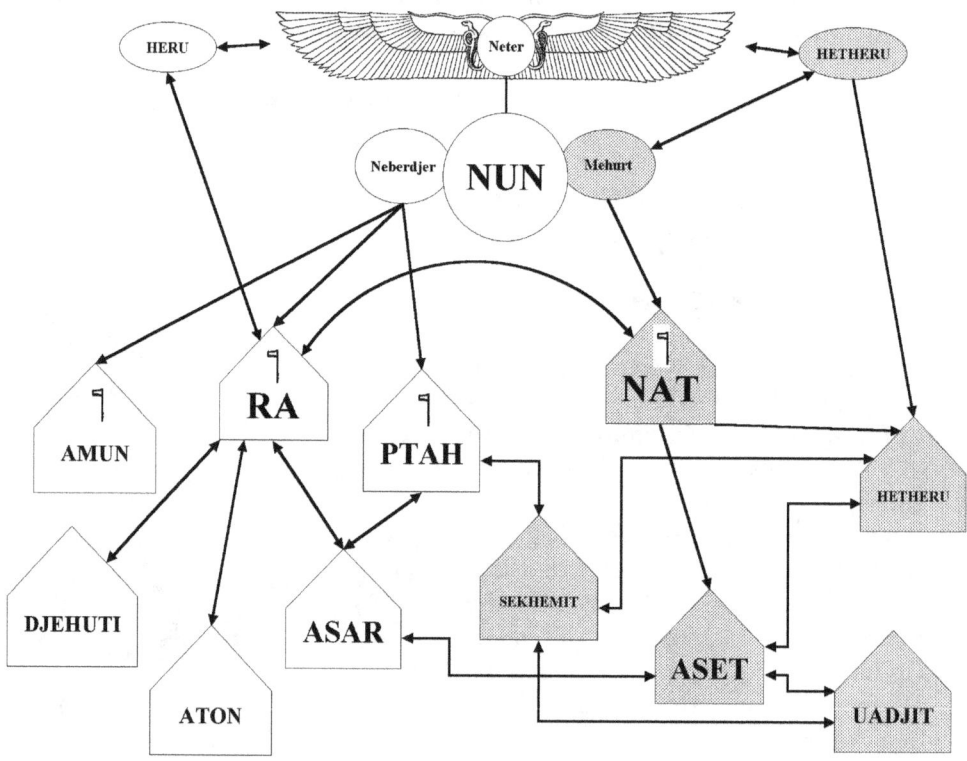

In the diagram above, the primary or main divinities are denoted by the Neter symbol (ᛉ). The house structure represents the Temple for that particular divinity. The interconnections with the other Temples are based on original scriptural statements espoused by the Temples that linked the divinities of their Temple with the other divinities. So this means that the divinities should be viewed not as separate entities operating independently, but rather as family members who are in the same "business" together, i.e. the Enlightenment of society, albeit through variations in form of worship, name, form (expression of the Divinity), etc. Ultimately, all the divinities are referred to as Neteru and they are all said to be emanations from the ultimate and Supreme Being. Thus, the teaching from any of the Temples leads to an understanding of the others, and these all lead back to the source, the highest Divinity. Thus, the teaching within any of the Temple systems would lead to the attainment of spiritual Enlightenment, the Great Awakening.

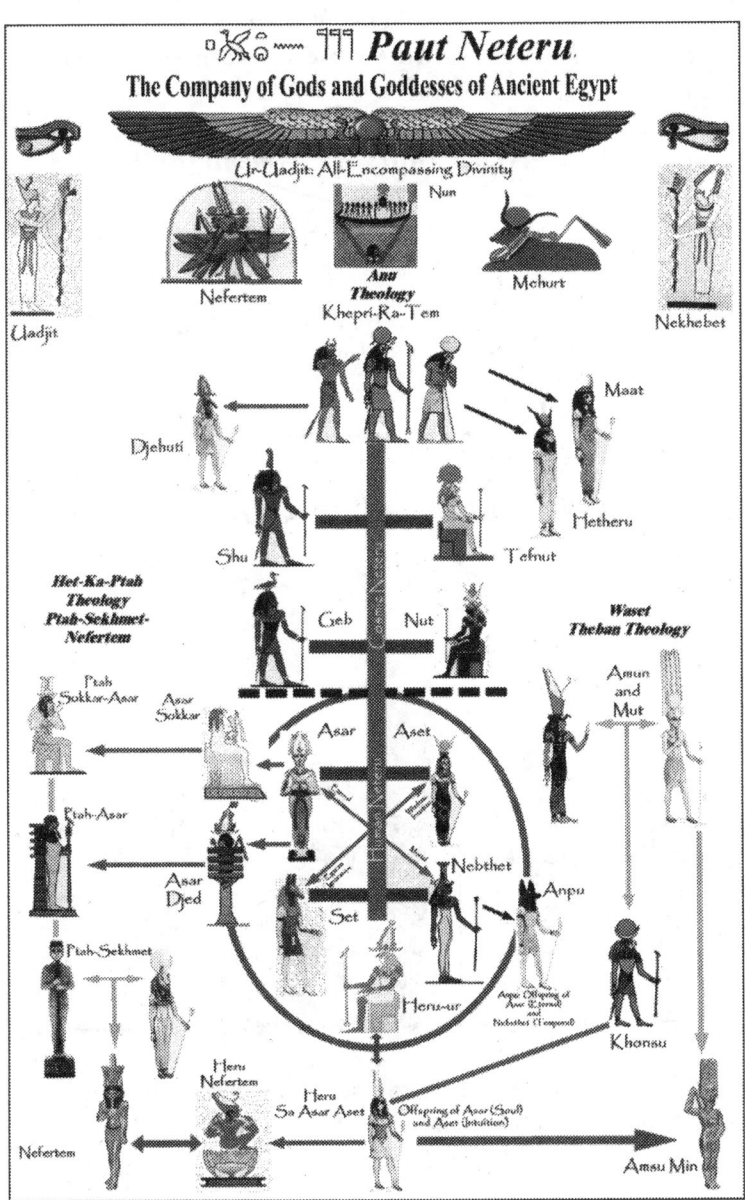

The Neteru and Their Interrelationships

Diagram: The Primary Kamitan Neteru and their Interrelationships. The same Supreme Being, Neter, is the winged all-encompassing transcendental Divinity, the Spirit who, in the early history, is called "Heru." The physical universe in which Heru lives is called "Hetheru" or the "house of Heru." This divinity (Heru) is also the Nun or primeval substratum from which all matter is composed. The various divinities and the material universe are composed of this primeval substratum. Neter is actually androgynous and Heru, the Spirit, is related as a male aspect of that androgyny. However, Heru in the androgynous aspect gives rise to the solar principle, and this is present in both the male and female divinities. This image provides an idea of the relationships between the divinities of the three main Neterian spiritual systems (traditions): Anunian Theology, Wasetian (Theban) Theology and Het-Ka-Ptah/Menefer (Memphite) Theology. The traditions are composed of companies or groups of gods and goddesses. Their actions, teachings and interactions with each other and with human beings provide insight into their nature as well as that of human existence and Creation itself. The lines indicate direct scriptural relationships and the labels also indicate that some divinities from one system are the same in others, with only a name change. Again, this is attested to by the scriptures themselves in direct statements, like those found in the **Prt m Hru** text Chapter 4 (17).[53]

The following is an overview of the main Neterian traditions based on the divinities of the diagram above.[54]

---

[53] See the book *The Egyptian Book of the Dead* by Sebai Muata Ashby

The Anunian Tradition

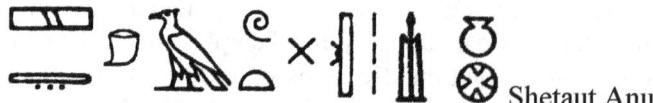 Shetaut Anu

The Mystery Teachings of the Anunian (Heliopolitan) Tradition are related to the Divinity Ra and his company of Gods and Goddesses.[55] This Temple and its related Temples espouse the teachings of Creation, human origins and the path to spiritual Enlightenment by means of the Supreme Being in the form of the god Ra. It tells of how Ra emerged from a primeval ocean and how human beings were created from his tears. The gods and goddesses, who are his children, go to form the elements of nature and the cosmic forces that maintain nature. The image of Ra on the following page comes from the Temple of Amun-Ra at Abu Simbel (southern Egypt).

Below: The Heliopolitan Cosmogony. The city of Anu (Amun-Ra)

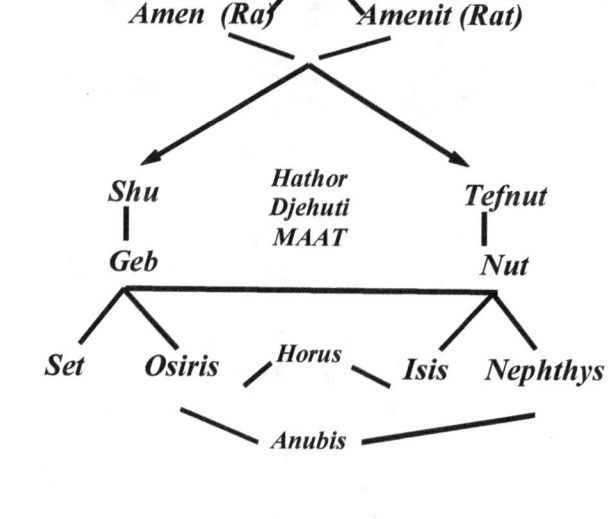

The Neters of Creation -
The Company of the Gods and Goddesses.
Neter Neteru
Nebertcher - Amun (unseen, hidden, ever present, Supreme Being, beyond duality and description)

Amen (Ra)   *Amenit (Rat)*

Shu   Hathor   Tefnut
      Djehuti
Geb   MAAT   Nut

Set Osiris Horus Isis Nephthys
            Anubis

Top: Ra. From left to right, starting at the bottom level- The Gods and Goddesses of Anunian Theology: Shu, Tefnut, Nut, Geb, Aset, Asar, Set, Nebthet and Heru-Ur

---

[54] See book *Egyptian Mysteries Vol. 2 Dictionary of Ancient Egyptian Gods and Goddesses* by Sebai Muata Ashby
[55] See the Book Anunian Theology by Sebai Muata Ashby

The Memphite Tradition

  Shetaut Menefer

The Mystery Teachings of the Het-Ka-Ptah/Menefer (Memphite) Tradition are related to the Neterus known as Ptah, Sekhmit, and Nefertum (Nefertem). The myths and philosophy of these divinities constitutes Memphite Theology.[56] This Temple and its related Temples espoused the teachings of Creation, human origins and the path to spiritual Enlightenment by means of the Supreme Being in the form of the god Ptah and his family, who compose the Memphite Trinity. It tells of how Ptah emerged from a primeval ocean and how he created the universe by his will and the power of thought (mind). The gods and goddesses, who are his thoughts, go to form the elements of nature and the cosmic forces that maintain nature. His spouse, Sekhmit has a powerful Temple system of her own that is related to the Memphite teaching. The same is true for their son, Nefertem.

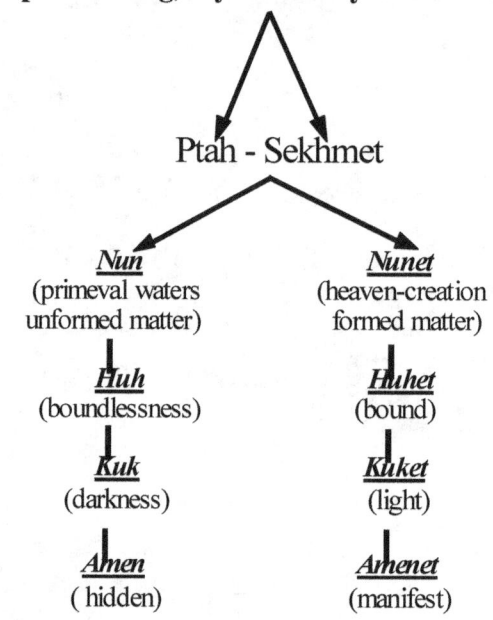

The Neters of Creation -
The Company of the Gods and Goddesses.
Neter Neteru
Nebertcher - Amun (unseen, hidden, ever present, Supreme Being, beyond duality and description)

Ptah - Sekhmet

Nun (primeval waters unformed matter) — *Nunet* (heaven-creation formed matter)
Huh (boundlessness) — *Huhet* (bound)
Kuk (darkness) — *Kuket* (light)
Amen (hidden) — *Amenet* (manifest)

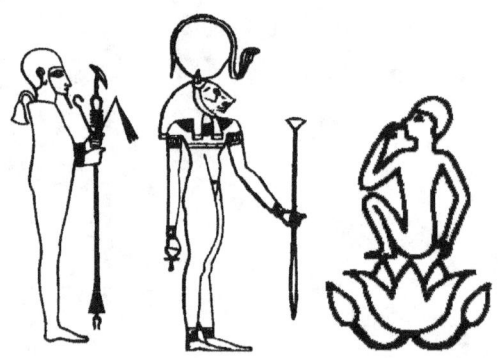

Ptah, Sekhmit and Nefertem

---

[56] See the Book Memphite Theology by Sebai Muata Ashby

The Priests and Priestesses of Ancient Egypt

The Theban Tradition

Shetaut Amun

The Mystery Teachings of the Wasetian Tradition are related to the Neterus known as Amun, Mut and Khonsu. This Temple and its related Temples espoused the teachings of Creation, human origins and the path to spiritual Enlightenment by means of the Supreme Being in the form of the god Amun or Amun-Ra. It tells of how Amun and his family (spouse Mut and son Khonsu), the Trinity of Amun, Mut and Khonsu, manage the Universe along with his Company of Gods and Goddesses. This Temple became very important in the early part of the New Kingdom Era.

Below: The Trinity of Amun and the Company of Gods and Goddesses of Amun

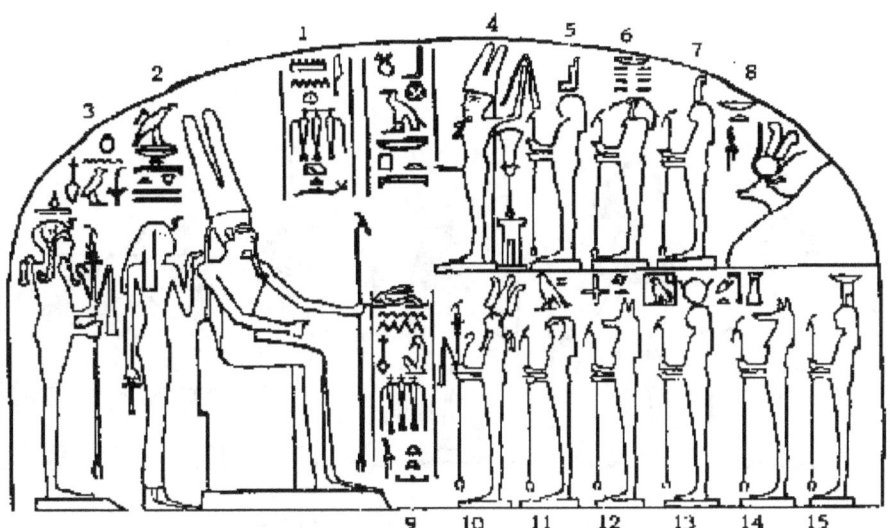

See the Book *Egyptian Yoga Vol. 2* for more on Amun, Mut and Khonsu by Sebai Muata Ashby

The Goddess Tradition

Shetaut Netrit

"Arat"

The hieroglyphic sign Arat means "Goddess." Generally, throughout ancient Kamit, the Mystery Teachings of the Goddess Tradition are related to the Divinity in the form of the Goddess. The Goddess was an integral part of all the Neterian traditions, but special Temples also developed around the worship of certain particular Goddesses who were also regarded as Supreme Beings in their own right. Thus, as in other African religions, the goddess as well as the female gender were respected and elevated similar to the male gender and male divinities. The Goddess was also the author of Creation, giving birth to it as a great Cow. The following are the most important forms of the goddess.[57]

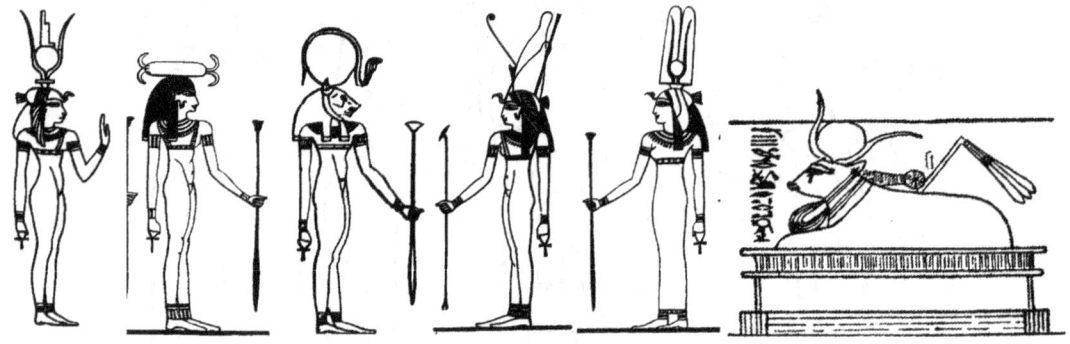

Aset, Net, Sekhmit, Mut, Hetheru
(Far right) The Cow goddess Mehurt ("The Mighty Full One")

---

[57] See the Books, *The Goddess Path, Mysteries of Isis, Glorious Light Meditation, Memphite Theology* and *Resurrecting Osiris* by Sebai Muata Ashby

The Asarian Tradition

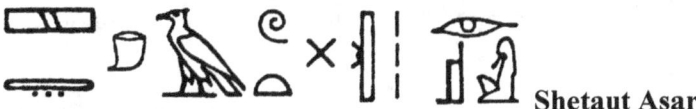 Shetaut Asar

This Temple and its related Temples espoused the teachings of Creation, human origins and the path to spiritual Enlightenment by means of the Supreme Being in the form of the god Asar. It tells of how Asar and his family, the Trinity of Asar, Aset and Heru, manage the Universe and lead human beings to spiritual Enlightenment and the resurrection of the soul. This Temple and its teaching were very important from the Pre-Dynastic era down to the Christian period. The Mystery Teachings of the Asarian Tradition are related to the Neterus known as: Asar, Aset, Heru (Osiris, Isis and Horus)

The tradition of Asar, Aset and Heru was practiced generally throughout the land of ancient Kamit. The centers of this tradition were the city of Abdu containing the Great Temple of Asar, the city of Pilak containing the Great Temple of Aset[58] and Edfu containing the Great Temple of Heru.

---
[58] See the Book Resurrecting Osiris by Sebai Muata Ashby

The Aton Tradition

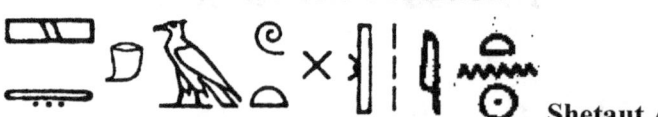
Shetaut Aton

This Temple and its related Temples espoused the teachings of Creation, human origins and the path to spiritual Enlightenment by means of the Supreme Being in the form of the god Aton. It tells of how Aton with its dynamic life force created and sustains Creation. By recognizing Aton as the very substratum of all existence, human beings engage in devotional exercises and rituals and the study of the Hymns containing the wisdom teachings of Aton explaining that Aton manages the Universe and leads human beings to spiritual Enlightenment and eternal life for the soul. This Temple and its teaching were very important in the middle New Kingdom Period. The Mystery Teachings of the Aton Tradition are related to the Neter Aton and its main exponent was the Sage King Akhnaton, who was often depicted with his family adoring the sundisk, symbol of the Aton.[59]

Akhnaton, Nefertiti and their Daughter

---

[59] For more on Atonism and the Aton Theology see the Essence of Atonism Lecture Series by Sebai Muata Ashby ©2001

The Priests and Priestesses of Ancient Egypt

The General Principles of Shetaut Neter
(Based on Teachings Presented in the Kamitan scriptures)

1. The Purpose of Life is to attain the Great Awakening-Enlightenment-Know thyself.
2. The Shedy (spiritual investigation) as the highest endeavor of life.
3. It is the responsibility of every human being to promote order and truth.
4. All human beings have the same Creator and are related
5. SHETAUT NETER enjoins the performance of Selfless Service to family, community and humanity.
6. SHETAUT NETER enjoins the Protection of nature.
7. SHETAUT NETER enjoins the Protection of the weak and oppressed.
8. SHETAUT NETER enjoins the Caring for the hungry.
9. SHETAUT NETER enjoins the Caring for the homeless.
10. SHETAUT NETER enjoins the equality for all people.
11. SHETAUT NETER enjoins the equality between men and women.
12. SHETAUT NETER enjoins the justice for all.
13. SHETAUT NETER enjoins the sharing of resources.
14. SHETAUT NETER enjoins the protection and proper raising of children.
15. SHETAUT NETER enjoins the movement towards balance and peace.

The Ultimate Goal of Neterian Spiritual Practices: The Great Awakening of Neterian Religion

Nehast means to "wake up," to Awaken to the Higher Existence.

Nehast is the ultimate goal of life. It means to resurrect, to have a spiritual rebirth. The goal of all the Neterian disciplines is to discover the meaning of "Who am I?," to unravel the mysteries of life and to fathom the depths of eternity and infinity. This is the task of all human beings and it is to be accomplished in this very lifetime. This can be done by learning the ways of the Neteru, emulating them and finally becoming like them, Akhus, (enlightened beings), walking the earth as giants and accomplishing great deeds such as the creation of the universe! (Below: The resurrection of Asar {Papyrus Ani})

Introduction to Egyptian Yoga

Most students of yoga are familiar with the yogic traditions of India and consider that the Indian texts such as the Bhagavad-Gita, Mahabharata, Patanjali Yoga Sutras, etc. are the primary and original source of Yogic philosophy and teaching. However, upon examination, the teachings currently espoused in all of the major forms of Indian Yoga can be found earlier in Ancient Egyptian scriptures, inscribed in papyrus and on Temple walls as well as steles, statues, obelisks and other sources.

What is Yoga?

As explained earlier, the word "Yoga" is an Indian Sanskrit term meaning to unite the individual with the Cosmic. The term has been used in certain parts of this book for ease of communication since the word "Yoga" has received wide popularity especially in western countries in recent years. Yoga is the practice of mental, physical and spiritual disciplines which lead to self-control and self-discovery by purifying the mind, body and spirit, so as to discover the deeper spiritual essence which lies within every human being and object in the universe. In essence, the goal of Yoga practice is to unite or *yoke* one's individual consciousness with Universal or Cosmic consciousness. Therefore, Ancient Egyptian religious practice, especially in terms of the rituals and other practices of the Ancient Egyptian Temple system known as *Shetaut Neter* (the way of the hidden Supreme Being), also known in Ancient times as *Smai (Sema) Tawi* "Egyptian Yoga," should as well be considered as universal streams of self-knowledge philosophy which influenced and inspired the great religions and philosophers to this day. In this sense, religion, in its purest form, is also a Yoga system, as it seeks to reunite the soul with its true and original source, God. In broad terms, any spiritual movement or discipline that brings one closer to self-knowledge is a "Yogic" movement. The main recognized forms of Yoga disciplines are:

- *Yoga of Wisdom,*
- *Yoga of Devotional Love,*
- *Yoga of Meditation,*
  - *Physical Postures Yoga*
- *Yoga of Selfless Action,*
- *Tantric Yoga*
  - *Serpent Power Yoga*

The diagram below shows the relationship between the Yoga disciplines and the path of mystical religion (religion practiced in its three complete steps: 1st receiving the myth {knowledge}, 2nd practicing the rituals of the myth {following the teachings of the myth} and 3rd entering into a mystical experience {becoming one with the central figure of the myth}).

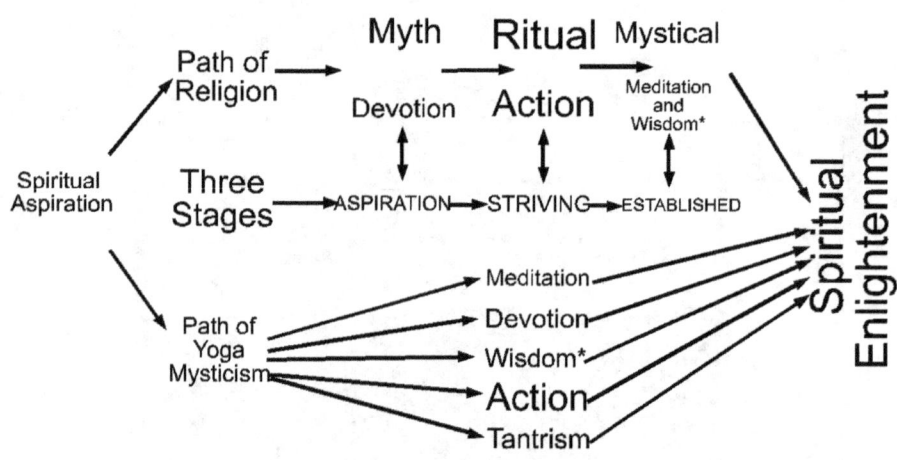

The disciplines of Yoga fall under five major categories. These are: *Yoga of Wisdom, Yoga of Devotional Love, Yoga of Meditation, Tantric Yoga* and *Yoga of Selfless Action.* When these disciplines are practiced in a harmonized manner this practice is called "Integral Yoga." Within these categories there are subsidiary forms which are part of the main disciplines. The emphasis in the Kamitan Asarian Myth is on the Yoga of Wisdom, Yoga of Devotional Love and Yoga of Selfless Action. The important point to remember is that all aspects of Yoga can and should be used in an integral fashion to effect an efficient and harmonized spiritual movement in the practitioner. Therefore, while there may be an area of special emphasis, other elements are bound to become part of the Yoga program as needed. For example, while a Yogin (practitioner of Yoga, aspirant, initiate) may place emphasis on the Yoga of Wisdom, they may also practice Devotional Yoga and Meditation Yoga along with the wisdom studies. So the practice of any discipline that leads to oneness with Supreme Consciousness can be called Yoga. If you study, rationalize and reflect upon the teachings, you are practicing *Yoga of Wisdom*. If you meditate upon the teachings and your Higher Self, you are practicing *Yoga of Meditation*.

Thus, whether or not you refer to it as such, if you practice rituals which identify you with your spiritual nature, you are practicing *Yoga of Ritual Identification* (which is part of the Yoga of Wisdom {Kamitan-Rekh, Indian-Jnana} and the Yoga of Devotional Love {Kamitan-Ushet, Indian-Bhakti} of the Divine). If you develop your physical nature and psychic energy centers, you are practicing *Serpent Power* (Kamitan-*Arat* or Indian-*Kundalini*) *Yoga* (which is part of Tantric Yoga). If you practice living according to the teachings of ethical behavior and selflessness, you are practicing *Yoga of Action* (Kamitan-Maat, Indian-Karma) in daily life. If you practice turning your attention towards the Divine by developing love for the Divine, then it is called *Devotional Yoga* or *Yoga of Divine Love*. In this manner, Yoga has been developed into many disciplines that may be used in an integral fashion to achieve the same goal: Enlightenment. Therefore, the aspirant is to learn about all of the paths of Yoga and choose those elements that best suit {his/her} personality or practice them all in an integral, balanced way.

Enlightenment is the term used to describe the highest level of spiritual awakening. It means attaining such a level of spiritual awareness that one discovers the underlying unity of the entire universe as well as the fact that the source of all creation is the same source from which the innermost Self within every human heart arises.

So What is Egyptian Yoga?

The Term "Egyptian Yoga" and The Philosophy Behind It

As previously discussed, Yoga (termed *Sema* in Ancient Egypt/Africa) in all of its forms were practiced in Egypt apparently earlier than anywhere else in human history. This point of view is supported by the fact that there is documented scriptural and iconographical evidence of the disciplines of virtuous living, dietary purification, study of the wisdom teachings and their practice in daily life, psycho-physical and psycho-spiritual exercises and meditation being practiced in Ancient Egypt, long before the evidence of its existence is detected in India (including the Indus Valley Civilization) or any other early civilization (Sumer, Greece, China, etc.).

The teachings of Yoga are at the heart of the Ancient Egyptian *Prt m Hru* spiritual text. The Ancient Egyptian equivalent term to the Sanskrit word yoga is: **"Smai (or Sema)." Smai (Sema)** means union, and the following determinative terms give it a spiritual significance, at once equating it with the term "Yoga" as it is used in India. When used in conjunction with the Ancient Egyptian symbol which means land, **"Ta,"** the term "union of the two lands" arises.

In Chapter 4 and Chapter 17 of the *Prt m Hru,* the term "Smai (Sema) Tawi" is used. It means "Union of the two lands of Egypt," ergo "Egyptian Yoga." The two lands refer to the two main districts of the country (North and South). In ancient times, Egypt was divided into two sections or land areas. These were known as Lower and Upper Egypt. In Ancient Egyptian mystical philosophy, the land of Upper Egypt relates to the divinity Heru (Horus), who represents the Higher Self, and the land of Lower Egypt relates to Set, the divinity of the lower self. So ***Smai (Sema) Taui*** means "the union of the two lands" or the "Union of the lower self with the Higher Self. The lower self relates to that which is negative and uncontrolled in the human mind including worldliness, egoism, worldly desires, ignorance, etc. (Set), while the Higher Self relates to that which is above temptations and is good in the human heart as well as in touch with Transcendental Consciousness (Heru). Thus, we also have the Ancient Egyptian term ***Smai Heru-Set,*** or the union of Heru and Set. So Smai (Sema) Taui or Smai (Sema) Heru-Set are the Ancient Egyptian words which are to be translated as **"Egyptian Yoga."**

The Ancient Egyptian language and symbols provide the first "historical" record of *Sema* Philosophy and Religious literature. The hieroglyph Sma, "Sema," represented by the union of two lungs and the trachea, symbolizes that the union of the duality, that is, the Higher Self and lower self, leads to Non-duality, the One, and singular consciousness.

The Ancient Egyptian Symbols of Yoga

The Ancient Egyptians called the disciplines of Yoga in Ancient Egypt by the term *"Smai (Sema) Tawi."* So what does Smai (Sema) Tawi mean?

(From Chapter 4 of the *Prt m Hru*)

The hieroglyphic symbols at the very top (†) mean: ***"Know Thyself," "Self knowledge is the basis of all true knowledge"*** and (±) abbreviated forms of ***Smai tawi***, signifies "Egyptian Yoga." The next four below represent the four words in Egyptian Philosophy, which mean ***"YOGA."*** They are: (A) ***"Nefer"*** (B) ***"Sema"*** (C) ***"Ankh"*** and (D) ***"Hetep."***

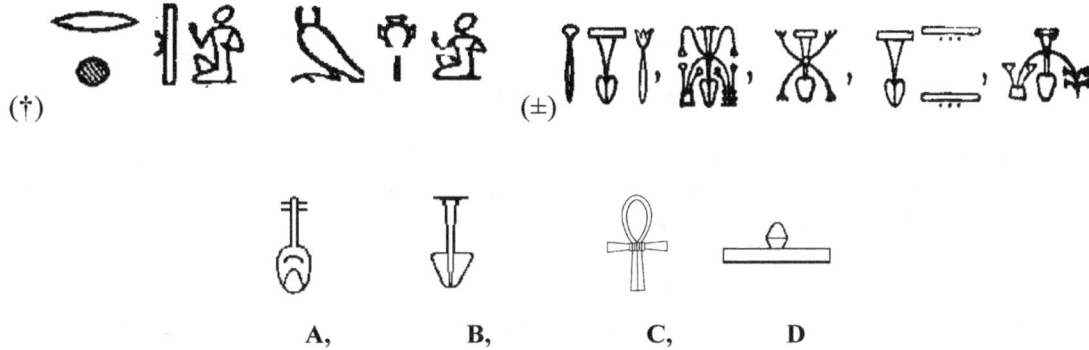

At right: Smai Heru-Set. The gods Heru and Set join forces to tie up the symbol of Union (Sema –see (B) above). The Sema symbol refers to the Union of Upper Egypt (Lotus) and Lower Egypt (Papyrus) under one ruler, but also at a more subtle level, it refers to the union of one's Higher Self and lower self (Heru and Set), as well as the control of one's breath (Life Force) through the union (control) of the lungs (breathing organs). The character of Heru and Set are an integral part of the *Pert Em Heru*.

One of the central and most popular characters within Ancient Egyptian Religion of Asar is Heru, who is an incarnation of his father, Asar. Asar was killed by his brother Set, who out of greed and demoniac (Setian) tendency, craved to be the ruler of Egypt. With the help of Djehuti, the God of wisdom, Aset, the great mother and Hetheru, his consort, Heru prevailed in the battle against Set for the rulership of Kamit (Egypt). Heru's struggle symbolizes the struggle of every human being to regain rulership of the Higher Self and to subdue the lower self.

The most ancient writings in our historical period are from the Ancient Egyptians. These writings are referred to as hieroglyphs. The original name given to these writings by the Ancient Egyptians is *Medu Neter*, meaning "the writing of God" or *Neter Medu* or "Divine Speech." These writings were inscribed in Temples, coffins and papyruses and contained the teachings in reference to the spiritual nature of the human being and the ways to promote spiritual emancipation, awakening or resurrection. The Ancient Egyptian proverbs presented in this text are translations from the original hieroglyphic scriptures. An example of hieroglyphic text was presented above in the form of the text-symbols of *Smai (Sema) Taui* or "Egyptian Yoga."

Egyptian Philosophy may be summed up in the following proverbs, which clearly state that the soul is heavenly or divine and that the human being must awaken to the true reality, which is the Spirit, Self.

"Self knowledge is the basis of true knowledge."

"Soul to heaven, body to earth."

The Priests and Priestesses of Ancient Egypt

"Man is to become God-like through a life of virtue and the cultivation of the spirit through scientific knowledge, practice and bodily discipline."

"Salvation is accomplished through the efforts of the individual. There is no mediator between man and {his/her} salvation."

"Salvation is the freeing of the soul from its bodily fetters, becoming a God through knowledge and wisdom, controlling the forces of the cosmos instead of being a slave to them, subduing the lower nature and through awakening the Higher Self, ending the cycle of rebirth and dwelling with the Neters who direct and control the Great Plan."

So *Egyptian Yoga* is an innovative way to understand and practice Ancient Egyptian Mysticism, the Ancient Egyptian mystical religion (*Shetaut Neter*). As stated earlier, Egyptian Yoga is what has been commonly referred to by Egyptologists as Egyptian "Religion" or "Mythology." This unique perspective from the highest philosophical system, which developed in Africa over seven thousand years ago, provides a new way to look at life, religion, psychology and the way to spiritual development leading to spiritual Enlightenment. So Egyptian Yoga is not merely a philosophy but a discipline for promoting spiritual evolution in a human being, allowing him or her to discover the ultimate truth, supreme peace and utmost joy which lies within the human heart. Every human being has the potential to discover the greatest treasure of all existence if they apply themselves to the study and practice of the teachings of *Sema* with the proper guidance. This is the vision of Egyptian Yoga.

Choosing a Sema Spiritual discipline as a Support for the Spiritual Tradition and Culture

The Sema disciplines are like an engine that allows the vehicle of the spiritual tradition to move forward. All Hm and Hmt (priests and priestesses) of Shetaut Neter must practice all of the Sema disciplines, but they may choose an area of Sema specialty along with their choice of spiritual tradition. The main sema disciplines are listed below.

Areas of Specialty *Sema* Paths -Kamitan Yoga Paths – Smai Tawi

- Sema of Wisdom– Rekh Sma
- Sema of Devotion– Uasht Merri Sma
    - Sema of Music– Divine Singing, Instrument and Chant – Shmai - Hesi

- Sema of Action– Maat Sma
    - Aru – Ritual- Ceremony-Theater
    - Udja Medut -   Law profession – Judge
    - Hekat – Government – civil service
        - Economics and Business

- Sema of Meditation– Uaa Sma
- Sema of Tantric – Shetaut Asar-Aset, Shetaut Min-Mut, Shetaut Geb-Nut.
    - Sema of Serpent Power -Arat Sekhem

- Sema of Movements and Posture - Tjef Neteru Sema Paut

The mythic tradition provides teachingsin a very special way through the language of myth. However, both sema (yoga) and religion go hand in hand. If you were to practice the teachings of mystical wisdom, the teaching of the Temple of Aset, a form of Rekh Shedy (Wisdom Yoga), you automatically are going to be immersed in the myths of Goddess Aset also (religion). The myths of Aset include the story of the God Ra and Goddess Aset, and the Asarian Resurrection myth. So the sema discipline as well as the religious discipline is practiced at the same time. The myth should lead to the high philosophy and the sema disciplines support both, but without the sema disciplines, the myth does not progress into the higher practice of religion. This is the condition of the ignorant masses that practice religion at the level of myth and ritual, but not mysticism.

Every Neterian tradition (in fact, every religion) needs to have an engine. Whatever tradition you choose has to have something to drive it and the term spiritual research, those we did earlier is the same as *Sema Tawi*. These are the disciplines that allow you to do your spiritual research and go beyond to the deeper mysteries. Remember the statement by *Plutarch*, talking about how some people are *"satisfied with the most superficial accounts of them"* ("them" means the mythic teachings), and some people go beyond that and study the depth of the teaching. This spiritual research, the mysteries, is not for those people who are satisfied with the outer form of the mythic teaching, the exoteric aspects; they are the masses, and not until they show worthiness and true devotion to the teaching are they invited to have entry into the higher philosophy. They can't make use of it even if it is given to them. They are not able to have entry into it; their own consciousness blocks (prevents) them from doing so. The dullness of their mind blocks their ability to do the research. This is an idea of what is involved in the practice of true religion. The idea is that the priests and priestesses become versed in these disciplines and in teaching the myth; they become avenues or conduits for the dissemination of them and the upholding of those rituals and those practices for the masses. In that way they assist the masses to maintain order in their life. They eventually cultivate people from the masses to become clergy also, to take their places as priests and priestesses to carry on the culture.

The Priests and Priestesses of Ancient Egypt

Summary of the Sema (Yogic) Disciplines Practiced by the Priests and Priestesses of Kamit

Yoga of Rekh (Wisdom)	Yoga of Maat (Action and Selfless Service)	The Yoga of Uasht-Merri (Devotion to The Divine)	Yoga of Uaa (Discipline of Meditation)	The Yoga of Tantrism and The Serpent Power
From Temple of Aset: *They (initiates) give themselves up entirely to study and meditation and to the listening and teaching of these divine truths which treat of the divine nature.* **Listening** Fill the ears, listen attentively- Meh mestchert. **SDJM** **Reflection** **MAUI** "to think, to ponder, to fix attention, concentration" **Meditation** uaa	**GENERAL DISCIPLINE** In all Temples especially **The Temple of Heru and Djebu (Edfu)** Scripture: Prt M Hru and special scriptures including the Berlin Papyrus and other papyri. 1- Learn Ethics and Law of Cause and Effect-Practice right action (42 Precepts of Maat) to purify gross impurities of the personality **Control Body, Speech, Thoughts** 2-Practice cultivation of the higher virtues (selfless-service) to purify mind and intellect from subtle impurities 3- Devotion to the Divine See maatian actions as offerings to the Divine 4- Meditation See oneself as one with Maat, i.e. United with the Cosmic Order, which is the Transcendental Supreme Self.	**GENERAL DISCIPLINE** In all Temples Scripture: Prt M Hru and Temple Inscriptions. 1- Listening to the myths and divine glories of the various forms of the divinity (god or goddess) 2- Effacement of the ego through cultivation of love for the Divine 3- Ritual, 4- Hekau (words of Power) Chanting 5- Praises, Hymns, Songs to the Divine God is termed *Merri*, "Beloved One" **Love and Be Loved** "That person is beloved by the Lord." PMH, Ch 4	**Basic Instructions for the Glorious Light Meditation System-Given in the Tomb of Sage Seti I. (1350 B.C.E.)** **(1)-Posture and Focus of Attention** *iuf iri-f ahau maq b-phr nty hau iu* body do make stand, within the Sundisk, (circle of Ra) **(2)- Words of power-chant**[60] *Nuk Hekau* (I am the word* itself) *Nuk Ra Akhu* (I am Ra's Glorious Shinning** Spirit) *Nuk Ba Ra* (I am the soul of Ra) *Nuk Hekau* (I am the God who creates*** through sound) **(3)- Visualization** *Iuf mi Ra heru mestu-f n-shry chet* "My body is like Ra's on the day of his birth	**Earliest manifestation of the disciplines** 10,000 B.C.E. in Anu The discipline of cultivation of the inner Life Force as described in the embalming papyri. 1-Cleansing the subtle body. 2-Cultivating the inner Life Force. 3-Harmonizing the two dual forces. 4- Uniting the individual Life Force with the Cosmic.

---

[60] The term "Words of Power" relates to chants and or recitations given for meditation practice. They were used in a similar way to the Hindu "Mantras."

The Priests and Priestesses of Ancient Egypt

Tjef Neteru Sema Paut Ritual Postures of Enlightenment

The Yogic Postures for Health and the Ritual of meditation in Motion are to be practiced as part of the daily Temple routine – and its basic discipline may be offered to the public as an open practice.

The name for the practice is *tjef neteru* – "movements of the gods and goddesses" or *sma paut n neteru* – "Union with the gods and goddesses," the art of meditative movements in a ritual format to discover harmony with and the power of the gods and goddesses within.

The discipline of the postures is an important practice for the Neterian Clergy. It is related to the Ancient Egyptian Theater. The book *Egyptian Yoga: Movements of the Gods and Goddesses* discusses the discipline of ritual movements for spiritual Enlightenment. This is a posture system similar to the Indian posture yoga system in some ways, although there are many differences. The Neterian system is more mythically based. The postures are directly based on the postures that were discovered in the Temple of Hetheru and other Temples as well as papyruses that were practiced by the priests and priestesses who were emulating the gods and goddesses. The priests and priestesses practiced these postures to emulate and meditatively identify with the divinities and the myth that extol their virtues and powers, thereby mastering these. So when we are speaking of the Sema Philosophy of the postures we are really referring to the metaphysical disciplines that were developed in ancient Kamit that lead a human being to spiritual Enlightenment. (For details see the book *Egyptian Yoga Movements of the Gods and Goddesses* by Sebai Muata Ashby.

Summary of The Great Truths and the Shedy Paths to their Realization

Great Truths

I
God is One and in all things manifesting through the Neteru

II
Unrighteousness brings fetters and these cause ignorance of truth (#1)

III
Devotion to God allows the personality to free itself from the fetters

IIII
The Shedy disciplines are the greatest form of worship of the Divine

Shedy Disciplines

I
Listen to the Wisdom Teachings (Become Wise)
Learn the mysteries as taught by an authentic teacher, which allows this profound statement to be understood.

II
Acting (Living) by Truth
Apply the Philosophy of right action to become virtuous and purify the heart

III
Devotion to the Divine
Worship, ritual and divine love allows the personality purified by truth to eradicate the subtle ignorance that binds it to mortal existence.

IIII
Meditation
Allows the whole person to go beyond the world of time and space and the gross and subtle ignorance of mortal human existence to discover that which transcends time and space.

Great Awakening
Occurs when all of the Great Truths have been realized by perfection of the Shedy disciplines to realize their true nature and actually experience oneness with the transcendental Supreme Being.

These disciplines, especially Devotion and Right Action, were practiced generally in all the Neterian Traditions. An aspirant can and should practice them all, but specialize in one. The choice is determined by the personality and inner inclination of the aspirant. If the aspirant likes to meditate a lot, or study a lot, the aspirant can choose the discipline of Uaa, Meditation, or Rekh, Wisdom, respectively, as his/her main path. So, the aspirant can choose a discipline that emphasizes their predilection as their main path.

Chapter 3- The Ancient Neterian Temple

Neter Het - house of divinity – Temple

The Purpose of the Neterian Temple

The priests and priestesses served the - *Het Neter*- house of God, i.e. the Temple. The Temple is a place where the priests and priestesses are able to be fully trained in the arts and philosophy as well as the disciplines of their chosen spiritual path. The Temple is also a focal point for the dissemination of the teachings to the general population as well as the management of the social order in that it is a planning headquarters as it were, to coordinate the practice of the disciplines of the Temple and the management of society. The priests and priestesses are responsible for maintaining the moral and spiritual health of the community. However, in Ancient Kamit (Egypt) that responsibility went much further. In Ancient Kamit the priests and priestesses managed the affairs of government as well as those of the national religion and its varied traditions. This required preciseness in organization, accounting and virtue. The system worked for thousands of years. The purpose of this volume is to present an outline of that system and how it is to be applied in present times for the reinstitution of the values and virtues of the Neterian religion. This chapter will present an overview of some of the most important rituals of the Temple, but will not be a detailed account of them, revealing deeper mysteries. It is presented to give potential aspirants an indication of what the mysteries are about and how the priests and priestesses conduct the practice of the mysteries through the Temple rituals in order to promote cosmic balance and spiritual attunement. Below: Peristyle court of the Temple of Heru (Egypt).

"Never go about revealing the rituals you see, in all mysteries, in the Temples."
Temple of Heru at Djebu (Edfu)[61]

---
[61] Chassinat, 1928, p.361, line3

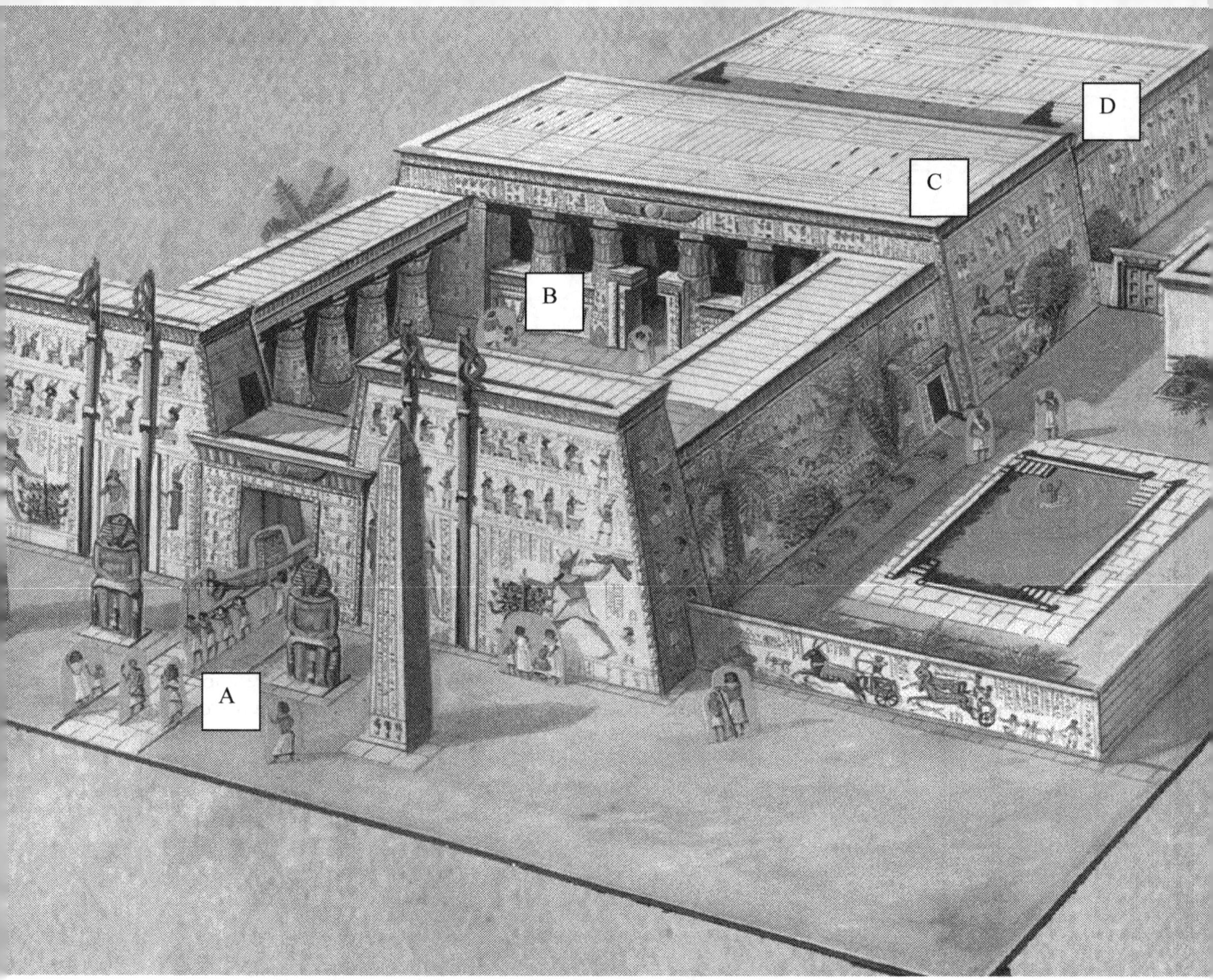

The Neterian Temple

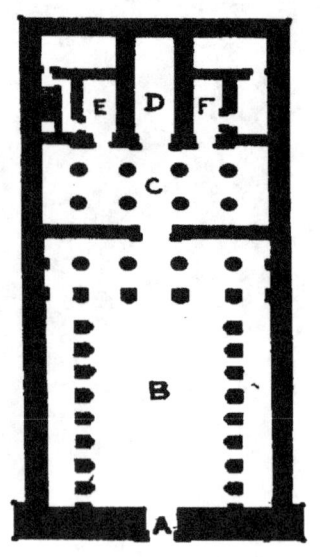
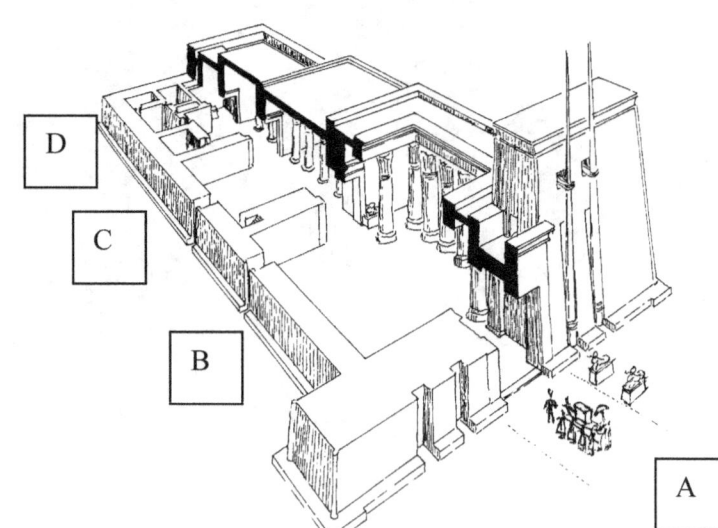

After entering the Temple through the pylons (A), the typical Neterian Temple has three sections: (B) Peristyle Court, (C) Hypostyle Hall, and D) Holy of Holies. These represent the areas where different levels of worshippers may enter. This follows generally the nomenclature of the triads of spirituality:

- The three levels of mind: **Unconscious - Subconscious – Conscious.**
- The three levels of relative consciousness (waking, dream, sleep) constitute the ego-personality of a human being.
- Religion encompasses three levels, *myth, ritual* and *mystical philosophy*.
- The Great Trinity of creation: Amun-Ra-Ptah.

The Three sections of the Temple, B-Open Court (Peristyle Hall), C-Hypostyle Hall (covered), D-Inner Shrine (Holy of Holies), also represent the three stages of religion and the Neterian three levels of aspiration:

1- The Mortals
2- The Intelligences
3- The Creators or Beings of Light

The Stages of African Religion

The Three Stages of African Religion		
Program of Religion (Universal Religion) 3-Stages	**African Religion**	**Sema (Smai) Tawi (Egyptian Yoga) Based on the teachings of the Temple of Aset (Aswan, Egypt)**
Myth	Storytelling (Myths – proverbs)	Listening (to spiritual scriptures, teachings)
Ritual	Ritual (Ceremony – Virtuous living)	Reflection (on & practice of the teachings)
Mysticism/Metaphysics	Ecstasy (Transcendental experience)	Meditation (on the teachings)

The complete program of religion has three steps, which are necessary to achieve the goal of religion, to discover and experience Neter (God). Any spiritual movement that includes these steps can be called authentic "religion" regardless of the name that it may be given by the culture that practices them. These steps include *Myth, Ritual* and *Mysticism* or *Metaphysics*. The table above shows how these three steps or stages manifest in African Religion (2nd column) and also how this same program is enjoined in the practice of Egyptian Yoga (3rd column). Egyptian Yoga (Sema Tawi)[62] may be thought of as the advanced disciplines to be practiced in order to promote the highest goal of the religious movement.

In African Religion, the tradition of storytelling achieves the purpose of transmitting myths that contain the basic concepts of human identity as part of a culture and offers insight into the nature of the universe. Those who aspire to become clergy must develop a competent knowledge of and ability to "tell" and

---

[62] See the books *Egyptian Yoga Vol. 1* for more on the disciplines of Egyptian Yoga and *Mysteries of Isis* for more on the teachings of the Temple of Aset, by Sebai Muata Ashby

otherwise disseminate the myths. In Neterian culture, during festivals and the observance of holidays, myth-telling was supplemented with special rituals for the public and for the clergy, in which reenactments were performed and ancient stories recounted. Myths contain a special language of self-knowledge, and also proverbs that provide moral education for an ethical society. Rituals are formal (ceremonial) and informal (virtuous living) practices which allow a human beings to come into harmony within themselves, the environment and the Spirit. This movement eventually leads to an ecstatic experience that transcends time and space, and allows a human being to discover and experience the Divine, first hand. The Neterian concept of the three levels of aspirants may be understood in more detail as:

- 1- **The Mortals**: *temmu* – {mortals-human men and women} Students who were being instructed on a probationary status, but had not experienced inner vision.
- 2- **The Intelligences**: *rekht*- {knowledgeable ones} Students who had attained inner vision and had received a glimpse of cosmic consciousness.
- 3- **The Creators or Beings of Light**: *Akhu*, {illumined men and women} Students who had become IDENTIFIED with or UNITED with the light (GOD).

The Temple architecture also signifies that there are three forms of actions: <u>Thought, Word and Deed.</u> The outer court is the place for deeds, work to propitiate the Divinity i.e. lower worship: physical rituals, offerings to the divine and prayers to the Divine. The Temple precinct is the House of Life (hospital) and University where the whole town gathers for instruction, healing and worship of the Divine.

The teaching is given in the appropriate section of the Temple in accordance with the level of the aspirant. Admittance to the inner portions of the Temple is based on the level of meritorious service, devotion, spiritual maturity, and understanding of the aspirant. The middle hall is the section of the Temple for words. In this section the wisdom teaching is espoused. The inner hall court is the section of the Temple for advanced ritual and metaphysics, meditations and mystical exercises that sustain creation and unite one to the Divine. Thus, the outer court is open to the lowest ranking practitioners of the Temple, the middle hall is open to more advanced practitioners and the innermost hall is open only to the most advanced aspirants. The innermost shrine is reserved for those who are ready to have union with the Divine. In this way, apprentice priests and priestesses, those who have been found to be worthy, are introduced to the teaching in the open court area. This is the area for developing faith in the Divine. The middle court is the area of philosophy, to promote understanding of the teaching and its application. The inner, third section is for transcending the teaching and entering into the experience of Knowing God. Thus, the teaching to the masses, which is outside the Temple, is of the nature of myth, ritual, festival, ceremony and ethics. Those who have developed virtuous character are able to apply for admittance to the Temple; they must show not only virtue, but also devotion to the Temple. Those who want to train for the priesthood must have that as their most important goal in life; all other worldly desires are secondary. This includes marriage, procreation, sex, food, travel, frivolous entertainments, wealth, social status, etc. The managing clergy oversee the teaching that is presented in the three levels of the Temple in a highly organized manner. This is among the primary duties of the Neterian Clergy who are *Tpy* or overseer priests and priestesses. Thus, the levels of teaching of the Temple may be summarized as follows:

Teaching of section 1 of the Temple (Peristyle Hall {open court}): Myth, devotional worship, virtue, purity.
Teaching of section 2 of the Temple (Hypostyle Hall {covered court}): Philosophy, reflection on the teachings.
Teaching of section 3 of the Temple (Peristyle Hall {open court}): meditation, transcendence and *sba-*illumination.

The Tutelary Deity

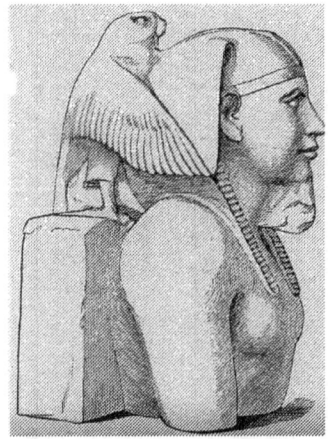

tu·te·lar·y (tōōt′l-ĕr′ē, tyōōt′-) also **tu·te·lar** (tōōt′l-ər, -är′, tyōōt′-) -- *adj.* **1.** Being or serving as a guardian or protector. **2.** Of or relating to a guardian or guardianship. --*n.*, *pl.* **tu·te·lar·ies** also **tu·te·lars**. One that serves as a guardian or protector. (American Heritage Dictionary)

Every Kamitan Temple has a tutelary deity. The tutelary symbol is a focal point for the aspirations, reflections and meditations of a spiritual aspirant. When we refer to the Temple of Asar or the Temple of Heru, we are speaking of the deity of the Temple; it means that particular Temple focuses on that particular divinity, not to the exclusion of the others, but rather as a highlight, as if there are many actors on a stage but the spotlight is on the one who is speaking. It is the same way with the Temple. The tutelary deity is presented as the prominent divinity of a Temple. Also, a Temple may be named after a divinity, ex. Per Aset "Temple of Aset." The divinity may be presented behind the aspirant, as the protective entity (at left statue of King Khafra with Heru behind him, see also the statue of the Pharaoh with the Ram of Amun –{overleaf}) or on a standard which is the icon of a divinity standing or sitting atop a pole (ex. Below).

Each deity offers some unique mode of insight into the teachings and leads to higher self-knowledge. The tutelary deity serves as the main icon of worship and shapes the focus of the energies of the mind of the aspirant through reflection and meditation and the cosmic energy that the Temple collects and manipulates. In the early stages of practice of religion the mind needs an object of worship. The tutelary icons satisfy this need and the rituals and festivals associated with it. These practices are a daily exercise in turning the mind towards the divine and provide an object of curiosity as well as focus of interest for the community and new aspirants who will eventually join the ranks of the Temple.

Ancient Egyptian (Neterian Temple) Flag

The ancient Egyptian Temple had another important icon, the flag. The flag represents a living symbol of an idea or national ideal. Most countries in modern times use the flag as an emblem of nationalist pride. In ancient times the flag was used to represent the ideals and philosophy of the Neterian Temple, and that is the national ideal of Kamitan culture and civilization; that is its foundation. The ancient flag is actually composed of three strips of material with three colors. Again, the triune aspect of the Temple is represented. The three colors are green, blue and yellow. Green symbolizes life force, *wadj*, greenery, vitality and health, which the divine infuses in all living things. Yellow symbolizes gold, *nub*, and the perfection of life, immortality, and purity. Blue represents divine consciousness, the transcendent consciousness, *Amun*. The following page shows a reconstruction of a model of the Ancient Egyptian Temple with flags (A) for worship (now located in the Brooklyn Museum). The second image is a modern rendering of the Ancient Egyptian Temple with flags (B). The third image is of a modern composite of the Ancient Egyptian flag combined with the Ancient Egyptian religious tutelary symbol of Heru (C) for use in modern times by the Neterian Clergy.

The Priests and Priestesses of Ancient Egypt

(A)

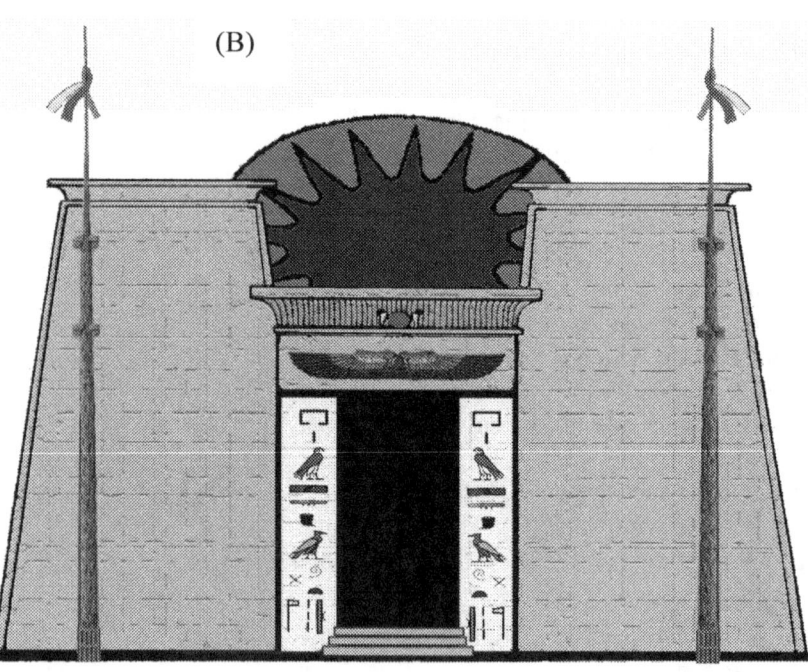
(B)

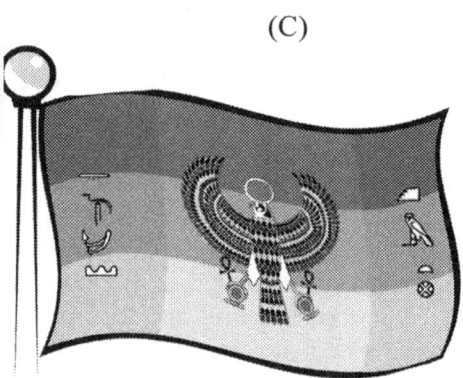
(C)

The flag (C) or similar can be used in modern times for public festivals and functions. This does not replace the ancient flag that will continue to be used for private functions and rituals. Above: Modern flag for Neterian Culture ©Copyright 2004 Sema Institute/Temple of Shetaut Neter

Chapter 4: The Benefits and Immeasurable Joys of Being the Priests and Priestesses

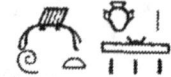

Awet ab -expansion of heart-joy-bliss.

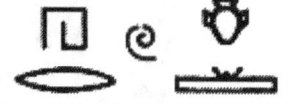

heru ab - inner peace and contentment- joy

reshwet – joy, gladness.

Funerary mask of Tuyu -1391 BCE.

The Benefits of a Spiritual Life and the Immeasurable Joy of Those who Serve as Priests and Priestesses

Many people may see the life of a priest, priestess or monk as austere and joyless. If the teaching is correctly understood and practiced, nothing can be further from the truth. Actually, the austerity is a discipline to assist the aspirant in gaining strength to oppose the worldly desires and entanglements which are actually the source of pain and sorrow in life, and therefore obstacles to the experience of real peace, joy and contentment. If life is correctly understood and lived, and if the true purpose of life is achieved, then there will emerge in the heart of the aspirant incomparable joy and peace which can be achieved in no other way. If life is led in this way, an aspirant can experience 𓈖𓏤𓏛 *menit-nefer* -a good death, a happy death. This is the implication of preserving the image of the deceased by creating a death mask that contains a smile, such as that of Tuyu (see above).

The following text from the Temple of Heru at Djebu (Edfu) conveys the feeling of those who tread the path of the clergy. It is unsurpassed by any other endeavor. Highlighted here is the exaltation born of surrender to God, knowing that all is in God's hands, so there is no need for worry or strife. All that is needed is to live off of God's offerings and serve God, being a divine instrument, doing the work of the Divine in peace.

> *"How happy are they {priests & priestesses} who celebrate Your majesty, oh Great God, and who do not cease serving Your Temple! Those {priests & priestesses} who elevate Your power, exalt Your grandeur, and fill their heart with You.... Those {priests & priestesses} who go on Your path, and come on Your water, and are concerned with Your majesty's plans! Those {priests & priestesses} who adore Your spirit with paeans[63] intended for deities, and who pronounce Your ritual.... Those {priests & priestesses} who conduct the regular service and the festival service, free of ignorance.... You who tread the path of Ra in His Temple; who keep watch in His home, conducting His festivals and presenting offerings, without cease: enter in peace, leave in peace, go happily! For life is in His hand, health is in His grip, and all goodly things are there where He is: there are the dishes that lie on His table, there is the food of those who eat His offerings! There is no ill or misfortune for those {priests & priestesses} who live on His goods; there is no damnation for those {priests & priestesses} who serve Him, for His care extends to the sky and His security to the earth: His protection is greater than that of all (other) deities."*[64]

There are some key points to be understood here. The joy that comes from living life free from ignorance is being elevated above the joy of life of people in the ordinary society. Speaking for myself, I would not trade being a priest in the Kamitan culture for being a regular person as I was before in the society, for any amount that you can pay me. I have less now than I had before, materially speaking, but I am happier now, more joyous now, more fulfilled now and this is what the scripture is talking about. Those who desire to tread the path of the Neterian clergy should learn to feel this way, content and at peace with the Self, realizing that all other things are perishable and illusory and therefore unworthy of desire.

Freedom from ignorance, doing the festival, making the common offerings again and again, unceasingly, are important disciplines to purify the heart and mind, to keep steady on the path. These offerings that are given to the Divine… where do they come from? The offerings come from the ordinary people who support the Temple. When those offerings come into the Temple, they are first presented to the Divinity, and when the Divinity is finished with them, then the priests and priestesses partake and are sustained by that; that's

---

[63] **pae·an** also **pe·an** (pē'ən) *n.* **1.** *Music.* A song of joyful praise or exultation. **2.** A fervent expression of joy or praise **3.** An ancient Greek hymn of thanksgiving or invocation, especially to Apollo (Heru)

[64] Chassinat, *Edfou*, Vol. V, 343, l. 13-344, l. 3: translated by M. Alliot, *Le Culte d'Horus a Edfou au temps de Ptolemees*, Vol. I 193.

how it works. The idea is that everything has a subtle body, just as you have a subtle body. Actually all human beings have three bodies, the Physical body, Astral body, and Causal body. There is physical food that is needed to sustain the physical body. The Divinity sustains itself with Astral food. Actually, the worship, devotion and love of aspirants comprise astral food for the Divine. The tutelary or *bes* –time and space manifestation of the Divine is what we are referring to here and not the Absolute and Transcendental Divinity. Actually, the offering is presented on the physical plane as well as the Astral plane since the food has physical and astral aspects. So the philosophy is that the Divinity is fed first, and the Divinity reciprocates, by sustaining you and taking care of you.

THE LIFE OF PETOSIRIS

The life and teaching of one priest of Ancient Egypt conveys the lofty feeling of one who has attained great heights of spiritual experience through the path of Neterian spirituality. In Middle Egypt, there is an ancient city, Khemenu, sacred to the god Djehuti, in which a certain priest-sage lived, c. 350 -330 B.C.E. His name was PetAsar (Petosiris), meaning heaven of Asar (Osiris). He was well known and revered. He held high titles:

...High priest who sees the God in His shrine, who carries His Lord and follows His Lord, who enters into the Holy of Holies, who performs his functions together with the great prophets, the prophet of the Ogdoad, chief of the priests of Sekhmet, leader of the priests of the third and fourth orders; the royal scribe who reckons the property in the Temple of Khnum.[65]

One who treads Your path will not stumble, for I have been on earth down to this day, when I attained this perfect realm, with no fault found in me ....[66]

Oh you who are alive on earth....
If you hear (my) words,
If you cleave to them,
You will find their worth.
Serving God is the good way,
Blessed is he whose heart leads him to it!
I speak to you of what happened to me,
I let you perceive the plan of God,
I let you discern knowledge of His might!
I have come here to the city of eternity,
Having done the good upon earth,
Having filled my heart with God's way,
From my youth until this day!
I lay down with His might in my heart,
I rose up doing His ka's wish;
I did justice, abhorred falsehood ...
I joined not with him who ignores God's might ...
I did this remembering I would reach God after death,
Knowing the day of the lords of justice,
When they separate in judgment![67]

Oh you living .... I shall instruct you in the will of the God. I shall guide you to the way of life, the goodly way of one who obeys the God; blessed are those whose hearts lead them to it. Those who are firm on the way of the God, confirmed is their existence on earth. Those with great awe of the God in their soul, great is their happiness on earth.[68]

It is useful to tread the path of the God, great are the advantages reserved for those who take care to follow it. It is a monument they raise for themselves on earth, they who set out to follow the way of the God. Those who hold to the path of the god, they will spend all their lives in joy, richer than their peers. They will grow old in their city, venerated in their nome, all their limbs as young as a child's. Their children will be numerous in their presence and considered the first of their city, their sons will succeed one another from generation to generation . . . They will reach the neterkhert (cemetery-lower heaven) *in joy, embalmed beautifully by the work of Anpu, and the children of their children will live on in their stead.... You have walked on the path of your Lord Djehuti, and after granting that these blessings be given to you on earth, He will bestow similar favors on you after death."*[69]

---

[65] M. Lichtheim, Ancient Egyptian Literature: A Book of Readings, Vol. X. The Late Period (Berkeley, 1980), 45; the Egyptian text was published by G. Lefebvre, Le Tombeau de Petosiris, 3 Vols. (Cairo, 1923 -1924), Vol- 11, 53.
[66] Lefebvre, Tombeau, Vol. 11, 82, text 115.
[67] Lichtheim, Ancient Egyptian Literature, Vol. 111, 50 -51; Lefebvre, Tombeau, Vol- 11, 83, text 116.
[68] Lefebvre, Tombeau, Vol. 11, 38, text 62.
[69] Lefebvre, Tombeau, Vol. 11, 36-37, text 61.

Above: Priests and Priestesses Purify Offerings

Again and again the testimonials of ancient times exalt the path of Neterian spirituality, and most revered in this path are the "servants" of God, the clergy. There is recognition that there is a wealth far surpassing money to be found in the path of *Shems*, or following God. What is necessary is full dedication to the path, observing the duties and responsibilities of performing the rituals, study and devotion to the Divine and observing the injunctions of Maat, keeping good association and obedience to the teaching. PetAsar is extolling the way of blessedness, the path that leads to joy while on earth and going to God after death. This is the supreme example for all aspirants.

ndj- protection

Who does not want to be sage, to be protected from the maladies of the world, to grow old and live in health, to be venerated, to be remembered through succeeding generations? Most people think they can do that by heaping up objects, amassing great wealth for their retirement fund, or by having many children, so that they have someone to take care of them in their old age. But those are not the ways. The way is by *"treading the path of The God."* This is the means to "raise" oneself up while on earth, to make a true monument for oneself. and then at the end of life, secure in the knowledge of higher consciousness, there is the divine journey to meet God. This is the kind of blessedness that is possible for a practitioner of Neterian spirituality. It is the purpose of life and the path that is extolled by all the saints and sages.

 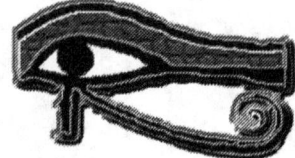

What does it mean to walk "on the path of your Lord Djehuti?" The teaching, the study, reflection and meditation upon the philosophy and disciplines of the Medu Neter (writings of Lord Djehuti containing the teaching of Shetaut Neter and Sema Tawi), must take precedence over all other worldly endeavors. Still, this does not constitute Enlightenment, the ultimate goal of the teachings. If the path is followed *Lord Djehuti* (*Djehuti Sheps* - Lord Djehuti) adds the special ingredient, that 64th part (stem), , of the eye of Heru, that special instruction that leads to whole understanding *udjat Heru*. Lord Djehuti repairs the defective eye, the ignorance that has led to sorrow and distance from the Divine Self. The eye is the organ for vision, and metaphorically it relates to the ability to understand, to wake up and be conscious. A person who is keen and even passionate about the teaching will not fail on the path.

In order to follow the path effectively, there must be Good Association. This is what PetAsar means when he says: *I joined not with him who ignores God's might.* Keeping company with those who believe in God and in the teaching is a necessity. To the extent possible, association with those who are unbelievers or naysayers should be avoided, or at least limited.

The priests and priestesses are teachers: *I let you perceive the plan of God, I let you discern knowledge of His might!* They illumine the people about the nature and power of the Divine. They help the ignorant to see and understand what is before them, and yet not known. They help those who are truly willing, to discover the mysteries of life that are self-evident, and yet unfathomable, and in such work there is incomparable satisfaction and inner peace.

GOD is hidden and no man knows God's form. No man has been able to seek out GOD's likeness.
GOD is hidden to Gods and men...GOD's name remains hidden...It is a mystery to his children (men, women, Gods)
GOD's names are innumerable, manifold and no one knows their number." (Ancient Egyptian Proverb)

Chapter 5: The Designations of the Clergy of Shetaut Neter, Their Functions and Spiritual Disciplines

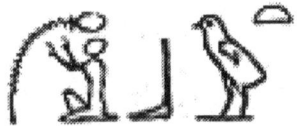

Uabut- priestly service

Offerings to Asar (E) with libations and incense by the Sem priest (C), Opening of the mouth with readings of the mystical text by the *Kheri heb* priest (B) and offering of the mystical haunch of beef by the uab priest (A). The Anpu priest (F) holds up the body of Asar upright, like the Djed pillar. The erect Djed pillar represents resurrection. [Papyrus Ani - Chap 1 B]

A   B   CD   E   F

The Priests and Priestesses of Ancient Egypt

It is essential for aspirants to understand that the tradition of Shetaut Neter (Ancient Egyptian/African Religion) is a highly advanced science of philosophy and spiritual disciplines. Therefore, the study and practice of the wisdom and mystical philosophy of life is an essential aspect of study for priests and priestesses. Thus, for those who wish to consider becoming priests and priestesses, a prerequisite is to succeed in specific academic studies that will allow them to gain greater understanding of the mysteries of life and death, and the nature of the Spirit and the Universe. The essential studies are enjoined in the academic program. These may be likened to the beginning academic studies for apprenticeship priesthood candidates.

Summary – main groups of clergy and leadership of the Temple

1. *sebai(t)*
2. *Sbait kheria*- assistant teacher instructor
3. *seba(t)*-philosophy teachers
4. *Hm(t)* {this level may have several sublevels-Ex. Fourth, Third, Second, First}
5. *Ab(t)*- Apprentice priests and priestesses
6. *Unut* – (Ministers)

The Specialized Disciplines and Education of the Hm and Hmt

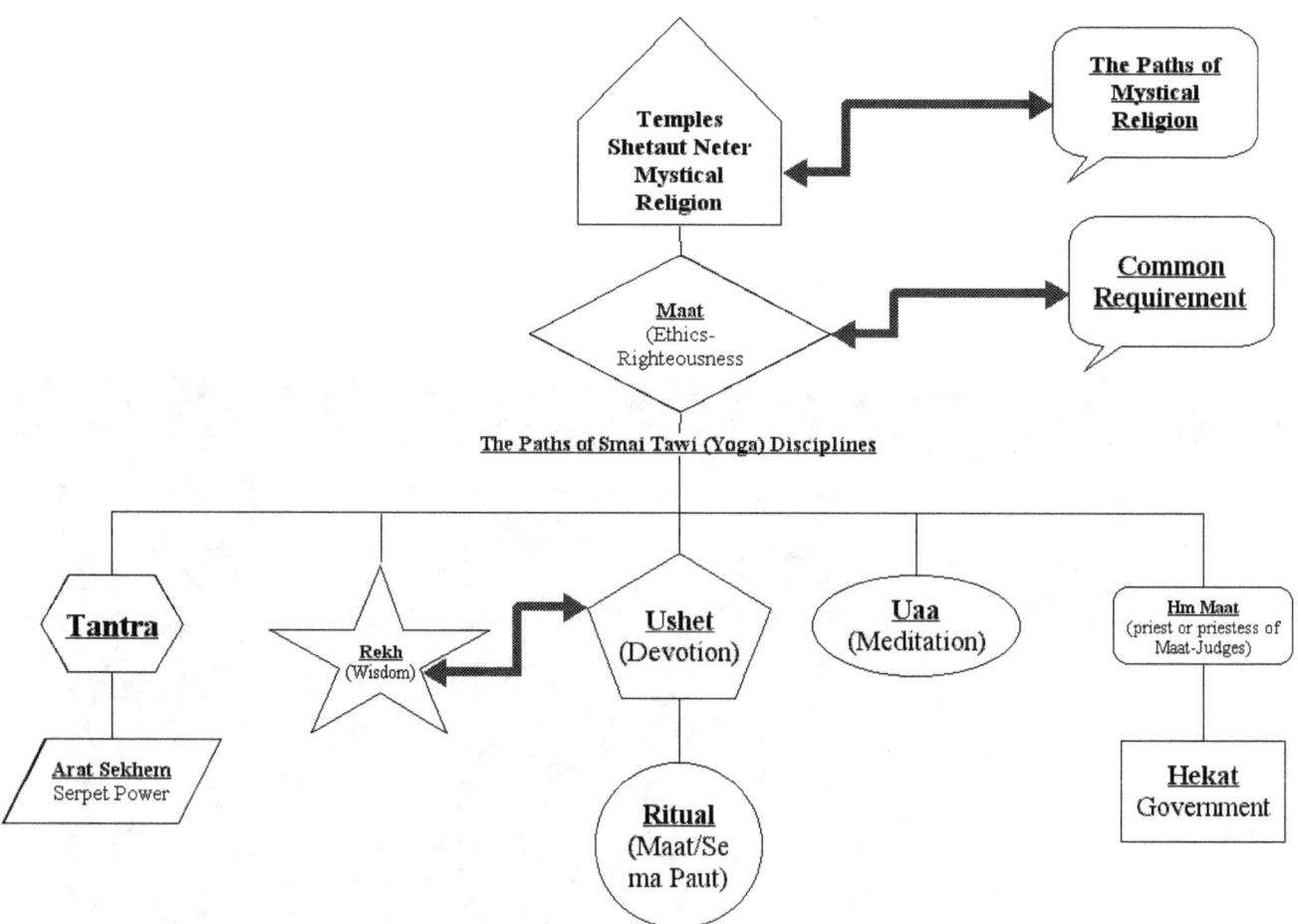

The Spiritual Disciplines of the Priests and Priestesses of Ancient Egypt

The diagram above underscores the importance of spirituality in Kamitan culture. The leaders in government and business were trained in the Temple by people who practiced the disciplines which are today known as "mysticism" and "yoga." Imagine how it was (as compared to how things are in today's world)… those running the country were people who practiced meditation, fasting, study of spiritual scriptures and they were able to at the same time manage the massive numbers of civil servants, farmers, armies and Temple workers, while at the same time providing for the spiritual upliftment of the country by administering the schools, training the professions, and conducting the cultural programs for the country which included weekly, monthly and annual festivals (religious services).

Specialization of the Hm and Hmt in Ancient times

All the priests and priestesses practiced one or more of the mystical religion paths. There were several traditions of Shetaut Neteru (mystical religion) within the monolithic construct of Kamitan religion (Shetaut Neter). They were all related and therefore, harmonious with respect to each other. The areas of specialization in the late period of Kamitan history were described by Clement of Alexandria[70] who witnessed processions of Ancient Egyptian priests.

The statement below is from Clement of Alexandria. He was a person who lived around the time when Jesus was supposed to have been born, when Gnosticism and Christianity were starting to develop in the Ancient Egyptian city of Alexandria. Clement was an ancient Egyptian person, but he was mixed with Greek culture and at this time the Greek culture was existing in parallel with the ancient Kamitan culture in Alexandria. He was talking about one of the processions of the ancient Egyptian Temple, describing how the priests or priestesses are differentiated as far as their particular duties of the Temple. He starts describing what he sees in the procession and how they are performing the ritual. He is something like a reporter, describing a ceremony as the procession passes by: "Now I see the priests who do the readings; now I see priests who do the libations; now I see the priests who do this, that, etc. This important record provides a foundation to show how the specializations of the priests and priestesses were handled in ancient times and how that supports the practice of the specialization of practices for today.

> "At its head walks a singer carrying a musical instrument; it is said that he was supposed to have memorized two books of Hermes, one containing hymns to deities and the other the royal biography. Behind him comes the soothsayer holding his insignia, the clock and the astronomical palm (leaf), in his hand. He must know by heart the four astrological books of Hermes: one of these treats the arrangement of the fixed stars, the second the movements of the sun and the moon and the five planets, the third the encounters and illuminations of the sun and the moon, and the last the rising of the stars. Next marches the sacred scribe wearing feathers on his head, with a book in his hands and the narrow palette containing the black ink and the reed pen they use for writing. This person is supposed to know the writing called hieroglyphic regarding Cosmography and geography, the path of the sun, the moon, and the five planets, the topography of Egypt and the description of the Nile, the prescriptions regarding sacred objects and the places dedicated to them, and the measures and utensils used in the ritual. Behind him walks the stolist, who carries the cubit (-long staff) of justice and the libation vase; he knows everything pertaining to the teaching called "moschosphragistic" (the science of the markings of animals), and the ten precepts having to do with the veneration of deities in the land, including Egyptian piety, treatises on fumigations, offerings, hymns, prayers, processions, festivals, and so forth. Finally, there is the prophet clutching a pitcher ostentatiously to his chest, followed by those who bear the offerings that are invoked aloud. In his capacity of chief of the Temple, he has thorough knowledge of the ten books called hieratic and knows all the priestly lore concerning the laws and the deities."[71]

---

[70] Early Christian church father who attempted to harmonize the Christian teaching with the Greek Gnostic and Egyptian in the Egyptian city of Alexandria. The Orthodox Roman church rejected these attempts and the reaction was the opposite of harmonization – a distinctly separate Christian teaching.

[71] Clement of Alexandria, *Stromateis*, VI, chap. 4, SS 35-36. The translation here follows that of P. Derchain, *Chronique d'Egypte* 26 (1951): 269-79.

Choosing a Spiritual Tradition

Areas of Specialty Theology Paths -Religious Path (Shetaut Neter)

All Hm and Hmt must choose and area of Theology specialty along with a tutelary deity for their personal spiritual practice. The tradition provides insights into the myth, ritual and metaphysics of spirituality. This allows the clergy to understand, practice and devote themselves to the Divine. So as in ancient times, the aspirant should choose a spiritual tradition or one should be assigned to them. The main traditions are: the Asarian tradition, the Anunian tradition, the Memphite tradition, the Theban tradition, the goddess Path, the Aton theology, etc. There are books or lecture series that have been created for all of them, specifically expounding on them, so anyone who wants to begin their studies could be directed thereby. The main traditions include:

- The Asarian Religion and the Asarian Trinity:
    - BOOK: *Resurrecting Osiris*

- The Teachings of Anunian Theology and the Anunian Trinity:
    - BOOK: *Anunian Theology*

- The Teachings of Memphite Theology:
    - BOOK: *Mysteries of Mind and Memphite Theology*

- The Teachings of Theban Theology and the Universal Trinity
    - BOOK: *EGYPTIAN YOGA VOL. 2: Theban Theology and The Supreme Wisdom of Enlightenment-The Mystical Wisdom of Ancient Egyptian Theban Theology*

- The Goddess Path:
    - BOOK: *The Mysteries of Isis*
    - BOOK: *The Goddess: Worship of the Divine Mother*
    - BOOK: *The Glorious Light Meditation*

Clergy Choosing an Area for Selfless Service as a Support for the Spiritual Tradition and Society, and Choosing a Tutelary Divinity

All Hm and Hmt must choose and area of Selfless Service specialty along with the tradition and sema (yoga) choice. This allows the gross aspects of the personality to be purified so that the aspirant may attain higher orders of personality integration and understanding of the teaching.

Service to the Temple

- Service to maintain Temple services (rituals – education – classes – spiritual disciplines {postures, chant sessions, meditation sessions})

Service to Humanity (Community – Society)

- Counseling – ministering – educating – healing
- Order and Righteousness in Society
- Maat Hem Rekhit – Maat service to humanity
    - Feed the hungry

- o Give drink to the thirsty
- o Give clothes to the clotheless
- o Give Shelter to the homeless
- o Give Opportunity to those who do not have opportunity

Spiritual Disciplines (Most important is meditation)
- Postures – ritual – meditation – chant – study of scriptures

Culture and Ritual
- Conduct Public rituals and proceedings

As stated earlier, a tutelary deity should be assigned to or chosen by an aspirant. An aspirant accepts a deity as a means to assist them in their spiritual research. When an aspirant has an image, a physical concrete image to focus the mind on, it assists in a more dynamic way in the beginning of the spiritual process, especially in the practice of meditation. When an aspirant elevates to a certain degree he/she can start going beyond that tutelary image of the Divine to a more abstract form of meditation practice and later transcend even that.

Priest making offering to Ancestors- Dyn 19.

The Organizational Structure of a Typical Ancient Egyptian Temple Clergy

In Ancient times there were Temples ranging from the very small to the very large. The smaller ones may have had as few as a handful of clergy while the larger might have had several thousands. In either case, the Neterian Temple was set up with a highly organized and specialized set of personnel, and the Temple rituals were performed by all the Temples, with scrupulous attention to detail.

There were priests and priestesses who were responsible for various duties that maintained the Temple, and others served the needs of the population where the Temple was located. The main divisions are the orders of priests and priestesses in varying ranks according to experience and training, headed by the *Hem* or *Hemt Neter Tpy* (Head priest or priestess). The next division is the Government (civil servants) and Army, overseen directly by the pharaoh and the Vizier (minister). The other division is the education division, headed by the *Sbaiu*. This division oversees the instruction of children and the apprenticeship programs of the priests and priestesses, who learn trades along with their spiritual studies.

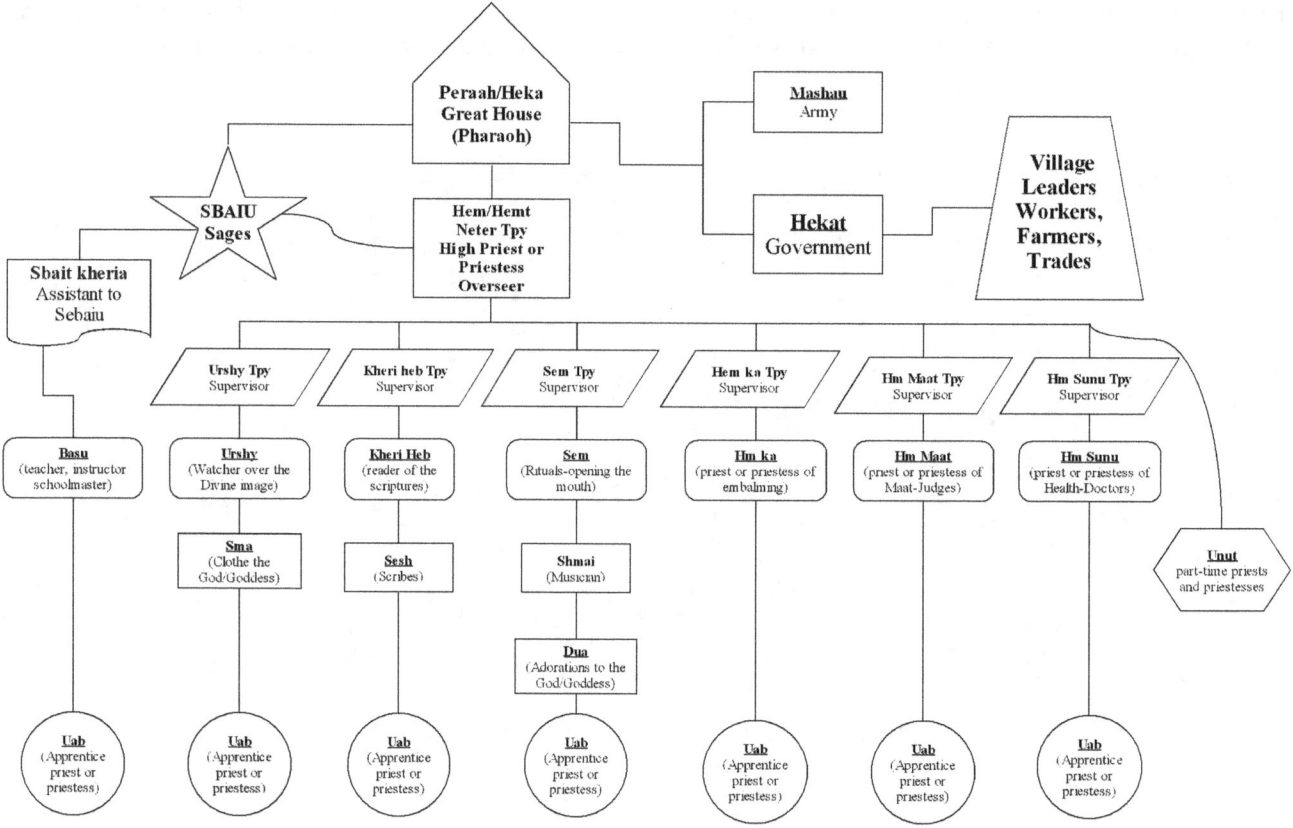

The *Peraah* (Pharaoh) is the leader of both the religion and the government. Together with the Vizier, who would be a priest or priestess, the Peraah (**Heka**) controls government (**Hekat**) and the civil servants as well as the **Mashau** (army). The Peraah may be a figurehead, or may be the religious leader as well as a political leader, thus heading up the Temple systems and not being just a figurehead. The Temple functions due to the work of priests and priestesses who are divided into various Temple occupations. Each occupation consists of **Uab** priests and priestesses who work under the direction of supervising priests and priestesses (**Hem or Hemt Neter Tpy**). The *Sba* is the disseminator of the high philosophical teaching, in charge of the instruction of all priests and priestess as well as directly overseeing the school of the Temple, which handles primary education of the children

Here we have the types of priests and priestesses, and the different orders and functions that they serve. This many personnel would be applicable to a very large Temple system like the Amun Temple. Most

Temple systems only had half a dozen full-time positions; the other positions were part-time. The different priests and their functions are listed in the chart. From left to right: there is the *Sbait kheria*. These are assistants of the Sebai. The Sebai is the sage, the wisdom teacher. *Seba* would be more like a college-level teacher, working independently or assisting the Sebai, and the *Basu* would be more like an Elementary-High School teacher. The *Abs* assists in the practice of the disciplines; they assist in anything that is related to the performance of the rituals, the readings, offerings, purifications, and they study under the Hm. The *Hmu* are the full-fledged priests and priestesses who manage the different departments or areas of specialization. Then the above them are the supervisor, priests and priestesses. The *Hemut Neter Tepy* are the female supervisor priestesses and the *Hmu Neter Tepy are the male* supervisor priests. Above the priests and priestesses is the Vizier, and above the vizier is the Pharaoh. As stated above, most Temple systems would have a smaller number of priests and priestesses, but this chart would be more like the Amun Temple. The Amun Temple complex was itself like a city. The Temple employed thousands of people. It was like the capital of the entire Kamitan empire that existed from the Nubia in the south all the way up into the Persia, India, and going up into Turkey, and Greece.

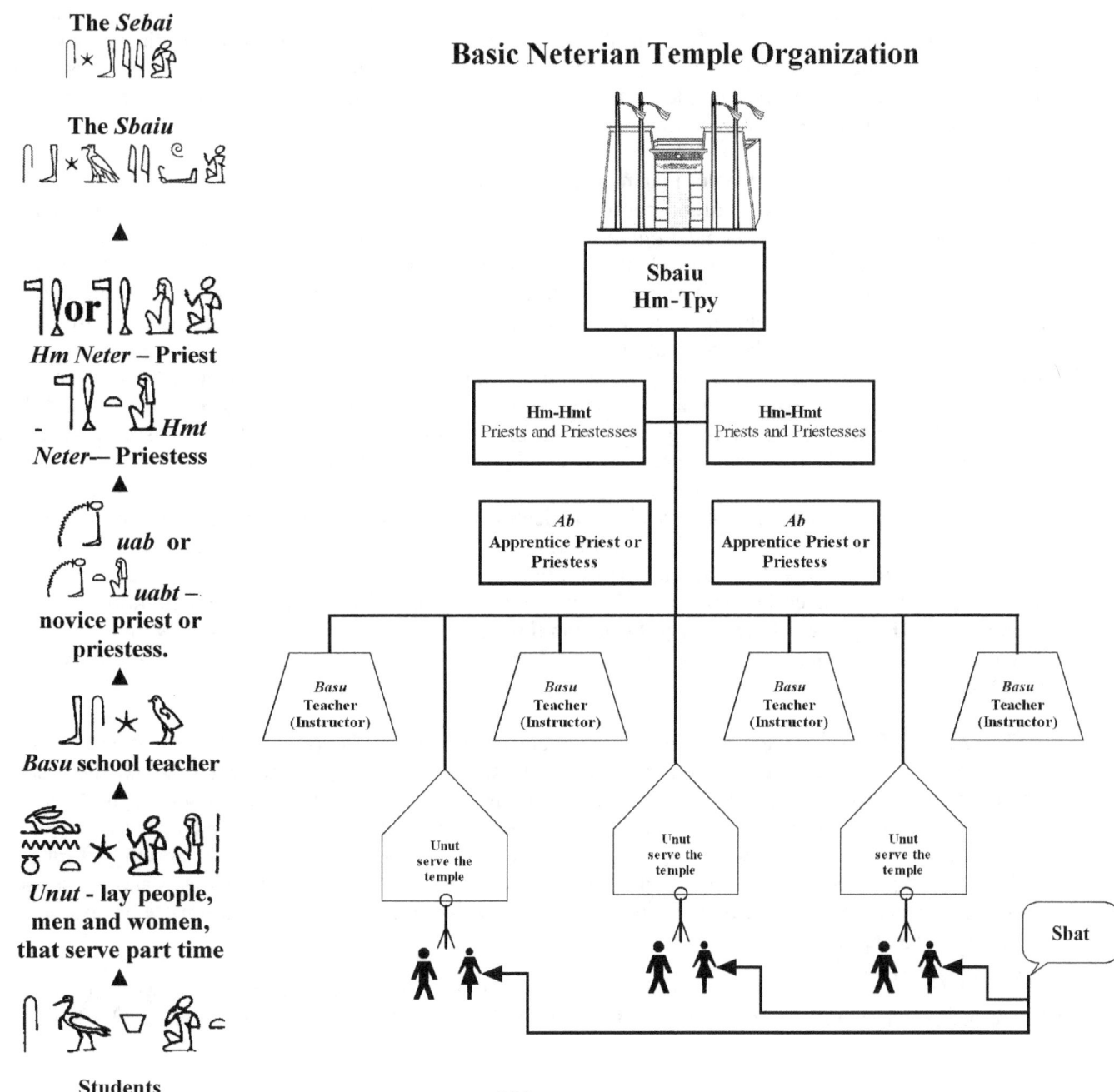

The Priests and Priestesses of Ancient Egypt

Now to break this down to its basic components the diagram above (**Basic Neterian Temple Organization**) shows something more like the basic small Temple arrangement. It contains the basic organizational pattern of the priests and priestesses. Starting at the bottom, there is the *Sbat*. Sbat means student. This includes laypersons that are interested in the teachings (i.e., anyone who comes off the street); there is no formal association between them and the Temple. Moving up from the Sbat are the *Unut*. Unut are the part-time priests and priestesses or part-time servants of God. They are not to be considered as full priests and priestesses, but rather as more like laypeople who have a formal association with the Temple. They assist in the practices of the Temple and the conduct of the Temple programs. They are like deacons in the modern Christian church, those who assist the priests and priestesses in their duties. The Basu are more like Sunday school teachers at the church or elementary school teachers. Above them are the novice (apprentice) priests and priestesses, the Ab, and the full priests and priestesses (Hemu) manage them. The *Sbaiu* teach them all.

Sbaiu are the sages, are the illumined teachers and another tem is *Djaasu* - sages wise ones - divine sages. The Sbai is the sage who teaches the *Sbait*. *Sbait* means spiritual teaching, the spiritual philosophy. The Sba is like a college level teacher. The Basu is like a high school level teacher. The Unut is like an elementary school level. It is all about managing the Sbat. Unut assist the ordinary people of the society, helping them to order their lives. On the other hand the Unut assist the priests and priestesses and those people who work at the Temple on their path to self-discovery. So the Temple has two functions, to espouse the higher mysteries and the lower mysteries.

The Sbat are the regular people, potential aspirants, those people who are interested in the teaching but they are uninitiated and uncommitted people. As for the term *Unut, Un* means existence and *nut* means heaven, and so Unut means *they who abide in heaven*. They are trying to abide in a higher plane and in a higher aspect of life. They are laypeople that volunteer their time part of the year, but also they can be more than that; they can be serious practitioners of the Neterian religion through their close association with the full priests and priestesses. They might work about two to three months out of a year or more, usually when the Nile was in flood after the planting season. They had ongoing training and were given duties to perform in assisting the management of the Temple; they have more of a formal agreement with the Temple. The teaching specifically says that they are the ones who support the Temple by making offerings and through their physical service. The Unut also assist in the dissemination of the teachings to the masses, assisting them to learn and practice the basic rituals and fundamental principles of Shetaut Neter.

The Basu are the ones who take special certifications in the classes they teach. They are the ones who teach in the primary school. The *Ab* or Uab priest is the apprentice level priest or priestess. They are the lowest rank of the full priesthood and the first level or tier of the full-time Temple. There are several levels of the *Uab* priesthood, increasing up to *Uab Tpy*, which means supervisor. One of the main duties of the Ab is purification. The symbol of the Ab priest is a man throwing water. Their duty is to purify things primarily by water. The priest will throw water on an object. The other symbol of the Ab is of a person throwing water over himself.

The *Hmu* or full priests and priestesses are the ones who manage the Temple. There can be several levels of rank (first, second, third, etc.). They are managed by the *Hm Neter Tepy*. This would be like the basic small Temple with a staff of 4-6 people. The *Hmu* and *Hm Neter Tepy* are in turn supervised by the *Sbait kheria*. The *Sbait kheria* are a higher level of *Hm* priest who assist the Sebai. They are advanced disciples of the Sbaiu. They are practitioners who are on a track towards becoming sages and saints, and they want to work and become experts in particular traditions and in particular disciplines. The *Hmu* (priests and priestesses) are proficient in usually one particular discipline or function (area of specialization). For example, The *sesh Neter* - scribe of holy books was in charge of codification work in the temple. There are priests who do nothing but clothing the divinity or taking care of the shrine, and this system of specialization becomes highly refined in a large Temple system. Note that the letter *"u"* at the end of the words means plural, i.e, Hm/Hmt means priest/priestess while Hmu means priests and priestesses.

The *official staff* of a Temple could consist, of comparatively few persons. The Temple at Siut for instance of had ten;[72] at Abdu (Abydos), there were only five priests.[73] Each of these had a special title; thus the secluded assembly of Asar of Abdu was composed of:

The great Ua'b," *i.e.* the high priest,'
The treasurer of the god,
The scribe of the god's house, The reciter-priest,
The *Mete-en-sa."*

Djed - Pillar of Asar

The Djed pillar is one of the single most important Neterian symbols/amulets/artifacts of the Temple. It represents the back or vertebrae of the god Asar, who was murdered by his brother in the Asarian Resurrection myth.[74] Asar was resurrected from the dead through the works of goddess Aset, and the gods Heru and Djehuti. In one relief from the Temple of Asar at Abdu the goddess (priestess) Aset may be seen receiving the pillar of Asar to resurrect him (A). Thus, the work of the priesthood is to effect a raising of the pillar of Asar in all spiritual aspirants.

The Djed symbolizes the four upper psycho-spiritual consciousness centers[75] of the spiritual body.[76] The work of the priests and priestesses *Uabut-* {priestly service} serves to raise the *Sekhem* –life force-divine power, which awakens the *Arat-Udjat-* Serpent Power. When that power which was manifesting as a duality, symbolized by the two serpent goddesses (Aset and Nebethet), is awakened and harmonized, it courses upwards through the pillar, carrying consciousness to the heights of Enlightenment. This image of Asar and the two serpents (C) is the mystic caduceus of life. Asar's back is made of a tree trunk; thus it is the tree of life. This process leads a practitioner of the mysteries to the *rekh-ab* knowledge of Self- to Know Thyself. The image on the following page (overleaf) is the actual relief of image (B) from the Temple of Hetheru.

---

[72] *A Z.*, 1882, 173.
[73] Mar. Cat. d'Ab., 711.
[74] See the book *Resurrecting Osiris* by Sebai Muata Ashby
[75] See the book *Egyptian Mysteries Vol 1.* by Sebai Muata Ashby
[76] See the book *The Serpent Power* by Sebai Muata Ashby

disciplines, but it is mostly concerned with *sba* Enlightenment, i.e. mysticism (mystical philosophy). It is not necessary for an aspirant to engage in that level of training (in all disciplines) in order to attain *nehast* (Enlightenment). All the above average aspirant needs is to become proficient in one system and that will lead the aspirant to Enlightenment. The reason to become Sebai is if the aspirant wants to be teaching on a level of nation building and to be disseminating teachings in several different areas or disciplines of specialization, like the ancient Kamitan sage, Imhotep, who had many degrees. But more generally speaking, what the aspirant needs to do is pick one system and become proficient in that. Then, along with other aspirants, there can be a growing group of clergy who are well versed in different areas and can work together to advance the Neterian culture as a group, as a whole community of Neterian clergy. They can start their own Temples based on their tutelary deities; then when approached by someone who is interested in a particular tradition or path they can say, "the priest or priestess of that tradition is at such and such Temple in such and such city." This kind of system could expand to be located in all countries, with the priests and priestesses working in a coordinated fashion to promote the Neterian Philosophy (the sbait) to uplift all humanity in modern times. So for those who aspire to be Neterian Priests and Priestesses, these are the kinds of ideas that need to de reflected upon.

Outline of Basic Designations of Priests and Priestesses of Ancient Egypt

The following is a general overview of the designations, functions and history of the priest(ess)hood of Ancient Egypt. The development of the priesthood entailed many changes and additions over the long history of the culture. Also, there were several local titles and assignments for priests and priestesses. However, there are some general aspects of the clergy in Ancient Egypt that can be delineated, which will add to our knowledge about the nature of the religious practice in Ancient Egypt.

Firstly, using the traditional Egyptological divisions of the main periods of Ancient Egyptian history (Predynastic, Early dynastic, Old Kingdom, Middle Kingdom and New Kingdom), there are two major phases or periods of the Kamitan clergy. The first phase is from the Predynastic era to the end of the Middle Kingdom and the other is from the New Kingdom to the Roman closing of all Temples in Egypt.

In the first Phase, the Temple service was the paramount defining aspect of Ancient Egyptian culture. There were two basic classes of service, the *Hem* and the *Uab*. There were other specific designations and functions.

The priests and priestesses served the - *Het Neter* - house of God, i.e. the Temple. The different grades or ranks of priests were referred to as - *sau* – which means "protectors." They were supervised by the overseer *Priest*. The full-time priests were assisted by *Unut Neter Het* - part time priests of house of God. One Priest may have been designated as *priest atf-neter* - *father of God* - for the temple.

Some important priesthood positions included the *Kheri heb* priest is in charge of the arrangements of the ceremonies and festivals. This person makes sure that the proper readings are done in the proper order and with the proper offerings. This priest(ess) also reads from the holy books. The *sesh Neter* - scribe of holy books was in charge of codification work in the temple. This included transcribing works from earlier periods that were becoming illegible due to the deterioration of papyri. It also included writing the Prt M Hru texts.

The general term for priests and priestesses is: ***Hm*** means "majesty" or "magnificence" or "splendor." Also, it means "servant" or "slave." This is what the ancient Egyptian concept of religious service was, a true source of happiness and glory in life through religious service in the Temple and service to humanity.

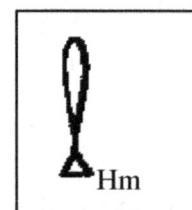

Hm Neter - servant or prophet of God – Priest

Hmt Neter - servant or prophet of God – Priestess

hmu ntr - servants, priests (priests and priestesses), prophets of god.

The Hmu Neter are considered as full priests or priestesses. In this capacity the term also implies Prophet or more accurately, "seer." They are seers in the sense that they have insights into the mysteries and foresight in life through the realization of the wisdom teachings. The relation of the term *Hm* (servant/prophet) and *maa* (see) is evident in the title *Maa - Ur* or "Great Seer" - title of High priest of Anu – (from the Palermo Stele).

The female gender is signified in an Ancient Egyptian word most often by writing the letter "t" at the end of a word and or adding a determinative symbol for woman. Thus the term *Hm* or Seer (servant of God-clergy) becomes "genderized" to the male *Hm Neter* and the female *Hmt Neter*. The use of the female appellation was mostly emphasized in the Middle Kingdom Period of Ancient Egyptian history.[77] Therefore, it is to be accepted as a legitimate designation but not an absolute requirement to denote the presence of a woman who is being discussed in the texts. When the Nubians took over Egypt, Nubian men and women also served as priests and priestesses.[78]

There are other important aspects of the term *Hm*. Present day scholarship has shown that the term Hm was sometimes used to refer to personalities that were clearly female. So the term should not be considered as an absolute determination of gender. *Hm* or *Hmu* should be seen as general terms referring to the clergy. Also, there are records of female priests who supervised both male and female priests. So the idea that men were dominant in Neterian spirituality is challenged by these findings. In the priesthood of the Temple of Hetheru, it is clear that there were more female priests than male priests. In the priesthood of Amun, there might have been more male priests, but also there is record of women assuming the position of High Priest(ess) of Amun, and at that time it meant that that person became the highest cleric of the entire country, something on the order of the Pope in the Catholic religion.[79/80] Therefore, the gender equality of Ancient Egyptian culture as reflected in the practice of religion was unparalleled in the ancient world for the size and scope of Ancient Egyptian religion, and even in the present day there continues to be no comparison. There is record of women who held priestly titles and who

---

[77] *Archeogender: Studies in Genders Material Culture*, Sheldon Lee Gosline
[78] *The Third Intermediate Period In Egypt. (1100-650 B.C.)* Warminster: Aris & Phillips.
[79] "Priestien" in *Lexicon der Agyptologie*, Vol. IV, 1100-1105. Weisbaden [edited by W. Helk and E. Otto], Fischer, 1982
[80] "Deux Monuments de la Princesse Anknasnofiribri," *ASAE 5*: 84-92. Meskell, Lynn

married men with honorific or unrelated titles.[81] Further, research has also shown that women could be priestesses in different Temples and also that positions within the Temple hierarchy were not inherited.[82] Moreover, women served in the Temples of male divinities such as Djehuti and Ptah.[83]

Below: West Wall of the Tomb of Nikauhor and Sekhemhatheru (Early Dyn. 5 Saqqara) Nikauhor was a priest of Ra and also judge. His wife, Sekhemhatheru was priestess of Hetheru and Net.

---

[81] *Seven Memphite Tomb Chapels.* BSAE 65; London. Quaegebeur, Jan 1952, Petrie, Hilda and M.A. Murray
[82] *The Priestesse of Hathor in the Old Kingdom and the 1st Intermediate Period.* (Brandeis University Dissertation) Ann Arbor: University Microfilm
[83] "Priestien" in *Lexicon der Agyptologie,* Vol. IV, 1100-1105. Weisbaden [edited by W. Helk and E. Otto], Fischer, 1982

The Hmt Neter - High Priestess — Tends to the needs of the Divinity — Oversees Temple

Certain elevated ranks of priestesses had a special function known as *Hemut Neter* – High Priestess-wife of the God. This term is derived from *Hmt* —woman, wife.

In ancient times in the Wasetian institution, there was a strong tradition of an earthly wife of the God, a priestess, the Divine Adoratrice (priestess in charge of adorations to the Divine), who commanded a high rank in the clergy of Amun. The presence of female musicians and singers in the varied Temples was consistent and extensive.

However, besides the more artistic role, unlike other religious traditions in ancient times and in the present day, women were also integral parts of the Temple ceremonies and rituals. One important example was when the mysteries were enacted. At those times two women played the role of the goddesses, Aset and Nebthet:

"there shall be brought in [two] women pure of body and virgin, with the hair of their bodies removed, their heads adorned with wigs, [...][84] tambourines in their hands, and their names inscribed on their arms, to wit Aset and Nebthet, and they shall sing from the stanzas of this book in the presence of this god."[85]

---

[84] lost or damaged text
[85] R. O. Faulkner, *Journal of Egyptian Archaeology* 22 (1936): 122. For the Egyptian text, see idem, *The Papyrus Bremner-Rhind*, Bibliotheca Agyptiaca 3 (Brussels, 1933), 1, ll. 2-5.

Male and Female Service in the Temple

A special tradition developed in the Temple of Amun wherein a priestess assumed the role of wife to the Divinity in the same way that modern day nuns consecrate themselves to Christ and remain celibate. However, the duties and practice of the Ancient Egyptian priestess were the same as that of the mystic priesthood. The Ancient Egyptian priestess remained celibate and tended on the needs of the icon in the Temple. Thus, the tradition of balance between the two genders, even in the service of the Divine, is a hallmark of Kamitan spirituality. This balance between the sexes translates into a harmony and prosperity in the family that promotes righteousness and peace in the community and strong marital relations. Thus, the balance between the sexes and the inclusion of females in all areas of the Temple service is essential to the proper execution of the spiritual tradition and the promotion of the kind of harmony in the society that will allow spiritual evolution instead of conflict and egoism to occur.

Gender bias is an obstacle to spiritual Enlightenment as it causes egoism and strife to develop between the genders. Therefore, it is not enjoined or supported by the Neterian teaching or the Kamitan culture. This is a development of Western and Middle Eastern cultures (ignorance and arrogance) and has no place in the practice of Kamitan spirituality. This is one of the great aspects of the Neterian legacy, our recognition of each other's worth and virtues.

The image above is a relief-panel of the Ritual of the Divine bull -priests reading – and offering incense and libations to Asar-Hapi.[86]

The specific clergy in charge of the funerary rights were the *Hm ka* priesthood of the Ka - funerary rights.

Hm Neter Tepy: Oversees Temple
There was an overseer priest or priestess for the lower order of clergy: *Hm Neter Tepy* -head servant of God.

The Uab – Ritual Purifications *uab* – purity, cleanliness, hygiene, morally pure.
Uab is the designation for priests and priestesses who were in charge of all purifications in the Temple.

or or *uab* - priest of purifications

uabt - priestess of purifications
This class of the clergy was supervised by the *uab aah* - Great priest of purifications.

The term for the *uab* is related to *uabti* – "morally pure" – noble, i.e. purity is not to be just considered as a physical hygienic condition but there must be purity of the morals in order to be considered noble, and as a candidate for the priesthood.

The *Neter Duat uabu* are a designation of priests and *Neter Duat uabut* priestesses who serve making adorations in the Temple.

Physical purity is to be considered a matter of very serious order. The male and female *uab* are clean-shaven, having no body hair at all. Sexual intercourse is considered a form of impurity and priests and priestesses who were married were required in ancient times to abstain from sex for a prescribed number of days before entering the Temple. In the Turin museum, there is a judicial document that describes an *uab* priest who was

---
[86] For more on the divinity Asar Hapi see *Egyptian Mysteries Vol. 2: Gods and Goddesses*

brought up on charges of "ritual impurity" because he was supposed to enter the Temple after 10 days of purification but did so after only 7 days.

The Kheri heb

There is also an order of clergy who read or recited texts and *hekau* (words of Power) at rituals. They were supervised by the  *Kheri heb Tepy*- head priest of the festival-ritual.

The Sm

Another class of clergy were the *Sm*, they wear leopard skins and side locks and perform libations, offering of incense as well as the "Opening of the Mouth Ceremony" of the Book of Enlightenment. *Sm* – priests were supervised by the *Sm Sekhem* – power priest.

Above (left) Sem Priest making and offering.

Above (right) Ancient Egyptian Sem Priestess.

The Sem (officiating) priest wears a leopard skin as a symbol of the power to dispel the evil of death and to open the mouth (mind) of the initiate.

Mafdet

Mafdet is a feline divinity that represents the fierce aspect of all cats, which is inimical with evil which manifests in the form of evil serpents (not all serpents are evil). When a priest or priestess wears the leopard pelt it means that they have that same power to destroy the evil forces, which promote ignorance, untruth, and suffering.

Figure: The Leopard Goddess Mafdet cutting the head of the Demon serpent Apep. (from the PertmHeru)

The Leopard Goddess Mafdet was associated with Sekhmet, the Eye of Ra and with Hetheru. She is the embodiment of the destructive force that can be unleashed on the negative impetus, symbolized by the serpent demon Apep. Mafdet is also identified with the execution blade itself.

Pharaoh Tutankhamun rides on a leopard.

The Priests and Priestesses of Ancient Egypt

Scenes from the King's Thirty Year Jubilee (Dynasty 4 – during the reign of Sneferu)

The priest (far left-wearing the leopard skin) presides over the festival as the goddess Merit chants "Come and Bring."

Sma

The Sma - Takes care of the Clothing, ornaments and offerings at the Altar

Another class of clergy is the ⚲ or ⚲ *Sma* or priest who clothes the God. The *sma* indicates a union with the Divinity, touching and communing with the Divinity to service the Divinity's personal needs. This term also of course relates the service as a unity of consciousness with the Divinity, i.e. the movement of Yoga mysticism or "union of individual consciousness (priest) with universal consciousness (God).

Urshy

The Urshy – Watches over the Image and those who Meditate upon it

The ⚲ *ursh* – is the watcher.

⚲ *ursht* - female watcher – of God.

⚲ *urshy* - watchers of God.

Their function was to watch over the divine image or initiate, i.e. assist them in remaining vigilant (meditating), as the goddesses Aset and Nebthet and the god Heru watched over the body of Asar and resurrected him.

Shmai Neter - Divine Musicians - The Music Discipline

Ancient Egyptian Priestess Playing Music

Ancient Egyptian Priests Playing Music

The Hieroglyphic texts of the discipline of music, chant and adorations:

⚲ *Shmait* - female musician singer

⚲ *Shmai* - male musician singer

⚲ *Hesi* -Chant, sing repeatedly praises.

Notice that the word for music and the word for chant or sing, all use the determinative sign, ⚲, which means with the mouth. Therefore, the primary musical instrument is seen as the voice, and all other instruments are viewed as accompaniments to the voice.

⚲ *Neter seshit* - priestess who plays sistrum for the Divinity.

Dua Neter – Divine Adorers

Another very important class of the clergy are the adorers. They are professional clergy who specialize in adorations of the Divine, through praises, hymns and ritual genuflections with incense and other artifacts.

⚲ *Neter Duait* - priestess adorer of the Divinity.

Neter duat abu - order of priesthood who serve making adorations and purifications in the Temple.

Dua - praises, adorations to the Divine (standing or sitting).

Hm Dua Neter - title of the priest who praises the Divine.

Hm Duat Neter - title of the priestess of Amun.

The priest who fills the role of touching the special instruments to the mouth is named *un ra* – "priest who opens the mouth."

Sba-Ur means "Great Star" or "Mighty Star." This is an allusion to the supreme light that opens up consciousness, the light that is steady and does not flicker, i.e. imperishable. Sba-Ur comes from the root word Sba. Sba means:

Sba – Star. Note the *Ra*, ☉, determinative, meaning illumination. Also it is a pun on the symbol for the soul, (ba). From S(ba), the star (the source of wisdom, i.e. illumination or Enlightenment) it is possible to teach the soul (ba).

Sba - to teach, bring up, educate, train, instruct.

The Sage instructs the wisdom teaching. *Sbai* – (wise man, teacher, instructor) of the imperishable star (i.e. wisdom about transcendental consciousness, the mysteries) with the *Sba-ur*, opening of the mouth instrument. So here the term's usage is related to the dual capacity of this priest or priestess function as an enlightened

Above: a priest offers Incense and Libations The Sbai – Spiritual Preceptor and the Unra

As the highest disseminator of the Mystery Teachings, the Sbai or Spiritual Preceptor is the key to the initiatic system.

(Vignette from the Opening of the Mouth Ceremonies from the Ancient Egyptian texts. Right with the Seba (Sba) ur instruments.)

personality (Sage) as well as the imparter of the spiritual wisdom (teacher-preceptor).

The teacher leads the ☧ *Sbat* – student (notice the female word ending {☉}), meaning receiver (this is tantric symbolism: male-electric correlates to Sbai who gives {i.e., metaphorically ejaculates} the teaching, female-magnetic correlates to the Sbat {male or female student} who receives the teaching) of the teaching or illumination from the teacher. The teacher illumines like the star and the student shines like the moon. When the moon waxes, ☽, it means the God of purified intellect, Djehuti, has fostered increasing wisdom and subtlety of intellect.

Thus, the Sbai (spiritual preceptor) leads the Sbat to Enlightenment by means of the Seba-ur or highest enlightening teaching. This is the initiatic philosophy in reference to the Kamitan term Sba.

Summary of the Sba Glyphs

1. ☧ *Sba* - to teach, bring up, educate, train, instruct

2. ☧ *Sba het* - schoolroom – school building

3. ☧ *Sbau* teachers instructors plural

4. ☧ *Sbat* or student (aspirant, disciple).

5. ☧ *Sbai* – Spiritual Preceptor – Espouses Mystical Philosophy

6. ☧ *Sbaiu* act as Spiritual Preceptors, or teacher of the high mysteries.

7. ☧ *Sbait kheria* - assistant teacher instructor of the Neterian philosophy.

8. ☧ *Sbait* - spiritual philosophy instruction teaching education.

9. ☧ *Sba* Star with Ra determinative, meaning illumination
Sba-ur opening of the mouth instrument

Overleaf: Ancient Egyptian Priests and Priestesses making adorations to the God Sobek

Chapter 6: Duties of the Servants of God

Akhut – wise men and women – enlightened people.

Left: Egyptian man and woman- (tomb of Papyri) 18th Dynasty displaying the naturalistic style (as people really appeared) in ancient times.

In order to be effective administrators, priests need to be proficient in several disciplines of social practice. These include, first and foremost, religion. They should be expert scholars, but more importantly, practitioners of spirituality. The Neterian clergy were always politicians, teachers, healers, farmers, scientists, economists, engineers, etc. This does not mean going to college to get four year degrees in all of those areas, but there needs to be competency in those areas of secular management along with expertise in their chosen area of spiritual practice.

What Does a Servant of God Actually Do?

The following teaching comes to us by Plutarch, who was a Greek initiate into the Temple of Aset and he states that this is the policy that was enjoined for Egyptian initiates.

> *"He alone is a true servant or follower of this Goddess who, after has heard, and has been made acquainted in a proper manner (initiated into the philosophy) with the history of the actions of these gods, searches into the hidden truths which lie concealed under them, and examines the whole by the dictates of reason and philosophy. Nor indeed, ought such an examination to be looked on as unnecessary whilst there are so many ignorant of the true reason even of the most ordinary rites observed by the Egyptian priests, such as their shavings[87] and wearing linen garments. Some, indeed, there are, who never trouble themselves to think at all about these matters, whilst others rest satisfied with the most superficial accounts of them: They pay a peculiar veneration to the sheep,[88] therefore they think it their duty not only to abstain from eating flesh, but likewise from wearing its wool. They are continually mourning for their gods, therefore they shave themselves."*

It is important to understand that there are two forms of religion. There is religion of initiates, that is the higher mysteries, and there is religion that is for the masses, that is the lower mysteries. The lower mysteries are the myths like the story of Asar which tells how Asar came down to the world, taught humanity, and was killed by his brother Set, as well as the festivals and ceremonies related to these myths; these are for the masses.

Now, for the initiates, the Sheti disciplines are enjoined to teach them how to meditate upon that mythic personality, how to realize their own Asarian nature, how to transcend the mortal consciousness and discover their Heru aspect, and so on. The wisdom and mysticism about the illusoriness of the world, the goal of resurrecting in consciousness and the true nature of Creation would not be divulged to the laypeople. The job of a priest or priestess is to research these high wisdom teachings, these high spiritual realizations, and elevate oneself so as to be able to provide leadership and moral support for each other, and the masses. The religion of the masses is at the level of ceremony, festival and holidays. That is the exoteric part of religious practice. But there is an esoteric practice, like the Neterian fire ritual, for example. What is really going on in the fire ritual is that the practitioner is burning their mortality into the fire. Laypeople may participate in this ritual, and they may like the music and the dancing, and feel that the moon is wonderful, and may become entranced by whatever else may go on, but they do not know about the higher mystical aspect of what is going on. They enjoy the program as a physical movement, as a physical enjoyment, like going to a party or some other social event, and also as an emotional catharsis, but the benefits of that lower practice are limited and temporary. That is the lower practice of religion; it is not enough to transform the human heart to promote full virtue and divine qualities such as compassion, universal love and understanding. That is why those people who practice the lower form of religion, fanatically going to church, shouting halleluiah, shaking uncontrollably, deluding themselves with the idea that they are possessed by the "spirit" are not transformed or fulfilled, but only temporarily relieved of stress. And at the same time, they are collecting more impressions of agitation, fanatical delusion and unrest, the opposite of critical thinking and higher insight into spirituality; therefore, they will actually be a danger to peace and harmony in their lives and in the world.

The priests and priestesses lead festivals and rituals that the ordinary (lay) people would be practicing, but they themselves would be initiated into the higher (mystical) aspects of those rituals. The lifestyle of the priests and priestesses is that of service to the God, and society. This philosophy of service to

---

[87] In the *Papyrus of Nes-Menu*, there is an order to the priestesses of Aset and Nephthys to have "the hair of their bodies shaved off." They are also ordered to wear fillets of rams wool on their heads as a form of ritual identification with the hidden (Amun) mystery. Wool was also used by the Sufis, followers of esoteric Islam. The name "*Sufi*" comes from "Suf" which means "wool." The name Sufi was adopted since the ascetic (an *ascetic* is one who practices severe and austere methods of spiritual practice.) followers of this doctrine wore coarse woolen garments (sufu).

[88] sacred to the Ancient Egyptian divinity Amun.

The Priests and Priestesses of Ancient Egypt

humanity as opposed to leaving humanity and dwelling in isolation is one of the hallmarks of Kamitan culture. Priests and priestesses were required to serve the laity in various capacities: ministerial, medical, legal, etc., and at the same time their duties to the Temple were maintained in a balanced manner. Again, this Kamitan culture is different from other kinds of cultures where the ideal of people is to go off and be hermits or monks, separated from society. That kind of understanding is not prevalent in Kamitan culture. There were retreats and sequestered periods however, periods of intensive practice. We can learn much from the descriptions of the priesthood relative to the manner in which the Neterian clergy comported themselves, because this reflects their inner spiritual attainments.

Priests and priestesses are there as leaders of society. They can be sequestered in the Temple for a time, but then they come out and lead society in various disciplines. Priests and priestesses have their inner attainment, their internal bliss, and yet they also serve society. The ancient writings state that the priests of ancient Egypt, having renounced all other occupations and human labor, devote themselves, their whole life, to contemplation and the vision of things divine and to selfless service to humanity. "By inner vision they acquire honor and safety, and piety by contemplation of knowledge and through a discipline of lifestyle, which is secret, and has the dignity of antiquity." Living always with divine knowledge and inspirations puts one beyond all greed, restrains the passion and makes life alert for understanding. They practiced simplicity, restraint, self-control, perseverance, justice and absence of greed. Their walk was disciplined and they practiced controlling their gaze so that if they chose, they did not blink. Their laughter was rare, and if it did happen it did not go beyond a smile. They kept their hands always within their clothing. Their lifestyle was frugal and simple; some tasted no wine at all and others very little. They accused it of causing damage to the nerves and a "fullness" in the head, which impedes research and of producing desire for sex. Of course, we now know scientifically that indulgence in alcoholic beverages destroys brain cells and leads to mental dullness and lower desires. This record was written by Greeks who were inducted into the ranks of the Egyptian priests and priestesses, such as Plato and Pythagoras.

"Do not pamper your body; this will make you weak.
And do not pamper yourself in your youth, or you will become weak in old age
-Ancient Egyptian Proverb

On Previous Page: Priests and Priestesses Bless Offerings

This gives an indication of the lifestyle of the Kamitan priests and priestesses. Remember that aspirants are cautioned to not be too extroverted and should not be too worldly-minded. They can have a certain amount of worldly fun and recreation however. But they have to put reins on it. If they do not put reins, those same activities will cause their consciousness to become dull. That is what is being really talked about here. Their research into higher spiritual matters would be impaired, and this also gives an indication of how initiates should comport themselves, how to carry themselves in a reserved manner. They should not allow themselves to get too happy or to get too sad either. They should not act with stone-like indifference, but also not with deluded sentimental attachment or greed. They are to find a balance; acting in a balanced manner purifies the emotions. Initiates should not act boisterously, shouting, "Hello how are you doing and my name is...," etc. Also, there is a problem if they act in the other extreme, very shyly, like a mouse. While one should promote good hygiene, there should not be excessive preoccupation with the body, and putting on oils and fragrances, and doing your hair, and about personal issues. That way of being will become an impediment to being free to understand the higher philosophy. Also it is admonished that aspirants should promote a charitable nature, being free from greed, living a life of simplicity. In ancient times, the Temples were the repositories of the riches of the country, especially in the early period. But the priests and priestesses did not see themselves as owning things; rather, they were managing the wealth for society, so they themselves were free internally. Priests and priestesses feel within themselves as paupers. So all those objects that are in the Temple which are worth thousands of dollars, the statues, etc, all of those objects are useful to the extent of their purpose in the relative world to promote the well-being of society, but beyond that they don't have any other meaning for priests and priestesses. All objects are composed of spirit stuff ultimately, and are also impermanent since they are part of a coagulated Paut "primeval stuff" that will one day dissolve back into its essential formless condition. That is why priests and priestesses live the way they do, being reserved. This is why they are not like restless people, constantly outgoing and running around back and forth, talking and yelling and screaming, and dancing and jumping, doing somersaults and screaming hallelujah, and all type of agitated behaviors such as that. What is being presented in this book are actual texts that describe the people who we are talking about, the Kamitan priests and priestesses, and how they were able to do the great things that they did. This is how they did it, through peace, detachment, inner harmony and spiritual transcendence that connected them to the power source of Creation and the boundless source of inspiration and unperturbed joy. Living in accordance with this discipline allowed them to control the senses so as not to be distracted by the worldly objects and the ignorance that arises through passion and delusion inherent in worldly desires.

Recall the instructions for the Glorious Light Meditation system.[89] It talks about how your gaze shall not leave your body when you sit for the meditation, which means that you must turn your senses internally; you must turn them in towards yourself. Inability to control the senses will prevent success in the meditation practice. The teaching specifically prohibits extraversion. If you do not have that kind of control, you will not be able to have concentration in your meditation practice because your senses will constantly wander. And even if you close your eyes, your senses will lead you in your mental vision towards objects of your desire, and they will distract you from the object of your meditation. The Glorious Light Meditation is to be practiced by all Neterian Clergy daily. Daily spiritual (Sheti) practice for Neterian Clergy should include: The daily worship program, study of philosophy, practice of the Maat virtuous teachings, practice of the Glorious Light Meditation system. These are essential to success in understanding the higher philosophy and the mystical expansion in consciousness.[90]

Suffice to say that if you do not exercise control over your carnal desires, you should understand that your sex desire is going to overwhelm your consciousness and prevent you from being able to practice the

---

[89] See the book *Glorious Light Meditation* for details.
[90] ibid

higher mysteries. Again, they are going to cause impediments to your ability to meditate and will also cloud the intellect, and your research will be impaired. Each time you engage in worldly activities, there are residues that enter and remain in your mind, which can be likened to a thin blanket or a thin haze on the glass of a window. Imagine just one year of haze on the glass in the windows of your house. And what if you do not wash them (the windows) for 20 years? You might not be able to see anything through the glass, similar to how a dark, thick cloud in the sky can block out the sun. That is what happens when you engage too much in sensory stimulus and with the ignorant idea that the world is real and abiding. That is why your desires, and the senses, must be controlled. Sexuality is one of the most powerful sensory activities that a human being engages in. And sexuality of course branches out into other forms of desire, so there must be controls on sexuality, meaning that there must be some regulation. The teaching enjoins regulations with respect to sexuality, as well as complete celibacy, depending on the level of spiritual maturity of the aspirant, which correlates to the intensity of practice of the disciplines. So this is something that an aspirant must decide about, how they fit into these categories, in terms your sexual life and spiritual practices? This is not something that the teachings impose on aspirants because it cannot. It is enjoined as a part of the discipline leading to higher practice of the teaching. Sexuality is something to be sublimated and fulfilled in a higher attainment. It cannot be fulfilled on the physical plane. The worldly attainment, conquest of some other human being in a sexual experience is a lower attainment; it is a transitory pleasure without higher fulfillment. So there must be control of the lower until you begin attaining the higher, and once you begin to realize that there is a higher fulfillment, the lower desires will be easier to control and eventually transcend. Look at the magazines and television. You are constantly being pushed to look at people's bodies and focus on the body: How does it look? How do you look in comparison?, and so on. There will never be peace in that way of life, because there is no perfection or abiding attainment in the world. There will always be someone who "looks" better, so there will always be disappointment and frustration in the end. But due to ignorance, desire and lust do not end, even while a person is suffering frustration; rather, they intensify.

Mysteries of the Gods and Goddesses and the Work of the Neterian Clergy

There are two important goals of the clergy. The first is to promote one's own spiritual evolution and spiritual Enlightenment and immortal realization. The second is to promote the welfare and evolution and Enlightenment of the society. One of the most important duties of the clergy for promoting their own evolution and that of the society is to learn the mystic symbolism of the gods and goddesses.

Neteru means "Gods and Goddesses." But the Neterian teaching of neteru represents more than the usual limited modern day concept of "divinities" or "spirits." The neteru of Kamit are also metaphors, cosmic principles and vehicles for the enlightening teachings of Shetaut Neter (Ancient Egyptian-African Religion). Actually they are the elements for one of the most advanced systems of spirituality ever conceived in human history. Understanding the concept of neteru provides a firm basis for spiritual evolution and the pathway for viable culture, peace on earth and a healthy human society.

Why is it important to have gods and goddesses in our lives? In order for spiritual evolution to be possible, once a human being has accepted that there is existence after death and a Transcendental Being who exists beyond time and space knowledge, human beings need a connection to that which transcends the ordinary experience of human life in time and space and a means to understand the Transcendental Reality beyond the mundane reality. Therefore, the sages of ancient times devised a system of symbols and metaphors that allow the mind to receive the wisdom of the Higher Consciousness. The gods and goddesses are the bridge between the world of human experience and the Transcendental Absolute. If the philosophy of the gods and goddesses were understood, the practitioner would have the keys to understanding the mysteries of life and the secrets of the universe as well as Cosmic Consciousness.

The discipline called *Tjef Neteru-Sema Paut* of emulating the gods and goddesses is ancient and glorious. It is predicated upon the idea that the gods and goddesses are symbols of cosmic forces in the universe.

(See the book *Egyptian Mysteries Vol 2: The Ancient Egyptian Gods and Goddesses*.) Those forces emanate from the Supreme Essence, like rays emanate from a sun, and like the rays of a sun, they are no different from the sun except in being a particular form or manifestation of it. If you learn about them, emulate them and discover them within yourselves, you can experience their forces within yourself and thereby be empowered to act with fuller consciousness of your essential nature and inner power. You can discover that you are a manifestation of that supreme power which is completely known when all of the rays or forces are reintegrated within your consciousness. Animal symbols are used because they embody the form of energy in question in a purer manifestation, unencumbered by the human mind, based with contradictions, quandaries and misconceptions. Animals act on instinct, which is free from diffidence or regrets. That form of being is harmony with nature, but it is not conscious harmony because the animals do not have the capacity for conscious reflection. Only human beings have the potential to develop conscious harmony with the universe and that is the discipline that leads to full consciousness, full power and full self-knowledge, the coveted goal of life. Therefore, those who attain this great height of consciousness achieve an unparalleled peace and contentment, but also great potential power, as their minds become unencumbered with lower desires, since they have discovered the fullness of their existence and no longer need to seek for fulfillment outside of themselves. They have great power to manifest their will and control their destiny. They have the capacity to know all things and experience the ecstasy of overflowing Life Force Energy, which is the fruit of fully integrating soul and spirit. That delight is the driving force behind all goodness in the world and is the true objective of all mystics; and that is the legacy of the Egyptian Mysteries. In that realization of true Self, the discoverer is supremely free from the foibles of human existence, the judgments of others and the inner quenchless fire of death, which consumes all but the deathless Spirit, because they have discovered themselves as that very Spirit which is beyond life, death, desire or opinions; they are free to love as they choose, to work as they choose, to speak as they choose, to think and feel as they choose. They also have the freedom to do nothing, go nowhere, and remain silent as all the world praises or mocks them; they are aloof, liberated, unbound and transcendental. They have forever broken the bonds of ignorant sentimental worldly desires, and so they can be like God because they are Gods.

Myth and Dreams and the Work of the Neterian Clergy

 *rasui*- dream- fancy-illusion.

The mysteries of life are explained in the esoteric teaching contained in the myths of the gods and goddesses. The Hemu are charged with learning the teaching of the myths so as to first of all "live" it, and then to be able to impart this teaching to the masses to the level of their capacity. Myths are not to be understood as absolutely real in physical or time and space or historical terms. They relate special teachings that may be grounded in the physical, but which also relate to realms beyond the physical plane and to states of consciousness that transcend ordinary mortal awareness.

Dreams may be considered as the means through which a mythic teaching is experienced by the individual mind. But that experience is often tainted by the neuroses, desires and ignorance of the individual. If a person is unwilling to progress on the spiritual path, that is, if they refuse to obey their conscience in order to indulge in unrighteous or worldly activities, the soul will force certain energies and projections into the mind. If the mind is lucid, the dream may express higher wisdom or a prophetic message. If the mind is agitated (containing some negative elements and some virtuous elements) the images can be a jumble of ideas, some making sense and others not. If the mind is dull, the images can become demoniac (nightmares). The inner awareness of conscience suffers the pain of ignorance, and this conflict builds stress in the personality that needs to be resolved. Sometimes these can cause people to become unbalanced, compulsive or psychotic. It is the duty of the clergy to promote the healthy dream state of the society so that the dreams may promote a healthy capacity to understand and practice the rituals of life, and eventually gain entry into the mysteries of the spirit.

 *Matnu* - legend, story, myth.

A mythic teaching as espoused by advanced religion provides the teachings of life in a coherent and methodical manner for all to partake. There is a level for the individual and for the society. Thus, a person who aspires to the clergy must be able to have a working understanding of the language of myth and how it manifests through dreams. The clergy learn to interpret dreams and how to know which are prophetic, deluded, dull or enlightening and how to translate them for the masses.

Basic Duties of the Priests and Priestesses

- ✓ **Neterian Priests and Priestesses** are primarily students of the Mystery Disciplines of **Shetaut Neter** which bestows the highest ecstasy and glory a human being can experience – self-mastery and Enlightenment to discover and commune with the Divine.
- ✓ They are practitioners and teachers of the Sema (yoga) disciplines.
- ✓ They perform certain rituals that promote and maintain cosmic harmony and peace (Hetep).
- ✓ They are teachers and ministers to the lower orders of aspirants who want to improve their lives and are contemplating becoming priests and priestesses as well.
- ✓ They are teachers and ministers to the community, promoting understanding and order for society, and keeping the higher vision of spiritual Enlightenment alive and accessible for those who are ready to tread the path of advanced spirituality.
- ✓ They publish books and other instructional media to lead and teach society in order to promote righteousness and order in all areas of human activity.
- ✓ They promote spiritual evolution for themselves and for humanity, and are guardians of the mystery tradition for future generations.
- ✓ They study the teachings of Shetaut Neter (Mysteries) so as to elevate their consciousness to the level of immortal and enlightened beings, to discover the heights of spiritual experience and to become conduits of Divine love and compassion for all creatures.

Opening the Mouth

One of the important duties of the Neterian clergy is the Opening of the Mouth Ritual. This ritual is actually an act performed by advanced clergy, in a ceremony which includes special readings and chants. It is actually part of a greater and elaborate philosophy related to awakening the higher spiritual consciousness. The "Opening of the Mouth Ceremony" where the priest uses the *Sba ur* instrument is one of the most important teachings of Neterianism. It is the force of spiritual awakening that is applied to the personality that allows it to experience full and perennial awareness of Higher Consciousness. It is not done by magic, but by leading the personality to awaken through the disciplines of *Shedy*, finally culminating in the fully illumined state. This is the task of every aspirant, to be worthy of this ritual and its psychic benefit. That awakening is the true resurrection, the rebirth into Higher Consciousness for which every aspirant must strive. The image overleaf shows a *Sem* priest opening the mouth of the Asar.

The mouth, ⌒, *ra,* is an important mystical symbol since it is through the mouth that consciousness expresses in the form of speech. If the consciousness is fettered, then the mouth is fettered (closed or blocked). That is why the philosophy and the ritual need to be applied to the personality, so that the mind may be unfettered. If the mind were to be unfettered it would mean full and complete experience of divine Consciousness. That is the goal of the philosophy, and the ritual makes the philosophy effective.

The opening of the mouth is more than a ritual and more than a concept. It is a ritual-philosophy of life, which is emphasized in the discipline of the mysteries of the inner Temple. It is a means by which the priests and priestesses transformed their consciousness so as to return to the world or ordinary human events in a transfigured form, in order to lead them (priests and priestesses) on the path to spiritual Enlightenment. So in this sense the Hemu are leaders who take the initiates by the hand, and guide them into the discovery of the mysteries of life. (See the section *The Concept of Guru and the Concept of Seba*)

Below: *The opening of the Mouth from Papyrus Ani Chap 23.*

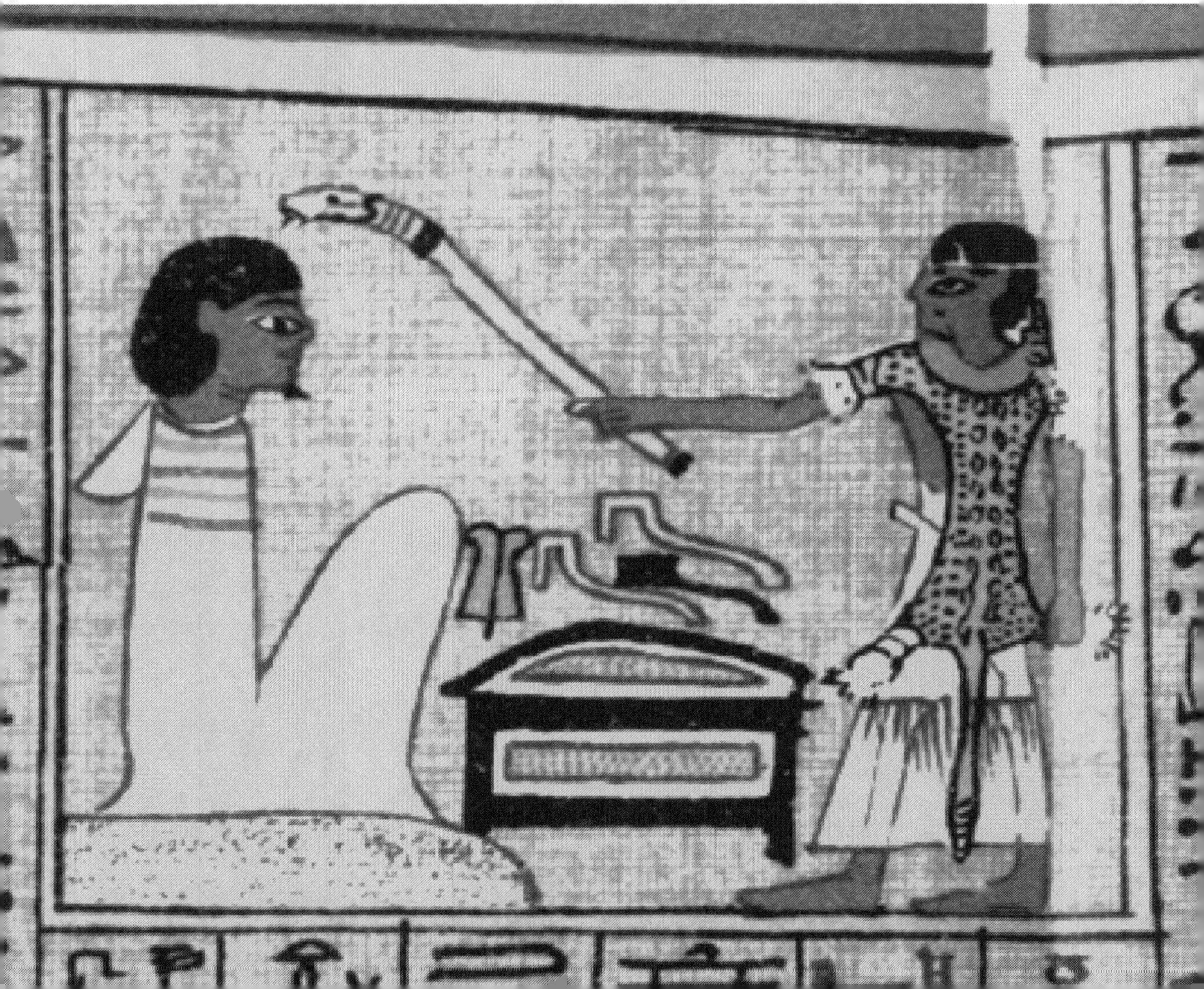

Above: the Ab (purification) priests purify the Asar who is in a coffin, being held upright, in preparation for the "Opening of the Mouth Ritual."

Below: Funerary procession. The coffin is carried by pall-bearers as the priest (Center) burns incense and pours libations for the deceased.

Insight into the Personal Disciplines of the Ancient Egyptian Priests and Priestesses

Plutarch outlined the teachings of the Temple of Aset (Isis) for the proper behavior of initiates in his writings about his experiences as an initiate of Aset. In the following excerpts Plutarch describes the purpose and procedure of the diet observed by the initiates of Aset, and the goal to be attained through the rigorous spiritual program.

To desire, therefore, and covet after truth, those truths more especially which concern the divine nature, is to aspire to be partakers of that nature itself (1), and to profess that all our studies and inquiries (2) are devoted to the acquisition of holiness. This occupation is surely more truly religious than any external (3) purifications or mere service of the Temple can be (4). But more especially must such a disposition of mind be highly acceptable to that goddess to whose service you are dedicated, for her special characteristics are wisdom and foresight, and her very name seems to express the peculiar relation which she bears to knowledge. For "Aset" is a Greek word, and means "knowledge or wisdom,"(5) and "Typhon," (Set) the name of her professed adversary, is also a Greek word, and means " pride and insolence."(6) This latter name is well adapted to one who, full of ignorance and error, tears in pieces (7) and conceals that holy doctrine (about Asar) which the goddess collects, compiles, and delivers to those who aspire after the most perfect participation in the divine nature. This doctrine inculcates a steady perseverance in one uniform and temperate course of life (8), and an abstinence from particular kinds of foods (9), as well as from all indulgence of the carnal appetite (10), and it restrains the intemperate and voluptuous part within due bounds, and at the same time habituates her votaries to undergo those austere and rigid ceremonies which their religion obliges them to observe. The end and aim of all these toils and labors is the attainment of the knowledge of the First and Chief Being (11), who alone is the object of the understanding of the mind; and this knowledge the goddess invites us to seek after, by being near and dwelling continually (12) with her. And this also is what the very name of her Temple promiseth to us, that is to say, the knowledge and understanding of the eternal and self-existent Being - now it is called "Iseion," which suggests that if we approach the Temple of the goddess rightly, we shall obtain the knowledge of that eternal and self existent Being.

Mystical Implications that the Discourse Above Teaches:[91]:

1- It is to be understood that spiritual aspiration implies seeking the union with or becoming one with the thing being sought because this is the only way to truly "know" something.

2- In order to discover the hidden nature of God, emphasis is placed on study and inquiry into the nature of things. Who am I? What is the universe composed of? Who is God? How am I related to God? These are the questions which when pursued, lead to the discovery of the Self (God). Those who do not engage in this form of inquiry will generate a deluded reality for themselves according to their beliefs.

3-4 The plan prescribed by the teachings of Shetaut Neter is the true means to effective spiritual development because it reveals the inner nature of the Self and it is experiential, i.e. it is based on your own personal experience and not conjecture.

5-7 The name "Isis (Aset)" represents "wisdom" itself which bestows the knowledge of the true Self of the initiate. In the Asarian Mysteries, when Set killed Asar (Osiris) by tearing him into pieces, Set was symbolically tearing up the soul. However, Aset reintegrates the pieces of the soul (Asar). Therefore,

---

[91] Note: The numbers at the beginning of each paragraph below correspond to the reference numbers in the text above.

Pride and Insolence (Set-egoism) destroy the soul and Knowledge of the Self (Aset) restores it to its true nature. The Greek name for Aset, Isis, is supported by the ancient Egyptian scriptures. One of the names of Isis (Aset) is: *Rekhåt or Rekhit* ⌢◦◉◯ 𓀁 meaning "knowledge personified." The variation, *Rekh-t* ⌢◦◉—◯ 𓀁, means Sage or learned person. So the task of a true devotee is to do the work of Aset, to put the pieces back together of one's soul.

8- True spirituality cannot be pursued rashly or in a fanatical way by going to extremes.

9-10 The foods referred to are flesh foods (swine, sheep, fish, etc.), pulse, and salt. Indulgence in sexual activity has important implications. It intensifies the physical experience of embodiment and distracts the mind by creating impressions in the subconscious that will produce future cravings and desires.

11- See #1.

12- Once again we are being reminded that good association or keeping the company of sages or other enlightened personalities is a powerful means to gain knowledge of the state of Enlightenment.

Plutarch further reports that the Egyptian Clergy:

...strive to prevent fatness in Apis[92] as well as themselves(1), for they are anxious that their bodies should sit as light and easy about their souls as possible, and that their mortal part (body) should not oppress and weigh down their divine and immortal part...during their more solemn purifications they abstain from wine(2) wholly, and they give themselves up entirely to study(4) and meditation(5) and to the hearing (3) and teaching of these divine truths which treat of the divine nature.

The following dietary guidelines for spiritual and physical health are derived from the statement above.

1- Preventing "fatness"- obesity. Physical weight is like a physical object that is possessed. The more you have, the more you try to hold onto, and the more stress you have trying to enjoy and hold onto "things." Desires of the body such as eating have a grounding effect on the soul because they engender the desire to experience more of the physical pleasure of consuming food. Also, excess weight on the body causes innumerable health problems to arise.[93]

2- The aspirant will notice that as they purify themselves, they will not want to tolerate even a small amount of intoxicants. Distilled liquor is not a natural substance and is injurious to the body and is therefore, not suitable at all for use by those advancing on the spiritual path. The same applies to narcotics and all other "recreational" drugs. Those who are using or addicted to drugs are not fit to be admitted to the Neterian Clergy. They must resolve the issues of addiction and dependency first.

3, 4, 5- The format for spiritual education and practice as outlined in the Temple of Aset constitutes the heart of the discipline of the priests and priestesses:

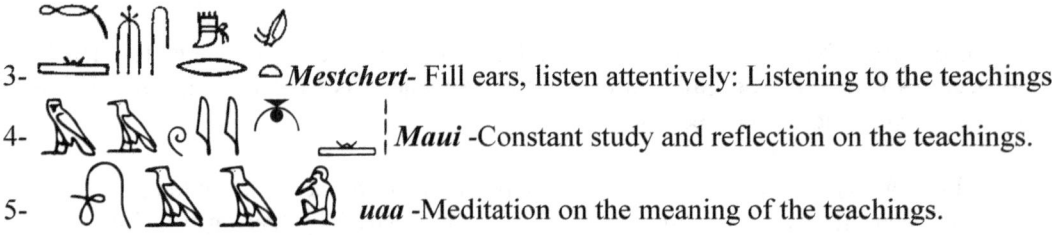

3- *Mestchert*- Fill ears, listen attentively: Listening to the teachings.

4- *Maui* -Constant study and reflection on the teachings.

5- *uaa* -Meditation on the meaning of the teachings.

---

[92] Bull which was kept as a symbol of Osiris and Ptah.
[93] See the book *Kamitan Diet* by Sebai Muata Ashby

Daily, Monthly and Annual Disciplines, Festivals, Rituals of Shetaut Neter

1- *Ra neb Aru* – "Ritual of every day"

2- *Abd neb Aru* – "Ritual of every month"

3- *Renpu Aru* – "Ritual of every year"

Daily Shedy -Threefold Daily Worship – Basic Discipline
(See the Shetaut Neter Daily Worship Manual)

- o Worship Ritual - Morning
  - Divine Song
  - Sema Yoga Postures
  - Reciting of the Great Realizations
  - Reading of scripture from one of the assigned Neterian Traditions
  - Chant – words of scripture
  - Meditation
  - Offering

- o Worship Ritual – Noon and Dusk
  - Reciting of the Great Realizations
  - Divine Chant
  - Meditation

Monthly Shedy - Basic Discipline for the monthly worship (See the Shetaut Neter Calendar)

- THE MONTHLY DISCIPLINES OF SHETAUT NETER: NEW AND FULL MOON RITUAL
- THE ANNUAL DISCIPLINES OF SHETAUT NETER: SUMER AND WINTER SOLSTICE RITUAL.
- FESTIVALS OF THE DIVINITIES OF THE MONTH - there are several holidays and rituals for individual divinities (see the Shetaut Neter Calendar).

Annual Shedy - Basic Discipline for the annual worship (See the Shetaut Neter Calendar)

As concerns the clergy, there were Annual Synod meetings, *sma ta hm neter,* "reunion assembly of priests and priestesses." They are to be held for conducting instruction, conferring on issues of the Temples and councils and for building the Neterian culture. Along with the different hierarchy of the Temple clergy there is the *udjatnu* - Chief of Council of priests. This position might serve as coordinator of a synod or as leader of a group of clergy in a particular district. The most important annual rituals are:

Api – Summer Solstice, *Nun* – Winter Solstice as well as the New Year, the battle of Heru and Set and the Resurrection of Asar.

The Priests and Priestesses of Ancient Egypt

Below: The Kheri Heb (lector priest far left) performs the discipline of reading the scriptures at a funeral.

The Main Temple Mystery Rituals

The typical New Kingdom Ancient Egyptian Temple is architecturally set up with three sections, the A-"Peristyle Hall," B-"Hypostyle Hall" and C-"Holy of Holies." An important aspect of the Temple festivals is the journey of the Divine Boat. The ritual of the boat is carried out by taking the Divine icon and placing it in the boat, which is attached to two poles. The priests carry it in procession out of the Temple through the pylons (D) to its destination. Upon its return the procession enters the Temple again and passes through the two first halls and into the Inner Shrine where it is placed back in its place. The deeper mystical significance of the boat ritual and other details about the meaning of the Temple architecture shall be discussed in a future text.

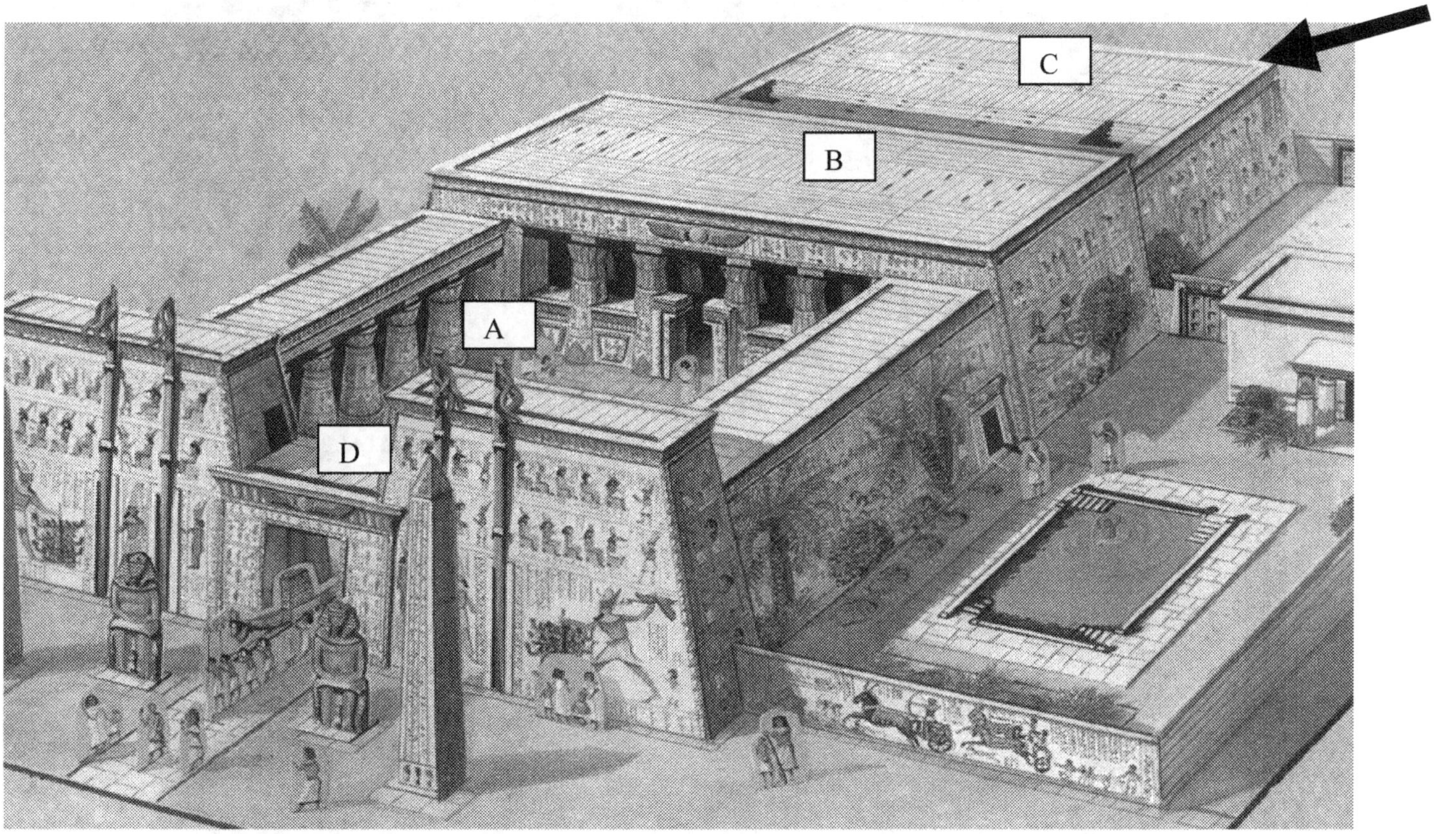

Opening the Temple and the Daily Worship Program

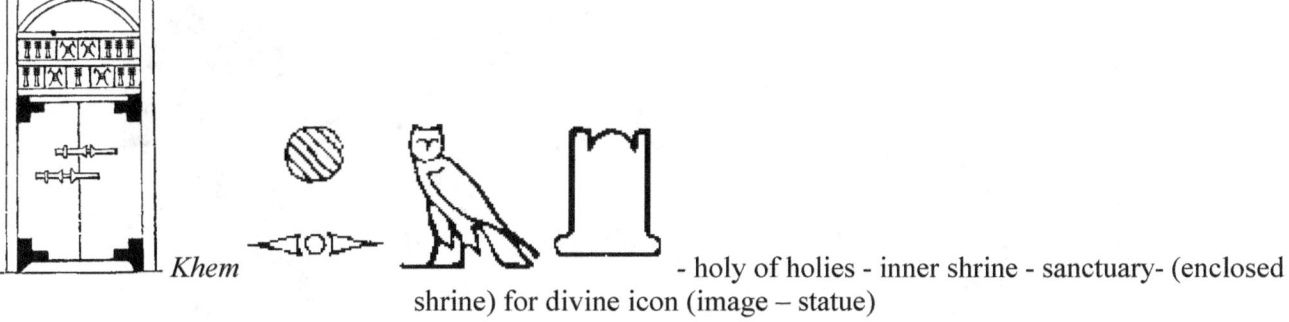

Khem - holy of holies - inner shrine - sanctuary - (enclosed shrine) for divine icon (image – statue)

The shrines are essentially model houses for the Divine icons (statues) to be opened only by the designated priest or priestess. The Temple is opened every day and the morning worship is performed, but only the designated clergy may open the shrine or handle the icon. After the noontime and evening ritual are performed, the door of the shrine is closed and sealed. The next morning the seal is broken and the cycle begins again. The shrine is placed atop a stone pedestal that is within the shrine room. The shrine room is also known as the "Holy of Holies." The floor in the Holy of Holies (C- above) is the highest point in terms of floor area elevation, in the entire Temple complex.

Naos- (enclosed shrine) for Divine image - statue- stone (door missing)- Louvre Museum. The shrine above has inscriptions showing images of the divine ritual

(A) (B)
A-*Naos*- (enclosed shrine) for Divine image - statue- stone (door missing)
B-*Naos*- (enclosed shrine) for Divine image - statue- wooden, with door and single bolt

The Morning Ritual

The morning worship consists in a simple but dignified series of rituals, chants and divine singing. Offerings are placed on an altar, which is at the feet of the Divinity. The chants and divine singing serve the purpose of extolling the glories and virtues of the divinity and propitiating the grace of God (who manifests as the Divinity in form and character as well as cosmic energy) to intercede and promote order, righteousness, prosperity and success. The ritual also serves to elevate the devotional feeling of aspirants so as to promote spiritual strength and concentration on the Divine. At the end of the program, the offerings, having been consecrated, are consumed – this is the source for the Christian eucharis ritual. It has its roots in the early period of Kamitan history and can be found in the Pyramid Texts (See Book of the Dead).

One of the most important duties of the clergy is to conduct the daily worship rituals. These consist of opening the Temple shrine for the day, making offerings, chanting, and cleansing the Temple, the altar and the Divine image. This program was to be followed in other Temples around the country in the same way, and at the same time, only changing the name of the particular Divinity of the particular Temple. The following is an actual account of a section of the ancient morning ritual.

Morning Song:

Awake (oh, great God) in peace, wake peacefully.[94]

The choir then repeats the song, in a chorus:

Wake peacefully, wake beautifully, in peace! Wake to life, oh (God of this city)! The gods rise early to honor your soul, oh august winged disk shining in the sky! It is you who break the seal in the heavens and spread gold dust over the earth, who come to life in the east and vanish in the west and sleep in (your Temple) each day.[95]

---

[94] M. Alliot, Le Culte d'Horus a Edfou au temps des Ptolemees, Vol. 1, Bibliotheque d' Etude 20 (Cairo, 1949), 152- On the morning invocation, see also D. Lorton, "The Invocation Hymn at the Temple of Hibis," Studien zur altdgyptischen Kultur zi (1994):159-217.
[95] Alliot, Culte, Vol. 1, 152-53.

The Priests and Priestesses of Ancient Egypt

The reader priest or priestess repeats the invocation again and again, but changing only the epithets, and then the chorus intones the same refrain. When the divine epithets are finished for that Divinity, the chanter invokes the other Temple deities, and body parts of the divinity, as they wake to life:

> *Your eyes spread flame; your eyes light the darkness! Your brows wake in beauty, oh radiant visage that knows no anger!* [96]

In this program there were forty-five invocations for the divine organs that each day are reborn, and the chorus repeats the chant:

> *May you wake peacefully ... and spread gold dust over the earth.*

Scenes from the daily Temple ritual –inscription from the Temple of Heru at Edfu

The prayers, chants and sequence of the modern program can be found in the *Shetaut Neter Prayer, Chanting and Kamitan Divine Singing Book* by Sebai Muata Ashby.

---

[96] Ibid., 153.

Ritual of the Carrying of The Divine Boat

kniu - portable shrine. The ritual of carrying the Divine Boat is one of the most important rituals of Neterian Spirituality. Several Temples had this ritual because the major male and female divinities had Divine Boats. In ancient times it was seen as a propitious and prestigious practice to be a pallbearer. In a stele at Abdu, the procession was described by *Akhernefert: "I conducted the Great Procession, following in the God's steps. I made the God's boat sail, with Djehuti at the helm...Decked in his beautiful tribunal, He proceeded to the domain of Peqer...I followed the God to His house."* The ritual entails the transportation of a Divine image from one Temple to another and in so doing enact the movement of the Divine Entity, to propitiate and participate in the cosmic movements of divine energy to promote peace, health, harmony and Enlightenment. The image is placed on a boat, which symbolizes the movement of the first boat that first stirred up the primeval waters and thus created the forms that became the objects of Creation. The ritual is to be carried out each year so that the act of creation may be renewed for another period of time. It constitutes a metaphysical reenactment, but also an actual participation in upholding the laws upon which the universe and the religion itself is based. In Ancient Kamit, the annual ritual of carrying the Divine Boat (vehicle of the god or goddess) from one Temple to another was a means to maintain the order of the cosmos, as the movement of the boat engenders and sustains Creation itself. This same act of Creation was re-enacted by the priests and priestesses of Ancient Egypt. In Kamit, pallbearers would carry the boat while a priest opened the way by burning incense on the path. A long procession would follow behind, some playing music, others dancing and others uttering chants.

Below is (A) a drawing of the actual Divine Boat of Sokkar, (A1) Temple relief of the Divine Boat of Sokkar and

the boat of Tem (B)   (A)   (B)

(A1)

On the following page: actual ritual boat of Heru (Temple of Heru, Edfu, Egypt)

Ritual of the Dawn of the New Year at the Temple of Hetheru

At the Temple of goddess Hetheru there was also another kind of ritual. Each year the image of the goddess Hetheru was brought out before dawn, following a procession of priests and priestesses uttering chants and bringing offerings to the roof of the Temple. There they waited for the dawn's first light, which would touch the goddess' naked body, and she would thereby be impregnated with the Life Force of the sun (Heru), thus continuing the cycle of life and prosperity for the next year.

Above: a stairway from the inner portions of the Temple of Hetheru leads up to the roof. The images of priests and priestesses carrying offerings and artifacts are inscribed in the wall itself. (Denderah, Egypt). One stairway was used for going upstairs and the other on the opposite side for going back down.

Overleaf: stairway going down.

Above: Roof of the Temple of Hetheru where the ritual of the priests and priestesses was carried out and also showing the boundary between the green Nile irrigated lands and the desert. (Denderah, Egypt)

The Wisdom Discipline

The Wisdom teaching learned by the clergy of Ancient Egypt consisted of the study and mastery of:

- ❖ Theology- the religious tradition
- ❖ Mystical philosophy
- ❖ Mathematics-geometry
- ❖ Symbolism
- ❖ Metaphor
- ❖ History
- ❖ Maat-ethics-law
- ❖ Maat-cosmic order
- ❖ Government
- ❖ Economics
- ❖ Ship building
- ❖ Medical science
- ❖ Music, prayer, chant
- ❖ Art
- ❖ Architecture

The Priests and Priestesses of Ancient Egypt

Maintaining The Neterian Library

One of the main tasks of the clergy is to document the teachings in order to then pass them on in an unchanged and complete fashion. Scribal work – collecting, studying and passing on the teaching – is a time honored tradition of the Neterian faith. The task is the concern of all Hm and Hmt and includes:

- Re-recording (transcribing) ancient text.
- Recording new texts that are commentaries of the ancient texts by the Sebaiu and Sebai Kheriau.
- Carrying on the language – so as to convey the feeling of the teaching through the text.
- Maintain a library of resources for all Hm and Hmt to use for study and as:
    - Historical records.
    - Precedents to consult when new situations arise.
    - Guides for the performance of rituals and other procedures.

Below: Relief of an Ancient Egyptian Scribe

Sacred Scriptures of Ancient Egypt and the Duty of the Clergy

The teaching of Neterian Spirituality is recorded in the Medu Neter. The Ancient Egyptian name for scribe is *sesh*. The cleric of Shetaut Neter must have a working knowledge of Medu Neter, the scribal art, and the written forms of language of Neterianism, including the hieroglyphic and cursive forms of writing. The Medu Neter is important not only because it was the first in history and gave rise to the modern forms of writing, from Phoenician to Greek and the European languages, but because it ties Neterian culture to an ancient literary tradition and also, it offers a special form of grammar that transforms the mind. This is the greatest secret of the Medu Neter, its transformative spiritual power. Scribes are to study and transcribe the texts for future generations. The cleric should also develop useful knowledge that will assist him/her to disseminate the appropriate knowledge to others by means of publishing, teaching, etc. The following scriptures represent the foundational scriptures of Kamitan culture. They may be divided into three categories: ***Mythic Scriptures***, ***Mystical Philosophy and Ritual Scriptures***, and ***Wisdom Scriptures*** (Didactic Literature).

MYTHIC SCRIPTURES Literature	Mystical and Ritual Philosophy Literature	Wisdom Texts Literature
Shetaut Asar-Aset-Heru The Myth of Asar, Aset and Heru (Asarian Resurrection Theology) - Predynastic **Shetaut Atum-Ra** Anunian Theology Predynastic **Shetaut Net/Aset/Hetheru** Saitian Theology – Goddess Spirituality Predynastic **Shetaut Ptah** Memphite Theology Predynastic **Shetaut Amun** Theban Theology Predynastic	Pyramid Texts (c. 5500 B.C.E.-3800 B.C.E.) **Coffin Texts** (c. 2040 B.C.E.-1786 B.C.E.) Papyrus Texts (c. 1580 B.C.E.-Roman Period)[97] Books of Coming Forth By Day Example of Famous Papyri: Papyrus of Ani Papyrus of Hunefer Papyrus of Kenna Greenfield Papyrus, Etc.	**Wisdom Texts** (c. 3,000 B.C.E. – Ptolemaic Period) Precepts of Ptahotep Instructions of Ani Instructions of Amenemope Etc. Maat Declarations Literature (All Periods) Songs of the Blind Harper

Many spiritual aspirants do not take the Neterian scriptures seriously. This is because of several problems. Firstly, they have studied them from the perspective of western scholarship, which is based on the Judeo-Christian-Islamic traditions that have a vested interest in portraying other forms of spirituality as primitive. Another problem is the lack of available teachers of the mysteries who can present the teachings as mysteries, that is, as mystical philosophy and a living religion (teachings are to be practiced and lived), and not just ancient myth or ancient cultural history. They may also mix up well-understood Neterian teachings with teachings from other traditions. Due to these deficiencies and other distractions, most people glean whatever mystical references they can find about Ancient Egyptian culture and spirituality and usually mix them up with their own researches or

---

[97] After 1570 B.C.E they would evolve into a more unified text, the Egyptian Book of the Dead.

those of others, and in this way come up with a "salad-bar" version of what they call the mysteries. Those who seriously desire to tread the path of Neterian priesthood must be of a mind to pursue the mysteries as mystics. This means, among other things, that a Neterian priest should be a Neterian priest, and not a priest of Judaism, Hinduism, Yoruba, etc., at the same time. An avid aspirant may study many traditions but they should know their own best, just as the clergy of other traditions know their own. Only by concentrating on their chosen tradition will they have the chance to delve into the deeper mysteries of life and death. Those who are unable to be centered on the Neterian tradition are not fit to be admitted into the ranks of the Neterian clergy, and should remain as aspirants, striving to improve their practice of the teachings. Further, in order to advance most effectively, the advanced aspirant on a track towards the priesthood should study under the guidance of a qualified spiritual preceptor and suspend all studies of other traditions until the Neterian culture, traditions and tenets are understood well and there develops a capacity to recite the main teachings, myths, and the nature of the divinities, their relationships and basic symbolic meanings, at will. Also, a qualified aspirant for the priesthood should have more than a working knowledge of his or her own special appointed Temple duty or duties. They should know the history, myth and hieroglyphic texts related to their specialty within the Neterian traditions, and the rituals they are specifically responsible for in the Temple.

The Medu Neter Of Neterian Culture

"Medu Neter"

The teachings of the Neterian Traditions are conveyed in the scriptures of the Neterian Traditions.
These are recorded in the Medu Neter script.
Below: A section from the pyramid of Teti in Sakkara Egypt, known as the "Pyramid Texts" (Early Dynastic Period) showing the cross (center-similar to the later Christian cross)

Old Period Hieroglyphic Script

The Old Period Hieroglyphic Script was used through all periods by priests and priestesses – mostly used in monumental inscriptions such as the Pyramid texts, Obelisks, Temple inscriptions, etc. – was used since Pre-Dynastic times⬇

Old Kingdom Cursive Hieratic Script
(Also known as Cursive Hieroglyphic- most resembles the Hieroglyphic script)

Hieratic is an adaptation of the hieroglyphic for ease of use in writing non-monumental texts, especially those that involve extensive expositions of the philosophical teachings and myths on papyrus paper, and other literary compositions; it was used since Pre-Dynastic times. This form of the script appears on various papyri known as *Coffin Texts* and *Book of the Dead* (*Prt m Hru*). This script developed into regional variants and period variants from the early period to the late period of Ancient Egyptian history.

Middle Kingdom to Late Period Hieratic Script
(Shorthand hieroglyphic, used by the priests and priestesses
Middle Kingdom Period to Coptic Period)

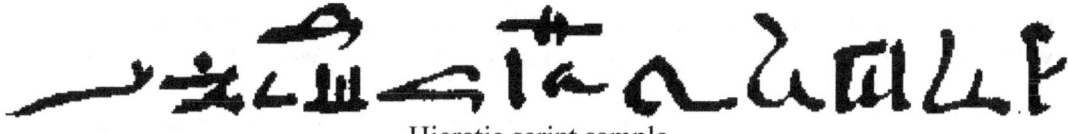

Hieratic script sample

Hieratic developed in succeeding levels of "cursiveness" from the Middle to the Coptic Period
⬇

Late Period Demotic Script

𓏥𓏤 (demotic script sample)

(Used by the general population for non-secular purposes
Late Period to Coptic period)

Demotic appears at the time of the Nubian Dynasty and remains in use until the closing of the Ancient Egyptian Temples in 450 A.C.E.
⬇

Coptic (Christian Period) Script

ϨⲚ ⲦⲈⲤⲞⲨⲈⲒⲦⲈ ⲚⲈϤϢⲞⲞⲠ ⲚϬⲒⲠϢⲀϪⲈ.

(Still presently used by the Coptic priesthood
and some families in Egypt and around the world)

While the Ancient Egyptian Medu Neter (hieroglyphic text) is a pictorial script, it should not be confused with primitive picture writing. It is a complete language with the capacity to transmit the basic needs of communication and convey the nuances of high philosophy in a way that a strictly syllabic script cannot. Thus, the aesthetic quality and beauty of the script is a combination of the syllabic, calligraphic as well as pictographic aspects of the language. Moreover, it is the language of the Temple inscriptions and the most important texts of Ancient Egyptian culture, the Pyramid Texts, the Coffin Texts and the Prt m Hru (Book of the Dead) Texts. So Medu Neter is as important to Ancient Egyptian religion and philosophy as Hebrew and later, Greek, (languages/scripts) are the original scripts of Old Testament of the Jewish religion or Arabic is the language and script of Islam. This language ties present day Neterian culture directly to the ancient and acts as a window into the mythic and philosophical teachings. So in this model of a revived language, the Hieroglyphic and Cursive Hieroglyphic are ideal choices for our purpose. The Cursive Hieroglyphic would be used for literary religious texts as well as day-to-day use by the general population, and the Formal Hieroglyphic script would be used for monumental inscriptions of the nation. A revised version of the hieratic (see above) could be used for the day-to-day necessities of the modern Temple, government, commerce and human interactions.

The Medu Neter was used through all periods by priests and priestesses – mostly in monumental inscriptions such as the Pyramid texts, Obelisks, Temple inscriptions, etc. – since Pre-Dynastic times. It is the earliest form of writing in known history.

Hekau, Medu Neter and Shetitu

"hekau" The concept of the divine word or *Hekau* is an extremely important part of Ancient Egyptian religion, and is instructive in the study of all African religions. One main difference between Ancient Egyptian religion and other African religions was the extensive development of the "written word." As explained earlier, the word religion is translated as Shetaut Neter in the Ancient African language of Kamit.

The Shetaut (mysteries- rituals, wisdom, philosophy) about the Neter (Supreme Being) are related in the *Shetitu* or writings related to the hidden teaching. Those writings are referred to as *Medu Neter* or "Divine Speech," the writings of the god Djehuti (Ancient Egyptian god of the divine word) – and also refers to any hieroglyphic texts or inscriptions generally. The term Medu Neter makes use of a special hieroglyph, , which means "*medu*" or "staff - walking stick-speech." This means that speech is the support for the Divine, . Thus, just as the staff supports an elderly person, the hieroglyphic writing (the word) is a prop (staff) that sustains the Divine in the realm of time and space. That is, the Divine writings contain the wisdom that enlightens us about the Divine, *Shetaut Neter*.

If Medu Neter is mastered then the spiritual aspirant becomes Maakheru or true of thought, word and deed, that is, purified in body, mind and soul. The symbol medu is static while the symbol of Kheru is dynamic.

The term Maakheru uses the glyph *kheru*, which is a rudder – an oar (rowing). It is a symbol of voice, meaning that purification that occurs when there is righteous movement of the word, when it is used (rowing-movement) to promote virtue, order, peace, harmony and truth. So Medu Neter is the potential word of the hieroglyphic text and Maa kheru is the perfected word.

The hieroglyphic texts (Medu Neter) become (Maakheru) useful in the process of religion when they are used as ⟨hieroglyphs⟩ hekau - the Ancient Egyptian "Words of Power," when the word is ⟨hieroglyphs⟩ Hesi, chanted, and ⟨hieroglyphs⟩ Shmai- sung and thereby one performs ⟨hieroglyphs⟩ or ⟨hieroglyphs⟩ Dua or worship of the Divine. The divine word allows the speaker to control the gods and goddesses, i.e. the cosmic forces. These concepts are really based on the idea that human beings are higher order beings if they learn about the nature of the universe and elevate themselves through virtue and wisdom.

Kamitan Proverbs:

"Men and women are to become God-like through a life of virtue
and the cultivation of the spirit through scientific knowledge, practice and bodily discipline."

"Salvation is the freeing of the soul from its bodily fetters; becoming a God
through knowledge and wisdom; controlling the forces of the cosmos instead of being a slave to them; subduing
the lower nature and through awakening the higher self, ending the cycle of rebirth
and dwelling with the Neters who direct and control the Great Plan."

The Duty of Scribal Illumination

Closely related to the scribal duty and the duty of the reenactment through the Temple theater is the duty of artistic illumination of papyri and Temple inscriptions. The artistic rendition of papyri and Temple inscriptions is also closely related to the *sebait-* or philosophy of Shetaut Neter. And it also represents a form of standardization of the form and procedure of the varied rituals of the mysteries. An exhortation from the Temple inscriptions illustrates this point: *"Do not perform the sacred services any way you please-what would be the purpose of looking at the old writings? The ritual of the Temple is in your hands, and it is what your children study-"*[98]

The *Pert m Heru* Text is a book of invocations, incantations and propitiations based on the myths of the divinities. These are to be reenacted, recited and lived so that the aspirant may be led to the triumphant resurrection that was experienced by Asar in ancient times. The following image is of the weighing of the heart of Priestess *Nesi-ta-neb-asher* in the Judgment Hall of Maat with the god Asar, and the goddesses Aset and Nebthet, presiding. The god Anpu handles the scale and the god Djehuti writes the results of the balance as the beast Ammit looks on, in the presence of the god Khepri and the gods and goddesses (British museum, Greenfield Papyrus).

---

[98] Chassinat, *Edfou*, Vol. III, 361-362, l. 4: translated by M. Alliot, *Le Culte d'Horus a Edfou au temps de Ptolemees*, Biblioteque d' Etude 20, Vol. I 186.

The Priestly art of Divine Worship and Divine Ritual

The priestly art of Divine Worship is an extremely important aspect of the work of the Neterian clergy. Its finer points are described by Iamblichus in his book *On the Mysteries*. The following excerpts provide insights into the principles of the priestly work of Divine Worship and the prospects for attaining higher consciousness through it. (highlighted text and Glosses by Ashby)

Iamblichus *On the Mysteries* Section 5, CHAP. 18:

According to another division, therefore, <u>the numerous herd [or the great mass] of men is arranged under nature, is governed by physical powers,</u> looks downward to the works of nature, gives completion to the administration of Fate, and to things pertaining to Fate, because it belongs to the order of it, and always employs practical reasoning about such particulars alone as subsist according to nature. <u>But there are a certain few who, by employing a certain supernatural power of intellect</u>, are removed indeed from nature, but are conducted to a separate and unmingled intellect; and these, at the same time, become superior to physical powers. <u>Others again, who are the media between these,</u> tend to things which subsist between nature and a pure intellect. And of these, some indeed equally follow both nature and an immaculate intellect; others embrace a life which is mingled from both; and others are liberated from things subordinate, and betake themselves to such as are more excellent.

This division, therefore, being made, that which follows will most manifestly take place. <u>For those who are governed by the nature of the universe, who lived conformably to this, and employ the powers of nature, these should embrace a mode of worship adapted to nature</u>, and to the bodies that are moved by nature, and should choose for this purpose appropriate places, air, matter, the powers of matter, bodies, and the habits of bodies, qualities, and proper motions, the mutations of things in generation, and other things connected with these, both in other parts of piety and in that part of it which pertains to sacrifice. <u>But those who live conformably to intellect alone, and to the life of intellect, and are liberated from the bonds of nature, these should exercise in all the parts of theurgy the intellectual and incorporeal mode of worship. And those who are the media between these, should labour differently in the paths of piety</u>, conformably to the differences of this middle condition of life, either by embracing both modes, of piety, or separating themselves from one of the modes [and adhering to the other], or receiving both these modes as the foundation of things of a more honourable nature. For without these they never can arrive at things supereminent. Or, in some other way, they should thus, in a becoming manner, labour in the paths of sanctity.

GLOSS

Worship is important, because it brings one closer to the transcendental essence of existence, which is manifested and operated through cosmic forces (gods and goddesses). Worship is to be melded with ritual that is devoted to the gods and goddesses. There are three forms or ways to worship the gods and goddesses. They can be worshipped as material beings with material objects; that is the path of the masses. They can be worshipped as incorporeal and transcendental beings, offering to them intellect alone, or they can be worshipped in combination. The forms of worship are suited to the level of the aspirant. The higher form cannot be practiced by one caught up in physicality, and one with abstract mentality should not practice the lower form. In any case, eventually there must be perfection in the worship, to look towards what is beyond the lower nature. Otherwise spiritual evolution will be slow and the higher attainment will be elusive.

Iamblichus *On the Mysteries* Section 5, Chap 20

"We must admit, therefore, that in each part of the world there is this visible body, and that there are also incorporeal powers, which are divided about bodies. Hence the law of religion distributes similars to similars, and thus extends from on high, through wholes, as far as to the last of things; assigning, indeed, incorporeals to incorporeals, but bodies to bodies, and this commensurately to the nature of each. If, however, some theurgist should participate of the supermundane Gods, which is the rarest of all things, he, indeed, in the worship of the
Gods will transcend both bodies and matter; being united to the Gods by a supermundane power. But that which happens to one person with difficulty and late, and at the end of the sacerdotal office, ought not to be promulgated as common to all men; nor ought it to be made a thing common to those who are commencing theurgic operations, nor to those who have made a middle proficiency in it. For these, after a manner, pay a corporeal-formed attention to sanctity."

GLOSS

The principle behind the science of Divine Worship is that like not only attracts like, but distributes like to its like. So the worship makes the worshipper like onto the object of worship, and if that object is the Divinity, then eventually the worshiper becomes Divine also. This attainment is rare in comparison to the masses, and the path of this discipline is not for all, but for those special personalities who are capable of training the mind, cultivating the intellect and entering into a meditative absorption through repeated acts of ritual-worship. The fruits of this practice can take a lifetime to manifest, and so this is not a path that is promoted to the masses. However, the discipline of Divine Worship purifies the emotions and prepares an aspirant for all other kinds of disciplines, for which they may be suited.

Iamblichus *On the Mysteries* Section 5, Chap 21

As, therefore, in the visible descents of the Gods, a manifest injury is sustained by those who leave some one of the more excellent genera unhonored, thus also in the invisible appearances of the Gods in sacrifices, it is not proper to honour one of them, and not honour another, but it is entirely requisite to honour each of them according to the order which he is allotted. But he who leaves some one of them unhonoured confounds the whole work of piety, and disturbs the one and whole orderly distribution of it; not, in so doing, as some one may think, imperfectly receiving the Gods, but entirely subverting all the ceremonies of religion.

Iamblichus *On the Mysteries* Section 5,CHAP. 22.

What then [it may be said], does not the summit of the sacrificial art recur to the most principal one of the whole multitude of Gods, and at one and the same time worship the many essences and principles that are [rooted and concentered] in it? Entirely so, but this happens at the latest period, and to a very few, and we must be satisfied if it takes place when the sun of life is setting. Our present discussion, however, does not ordain laws for a man of this kind; for he is superior to all law; but it promulgates a law such as that of which we are now speaking, to those who are in want of certain divine legislation.

GLOSS

In the practice of Divine Worship. the ritual is performed by first acknowledging the lower divinities, the divinities of the mundane world. Then it proceeds to the higher divinities, beginning with the divinity that opens the ways, the paths, and clears obstacles so that spiritual evolution may proceed. In Neterianism, that divinity is *Wepwawet* -"Opener of the paths." All divinities need to be appeased so that there may be clarity of mind and transcendence of the mundane reality. That is what *htp* (Hetep, Hotep) means. It means "offering that appeases the gods and goddesses." It is composed of symbols that represent the opposites. The opposites represent the mundane reality, separation and agitation. When they come together (through Divine Worship) they signify unity, oneness, peace and the cessation of movement. If the lesser divinities are not paid due respects there will be disruption in the subtle matter which they inhabit, that is, the lower mind, which will be filled with worries, anxieties and distractions. Those who have transcended worldliness, desire, egoism, ignorance and greed are beyond the effects of the lower divinities, and so are not bound by this regulation. However, those who are not yet advanced to be able to experience the transcendental reality through pure intellect are indeed bound by this regulation of Divine worship.

Iamblichus *On the Mysteries* Section 8, Chap 4

The Egyptian Priests likewise arrange the Demiurgus as the primary father of things in generation; and they acknowledge the existence of a vital power, prior to the heavens, and subsisting in the heavens. The Egyptian Priests also establish a pure intellect above the world, and one impartible intellect in the whole world, and another which is distributed into all the spheres. And these things they do not survey by mere reason alone, but through the sacerdotal theurgy, they announce that they are able to ascend to more elevated and universal essences, and to those that are established above Fate, viz. to God and the Demiurgus; neither employing matter, nor assuming any other thing besides, except the observation of a suitable time.

GLOSS

This teaching is not supported by intellectual theorizing, but through the practice of the priestly arts which were proven over a period that spanned more than 5,000 years.

Ancient Egyptian Theater and Music

Divine Worship is intimately related to the performance of the Temple Play or reenactment of the Divine myths. Illumination and Temple art are closely associated with the Temple ceremonies and rituals that constitute the Ancient Egyptian Temple Theater. The Temple Theater, rituals and pageantry are integral aspects of the mystical disciplines of the priests and priestesses. Many people believe that the art of theater began with the ancient Greek theater. Thespis, the first actor-dramatist (about 560 B.C.E.), is considered to have been the first person to give the Greek drama its form; actors are still called "thespians." However, upon closer examination, it must be noted that just as Greek philosophers such as Thales and Pythagoras learned their wisdom from the Ancient Egyptians and then set up their schools of philosophy in Greece, it is likely that the first Greek actors and playwrights learned their profession from the Ancient Egyptian Sages when the Greeks came to Ancient Egypt to learn the religion and the sciences from the Ancient Egyptian Sages.[99] Actually, a great debt is owed to the Greek writers of ancient times because their records attest to many details which the Ancient Egyptians did not record about the Ancient Egyptian mysteries.

Ancient Greek theater had its origin in the mysteries of Dionysus. It is well known to scholars of Ancient Greece and Greek mythology that Orpheus is credited with introducing the cult of Dionysus to Greece along with its initiatory rites.

> Orpheus, king of the Ciconians, is counted among the ARGONAUTS. Orpheus practiced minstrelsy and by his songs moved stones and trees, holding also a spell over the wild beasts. He descended to the Underworld in order to fetch his dead wife, but had to return without her. Orpheus, whom Apollo taught to play the lyre, traveled to Egypt where he increased his knowledge about the gods and their initiatory rites, bringing from that

---
[99] see the book "From Egypt to Greece" by Sebai Muata Ashby available through the Sema Institute and bookstores.

country most of his mystic ceremonies, orgiastic rites, and his extraordinary account of his descent to the Underworld. Orpheus became famous because of his poems and his songs, excelling everyone in the beauty of his verse and music. He also reached a high degree of influence because he was believed to have discovered mysteries, purification from sins, cures of diseases, and means of averting divine wrath. Some say that Orpheus introduced a cult of Dionysus that was very similar to the cult of Osiris, and that of Isis, which resembles the cult of Demeter.[100]

As we saw earlier, (and it is important to reiterate) Dionysus is the Greek name for the god Asar (Osiris). The Greek writings attest to the fact the Dionysus was the same Osiris, brought into Greece from Egypt. The dates of the prominence of Dionysus coincide with the association of the first Greek philosophers of the Greek classical period with the Ancient Egyptian priests. The qualities of Dionysus are the same as those of the Egyptian Asar, and the Temple mysteries, including vegetation, death and resurrection, were also the same. The enactment of those mysteries constitutes the Egyptian "Theater" ritual that was adopted by the Greeks, and which was later developed by the Greek playwrights into other themes.[101] (Highlighted text by Ashby)

> Born of the union of Zeus and a mortal, Semele, **Dionysos rose to prominence around the 6th century B.C. under many names and forms.** The principles of life and generation, as well as the cyclical life of vegetation (death and rebirth), are central to the worship of Dionysos: lord of the vine, but also god of the tree. He is often considered in reference to the fig tree, ivy (undying life), and all blossoming things -- symbols of life and vitality. His celebration is marked by the joy of his epiphany in the Spring, and the sorrow of his death or descent in the Winter. Dionysos also appears as a bull god, long considered an important symbol of fertility in the Ancient World. Other symbols that are associated with him include snakes, goats, lightening bolts, as well as moistness, madness and the phallus. Dionysos is typically followed by satyrs and maenads who participate in the music, wine, and dancing which make up an integral aspect of his mystery. Satyrs, or primitive, goat-like men, usually lurk in the shadows of the more primary maenads, or mad women, which typified Dionysian worship. These maenads, "the frenzied sanctified women who are devoted to the worship of Dionysos."(Harrison -401), are 'nurses' who look after and follow the infant Dionysos-- likely referring to the largely female following he inspired and the great Mother goddess he came from.[102]

This section has been included to show the importance of theatrical-ritual in Neterian spirituality. It must be clear though that this form of art (theater) is reserved for the realm of spirituality and not for frivolous entertainment.

There was no public theater in Ancient Egypt as the modern world knows theater at present. Theater in present day society is performed publicly for the main purpose of entertainment, but in Ancient Egypt the theatrical performances were reserved for the Temple and the Temple festivals exclusively. This was because the performing arts, including music, were held to be powerful and sacred endeavors, which were used to impart spiritual teachings and evoke spiritual feeling, and not as frivolous forms of entertainment. The Greek writer, Strabo, relates that multitudes of people would flock to festival centers (important cities and Temples) where the scenes from myths about the gods and goddesses would be acted out.

Sometimes the main episodes of the religious dramas were performed outside the Temple, in the courtyard or between the pylons of the "Peristyle Hall" or "Hypostyle Hall" areas; they were the most important attraction of

---

[100] *Greek Mythology Link*, created and maintained by Carlos Parada. Since 1997© 1993-2004 http://homepage.mac.com/cparada/GML/index.html
[101] Origin of the Greek Theater by B. H. Stricker, Journal of Egyptian Archeology
[102] *Greek Mythology Link*, created and maintained by Carlos Parada. Since 1997© 1993-2004 http://homepage.mac.com/cparada/GML/index.html

the festivals. The most esoteric (mystical) elements were performed in the interior portion of the Temple for initiates, priests and priestesses only. The priests and priestesses took great care with costumes and the decorations (modern terminology-direction and set design). The spectators knew the myths that were being acted out, a retelling of the divine stories, but never stopped enjoying their annual performance, which bring purpose and meaning to life. Thus, the art of acting was set-aside for spiritual purposes and was not to be used for mindless entertainment, which serves only to distract the mind from reality and truth. The spectators would take part by clapping, lamenting at sad parts, and crying out with joy and celebrating when the ultimate triumph came. In this manner the spectators became part of the myth. As the myths are essentially about the gods and goddesses whose lives not only sustain the world, but also lead to understanding the connection between the physical, material and spiritual worlds, the reenactment of these dramas serves to teach and reinforce the spiritual values of the Kamitan culture in the general population. Further, the occasions were used as opportunities for enjoying life, though it was understood to be fleeting. Thus, the bridge between the mortal world and the eternal world was established through mythological drama and the performing arts.

In the Ancient Egyptian view, life cannot be enjoyed without affirming the Divine, the Spirit. Further, theater, religion and mystical philosophy were considered to be aspects of the same discipline, known as "Shetaut Neter" or the "mysteries." Every aspect of life in Ancient Egypt was permeated by the awareness and inclusion of spiritual philosophy. For example, lawyers and judges followed the precepts of Maat, and medical doctors followed and worshipped the teachings of the god Djehuti, who was adopted by the Greeks as the god Asclepius. This idea is also evident in the Ancient Egyptian manner of saying grace before meals even by ordinary householders. Prior to consuming food, the host of an ordinary household would invite the guests to view an image of a divinity, principally Asar (Osiris) the god of the afterlife, thereby reminding the guests that life is fleeting, even as they are about to enjoy a sumptuous meal and pleasing entertainment. In this manner, a person is reminded of the ultimate fate and purpose of life and a reflective state of mind is engendered rather than an arrogant and egoistic state. This theme is present in every aspect of Ancient Egyptian culture at its height.

The Ancient Egyptian clergy instituted tight controls on theater and music because the indulgence in inappropriate entertainments was known to cause mental agitation and undesirable behaviors. The famous Greek Philosopher and student of the Ancient Egyptian Mysteries, Pythagoras, wrote that the Ancient Egyptians placed particular attention to the study of music. Another famous Greek Philosopher and student of the Ancient Egyptian Mysteries, Plato, states that the Ancient Egyptian clergy thought music was beneficial to the youths. Strabo confirms that music was taught to youths along with reading and writing, however, it was understood that music meant for entertainment alone was harmful to the mind, making it agitated and therefore difficult to control oneself, and thus was strictly controlled by the state and the priests and priestesses. Like the sages of India, who instituted Nada Yoga, the spiritual path of music, the Ancient Egyptians held that music was of Divine origin and as such was a sacred endeavor. The Greek writer, Athenaeus, informs us that the Greeks and barbarians from other countries learned music from the Ancient Egyptians. Music was so important in Ancient Egypt that professional musicians were contracted and kept on salaries at the Temples. Music was considered important because it has the special power to carry the mind to either elevated (spiritual) states or (worldly) states. When there is overindulgence in music for escapism (tendency to desire to escape from daily routine or reality by indulging in fantasy, daydreaming, or entertainment) or to promote other egoistic experiences (violence, hate, lust, greed, sentimentality, desire, etc.), the mind becomes filled with worldly impressions, cravings, lusting and uncontrolled urges. In this state of mind, the faculties for right thinking and right feeling are distorted or incapacitated. The advent of audio and visual recording technology and their combinations in movies and music videos are more powerful because the visual element, coupled with music, and the ability to repeat with intensity of volume, acts to intoxicate the mind with illusory, egoistic and fantasy thoughts. The physical body is also affected in this process. The vibrations of the music and the feelings contained in it through the lyrics and sentiment of the performer evokes the production of certain psychological and corresponding bio-chemical processes in the mind and body, respectively. This capacity of music is evident in movies, musicals, concerts, audio recordings, etc., in their capacity to change a person's mood. Any and all messages given to the mind affect it, and therefore, great care should be taken to fill the mind with the right kinds of messages in the form of sublime ideas and feelings.

The Priests and Priestesses of Ancient Egypt

Those societies which produce and consume large quantities of audio and audio-visual entertainment for non-spiritual purposes will exhibit the greatest levels of cultural degradation which will express as mental agitation, violence, individual frustration, addiction, mental illness, physical illness, etc., no matter how materially prosperous or technologically advanced they may become. So true civilization and the success of a society should not be judged by material prosperity or technological advancement, but rather by how successful it is in producing the inner fulfillment of its citizens. Being the creators and foremost practitioners of Maat Philosophy (adherence to the principles of righteousness in all aspects of life[103]), the Ancient Egyptians created a culture which existed longer (at least 5,000 years) than any other known society, and the construction methods of many of their monuments still defy explanation and cannot be duplicated. Therefore, the real measures of civilization and human evolution are to be discerned by the emphasis on and refinement of the performing and visual arts and spiritual[104] philosophy, for these endeavors serve to bring harmony to the individual and to society. It should be clearly understood that art should not become stagnant or rigid in its expression since this is the means by which it is renewed for the understanding of new generations. Rather, the principles contained in the arts should be kept intact in the performance of the rituals, paintings, sculptures, music, etc., since these reflect transcendental truths which are as effective today as they were 5,000 years ago in the Ancient Egyptian Temple and will be effective until the end of time. The loss of these is the cause of disharmony in society, but societal dysfunction is in reality only a reflection of disharmony in the individual human heart that has lost its connection with the Higher Self within.

Dance was also an important part of Ancient Egyptian life. Dance, along with music, was used for worship of the gods and goddesses, especially Asar and Hetheru. However, dance was also present at private dinner parties. Private parties were also the scene for entertainments for games such as Senet, as well as music. Men and women would dance together or alone, and would improvise more so than in the dances of the Temples and special ceremonies. As is the custom in modern day India and Japan, the Ancient Egyptians would take off their shoes when entering a house or the Temple as a sign of reverence for the host and a symbolic gesture of leaving the world outside when practicing higher endeavors. The Medu Neter (hieroglyphic texts) of the priestly discipline of music are:

Ancient Egyptian Priests and Priestess Playing Music

 *Shmait* - female musician- singer

Shmai - male musician- singer

Hesi -Chant, sing repeatedly praises

Notice that the word for music and the word for chant or sing, all use the determinative sign, which means with the mouth. Therefore, the primary musical instrument is seen as the voice, and all other instruments are viewed as accompaniments to the voice.

Dua - praises, adorations to the divine (standing or sitting)

Dua Neter - title of the adoring priestess of Amun

---

[103] See the book "The Wisdom of Maati" by Dr. Muata Ashby
[104] The word spiritual here implies any endeavor which seeks to bring understanding about the ultimate questions of life: Who am I? and What is life all about? So spirituality may or may not be related to organized religion.

Above: Section of a relief depicting priestesses playing music and offering libations and singing to the *"cobra goddess of gold"* (New Kingdom Sakkara –Egypt-Brooklyn Museum)

For more on the art of Kamitan Music, see the book *Shetaut Neter Daily Chant and Songbook* and see the listing of recorded chants and musical compositions based on the original Kamitan texts –at the back section of this book. Thus, the question of whether or not music and entertainment has an effect on youth and the mind of a person was resolved in ancient times. The Ancient Egyptians observed that the people from Greece and the Asiatic countries were more aggressive, and that their behavior was unstable.[105] They attributed these problems to their lifestyle, which was full of strife due to life in harsh geographical regions, meat eating, overindulgence in sense pleasures, and the inability to control the human urges and the consequent disconnection from the natural order of the universe as well as the spiritual inner Self. These observations of the psychology and lifestyle of the foreigners prompted the Ancient Egyptian Sages to refer to the Greeks and Asiatics (Middle Easterners) as "children" and "miserable"..."barbarians." Their observations allowed the Ancient Egyptian Sages to create a philosophy of life and a psycho-spiritual environment wherein the Kamitan people could grow and thrive in physical, mental and spiritual health. As stated earlier, the Greek writer, Athenaeus, informs us that the Greeks and barbarians from other countries learned music from the Ancient Egyptians.

From: The Republic (by Plato) – the Socrates character, in the book, asserts:

> The Egyptians rated music highly, and Plato considered their music superior to the Greek, both for melody and energy. But harmony and rhythm were always subordinate to the words, and the subject matter was paramount. There were two sorts of Harmonies known to the old Egyptians, which the Greeks designated as "Dorian" and Phrygian" – the former, grave, slow and tranquil, the latter, a dithyrambic form, probably employed in these chants (Laments of Aset and Nebthet), which was forceful, appealing and energetic.[106]
>
> The Egyptians based their music on seven diatonics, which Demetrius of Phalerus attributes to the "seven vowels;" others say seven senses, or seven planets. Dion Cassius corroborates him, while Dionysos of Halicarnassus says: "Melody embraced an interval of five-it never rose

---

[105] See the books Egyptian Yoga Vol. 1 and 2 and The 42 Laws of Maat and the Wisdom Texts
[106] The Republic – the Socrates character, in the book, asserts this.

more than three and one-halftones towards high, and fell less towards bass." This probably was a result of the use of the three stringed lyre.[107]

In ancient Greece, theater became a practice that was open to the public, and later on in the Christian era it deteriorated into mindless entertainment or a corrupted endeavor of con artists. In present times, it is a big business, a "show business," wherein its participants are paid excessive and disproportionately high salaries for their entertainment skills, or otherwise said, their ability to sell merchandise. In modern times, the almost unfettered creation and promotion of movies, videos, music and other forms of entertainment containing elements designed to promote sense pleasures and excitement, leads to mental agitation, but with little true satisfaction of the inner need of the heart. Thus, while the entertainments may cause excitation, they do not lead to abiding fulfillment and inner peace, but to more desires for more excitement in a never-ending cycle that is impossible to fulfill. This process leads to mental confusion and stress, which in turn lead to strife, conflict and internal frustration. Corresponding with the emergence of Western and Middle Eastern culture, with its negative lifestyle elements noted by the Ancient Egyptians, the world has also seen an increase in wars, violence against women and children, environmental destruction, enslavement and taking advantage of weaker human beings, drug abuse, crime, divorce, and overall personal dissatisfaction with life. In other words, the lack of restraints, in both individuals and in societies as a whole, has led to frustration with life, a kind of cultural depression and degradation, which has led to record numbers of people suffering from mental illnesses such as depression, schizophrenia, psychosis, as well as medical disorders of all kinds which were not present in ancient times due to self-control and the direction of life being guided by spiritual pursuits as opposed to egoistic pursuits. The Ancient Egyptian Mystery theater provides the means for allowing a human being to come into harmony with the spiritual reality (mental expansion and self-discovery) while frivolous entertainment serves to dull the intellectual capacity to discover and understand anything beyond the physical world and the physical sense pleasures of life (mental contraction and hardening of the ego). This inability to go beyond sense pleasures and experiences in the world of human activity is what leads a person to mental stress, which in turn leads to mental and physical illness.

Therefore, understanding the message of Ancient Egyptian Theater is of paramount importance to human evolution. In Ancient Egypt, theater and music were used for spiritual education and to maintain harmony between the individual and the universe, the soul and the Divine. Thus, spiritual plays were acted by the priests, priestesses, initiates and sometimes by the relatives of the deceased (especially in the case of the Pert Em Heru Mysteries). The use of masks in theater did not originate in Greece. Their use already existed in Ancient Egypt. Unlike the Greek theater, which placed great importance on tragedy in life, masks, such as those presented in this volume were sometimes used by those playing the characters of the mystery in an effort to understand the mystery by becoming one with it, to embody the qualities of the divinity being portrayed and in so doing ultimately becoming one with the Divine. Also, the purpose was to promote the well being of others by directing one's mind and heart towards what is righteous, beautiful and good in the world and beyond. This was the motivation and source of strength which allowed Ancient Egyptian Culture, led by the priests and priestesses, to achieve a high degree of "civilization" and spiritual Enlightenment.

Thus the earliest religious rituals in Egypt were performed as plays that were often part of festival periods. This tradition began with the early Dynastic Period and the Asarian Resurrection myth (5,000 B.C.E. or earlier), which surrounds the death and resurrection of the god Asar (Osiris). This was the main play that was performed universally in Kamit, and then in Greece and Rome in later times, after the Greeks came to Kamit to learn the arts, sciences, and spiritual philosophy upon which they then established their civilization. In Ancient Egypt, the story of Hetheru was revered so highly that an annual play and festivity commemorating her saga was held in her honor, even down to the early Christian era. It was so popular that it was observed widely throughout the entire country of Egypt. Remnants of it and other Ancient Egyptian festivals survive even today in the rituals of the Muslims who live in present day Egypt. Thus, theater emerged in ancient Africa and influenced Europe, and what would later develop into Greek and Christian theater. The practice of the mystery play was done for the purpose of worshipping the Divinity, and also as a method of imparting some important mystical teachings. These have

---

[107] BURDEN OF ISIS by James Teackle Dennis 1910

been presented at length in the gloss following the presentation of the play, which discusses the main themes of the myth of Hetheru.[108] Therefore, anyone wishing to learn more about the teachings and practice of Ancient Egyptian philosophy can learn much from participating in the play and studying Ancient Egyptian Philosophy (Shetaut Neter-Smai Tawi-Ancient Egyptian or Kamitan Yoga).

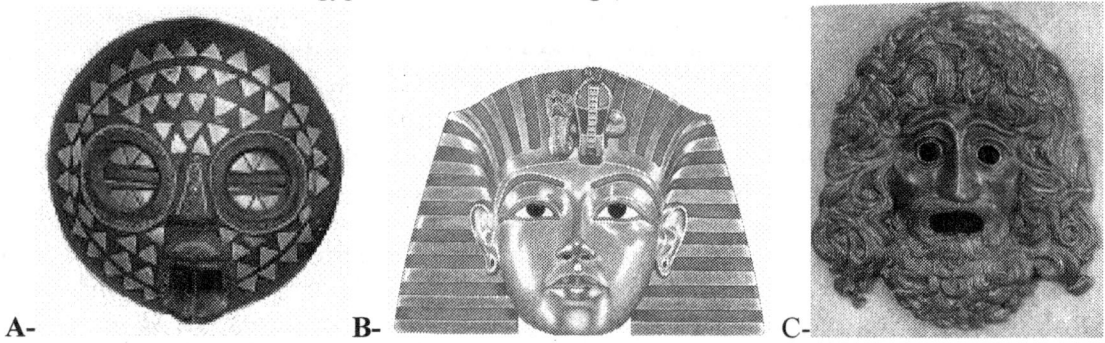

A- Baluba mask of Ghana, B- Mask of Tutankhamun, C- Ancient Greek tragedy mask

Reenactment of the Mysteries

Below: Lord Anpu priest embalming the god Asar as goddess Aset and goddess Nebthet look on. One of the common reenactments is of the mummification and resurrection of Asar.

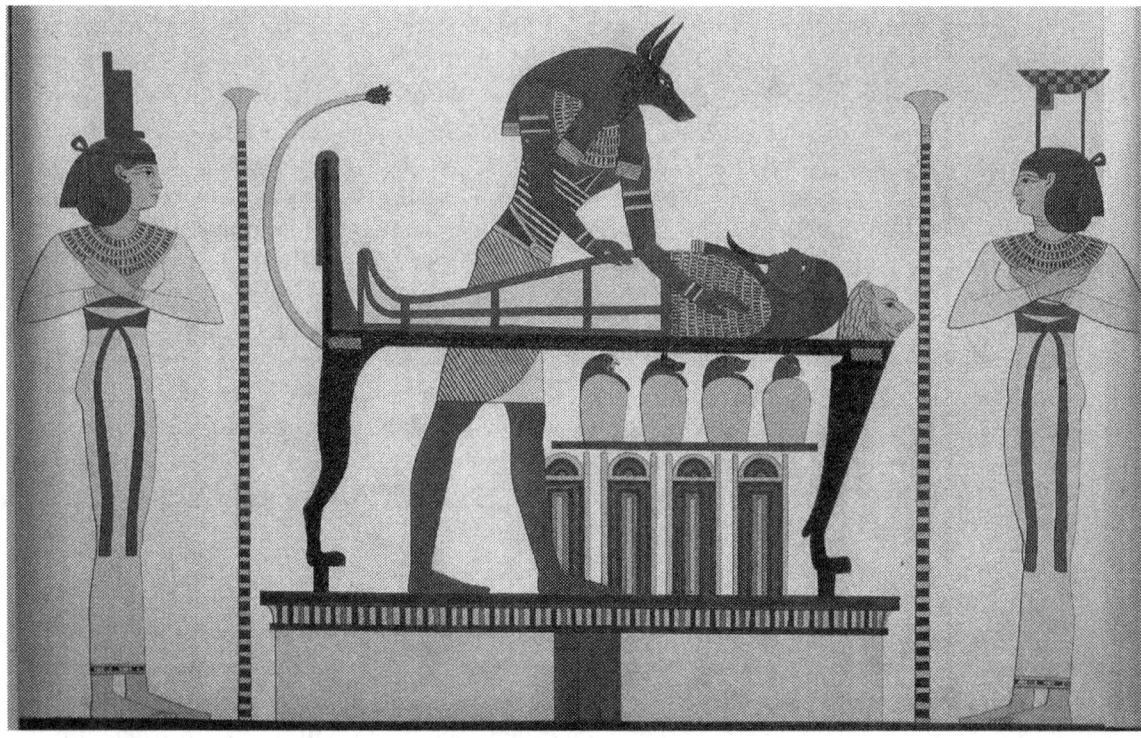

One of the main duties of the advanced priesthood (not the lower ranks) is the reenactment of the myths of the tutelary Divinity of the Temple. This reenactment is the ritual in the form of a theatrical performance and has the effect of promoting a communal meditative experience in the participants in which they eventually identify with the Divinity whose drama is being reenacted.

---

[108] See the book *Theater and Drama of the Ancient Egyptian Mysteries* by Sebai Muata Ashby

The Priests and Priestesses of Ancient Egypt

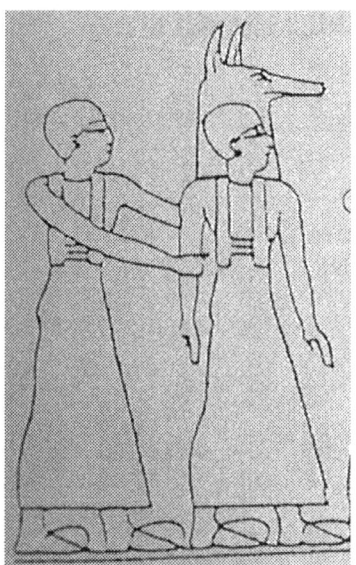 

At left: Actually, the character of Anpu is an Ancient Egyptian priest who performs the rites of the dead while wearing a mask/helmet having the likeness of the god Anpu (actual surviving Anpu helmet -above right), who is the divinity of embalming.

Below: The priest as Anpu holds the mummy of Asar Ani upright.

What do the Priests and Priestesses Teach and How do They Teach It?

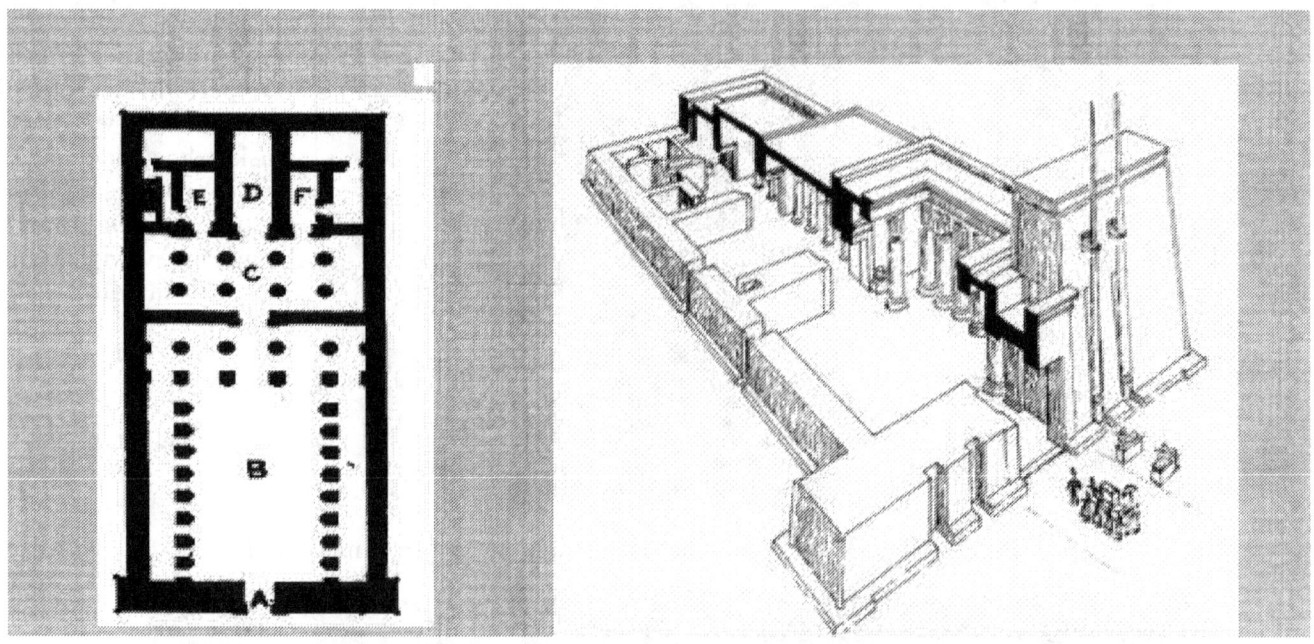

The Neterian Temple has three main sections: the Peristyle court, the Hypostyle hall, and Holy of Holies. These represent the areas where different levels of worshipers may enter, and the form of teaching they are to receive. This conception follows, generally, the nomenclature of the triads of spirituality: The three levels of mind - unconscious, subconscious and conscious; the three levels of relative consciousness - waking, dream and deep sleep; the three levels of religion: myth, ritual, and mystical, and the great trinity; the three levels of aspiration – aspiration, striving and established. The three sections of the Temple also represent the three levels of human existence: Mortals, Intelligences and Creators or Beings of Light.

The outer court (B) is open to the lowest ranking practitioners of the Temple, the middle (C) is open to the more advanced, and the innermost (D) is open to the most advanced. The innermost is reserved for those who are ready to have union with the Divine and experience Transcendental Consciousness, and become established in that higher consciousness, leaving the lower (egoistic consciousness) behind. They are ready to let go of the world and all that is temporary, fleeting and evanescent in life.

There are three modes of actions: thought, words and deed. The outer most court is the place for deeds, that is, work to propitiate the Divinity, the lower worship. Lower worship is not inferior, but rather, it means physical rituals, making offerings to the Divine, offering prayers to the Divine, and chanting, self-purification, etc. It is foundational to the higher worship.

The middle hall is the section of the Temple for words. This section is reserved for the wisdom teachings, and this is where classes would be held and spiritual wisdom imparted.

The inner hall court is the section of the Temple for advanced rituals, metaphysics, meditations and mystical exercises that sustain creation and unite one to the Divine. So there is an alchemy that goes on in the inner court – a transformation of mortal consciousness to immortal, from worldly to spiritual, from mundane to cosmic, from physical body to the body of light, called *Akh*.

The Temple complex houses different buildings where various services are provided to the community. There is the Per Ankh (House of Life - hospital), a school for children, and university rooms for instruction of varied disciplines, healing and worship of the Divine. Again, the hospital is not located inside the Temple itself; it is a building within the Temple complex. There would be special buildings in the Temple complex that would serve as the schoolrooms for disciplines other than spirituality.

The symbol above is called "Rekhyt." The "Rekhyt" symbol means the "common folk." The rekhyt symbols are inscribed on the pillars where the common folk offer praises, adorations, and perform devotional practices to the Divine. The term "common folk" here means ordinary people who are not priests and priestesses. However, this should not be taken to mean that non-devotional people, i.e., non-believers, are allowed to enter. This is meant for followers of the tradition who are also laypersons and not professional clergy or initiates. The upraised arms of the rekhyt bird symbolize the "Dua" posture.

Below: The initiate adores the Bennu.

Above: An Ancient Egyptian woman in the "Dua" posture

The Dua posture is performed with upraised hands, and palms facing outwards, towards the image of the Divinity being worshipped; it means "adorations." In serving the masses, the Neterian clergy invite those interested in the teaching only to the outer section of the Temple where they are to be instructed in the exoteric teachings, concentrating on the myths, devotional exercises (chanting, divine singing, religious festivals, meditations) and Maat virtuous philosophy. This is to be done until the life of an individual is orderly; they develop virtue, true devotion and dedication to the teaching as well as respect for the clergy.

The priests and priestesses study the sacred scriptures and impart these to those who are ready to understand and practice the teachings that are contained in them. There are three kinds of scriptures in Kamitan culture. We have Mythic scriptures, Mystical scriptures, and Wisdom Text scriptures. In addition to these, there is also the genre of the Harper's songs. Though belonging in the category of music, they are also to be considered as part of the wisdom literature. All the books in this series are based on these scriptures.

The Glorious Duty

The end and aim of all these toils and labors is the attainment of the knowledge of the First and Chief Being, Who alone is the object of the understanding of the mind; and this knowledge the Goddess invites us to seek after, as being near and dwelling continually with Her. – Teaching from the Temple of Aset

saa-{understanding}, ab {mind}, haui- {close by-near by}, menta – {continuously}, Aset {the goddess}, nemm – {to sit to dwell}, aset s-gera- {place of making silent}, ast htp – {abode of the heart's peace}.

Divine Worship leads to introspection and meditation. What is the most important duty of a priest or priestess? Of all the duties of the clergy, one stands out because it is the foundation and goal of life. That goal is to always dwell with the Divine. In the Temple of Aset, a special discipline is enjoined for true devotees. It is to continually remain concentrated on the Divine, to listen, reflect upon and meditate on that. That practice is to be done in the abode of peace, in silence. The term silence is phonetically related to the term gereh-darkness. So to dwell (remain) in peace and silence in proximity to the Divine is the practice of this discipline.

It is this discipline that (Sba) illumines and teaches so that the aspirant may become *nehast* spiritually awakened-enlightened. That discipline is incomparable because it allows one to discover the source of Spirit, within. No pleasure can match it. No worldly attainment surpasses it. When the personality finds solace in silence and contemplation, there is a special peace that emerges, a peace that transcends problems, faults and misgivings. It is a peace wherein the opposites are cancelled out. That is what Hetep means, when the gods and goddesses are appeased. Those gods and goddesses are the opposing energies, the desires, the ideas, imaginations and delusions of the mind. To appease them there must be understanding of the teaching of life and death. There must be constant reflection upon it, even while working, talking, sleeping, studying, eating, bathing, breathing, and doing anything. Then there emerges a meditative absorption, and that is the divine act of dwelling. Dwelling always in the glory of the Self is indescribable and yet all encompassing, wholistic and most satisfying. It is a different way of relating to the world in which there is a realization that silence is the only answer to everything, because everything is in reality no-thing. The sense of the mind that relates to the world gives way to the mind of thoughtless form, the world of the thinking mind falls apart, and the rationale of the things that must be done or should have been done or are hated or loved or imagined show their true nature as demons and tricksters of senseless grief. And that mind that dwells with that wisdom of timeless nature that is sought after by all who pursue "the aim of all toils" discovers the first and the chief being, and there is a realization of "that is I." And this is why the priests and priestesses say: 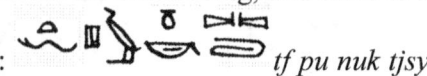 *tf pu nuk tjsy wdjb* - he is me tied to each other- *"He is I and I am He."*

Special Meditation Discipline of the Priests and Priestesses of Shetaut Neter

In **CHAP. XVIII.** of the book *On the Mysteries*, the Ancient Egyptian priest and Sage (Sebai) Iamblichus speaks of a special form of meditation that is practiced by the priesthood. It is a practice enjoined for those who enter into the correct form of spiritual worship. There are three classes of worshippers: those who worship the Divine in material forms (the things controlled by higher powers), those who worship the Divine in immaterial forms (pure intellect), and of those who worship the Divine in combination forms. But there are those who do not become "liberated" from the lower nature that is subordinate to the forces of nature, and are therefore a slave to them. Those who worship in the lower ways also are slaves. Those who take up the "more excellent" form are "removed from nature" and "become superior to the physical powers" that control the "things subordinate." The latter is of course the highest goal. (Highlighted text by Ashby)

> "ACCORDING to another division, therefore, the numerous herd [or the great mass] of men is arranged under nature, is <u>governed by physical powers</u>, looks downward to the works of nature, gives completion to the administration of Fate, and to things pertaining to Fate, because it belongs to the order of it, and always employs practical reasoning about such particulars alone as subsist according to nature. But there are a certain few who, by employing a *<u>certain supernatural power of intellect, are removed indeed from nature, but are conducted to a separate and unmingled intellect; and these, at the same time, become superior to physical powers.</u>* Others again, who are the media between these, tend to things which subsist between nature and a pure intellect. And of these, some indeed equally follow both nature and an immaculate intellect; others embrace a life which is mingled from both; and others are liberated from <u>things subordinate</u>, and be take themselves to such as are more excellent."

Plotinus was born in Egypt, and he followed the teachings of Plato and Pythagoras as well as the Egyptian Mysteries. He also taught asceticism in (70-205 A.C.E.). The class to which the practitioners that become liberated belong is further expertly elucidated, as follows, by Plotinus, in the beginning of his *Treatise on Intellect, Ideas, and real Being.* --- (Highlighted text by Ashby)

> "Since all men from their birth employ <u>sense prior to intellect</u>, and are necessarily first conversant with sensibles, <u>some proceeding no farther</u>, pass through life, considering these as the first and last of things, and apprehending that <u>whatever is painful among these is evil, and whatever is pleasant is good</u>; thus thinking it sufficient to pursue the one and avoid the other. Those, too, among them who pretend to a greater share of reason than others, <u>esteem this to be wisdom</u>, being affected in a manner similar to more heavy birds, who collecting many things from the earth, and being oppressed with the weight, are unable to fly on high, <u>though they have received wings for this purpose from nature</u>. (2) But others are in a small degree elevated from <u>things subordinate</u>, the <u>more excellent part of the soul recalling them from pleasure to a more worthy pursuit</u>. As they are, however, unable to look on high, and as not possessing anything else which can afford them rest, they betake themselves, together with the name of virtue, to actions and the election of things inferior, from which they at first endeavored to raise themselves, though in vain. (3) In the third class is the race of divine men, who, <u>through a more excellent power, and with piercing eyes, acutely perceive supernal light, to the vision of which they raise themselves above the clouds and darkness, as it were, of this lower world</u>, and there abiding despise everything in these <u>regions of sense</u>; being no otherwise delighted with the place which is truly and properly their own, than he who after many wanderings is at length restored to his <u>lawful country</u>."

Following the scheme also followed by Iamblichus, Plotinus describes in more detail the experience of those who go beyond the senses and duality in the form of hatred and love (<u>whatever is painful among these is evil, and whatever is pleasant is good). The passage "though they have received wings for this purpose from nature" signifies that all have the capacity to transcend the objects of the senses and yet most people choose the path of "proceeding no farther" with inquiry. So they get caught up in the "regions of sense" (mind and senses, the physical world), which is the subordinate. Intellect is above mind and the region of pure intellect that is free of sense perception is that realm which bestows a vision of the true nature of Self, the "lawful country" wherein reside **the Creators or Beings of Light:** *Akhu*, {illumined men and women} initiates who become IDENTIFIED with or UNITED with the light (GOD).

Once the personality is properly prepared through vegetarian diet, virtuous living and right worship, the advanced meditation techniques can be practiced. The technique involves certain posture, visualizations, breath-work, and subtle energy manipulation techniques to promote withdrawal of the senses and cessation of sense perceptions. In order to be able to withdraw the senses, to make the mind introspective instead of extroverted, there must be virtue and order in life. Virtue allows the mind to be peaceful. A mind that is turbulent will not succeed in sense withdrawal and if per chance there are some fleeting periods of success, the agitated mind will suffer from delusions and sometimes attacks from its own agitated nature in the form of images and feelings that are negative (demons). Those negative experiences can have a deleterious effect on the spiritual capacity. Also, it is important to be well schooled in the philosophy of Shetaut Neter and the teaching of the impermanence of life, contained in the *Harper' songs* and *Prt M Hru* texts. Therefore, training in the philosophy and discipline of Maat precedes the instruction in the techniques and discipline of the sense withdrawal meditation technique here described in most general terms.

When the senses are withdrawn, it becomes possible to experience mind in its purer state (intellect). However, in the withdrawn state it is possible to have experiences based on subtle senses, so those must be transcended as well. The experiences of the astral plane (Duat) can be more intense than those of the physical world. Those experiences can be powerful enlighteners for those who are prepared, but can also be powerful frighteners to the uninitiated and unprepared. So it is important to have a gradual progress and proper initiation into the practice in order to promote an integrated and successful movement into higher realms of existence and Transcendental Being. Going further there is a special realm where all sense perceptions are transcended (*Yanrutf*). That is the state that is completely "removed indeed from nature," that was described by Iamblichus earlier. Within that realm there will be discovered a special effulgent light ("supernal light"), more powerful than any other. The individual self is merged in that light, like a drop of water merging with the ocean, thus allowing ultimate self-knowledge and the ultimate (over a period of time) becoming of a Being of Light (one with the Light). The "certain supernatural power of intellect" described by Iamblichus is the power to control one's attention and through strength of will direct oneself away from the sense perceptions and towards the inner recesses of Being. That comes through virtue, philosophy and right worship. These are the secrets to spiritual realization that every Neterian cleric MUST pursue and not be satisfied as those who accept the sense perceptions as final realities and "proceed no farther" with their researches. However, there are those who attain certain glimpses of expanded consciousness in the Duat, who may have visions or intense sense experiences and consider those to be illumination, and they also "proceed no farther." It is important to understand that the subtle sense perceptions of the astral plane are also part of the realm of generation, of "things subordinate," and "governed by physical powers." That is not the "lawful country," spoken of by the illustrious teachers quoted above.

During the conscious, integrated and peaceful entry into the experience of transcending time and space, there is a feeling of incomparable peace and a sense of well-being, and comfort that cannot be equaled by any pleasurable state of the physical realm or the sense perceptions. This is concomitant with the ascendancy of the Arat Sekhem (Serpent Power). During the even more elevated but indescribable experience of touching that transcendental Light, there is no conscious awareness of time and space and no awareness of self as individual subject, but upon return to the physical realm of the senses and individuality, there is a feeling not unlike the afterglow[109] that remains for a time after the climax of a sexual experience. That feeling is much deeper than the physical sexual experience, but is a remnant of the spiritual transcendental experience. This also is the cause for the sex desire in all life; it is a search for that pleasure, that peace, that bliss which is born of union with Spirit that people truly yearn for in life. However, ignorant people can only glimpse that glory through physical acts such as drugs, mindless entertainments and thrill seeking, or sexual experiences which are fleeting. A fully integrated, illuminated person, enters into that experience many times until finally they become one with it, and experience it perennially. Along with that exhaled feeling there is expanded consciousness and awareness of undivided and unbroken consciousness that transcends the waking, dream and deep sleep states; i.e. there is a constant awareness of Consciousness that is the same, unlike the ordinary waking experience, dream experience and sleep experience of most people that is broken, erratic and different. Most people experience themselves as different personalities in the three states. The enlightened state opens the awareness to the underlying "Higher Self" which is undifferentiated and immortal Spirit. The writings of Iamblichus and Plotinus occur in the later period of Ancient Egyptian history. They reflect the ages old teaching of withdrawal of the senses that is contained in the Pert M Hru texts of Ancient Egypt. An example is contained in Chapter 31:69:

"This Chapter can be known by those who recite it and study it when they see no more, hear no more, have no more sexual intercourse and eat no meat or fish."

The Duty of Offering

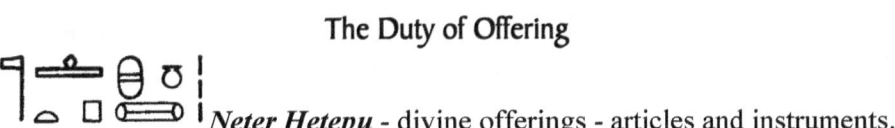*Neter Hetepu* - divine offerings - articles and instruments.

Intimately related to Divine Worship is the Divine Offering. One of the most important duties of the Neterian clergy is to make the prescribed offerings. Making Divine Offerings –*Neter Hetep*- is of paramount importance because offering is the key to propitiating divine grace. Divine grace is a divine act that assists the spiritual aspirant to progress spiritually. There are three main forms of the Neterian offering. One is the Maat offering. The Maat offering is the offering of a Maat icon to the Divine (god or goddess receiving the offering). There is more to making this offering just the ritual; it means becoming virtuous, balanced, just and pure. Another important offering is the *arit*. The arit is the *udjati or eye of Heru* in the form of consecrated food items, including bread, wine, beer, cakes, etc. This offering represents the essence of Asar, and Heru that makes consciousness whole again. This offering was in place from the earliest period of recorded history in Ancient Egypt, and its teaching can be seen in the Ancient Egyptian Pyramid Texts. The next form of offering is the *Hetep (Hotep)*. The "Hetep Slab" or Offering Table is typically composed of a stone slab with male ⌒, thigh, and female ⌒, duck, symbols carved into the top, along with the symbol of Supreme Peace, ▵, or Hetep, which consists of a loaf of bread, ⊖, and an offering mat, ▭, which was composed of woven reeds (in Pre-Dynastic times), and two libation vessels ⁞⁞. The Hetep offering is an offering of duality. It is a tantric teaching that relates to offering one's individuality, merging oneself with the Divine and thereby dissolving the separation between individual consciousness and the Divine Self. There are many types of the Hetep symbols, in size and shape, but they all have the same objects incised on them, and they are all used in the same ritualistic way, with libations and special prayers. The image on the next page (overleaf) is of an Ancient Egyptian priest holding a Hetep offering tray. Hetep also means peace, and pacification of the gods and goddesses. This is a kneeling bronze figure from the Late Period. This figure is now housed at the Brooklyn Museum.

Amenit ent ra neb- "daily offerings."

---

[109] A lingering impression of past glory or success.

The Priests and Priestesses of Ancient Egypt

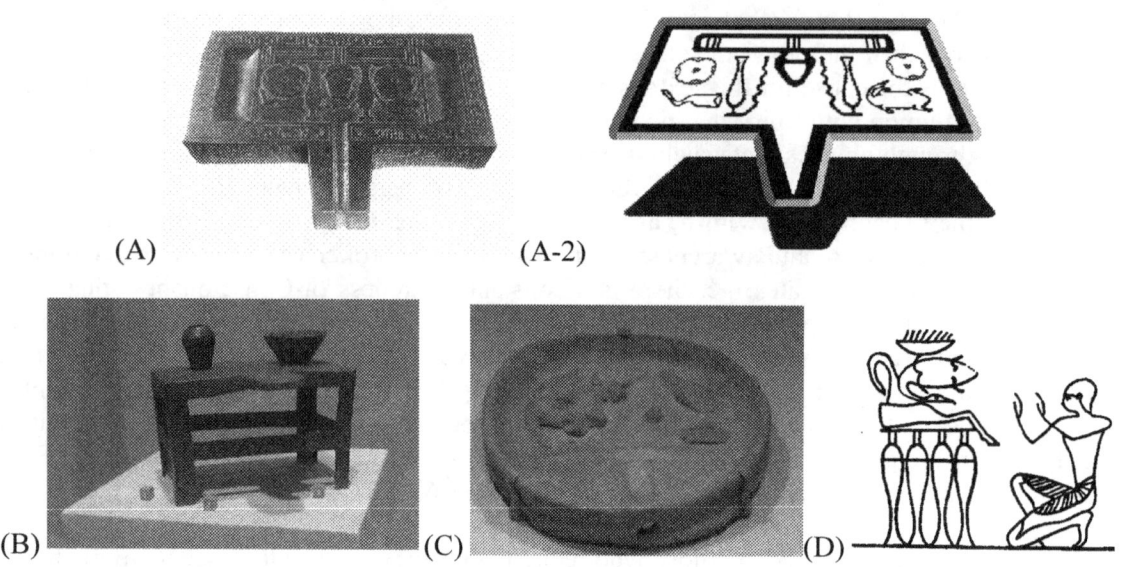

(A)   (A-2)

(B)   (C)   (D)

The greatest offering is *Arit Heru Arat Hetep* – "Eye of Heru the goddess as offering." This is the offering that restores Divine Consciousness, it is the original Eucharist.

Below: Priest presents HTP (Hetep) Offering Table

The Priests and Priestesses of Ancient Egypt

Offering of Maat

The following image is a relief that shows a "God's Wife of Amun" (priestess of Amun) who is making a Maat offering of a seated figure of goddess Maat (A), the divinity of truth, righteousness, order, balance, to the god Amun-Ra. The son of Amun, Khonsu, stands behind Amun. (Late Period– Waset-Thebes, Egypt) (Brooklyn Museum). The Peraah (king) is often depicted making the Maat offering on Temple reliefs (B). However, the image below is proof that the Maat offering is to be practiced by the Neterian clergy, as well as the nobility and advancing aspirants of Neterian spirituality.

Chapter 7: Qualifications of the Clergy and Admonition to Priests and Priestesses for Righteous Conduct

Admonition to Priests and Priestesses from the Ptolemaic Period

"Oh you prophets and great pure ones, guardians of what is secret, pure priests of the god, all you who enter into the presence of the deities, you lector priests who are in the Temple! All of you, judges, administrators of the domain, stewards who are in your month .... turn your faces to this house in which his (divine) majesty has placed you! As he sails in the sky (Ra), he looks down, and he is satisfied with it if his law is being observed. Do not present yourselves in a state of sin! Do not enter in a state of impurity!

Tell no lie in his home! Do not misappropriate any of the provisions; do not raise taxes injuring the small in favor of the powerful! Do not add to the weight and the measure, rather diminish them! Do not plunder with the bushel.... Do not reveal what you see in any secret matter in the sanctuaries! Do not lay a hand on anything in his dwelling, do not go so far as to steal before the lord with sacrilegious thought in your heart! One lives on the provisions of the deities, but one calls 'provision' that which leaves the altar after the god has satisfied himself with it! See, whether he sails in the sky (or) traverses the netherworld, his eyes remain (fixed) on his goods, there where they are."[110]

The passage above contains several important regulations that the priests and priestesses need to observe. Lying and stealing in overt or subtle ways is addressed. The clergy is in a special position of trust and therefore has special temptations. There is the temptation to misuse the power of the office. The clergy have special responsibilities, which includes not stealing from those who do not know how to measure weights, or to read. There is another more grievous transgression being listed here, the *sacrilegious thought in your heart!* This is recognition that not only actions of the body but also thought-actions of the mind are important. The sinful behaviors arise from the highly egoistic notion that one is getting over on god, that one is taking something and profiting by it as if God is like a person who can be burglarized secretly, without God knowing what has happened. This idea is based on the notion that God is like a person, with limited senses and limited presence. This kind of ignorant notion occurs in the mind of a person who is so egoistically involved that they believe the personalities and divinities of the world are like individuals, in competition for the meager scraps of the world. This is a very degraded mental process and such people are not fit to practice at any level of the priesthood. Those who have ideas of getting rich by stealing from others will be dealt with severely by their karmic fate. Those who steal from others and use the Temple or who steal from the Temple itself will be dealt with more harshly. Even if they are not caught, they will suffer tremendously in life and later on after death also. They will have no peace in life and they will endure punishments after death.

Some of the duties of a person who aspires to the clergy are to bring balance and order to the practical realities of life, and learn to be satisfied with what is needed to survive and not entertain greedy thoughts or actions. Living unrighteously and pursuing desires and intense suffering leads to insanity. Those who are insane (depressed, psychotic, sociopathic, vengeful, greedy, bipolar, schizophrenic, self-destructive, etc.) are not fit for priesthood studies, and must resolve the issues of mental instability first before applying for the clergy. Living by Maat brings order, peace and health. This way of life will bring peace, and that peace will allow concentration on the teaching, and allow the teaching to enter into the private regions of the heart.

---

[110] Chassinat, *Edfou*, Vol. III, 361, l. 12-362, l. 5: translated by M. Alliot, *Le Culte d'Horus a Edfou au temps de Ptolemees*, Biblioteque d' Etude 20, Vol. I (Cairo, 1949), 184-85.

Admonition to part-time Priests and Priestesses (Unut) from the Ptolemaic Period

"Do not raise lies against truth in invoking the lord! You who are people of importance, never spend a long period of time without invoking him when you are relieved of (the duty of) presenting offerings and praising (him) in his home in the Temple. Do not frequent the place of the women, do not do what (should) not be done there.... Open no vessel in the Temple; it is the lord (alone) who drinks there! Do not perform the sacred services any way you please-what would be the purpose of looking at the old writings? The ritual of the Temple is in your hands, and it is what your children study- [111]"

What does this mean? It is important to understand that the virtuous conduct in the Temple precincts must be maintained in the secular world as well. So the regulations of Maat must be followed in as well as outside of the Temple. Those who hold the degraded notion of behaving virtuously and with humility when in the presence of other clergy and within the Temple, but think that they can act unrighteously or egoistically in the city, in business or in other human activities, are committing a grave error. Those who do the Temple ritual faithfully at the appointed times but neglect it when they are away from the Temple, or traveling, etc., are also committing error. The practice of the teaching should be perennial, i.e. constant. That is the way to steer clear of worldly entanglements and to have positive progress on the spiritual path. Those aspirants who practice the teaching in a way that is not consistent, meditating, practicing the postures and perhaps the other disciplines a lot one day, but then don't' do anything for two to three days, are in error. This is not enjoined by the teaching. There needs to be regularity. A disjointed movement is not going to allow you to have the consistent evolution that you need to have.

Some priests and priestesses serve as *Unut*, part-time clergy, and they do the presentation of offerings, cleansing, chanting and other duties. They do it at certain times of the year on a rotating basis. The statement *'do not open any vessels, do not be eating in the Temple'* is a ritual of reverence, and respect for the sacred space, so it is not treated as a mundane worldly locale. So you show the respect, because you are in a special place, otherwise you are bringing it down to a mundane level, and will not be benefitted. You may as well go and sit in front of the TV, eat your food and talk, etc. The statement *"Do not perform the sacred services any way you please-what would be the purpose of looking at the old writings?"* relates to people who have a self-willing nature. They want to do things their way as opposed to that which has been laid out by the sages of ancient times. They do not respect the teachings of the ancients, and so also they do not have respect for the teachings of present day sages. They should start their own religion or practice in whatever way they choose on their own and not try to change the teaching that was set from ancient times. This is why I have sought to bring forth the Neterian teaching based on the Neterian scriptures and not on synthesized teachings from many traditions or previously unknown teachings. What you see here are actual texts, which are authentic and effective.

The *Unut* level of priesthood is important because this group provides an important supportive role for the Temple. An Unut (deacon-minister) is one who takes care of the needs of rekhyt (lay people-congregation) on behalf of a higher authority of the Temple. In this capacity, the ministers assist in the dissemination of the teachings and disciplines of Shetaut Neter and Sema Tawi. They assist the community by giving classes in the disciplines to help people better their lives. They also assist in the work of the higher authorities of the Temple as they conduct programs for aspirants, the general public and for the priesthood. In so doing they develop spiritual merit through service, and the enlightening effect of teaching others what they know. In this manner they become more proficient and hasten their own movement towards Enlightenment.

---

[111] Chassinat, *Edfou,* Vol. III, 361-362, l. 4: translated by M. Alliot, *Le Culte d'Horus a Edfou au temps de Ptolemees,* Biblioteque d' Etude 20 , Vol. I 186.

Guarding Against Impatience, Self Willed Nature and Irreverent Attitude

The modern world has developed many technological advances that have assisted human beings to provide for themselves and have more conveniences. The advancements have also led to unprecedented levels of stress on the psycho-physical (mental and physical) constitution of human beings, and also on nature. The conflict over resources and the pursuit of leisure have led to impatience in all areas of life, including the spiritual life. Just as people like to get a pill to relieve a headache quickly, they would like to get a pill to attain Cosmic Consciousness. But that is not possible, just as a mango tree cannot bear fruit before its time. This impatience and irreverence lead to lack of respect for authentic spiritual personalities, and an inability to progress on the spiritual path, because the movements of such a person are shallow and ineffective. Such aspirants are not worthy to receive teaching, let alone admittance to the ranks of the apprenticeship for the clergy. All prospective aspirants must prove their merit and constant desire to follow the teachings by their speech and their consistent actions. The following story was written by Lucian,[112] called *Philopseudes,* about a sacred scribe of Memphis and the misadventures of his hero Eucrates:

"In my youth, when I was living in Egypt-my father sent me there to finish my education-I thought it would be nice to sail up the Nile as far as Coptus, travel on from there to the statue of Memnon and hear the strange sound that it makes at sunrise. Well I heard it all right, but it was not just the meaningless noise that most people hear. On the contrary, Memnon actually opened his mouth and gave me a seven-line oracle in verse, which I could repeat to you word for word, if there were any point in doing so. On the voyage back, one of my fellow-passengers was a holy scribe from Memphis, an incredibly wise man who'd mastered all the mystic lore of Egypt. He was said to have lived for twenty-three years in an underground shrine, receiving instruction in magic from Isis."

"Why that sounds like the man that taught me!" exclaimed Arignotus. "Pancrates, his name was-a very holy man, clean-shaven, always wore linen, highly intelligent, spoke rather bad Greek, tallish, snub nose, thick lips, and rather thin legs."

"Yes, Pancrates! That's exactly who it was," said Eucrates. "I'd never heard of him before, but when I saw the amazing things he did every time we landed, like riding about on crocodiles and going for swims with them-when I saw the great brutes crouching at his feet and wagging their tails, I realized that he must be a Holy Man. Very gradually, by various small acts of courtesy, I managed to make friends with him and he told me all his secrets. Finally he persuaded me to leave my own employees at Memphis, and go off with him. He said there wouldn't be any problem about servants. So off we went.

"Whenever we stopped at an inn, he used to take a broom, or a rolling-pin, or the bolt off the door, dress it up, and then, by saying, a spell, make it walk about just like a human being. It went and fetched us hot water, did all the shopping and the cooking, and generally acted as a most efficient domestic servant. When there was nothing more for it to do, he'd say another spell, which turned it back into a broom, or a rolling pin, as the case might be. Much as I wanted to, I could never get him to show me how he did it, for he was very jealous of this particular accomplishment, though he was quite prepared to tell me everything else.

"However, one day I hid in a dark corner while he was doing it, and overheard the spell-it was only three syllables long. Having told the rolling-pin what he wanted done, he went off

---

[112] Lucian (c. AD 120- c. 200), Greek satirist, born in Samosata on the Upper Euphrates. Lucian is best known as the contributor of the satiric dialogue to Greek literature. He made use of this unique form of dialogue in some 80 works. His writing was witty, and drew attention to the foibles of contemporary life and manners. Religion and philosophy were among Lucian's favorite targets. Copyright (C) 1983,1990 by Random House Inc.

into the town. So next day, when he again had business in town, I seized the rolling-pin, dressed it up, pronounced the three syllables, and told it to fetch some water. When it came back with a bucketful, I said: 'That'll do. Don't fetch any more water, but turn back into a rolling-pin.' This time it refused to obey me, but went on fetching bucket after bucket of water, until the whole house was flooded. I couldn't think what to do, for I was afraid Pancrates would be rather annoyed when he got back-as indeed he was. In despair, I seized an axe and chopped the rolling-pin in two whereupon each half grabbed a bucket and went on fetching water, so now I had twice as much water coming in! At this point Pancrates turned up, and realizing what had happened, turned both halves back into wood again. He then abandoned me in disgust, and mysteriously disappeared."[113]

The story above illustrates several important issues related to the Ancient Egyptian sages, discipleship and the manner for approaching elevated personalities. Clearly the Greek aspirant illustrates a desire to attain the teaching with sufficient guile to get the sage to take him on. However, impatience gets the better of him and he acts as a spy in order to secretly listen to the teaching that the sage knows he is not yet ready for. That act shows immaturity of character, but also disrespect and irreverence. The disastrous results of his act damaged the room, but also irreparably damaged his relationship with the sage, a relationship that could have been most fruitful. The moral (*maut* -moral of story- tale -myth to be remembered) of the story is that aspirants should be mature, reverent and patient. Teachers watch them allowing them to prove their character and readiness to receive teachings. Without those qualities the teaching is fruitless, and even dangerous, and from such people the sages pass out of sight. The passage, *seized an axe and chopped the rolling-pin in two,* illustrates the danger of the ignorant possessing certain knowledge. The misuse of the knowledge and the subsequent ignorant way of dealing with the problem that ensued led to a problem twice as large as it was originally. So the ignorant are liable to mess up their lives more if they receive spiritual teaching and follow it in a wrong way than, they would if they did not receive any spiritual teaching at all. For example, an aspirant may hear teachings on the illusoriness of the world and detachment and feel that she or he is being spiritually minded and practicing the teachings by disregarding their practical realities and responsibilities in favor or meditating all the time, when in fact such actions will create severe negative ariu (karmic impressions) which will negate spiritual progress. Such aspirants are not worthy and will not be assisted. There must be worthiness, and that comes with maturity, devotion to the teaching, reverence, patience, time spent listening to, studying, reflecting and meditating upon the teaching, purification of the personality through physical hygiene, providing selfless service to society in accordance with the injunctions of Maat, and living in accordance with the precepts of Maat to purify the heart (mind). Another important point brought out by this story is that there seems to be an eagerness among the ancient Greek peoples to admit traveling to Ancient Egypt, as if it were a stamp of approval for their entry into society as professionals in their fields.

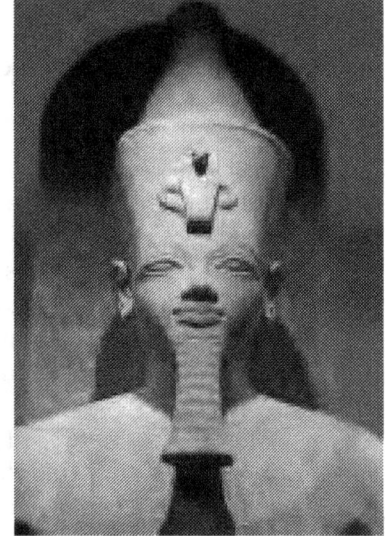

Figure: The Ancient Egyptian-African Pharaoh Amenhotep III (Memnon of the Greeks)

---

[113] P. Turner, trans, *Lucian: Satirical sketches* (Baltimore 1961), 215-217

Above: The Colossi of Memnon- built under Amenhotep III, 1,417 B.C.E. -1,379 B.C.E. 59 feet tall

Admonitions to Servants of the Temple and other Admonitions to Aspirants.

The Ptolemaic period texts (above) from Djebu (Edfu) Temple exhibit the same kind of impetus that is present in the "Instructions for Merikara," that were written over 2000 years earlier (Middle Kingdom Period):

> In the monthly service (Unut), wear the white sandals.
> Visit the Temple, observe the mysteries,
> Enter the shrine, eat bread in god's house.[114]

These kinds of injunctions are recorded in several places. The important point here is maintaining the rituals of spiritual life: visiting the Temple, wearing the special clothing, participating in the mysteries, etc. When the ritual of the Temple is maintained, the order of the individual spiritual practice as well as the society is maintained also. Actually the cosmic order is also maintained. If the offering is stopped, the sustenance is also withdrawn. Being with God is like a child who has a big brother or big sister. If the child is in a playground and the big bully comes after the child, the child will be beaten up, but what happens when the child's big brother comes in? There will be no problem any more. That is like being with God, what living in security is all about.

---

[114] M. Lichtheim, *Ancient Egyptian Literature,* Vol. I: *The Old and Middle Kingdoms* (Berkley 1973), 102

FROM: THE STEALE OF ABU:

"Be chief of the mysteries at festivals, know your mouth, come in Hetep (peace), enjoy life on earth but do not become attached to it, it is transitory."

Again, the important teaching about practicing the mysteries occurs in the stele of Abu: "Enjoy life" but don't become attached to it. The avid aspirant should reflect on these injunctions again and again, control, regulation of your senses, not going off like people like to do, with exuberance and having fun and constantly flying off in to activity and boisterousness. All that is counterproductive to your spiritual evolution and the deportment of the Neterian clergy. Those people who do not want to think about death and who want to "live life to the fullest" by pursuing thrill seeking activities or those who like to get caught up in entertainments so they do not think about the misery in their lives are not fit to be part of the Neterian clergy. The path of the clergy is not easy, but it is most rewarding, and in the end, the pleasure and peace of self-knowledge is greater than any temporary relief from worldly activities.

FROM THE STEALE OF DJEHUTI-NEFER:

"Consume pure foods and pure thoughts with pure hands, adore celestial beings, become associated with wise ones: sages, saints and prophets; make offerings to GOD."

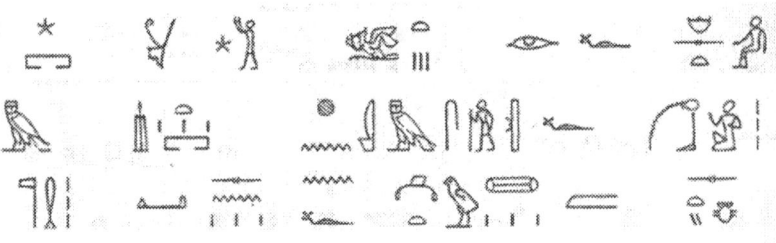

The celestial beings are the *neteru* (gods and goddesses). Saints are considered to be the *Shepsu*. The Shepsu would be more of the ancestral veneration, the departed enlightened ancestors. The enlightened human beings are *Akhu*. The sages and "wise ones" are the *Sebaiu*, who have attained insight into Akhu and prophets (seers) *Hemu* are the priests and priestesses.

Finding a place in the Sanctuary of God through Selfless Service

> (30) Set your goodness before people,
> Then you are greeted by all;
> One welcomes what is good, Spits upon what is bad.
> (31) Guard your tongue from harmful speech. Then others will love you.
> You will find your place in the Sanctuary, the house of God,
> Be kind to the poor.
> Get thee a seat in the sanctuary.
> Be strong to do the commandment of God.
> You will share in the offerings of your Lord.
>
> -Ancient Egyptian Teachings of Sage Amenemope.

The concept of being good to others implies caring for them and loving them; this is a fundamental aspect of Maat philosophy within Ancient Egyptian religion. This is a purifying practice, essential for developing the level of virtue that qualifies one to become one of the clergy. The important statement in the passage above is *Get thee a seat in the sanctuary*. Finding a place in the sanctuary means becoming part of the Temple ritual and that requires maturity, austerity, service and study of the teaching. Most people are strong in doing what they desire to do, to pursue pleasure, entertainments or wealth. Some pursue the teaching, but do so in their own way, according to the way that is comfortable to them so they do not have to follow difficult instructions or go against their egoistic notions. Others seem to be strong in going to church, but their strength is bogus because they are not doing so out of true desire, but out of fanaticism. There are many people who go to church every day, who speak about religious matters constantly, however this does not mean that they are enlightened beings or even pious beings necessarily. When there is sufficient ignorance, mental agitation and degradation in the mind due to guilt or fear, the mind seeks that which will offer relief. Some people choose movies, drugs or sex. Others choose religious fanaticism. Those who are part of cults or who fanatically go to the "legitimate" churches, mosques or Temples are actually suffering from the same illness, mental degradation. They are not fit for the practice of the higher mysteries. They must resolve their issues and find a balance between the spiritual life and the secular duties. They need to normalize before they spiritualize. The practice of the mysteries is intensive and all consuming, but it is not fanatical. It is an intelligent and enlightened predilection for the teaching and the Divine, born of maturity, balance and peace. That takes time to develop. This is why the early Greek initiates such as Pythagoras and Plato spent so much time in Egypt, decades in fact. Those who pursue the teaching and remain unbalanced are doing so in the wrong way, and will not be successful.

What is the Role of the King or Queen?

The King and Queen as High Priest

The "Per-Aah" or "Great House," is the institution of the seat of leadership in Ancient Egyptian civilization. The word Pharaoh is a corruption of the Ancient Egyptian word Per-Aah, and it is also erroneously translated as king. It is more related to caretaker, guardian and protector or shepherd. The Per-Aah was also the High Priest of the country in some periods. He or she was the political ruler and or the head of the religion. The main function was as promoter and protector of the spiritual traditions, economy, safety and general welfare of the country. The Per-Aah was seen as an incarnation of Heru, the divinity of order, truth, righteousness, and redemption. And the Per-Aah could be a man or woman. As such, the first duty of the Per-Aah was to maintain order and keep chaos (disorder, unrighteousness, famine, injustice, etc.) under control. High priests and priestesses assisted the Per-Aah and the day-to-day administration of the country was delegated to educated officials. In later times, the control of the priesthood was eroded and the nobility as well as military leaders ruled with more autonomous control. This, along with invasions and internal corruption, led to Egypt being conquered in the Late Period by Persians, Assyrians, Libyans, Greeks, Romans and Arabs. There were several Per-Aahs who were heads of state and at the same time not just heads of the Temples, but also spiritual philosophers. Some examples are Asar, Aset, Seti I, and Akhenaton. They promoted or introduced expansions into the spiritual philosophy and elevated particular divinities for general worship and social edification.

The Concept of Maat as the Foundation of the Neterian Priesthood

Udja medut means "weighing of words – the law – to judge." This is a science of ethics in which every aspirant in the Neterian clergy must become proficient. It is based on the Ancient Egyptian teachings of the Prt M Hru. In Ancient Egypt, the judges and all those connected with the judicial system were initiated into the teachings of Maat. Judges were priests and priestesses of Maat. Thus, those who would discharge the laws and regulations of society were well trained in the ethical and spiritual-mystical values of life. These principles included the application of justice, and the responsibility to serve society and promote harmony and the possibility for spiritual development in an atmosphere of freedom and peace, for only when there is justice and fairness in society can there be an abiding harmony and peace. Harmony and peace are necessary for the pursuit of true happiness and inner fulfillment in life. The opposite of *Maat* (righteousness) is *n-Maat* (unrighteousness) or *Isfet*-wrongdoing. Those who aspire to work as the clergy, upholding the Neterian culture, must gain a keen insight into the philosophy and practice of Maat Philosophy.[115]

Maat Philosophy and its Influence on Present Day Social Ethics

Since ancient times, beginning before 4,000 B.C.E., the Ancient Egyptian civilization based its system of social order and justice on Maat Philosophy. This philosophy has influenced present day African culture as well as present day societies and religious systems outside of Africa. Maat Philosophy is a system of values prescribing a way of life that is based on order, truth and justice, which was developed in Ancient Egypt (Kamit)/Africa. The Maat philosophy writings of Ancient Egypt encompass the Precepts of Maat, contained in Ancient Egyptian *Prt M Hru* Texts (more commonly known as the *Book of the Dead* or the *Book of Coming Forth by Day*), *The Ancient Egyptian Wisdom Texts*, *The Ari Maat Tomb Inscriptions*, *Blind Harpers Songs* and the *Hymns to Maat*. The most popular Maatian writings are known as the "Forty Two Laws (or Precepts) of Maat" which are contained in the *Prt M Hru* Texts.

After centuries of trying to stop the practice of African Religion and convert Africans to Christianity, the Catholic Church reversed itself and at the 1964 Vatican II conference of Bishops in Rome, officially accepted African Religion into the family of World religions as a full partner. Years later, on a visit to Benin, Pope John Paul II again apologized for centuries of denigration of African religion by the Western Culture. African religion is universally accepted as a distinct and legitimate form of spirituality and continues to be practiced by a substantial number of people in and outside of Africa. African religion is in a sense a conglomeration of seemingly different religious traditions. However, upon closer examination it becomes evident that most, if not all of them, exhibit certain common fundamental tenets that reveal their common origin and spiritual ideal. The factor of the compatibilities and fundamental agreements of the canons, Creeds, systems of belief, may be termed *African Religious Concordance* (ARC). Therefore, they are not different, but may be practiced differently in different countries in Africa.[116] African religion is practiced by many who on one hand profess to be converts to the western religions, while at the same time retaining the practice of some aspects of African religion in their life.

Two reasons for the persistence of African religion are the qualities of pantheism and *Humanism* that characterizes it. The African term *Ubuntu* means humanism. Humanism is a fundamental concern for the human condition, a caring for fellow human beings with respect to their well-being, but also it means a kind of openness, hospitality and compassion for those in need. The quality of Ubuntu has had the effect of tempering the harshness of other religions, as well as bringing to the forefront the sufferings and needs of others, and sometimes the inequities that are endured by others. Ubuntu is a kind of empathy and sympathy for others, and a heartfelt desire to share with others. Maat and Ubuntu are antithetical to the notions of egoistic hoarding, property ownership and wealth accumulation. Therefore they are in contradiction with capitalist, oligarchic, and tyrannical socio-economic systems. One important example of the effect of African religion and its quality of Ubuntu is the Aldura Church of Yoruba. In this church the Christian emphasis on salvation has given way to an approach that is more in line with the traditional needs of the people. The priests function as diviners, healers and ritual leaders. Those functions are not present in the western form of Christianity. The concept of humanism may be best expressed in the following quotations:

---

[115] See the book *Wisdom of Maati* by Sebai Muata Ashby
[116] See the book *African Origins of Civilization, Religion, Yoga Spirituality and Ethics Philosophy*, by Sebai Muata Ashby

The Priests and Priestesses of Ancient Egypt

About Ubuntu: N. Adu Kwabena-Essem is a freelance journalist, based in Accra, Ghana

> "African belief is basically the humanistic belief that doing good is good, while doing anything bad is bad. You are rewarded here on earth for your good deeds and punished for your iniquities. Indeed, many Africans believe that the ultimate punishment for bad or iniquitous behavior is death."

About Ubuntu: South Africa's Archbishop Desmond Tutu, winner of the Nobel Prize 1984:

> "You know when it is there, and it is obvious when it is absent. It has to do with what it means to be truly human, it refers to gentleness, to compassion, to hospitality, to openness to others, to vulnerability, to being available for others and to know that you are bound up with them in the bundle of life, for a person is only a person through other persons."

When compared to the concept of Ubuntu, the Kamitan concept of Ari Maat (Maatian Actions) is found to be in every way compatible with this concept of humanism or social awareness and caring. Maat is a philosophy, a spiritual symbol as well as a cosmic energy or force which pervades the entire universe. Maat is the path to promoting world order, justice, righteousness, correctness, harmony and peace. Maat is also the path that represents wisdom and spiritual awakening through balance and equanimity, as well as righteous living and selfless service to humanity. So Maat encompasses certain disciplines of right action that promote purity of heart and balance of mind. Maat is represented as a Goddess with a feather held to the side of her head by a bandana. She is sometimes depicted with wings, a papyrus scepter in one hand and holding an ankh (symbol of life) in her other hand.

In Kamit, the judges were initiated into the teachings of Maat, for as stated earlier, only when there is justice and fairness in society can there be abiding harmony and peace, which are necessary for the pursuit of true happiness and inner fulfillment in life. Thus, Kamitan spirituality includes a discipline for social order and harmony not unlike Confucianism of China or Dharma of India. Maat promotes social harmony and personal virtue that lead to spiritual Enlightenment.

Many people are aware of the 42 Laws or Precepts of Maat. They are declarations of purity (also known as *negative confessions)*, found in the *Prt M Hru* Texts, which a person who has lived a life of righteousness can utter at the time of the great judgment after death. All of the precepts concern moral rectitude in all aspects of life, which leads to social order. Order leads to peace, prosperity and harmony.

There are other injunctions given in the Wisdom Texts that serve as adjuncts to the 42 Precepts. The wisdom texts are elaborated in the tomb inscriptions of Ancient Egypt. In Chapter 125 of the *Prt M Hru* Texts , the person uttering the declarations states:

> "I have done God's will. I have given bread to the hungry, water to the thirsty, clothes to the clotheless and a boat to those who were shipwrecked. I made the prescribed offerings to the gods and goddesses and I also made offerings in the Temple to the glorious spirits. Therefore, protect me when I go to face The God." (For the full text see the *Book of the Dead* -translated by Sebai Muata Ashby)

In ancient times, the early Greeks adopted many teachings in relation to ethics and the concepts of Justice. This is attested to in the writings of classical Greek philosophers and historians such as Plato. Later the Judeo-Christian tradition adopted many tenets from the Maatian philosophy of Ancient Egypt. The Judeo-Christian Bible states that Moses led the Hebrews, who were by this time in reality people of Egyptian blood, out of Egypt into the Sinai desert where he was given the Ten Commandments by God. Moses, according the to the Old Testament scriptures, subsequently wrote the Pentateuch (the first five books of the Hebrew Scriptures) and gave these teachings to the people. Under the rulership of Joshua, the Hebrews gained control over the land of Palestine where they continued to mix with other Canaanites, who were themselves descendents of the Ethiopians and Egyptians. Under the rulership of King David (circa 1000-961 B.C.E.), the Hebrews became a local power. David's son, Solomon, ruled from around 961 to 922 B.C.E. and was famed for his wisdom. Many scholars have noted the close parallels between the Jewish teachings and the Ancient Egyptian teachings of Sage Amenemope. Solomon commissioned the building of the first Jewish Temple in Jerusalem. The term "Jewish" means specifically those tribes of the Egyptian/Canaanites that accepted the god Yahweh as their deity.

When the Biblical teachings known as The Beatitudes (group of blessings spoken by Jesus at the opening of the Sermon on the Mount, as recorded most fully in Matthew 5:3-12), the Ten Commandments Laws (given from God to Moses), the teachings of King Solomon (Proverbs), and the Prayer of Jesus (Our Father)[117] are compared to the Maatian and other Kamitan writings, the close similarities have led many scholars to conclude an ancient Egyptian origin for the teachings. Many Egyptologists now believe that the early Jews were well aquatinted with the Ancient Egyptian Wisdom Texts, especially the *Instructions of Amenemope*. The *Instructions of Amenemope* is particularly strikingly similar in concept and the form of the literary expression to the book of Proverbs in the Bible.

This section has not been presented just to show that the Judeo-Christian tradition developed primarily out of the Neterian tradition, but to also introduce the notion that Judaism, Christianity and Islam are latecomers in human religious history. Many people see the later, the newer, as something better and more advanced. That could be true if the new makes use of the old, builds on it and expands on it. That was not the case with the Western religious traditions. Actually, those western traditions originally sought to distance themselves from the African religious roots and in so doing they cut themselves off from the deeper teachings contained in the original spiritual system. They were left with the superficial religious teachings based on dogma and orthodoxy, devoid of mysticism and pantheistic insight which renders them intolerant and prone to fanatical idolatry. Actually, the early Jews, Christians and Muslims tried to destroy all traces of the earlier tradition and openly repudiated it, and in so doing, created a new form of religion that digressed instead of progressed. Therefore, it is important to examine the original teaching in order to discern the deficiencies in the western traditions and thereby restore humanity, harmony, peace and mysticism to human life. This should be the mission of the Neterian cleric as concerns the uplifting of society, and as for themselves, this same path will lead to the practice of authentic and powerful spirituality that will elevate them (the clergy) most effectively.

We close this section with the writings of Plato, who, while describing the experiences of Solon in Egypt, shows that there is a value in the ancient tradition, its age itself becoming like an investment that appreciates with time by virtue of its age. He also chides the Greek culture for not having such a tradition.

> "Solon said that, when he traveled thither (i.e., to Sais), he was received with much honour; and further that, when he inquired about ancient times from the priests who knew most of such matters he discovered that neither he nor any other Greek had any knowledge of antiquity worth speaking of Once, wishing to lead them on to talk about ancient times, he set about telling them the most venerable of our legends, about Phoroneus the reputed first man and Niobe, and the story how Deucalion and Pyrrha survived the deluge. He traced the pedigree of their descendants, and tried, by reckoning the generations, to compute how many years had passed, since those events.
> Solon, Solon, "said one of the priests (ancient Egyptian)," a very old man, "you Greeks are always children; in Greece there is no such thing as an old man." "What do you mean?" Solon asked.
> You are all young in your minds," said the priest, "which hold no store of old belief based on long tradition, no knowledge hoary with age.""[118]

---

[117] Likened to the Hymns of Amun
[118] F M. Cornford, trans., *Plato's Cosmology: The "Timaeus" of Plato* (Indianapolis, n.d.), 14-15 *(= Timaeus,* chaps. 21-22).

Selfless Service is the Mainstay of the Life of the Neterian Clergy

Service is an important ingredient in the development of spiritual life. In selfless service one adopts the attitude of seeing and serving the Divine in everyone and every creature, and one is to feel as an instrument of the Divine, working to help the less able. The following are some important points to keep in mind when practicing selfless service.

Having controlled the body, speech and thoughts, a person who lives by Maat should see {him/her} self as an instrument of the Divine, being used to bring harmony, peace, and help to the world. All human beings and nature are expressions of the Divine. Serving human beings and nature is serving the Supreme Divine Self (God).

In Chapter 34, Verse 10 of the *Pert M Hru* scripture, the initiate states that {he/she} has become a spiritual doctor: *There are sick, very ill people. I go to them, I spit on the arms, I set the shoulder, and I cleanse them.* As a servant of the Divine Self, a person who lives by Maat is also a healer. Just as it would be inappropriate for a medical doctor to lose {his/her} patience with {his/her} patient because the person is complaining due to their illness, so too it is inappropriate for an initiate to become angry with the masses of worldly-minded people, suffering from the illness of ignorance of their true essence. So, it must be clearly and profoundly understood that in serving, you are serving the true Self, not the ego. Again, Chapter 33 of the *Pert m Heru* text provides three important verses that every cleric must always remember and always practice.

Excerpts of Chapter 33(125) of the *Pert M Heru*

1. I have lived by righteousness and truth while on earth. I live in righteousness and truth; I feed upon right and truth in my heart. I have done what is required to live in harmony in society and the gods and goddesses are also satisfied that I have worshipped rightly.
2. I have done God's will. I have given bread to the hungry, water to the thirsty, clothes to the clotheless and a boat to those who were shipwrecked. I made the prescribed offerings to the gods and goddesses and I also made offerings in the Temple to the glorious spirits.
3. Therefore, protect me when I go to face The God.

A person who lives the higher aspects of Maat should not expect a particular result from their actions. In other words, one does not perform actions and wait for a reward or praises, and though working to achieve success in the project, one should not develop the expectation that one's efforts will succeed, because there may be failure in what one is trying to accomplish. If a person who lives by Maat focuses on the success of the project or on the success as being a source of pleasure and peace, and failure occurs, the mind will become so imbalanced that it will negate the positive developments of personality integration, expansion and concentration which occurred as the project was pursued. Therefore, one's focus should be on doing one's part by performing the service, and letting the Divine handle the results. This promotes selflessness and effacement of the ego and provides a person who lives by Maat with peace and the ability to be more qualitative in the work being performed (without the egoistic content), and more harmonious, which will lead to being more sensitive to the needs of others and of the existence of the Spirit as the very essence of one's being.

The Lifestyle of Priests and Priestesses and their Service to God and Society

This philosophy of service to humanity as opposed to leaving humanity and dwelling in isolation is one of the hallmarks of (Kamitan) culture. Priests and Priestesses were required to serve the laity in various capacities, ministerial, medical, legal, etc., and at the same time their duties to the Temple were maintained in a balanced manner. At some point the clergy could also follow the path as a monastic order, after a life of service. The following passages from the writings of Porphyry illustrate the ideal of the Neterian priests and priestesses of ancient times.

> "The priests (of Ancient Egypt), having renounced all other occupation and human labour, devoted their whole life to contemplation and vision of things divine. By vision they achieve honour, safety and piety, by contemplation of knowledge, and through both a discipline of lifestyle which is secret and has the dignity of antiquity. Living always with divine knowledge and inspiration puts one beyond all greed, restrains the passions, and makes life alert for understanding. They practiced simplicity, restraint, self-control, perseverance and in everything justice and absence of greed.... Their walk was disciplined, and they practiced controlling their gaze, so that if they chose they did not blink. Their laughter was rare, and if did happen, did not go beyond a smile. They kept their hands always within their clothing... Their lifestyle was frugal and simple. Some tasted no wine at all, others a very little: they accused it of causing damage to the nerves and a fullness in the head which impedes research, and of producing desire for sex."[119]

The passage above was presented earlier in this book, and is being repeated here again due to its great significance, in order to highlight different teachings in reference to the character and philosophy of the priests and priestesses of Ancient Egypt. It must be clearly understood that the primary social comportment of the Neterian clergy is reserved. They are not extraverted in mixed company, with the worldly. They do not seek attention, to stand out in a crowd as celebrities or to be admired. They are not vain or conceited, but humble and unassuming. Any glory they achieve through their work is ascribed to God who operates behind all. Those who are not prepared to take up this form of lifestyle should pursue other goals until they have finally realized the falsehood of worldly social interactions and the meaninglessness of worldly attainments as pertaining to human existence.

Shaved Hair, Baldness and the Philosophy of Nothingness of the Ancient Egyptian Priests and Priestesses

Diodorus Siculus (Greek Historian) writes in the time of Augustus (first century B.C.):
(highlighted portions {italics} specifically refer to the clergy-highlighted portions by Ashby)

> "*for all (ancient Egyptian priests) are clean who are engaged in the service of the gods, keeping themselves shaven, like the Ethiopian priests, and having the same dress and form of staff, which is shaped like a plough* and is carried by their kings ...."

One important feature of Kamitan culture is the practice of shaving off the hair of the body and wearing wigs, which was practiced by men and women alike. It has been found that this is a highly effective way to protect the head from the great heat of the desert sun during the day and provide coolness at night. It is even better than wearing a turban. Personal hygiene is a peculiar and highly important feature of the Neterian clergy. It was to this feature of the lifestyle that Ancient Egyptian culture owed a great deal for its renowned health and longevity. It was a longstanding practice of the Egyptian clergy to bathe three times daily. Their hygiene was legendary in the ancient world.

---

[119] *Porphyry*, On Abstinence from Killing Animals, trans. Gillian Clark (Ithaak, 1999). (= *De abstentia*, Book IV, chap 6)

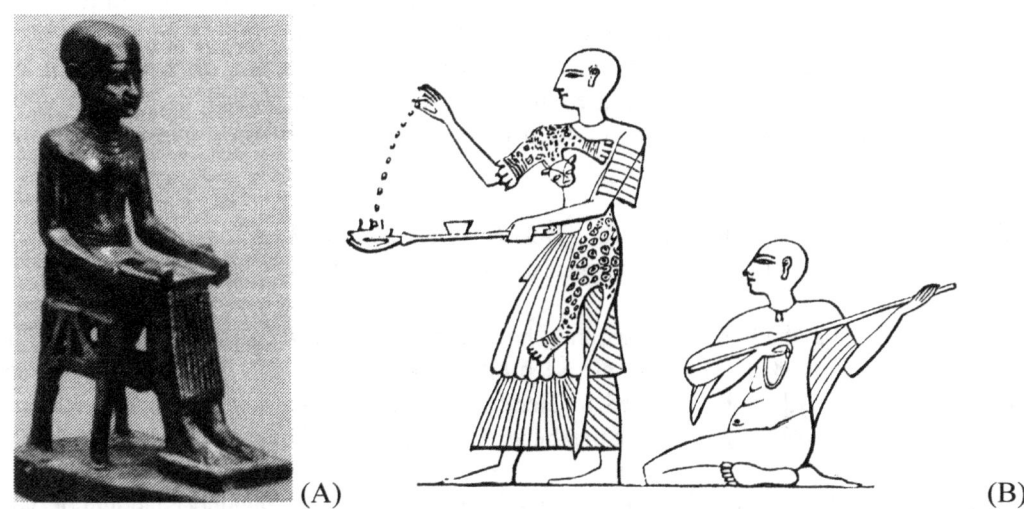

Imhotep, an Ancient Egyptian Sage who lived in the Old Kingdom Period (5,000-2,500 B.C.E.) is often depicted as a seated baldheaded man wearing a skullcap (A). The priests (B) are often depicted in this way as well. Certain prominent divinities were also bald and wore skullcaps. The god Ptah and the goddess Net are primary examples.

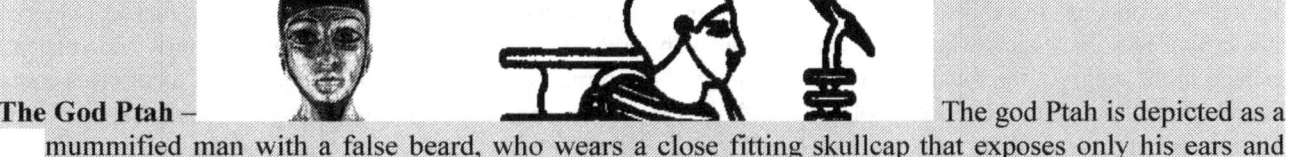

The God Ptah – The god Ptah is depicted as a mummified man with a false beard, who wears a close fitting skullcap that exposes only his ears and face.

Goddess Nat- (Net Anet, Anat {Neith to the Greeks}). Goddess Nat is depicted wearing the hawk, the crown of Lower Egypt or the weaving spool. She may also be depicted wearing the shield that has two crossed arrows, or the red crown of Lower Egypt. Sometimes she is seen wearing a skullcap similar to that of Ptah.

The concept of baldness *ushu* – [empty-bald- effaced- hairless-hair falling out- lacking-deprived] is related to the concept of nothingness *ush* – [nothingness- emptiness]; these are also related to the concept of voidness or absence of created things *Nerutef* -[*Growthless, barren*]. In the deepest and darkest realm of the Duat (Astral Plane) is Asar, Himself, and this is why Asar is referred to as the "Lord of the Perfect Black" and is often depicted as being black or green of hue. It is also why Nut, Aset, and Hetheru are also described as "dark-skinned." They are emanations from this realm of blackness, which is described as a void or "*nothingness*" in the hieroglyphic papyrus entitled *The Laments of Aset and Nebthet*. This notion of nothingness is akin to the Buddhist notion of *Shunya* or the "void," which refers to the area of consciousness that is devoid of mental concepts and thoughts. When there are no thoughts or forms in the mind, it becomes calm, expansive and peaceful. When there are thoughts in the mind, the mental awareness is narrowed and defined in terms of concepts. If the mind is confined to these concepts and narrow forms of thought, then it is confined to that which is limited and temporal. If it eradicates its desires, cravings and illusions, then it becomes aware of the innermost reality and realizes its connection to the entire cosmos.

The following passage from Chapter 33 of the *Prt M Hru (Egyptian Book of Coming Forth By Day)* provides insight into this important concept of nothingness as the place to discover the highest wisdom.

> "I have entered into the House of Asar and I have removed the head coverings of him that is therein. I have entered into Rastau, [1] and I have seen the Hidden One[2] who is therein. I was hidden but I found the boundary.[3] I journeyed to Nerutef[4] and He who was therein covered me with a garment....Verily He (Asar)[5] told me the things which concerned Himself."

The mystical meaning behind the hekau just presented is very important to the understanding of what is meant by the terms "Enlightenment" and "mystical experience." 1-Rasta or Restau refers to the site of the grave of Asar, 2- The "Hidden One" refers to the Shetai or Hidden Supreme Being who is known as Asar-Amun. 3-Here the Initiate discovered that he/she was able to find the boundary and was able to discover the abode of the "Hidden One"; he / she was able to discover the difference between what is real and what is illusion, and was able to traverse the illusory Duat and discover the special location wherein there is Supreme Peace and Immortality. 4-Nerutef (Nrutef, Anrutef, Yanrtf) refers to the mythological site of the grave of Asar or the innermost shrine. 5-This line imparts the wisdom that God Him/Herself is the one who ultimately gives the highest wisdom about God. All of the teachings of the scriptures are only incomplete and indirect descriptions of God because God transcends any and all mental concepts. Even though the spiritual scriptures are given by Sages and Saints who are in communion with God, the mediums of communication, words and concepts, remain in the realm of the mind. Therefore, the study of the scriptures and various rituals cannot in themselves confer Enlightenment or mystical experience of union with the Divine. For that to occur it is necessary to actually experience the Divine, and in order for this to occur it is necessary to discover one's true essence as one with God, for only by becoming one with something can that thing be known. In this form of knowing there is experience, unlike intellectual knowledge, which does not include experience, but only theory.

Marriage, Sexuality and Celibacy for Neterian Priests and Priestesses

In Ancient Egypt, marriage was considered a stabilizing aspect in society. This is evident from the hieroglyphic text which denotes the word for marriage in the Ancient Egyptian language itself. These hieroglyphs provide important keys to understanding the Kamitan culture as it relates to the concepts of male-female interrelations and the purpose of marriage.

The following Ancient Egyptian hieroglyphs about the concept of marriage give insight into its nature as a social institution and the human marital relationship.

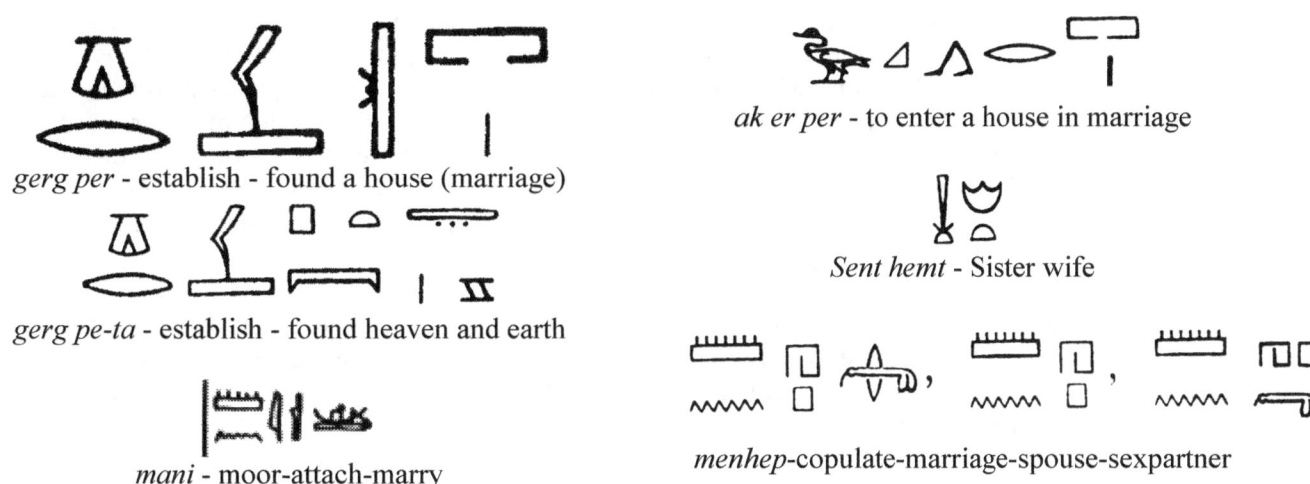

gerg per - establish - found a house (marriage)

gerg pe-ta - establish - found heaven and earth

mani - moor-attach-marry

ak er per - to enter a house in marriage

Sent hemt - Sister wife

menhep-copulate-marriage-spouse-sexpartner

The following are guidelines based on the teachings; they should be adjusted in their application relative to the present day conditions. The main objective of marriage from the perspective of society is to engender the continuation of humanity. From the perspective of the ignorant soul, its purpose is to provide a framework through which the soul can have certain experiences in time and space within a marital context. Two people of the opposite sex come together to make a household wherein they can cooperate to raise a family. The man enters the house with his sister, and the woman enters the house with her brother (not blood relative – metaphorically all men and women are brothers and sisters…children of the one Father-Mother God).

It is important to understand that in ancient times the priests and priestess discovered the best arrangement for human beings who want to practice advanced spirituality, that is, pursue the path of spiritual Enlightenment and immortality. It is to serve humanity by serving God. The instructions given in the Neterian texts provide guidelines for that service. Human beings should study the mysteries, participate in the Temple rituals, become virtuous and give drink to the thirsty, food to the hungry, clothes to the clotheless and shelter to the homeless. One way to serve humanity is to promote peace and prosperity for society. Marriage is a means to achieve that peace in a well ordered and mentally balanced society. Marriage allows the wild tendencies of the personality to be channelized into productive endeavors. Marriage allows the desires for companionship and procreation to be expressed in an orderly manner, in such a way that these endeavors lead to eventual sublimation of those desires into fulfillment in insight and love of the transcendental Divine. If they are allowed to run free society, will degrade to chaos, with rampant promiscuity, divorce, children born without responsible parents to take care of them, disease and many other problems. So those human beings who are at a level of consciousness that they desire the experience of worldly human romantic and sexual relationships should be encouraged to follow the householder life. Through such a relationship, a person with worldly tendencies and egoistic notions can develop into a caring and insightful personality. If the worldly tendencies of the personality are controlled, the egoism and selfishness turns into caring and service through love of someone other than self. Actually, that is a lower mystery of life. When a person is through with the lower mysteries of human interrelationships, then they can seek higher knowledge from interacting with the neteru through myth and ritual. That knowledge allows a person to grow to the capacity of having the divine marriage, the marriage with the Neter, the Divine itself.

In ancient times, since the population was low and society was well ordered along agrarian lines, it was possible to freely have children, and then look forward to old age and greater time spent at the Temple. In the present day, the chaos of society does not allow for such freedom. Another issue is that due to economic concerns and the limited number of suitable partners, it is very difficult to find elevated members of the opposite sex to enter into a Neterian marriage. Most people in the general society are ignorant of the Neterian culture and have been inculcated with orthodox western religious beliefs or western secular ideals. Therefore, it is very challenging for a person practicing Neterian spirituality, especially at the level of the priesthood, to be married to someone who is of a different faith or philosophy, especially orthodox, and be able to develop a relationship that can promote peace and prosperity and the service of Neter. Further, the unprecedented level of social psychosis and frustration has generally reduced the pool of reasonably well-integrated human beings, even by worldly standards of normalcy. Therefore, sexual and marital as well as close business relationships and partnerships with members of other traditions that are not compatible with the Neterian culture are to be discouraged.

The Neterian marriage is an agreement made by two individuals to come together to make a home and produce a family. However, for priests and priestesses, the discipline is different than that of the masses. The higher purpose of spiritual living is to grow in patience, forbearance, nonviolence, self-control, detachment, and cosmic love, love beyond family, community and country.

Priests and priestesses may be married or unmarried. If they are married, they must practice ritual cleansing before entering the Temple if they have engaged in sexual intercourse. So whether married or not, the discipline of celibacy is to be observed by all who work as priests and priestesses. Celibacy allows the energy of the sexual encounter to be dissipated and the personality will be able to apply him/herself to the worship of the Divine. Also, realize that in ancient times, the pressure to have sex that is so prevalent in modern culture was not there. Therefore, an aspirant needs to control the sensory input of the world, avoiding company with those who are lewd, vulgar or of degraded culture, as well as those forms of entertainment that promote lewdness, profanity and vulgarity.

The ideal of marriage in Neterian culture is not the same as the modern culture. Partners are not forced to stay together if they do not want to be married, nor are they forced or coerced to marry in a Temple. They unite by choice and they can separate by choice. Also, unions are not arranged by the parents. However, their relationships are not based on externalities such as sex or unnatural pleasure-seeking. Those things will always lead to frustration and eventual divorce, because a mind that is in a relationship for pleasure only, seeking externalities such as sex-appeal and good looks, will be constantly engaged in adulterous thought processes that will eventually compel the mind to act impulsively and promiscuously with the senses, and eventually with the genitals. Marriage is to be based on Maat, righteousness. Any relation that is based on truth will be fruitful and lead to the evolution of all concerned. In such a relationship, there is a greater capacity to grow and a greater capacity for forgiveness and selflessness. So if a Neterian follower wishes to marry in order to experience the householder life, they may do so, but that should not interfere with the work at the Temple and the practice of control of the sex urge. It is more difficult in the present day to have the householder-priesthood lifestyle due to economic reasons and other forms of social strife. If there is a conflict between these two choices, the aspirant should reflect on what is most important to them and follow that.

Those who are married and cooperating with each other to follow the path of advancing spirituality should continue in their partnership, but with the ideal of growing in independence and greater devotion to the Temple work. Partners may or may not work in the same projects (Temple) together. Those who are ready to be unmarried and dedicate themselves fully to the path of Neterian spirituality should do so.

The important point to understand is that in order to have positive spiritual evolution, there can and should be "some" friction in a relationship. Their needs to be some challenge, some obstacles in the interpersonal relationships as well as the outer social environment as well (at work, at school, in politics, etc.); otherwise the ego becomes complacent and the soul will not evolve. But if there is too much strife, sufficient strife to interfere with the practice of the teachings or if there is unrighteousness (one person acting in contradiction with the precepts of Maat) that interferes with the proper practice of the spiritual disciplines and rituals, partners should consider separating if the conflicts cannot be resolved. Couples should take regular spiritual retreats and they should also spend time alone, away from each other. It should be understood that there is no abiding happiness in the world and no abiding sorrow either; however, both can be a trap if encountered in excess. Too much pleasure can lead to stagnation in the spiritual life because when everything is seen as good and wonderful (from an egoistic perspective), there is no impetus to seek a better answer to the mysteries of life. Also, too much strife does not allow the movement of spiritual inquiry to proceed properly because there will be too much stress. (For more details on relationships, see the book *Egyptian Tantra Yoga* by Sebai Muata Ashby)

Below The Priest and Priestess (fir right) Present offerings to the tomb owner and spouse

Neterianism and Sexual Misconduct.

 *nedjmmit* – "sexual delights".

The goal of Kamitan spirituality is for an individual to come into harmony with the cosmos (attain Nehast). It must be clearly understood that Neterian spirituality is founded on Maat Philosophy. Maat Philosophy recognizes the harmony in the natural order of the universe, i.e, the sun rises in the East, and sets in the West, water runs down hill, not uphill, fire burns upwards, not downwards, etc. Within this order, sexual union is harmonious (Maat) between man and woman. This kind of union leads to the conception of a child. So the union between a man and a woman perpetuates life just as nature strives to perpetuate life in its natural order. Same sex unions do not produce offspring so they do not promote the natural order of nature.

Persons who label themselves as homosexuals have maintained extreme attachments to a particular sex, which carries over into future lifetimes, giving them urges that, due to weak will and ignorance of the higher spiritual teachings, they are unable to control. Thus, they are correct when they say they are born with these urges, born the way they are. The erroneous impressions they created in previous lifetimes were so strong that they manifested in this present lifetime as a homosexual personality. But this is not their true identity, and therefore, not an abiding reality. Just as heterosexual people are not either. Through reincarnation, souls have existed as female, male and homosexuals in the past. As the Neterian scriptures instruct: "Sex is a thing of bodies, not of souls." Thus, some persons who previously considered themselves to be homosexuals have been able to move beyond such relationships to engage in heterosexual relationships. In other words, they were able to convert/transform their mental impressions from being homosexually inclined to being heterosexually inclined.

In any case, the goal of higher spirituality is to transcend gender altogether to realize the deeper genderless essence of the spirit within. Thus, the practice of Kamitan spirituality would be the same for hetero or homo - sexual personalities. Heterosexuals and homosexuals alike need to control the sex urge and the Pert M Heru texts provide guidelines on what the regulations are for those who want to follow Neterian spirituality and culture.

Firstly, sexual misconduct is not a sin in the sense of the western Judeo-Christian-Islamic culture. In Neterian philosophy it is seen as a movement in ignorance away from order and truth towards unrighteousness and ignorance. In Neterian culture, ordinary people are encouraged to form families to perpetuate the culture and so that people may grow through family relationships. From the Prt M Hru we learn that: *nek* - sexual intercourse with a woman *zthken* - is allowed for a man. However, adultery is prohibited and excessive ejaculation (masturbation) is also not permitted. Also, sodomy or fornication is not permitted. Sodomy *nekek* and *nek nekek* - sex with a sodomite are not permitted.

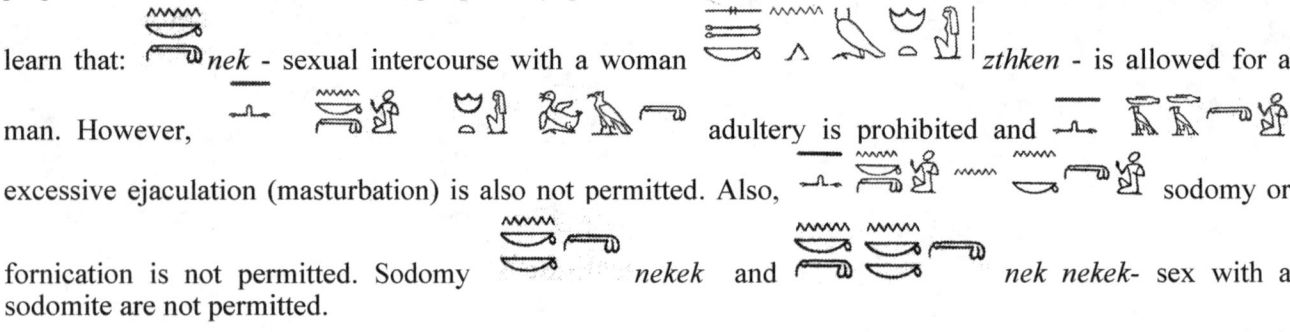

Sodomy is contrasted from the mysticism of Gods union with himself as an androgynous being. *Nekim-f-djesef* sex with himself – is what Ra did to create the world. He encompasses the male and female creative principles within himself. Homosexuality is not the same as androgyny because homosexuality is an egoistic desire for another sexual being, just like heterosexuality. Androgyny is the unity of opposites and the extinguishing of sex desire in the oneness of the creative Divine principle.

So the focus of mystical spirituality, for all aspirants, regardless of their sexual orientation, is to purify themselves from seeking the transient pleasures of the world, to seeking the source of all pleasure, and the only source of true, abiding happiness, Nehast or Enlightenment. Thus, everyone needs to practice control of the sex urges as well as dispassion and detachment.

Yes, this does mean that eventually one is to discover a form of transcendental fulfillment beyond sex. That is hard even for most initiates to believe and accept. This teaching was explained in Chapter 175 of the Prt M Hru texts.[120] If one has this level of understanding, then the question of being involved in a sexual relationship with someone of the opposite or same sex becomes moot. Seeking and engaging in sexual relationships with others (of the opposite or same sex) to fulfill one's desire for happiness reinforces two erroneous concepts: First, that one is a physical being, and the physicality of one's existence, rather than one being a soul that is beyond physical existence, and therefore, sexual relationships, and secondly, that true abiding happiness can be found through outer (worldly) experiences and interrelationships, rather than through one's inner experience of oneness with the Divine. Thus, the desire to have sex for pleasure, as with the desire to seek abiding pleasure (happiness) in the world of time in space by any other means, is erroneous and will be fleeting and unfulfilling in the end. True abiding happiness cannot be acquired through sexual relationships with other human beings, or through any attainments in the world of time and space.

Furthermore, at the highest level of the teachings, there are no individual souls....there is only the one Divine Self. Believing that an individual exists as an individual soul is a lower level of spiritual teaching to assist the transition of the understanding of aspirant's from knowing themselves as a physical individual being, to understanding that they are not physical beings, but spiritual beings. Thus, the teachings support the idea of the existence of individual souls for those who are at the lower level of understanding, but eventually one must let go of their individuality even at the soul level to attain Nehast, and discover one's true Self, the only being in existence.

When one has this perspective, there is no need to become involved in relationships to attain happiness and fulfillment... because it is all you. And since you are complete, encompassing all, there is no need to connect with others to feel wholeness. The ocean, encompassing all waves and being full and complete, has no need to unite with an individual wave to feel complete, whole and full. This is why sages generally are celibate.... it is not a strain for them as it is for striving aspirants, since having discovered their true all-pervasive, all-encompassing essence, there is no need for them to seek lower levels of transient pleasure since they are experiencing the higher peace and fulfillment. Thus, enlightened sages engage in relationships at a practical level, in accordance with their past *ariu (*karma) that is running its course.

All this being said is more for your own understanding, rather than facilitating you to be able to bring the teachings to homosexual personalities, because most homosexual personalities, and this is even more reinforced because they are / have been struggling for acceptance and validation from general society, identify themselves, their very essence with their homosexual ego-personality, rather than seeing their homosexuality as something that they do, separate from their true essence. They often make statements to the effect, "I have been this way since I was a child. I always knew this is who I am." Of course these types of statements, {reinforcing one's identity as being an individual, other than the one Divine Self} from the perspective of homosexuality or heterosexuality, are erroneous from a spiritual point of view. But you will not find many homosexual personalities willing to let go of their homosexual identity, and thus, they will not be able to practice higher mystical spirituality, which requires letting go of the physical identity and identification of oneself as male or female (except as fitting to deal with practical reality)... and of course the same goes for heterosexuals who are also unable to let go of their physical or individual identity.

The spirituality practiced by many homosexuals is more of a quasi spirituality...something they have created to validate their lifestyle, and themselves as human beings, just as heterosexuals have created a culture that supports and affirms heterosexuality. Heterosexuality is more acceptable to the teachings because it is closer to the order of nature and when a human being lives in harmony with nature they are

---

[120] See *The Egyptian Book of the Dead* by Muata Ashby

more apt to be able to transcend it. Thus ultimately, if one's spiritual movement does not include all three levels of spiritual practice in advanced religion: Myth, Ritual and Mysticism, which includes the precepts of Maat discussed above related to sex regulations, it cannot be considered as true, authentic religion or spiritual practice. More can be found on what authentic spirituality is in our books: *Resurrecting Osiris, Initiation into Egyptian Yoga*, and the *Book of the Dead*, as well as some of the other books.

Thus, though the path of Kamitan spirituality is open to all, all are not able to practice it in an advanced manner due to the intensity of the disciplinary nature of it, including mastering the precepts of Maat. Such personalities would have difficulty following any other authentic mystical tradition for the same reason. "Many are called, few are chosen." Therefore, just as those who practice adultery cannot be allowed to serve as priests and priestesses, those who are homosexual cannot be allowed either. Priests and priestesses are leaders and examples for the community to follow. Those who would desire to become Neterian clerics must be willing to renounce the lower erroneous notions and adhere to the regulations of Maat in all sexual matters. Being a teacher of the Neterian path means following a life of order and truth, that is, the Maati, the truth of the practical world, but ultimately also the truth that transcends the world and time and space.

Vegetarianism, Celibacy and Self-Control of the Neterian Clergy

The teachings of vegetarianism and control of the sex urge of the clergy are well documented. If there is no control in these areas, the higher aspects of the teachings and their practices will not be understood easily or correctly. Therefore, it is enjoined that aspirants should gradually turn towards a live of self-control, discipline and purity in order to allow the mind and body to settle so as to be able to peacefully enter into higher states of consciousness.

Teachings from the Temple of Aset (Isis) on Vegetarianism for the Initiates (Spiritual Aspirants): "Plutarch, a student of the mysteries of Aset, reported that the initiates followed a strict diet made up of vegetables and fruits and *abstained from particular kinds of foods* (swine, sheep, fish, etc.)..."

Teachings from the *Egyptian Book of the Dead (Pert em Heru* Text *)* on Vegetarianism and Celibacy. (Note: Chapter numbers refer to Chapters in the text. Translated text by Dr. Muata Ashby) In Chapter 36, of the *Pert Em Heru*, the chapter of "Entering the inner shrine, making the offering and becoming one with Asar:"

> "Henceforth, this chapter shall be recited by a person who is purified and washed;
> one who has not eaten animal flesh or fish."

Chapter 10, Verse 11:

> "...And behold, these things (mysteries of the Temple) shall be performed
> by one who is clean and pure,
> a person who has eaten neither meat nor fish and who has not had sexual intercourse."

Chapter 31:69:

> "This Chapter can be known by those who recite it and study it when they see no more, hear
> no more, have no more sexual intercourse and eat no meat or fish."

From Herodotus:

> It was the Egyptians who first made it an offence against piety to have intercourse with women in Temples, or to enter Temples after intercourse without having previously washed. Hardly any nation except the Egyptians and Greeks has any such scruple, but

nearly all consider men and women to be, in this respect, no different from animals, which, whether they are beasts or birds, they constantly see coupling in Temples and sacred places-and if the god concerned had any objection to this, he would not allow it to occur.[121]

The practice of vegetarianism may be considered both a discipline and also a lifestyle. There are several references to the practice of vegetarianism in Ancient Egypt. The cow was revered there since ancient times, well before the emergence of Hinduism, which also upholds this custom of revering the cow. The general diet of the Ancient Egyptians included a mostly vegetarian diet and fasting. The dietetic concept adopted by Hippocrates, that improper foods are the cause of disease, was espoused by the Ancient Egyptians in the early Dynastic Period.

Kamitan Proverb:

>"The source of illness is the food you ingest;
> to purge the dreadful UKHEDU which lurks in your bowels,
> for three consecutive days each month purge yourself with a cattle horn,
> its sharp end clipped off so as to create a small opening (for water to run through)."

The initiates were required to keep a much more restrictive dietary regimen than the general populous, which excluded not only meats (including fish), but also alcoholic beverages and carnal indulgences. These austerities constituted an advanced form of ascetic lifestyle that allowed the Ancient Egyptian initiates to pursue the paths of spiritual development, unhindered by the proclivities of the lower nature. Ancient Egyptian Temple practices led to the development of Western Monasticism in Christianity, Judaism and Islam. The following ancient texts are instructive in these disciplines.

> "The priests (of Ancient Egypt), having renounced all other occupation and human labour, devoted their whole life to contemplation and vision of things divine. By vision they achieve honour, safety and piety, by contemplation of knowledge, and through both a discipline of lifestyle which is secret and has the dignity of antiquity. Living always with divine knowledge and inspiration puts one beyond all greed, restrains the passions, and makes life alert for understanding. They practiced simplicity, restraint, self-control, perseverance and in everything justice and absence of greed.... Their walk was disciplined, and they practiced controlling their gaze, so that if they chose they did not blink. Their laughter was rare, and if did happen, did not go beyond a smile. They kept their hands always within their clothing. . . . Their lifestyle was frugal and simple. Some tasted no wine at all, others a very little: they accused it of causing damage to the nerves and a fullness in the head which impedes research, and of producing desire for sex."[122]

Plutarch outlined the teachings of the Temple of Aset (Isis-Ancient Egypt) for the proper behavior of initiates in his writings about his experiences as an initiate of (Aset) Isis. In the following excerpts Plutarch describes the purpose and procedure of the diet observed by the initiates of Aset, and the goal to be attained through the rigorous spiritual program. Though presented earlier, the importance of this text merits revisiting it again for some other important teachings.

> "To desire, therefore, and covet after truth, those truths more especially which concern the divine nature, is to aspire to be partakers of that nature itself (1), and to profess that all our studies and inquiries (2) are devoted to the acquisition of holiness. This occupation is surely more truly religious than any external (3) purifications or mere service of the Temple can be (4). But more especially must such a disposition of mind be highly acceptable to that

---

[121] De Selincourt, *Herodotus,* 154 (= *Histories,* II, chap. 64).
[122] *Porphyry,* On Abstinence from Killing Animals, trans. Gillian Clark (Ithaak, 1999). (= *De abstentia,* Book IV, chap 6)

goddess to whose service you are dedicated, for her special characteristics are wisdom and foresight, and her very name seems to express the peculiar relation which she bears to knowledge. For "Isis" is a Greek word, and means "knowledge or wisdom,"(5) and "Typhon," (Set) the name of her professed adversary, is also a Greek word, and means " pride and insolence."(6) This latter name is well adapted to one who, full of ignorance and error, tears in pieces (7) and conceals that holy doctrine (about Asar) which the goddess collects, compiles, and delivers to those who aspire after the most perfect participation in the divine nature. This doctrine inculcates a steady perseverance in one uniform and temperate course of life (8), and an abstinence from particular kinds of foods (9), as well as from all indulgence of the carnal appetite (10), and it restrains the intemperate and voluptuous part within due bounds, and at the same time habituates her votaries to undergo those austere and rigid ceremonies which their religion obliges them to observe. The end and aim of all these toils and labors is the attainment of the knowledge of the First and Chief Being (11), who alone is the object of the understanding of the mind; and this knowledge the goddess invites us to seek after, as being near and dwelling continually (12) with her. And this also is what the very name of her Temple promiseth to us, that is to say, the knowledge and understanding of the eternal and self-existent Being - now it is called "Iseion," which suggests that if we approach the Temple of the goddess rightly, we shall obtain the knowledge of that eternal and self existent Being."

The practice of vegetarianism is important because non-vegetarian foods intensify the physical experience of embodiment and distract the mind by creating impressions in the subconscious and unconscious, which will produce future cravings and desires. This state of mind renders the individual incapable of concentration on significant worldly or high spiritual achievements. Secondly, control of the sexual urge leads to control of the sexual Life Force energy,[123] which can then be directed towards higher mental and spiritual achievement. Further, overindulgence in sexual activity tends to wear down the immunity as it wears down the mental capacity, and one becomes a slave to sensual passions and susceptible to sexual and non-sex related diseases. Sexuality also has the potential to entangle a person in relationships which may not be conducive to the proper conduct of spiritual life and may draw the aspirant away from their studies and disciplines.

(For more details see the books *Egyptian Tantra Yoga* and *Kamitan Diet* by Sebai Muata Ashby)

---

[123] The concept of the Life Force will be explained in detail later.

The Priests and Priestesses of Ancient Egypt

Below: Fragment of the Stela of Priest Userhat. He is shown with his wife. He is testifying to his virtues and his trust in God.

Faithfulness to the Tradition

In the modern day technically advanced society, it has become fashionable to take things and rework them and call them something else that can be owned, marketed and sold. One example of that is taking a style of clothing from another country, making changes in it and selling it. In Neterian spiritual culture the problem is compounded because if changes are made in a teaching, it loses its character. Note that changes are allowed in the method of dissemination of the teachings, but not in the transcendental and perennial principles of the teachings.

"Do not perform the sacred services any way you please-what would be the purpose of looking at the old writings? The ritual of the Temple is in your hands, and it is what your children study-"[124]

There are many people who like to make adjustments in fundamental aspects of the teachings and that is incorrect. The teaching should be carried forth as the ancient founders intended, but this does not mean that the teaching remains stagnant or that there should be a blind reenactment of a ritual without knowing its deeper meaning. That too would be a degraded movement in the practice. However, the ancient texts should be consulted and the fundamental elements of the teaching, which are universal and timeless, should be followed faithfully, even if minor changes are made to accommodate present day technological advances. Also, it is allowed for qualified priests and priestesses to add (expound) to the teaching as long as it is in keeping with the original tradition.

The writings also serve as a record of the teaching and its practice. This is the single most important aspect of Neterian spirituality that allows our understanding of the ancient tradition and how it should be carried forth in the present and for the future. This is also why it is important to study the Neterian scriptures. They offer insights into African Religion as well as the Western religions, and some eastern faiths as well (Hinduism and Buddhism). So the clergy must make the effort to resist the temptation to create new traditions based on conjecture or deluded notions and instead follow the guidelines set forth by the enlightened ancestors (Shepsu) of ancient times. Those who want to "remake" the teaching to suit themselves will fail in the practice, because they are removing the challenge of the teachings; therefore, they will not transform themselves, but rather they will delude themselves into believing that they are following the teaching.

Right: Statue of Amun-Anen, High Priest of Anu (Ra),
Amun-Anen
He wears the characteristic priestly mantle of a leopard pelt.
He also wears an insignia which denotes his position.

---

[124] Chassinat, *Edfou*, Vol. III, 361-362, l. 4: translated by M. Alliot, *Le Culte d'Horus a Edfou au temps de Ptolemees*, Bibliotheque d' Etude 20, Vol. I 186.

Personal Standards for Kamitan Priests and Priestesses and Criteria for Evaluating Spiritual Maturity and Spiritual Evolution and Spiritual Qualities in their Students

Priests and Priestesses need to learn how to evaluate their own spiritual standing with honesty and sincerity. After completing their own course of study and years of service the Neterian priests and priestesses teach those who are below them in rank. For example, the Hemu (full priests and priestesses) teach and oversee the Ab (apprentice priests and priestesses). They will also judge the progress of the aspirants (congregation) assigned to them by the same criteria. They should base their judgment on the following initiatic criteria. The aspiring priests and priestesses should reflect upon these criteria and then it is to be applied to the instruction of novice aspirants when the time comes.

Consistency & Balance:
Does a person follow through with doing what they say that they will do? Do they say what they mean and mean what they say? Or are they fickle, following their senses? Is the person emotionally unstable or balanced? Is the person infirm or healthy (body and/or mind)? Does the person practice the disciplines of Sema regularly?

Reliability:
Is this person reliable? Do they show up at the appointed time? Do they pay dues/tithes on time or do they come up with excuses frequently? Do they need to be reminded of meetings or are they in attendance on time? There are three forms of participation-where do they fall?
- Regularly attend meetings and participate in programs and activities of the organization.
- Intermittently attend meetings and participate in programs and activities of the organization.
- Seldom attend meetings and participate in programs and activities of the organization.

Integrity-Honesty:
Does this person tend towards truth as opposed to delusion, and can they be trusted to do what is righteous, even if it contradicts the ego's desires? Does the person face the truth or lash out in anger or resentment when they are told something about themselves?

Intelligence:
Is this person well informed? Do they have the capacity to think clearly and follow logical arguments or are they dull, unwilling to read, study and cooperate with the spiritual teacher? Do they ask intelligent questions and build on their knowledge or do they ask the same questions again and again without attempting to practice the advice that was given?

Competency-Initiative:
Does the aspirant do what is asked efficiently or haphazardly and without reflection (thinking about what they are doing- conscientiously)? Do they go above and beyond the call of duty or are they content to be an average follower? Does the person take initiative and check with the person in authority when they need to do something and are not sure how to proceed or do they do things on their own without consultation? Do they ask a lot of questions when they should already know what to do (sign of an insecure personality)? Note: the insecure personality should not be encouraged to stop asking so many questions- rather bolster their confidence when tasks are performed well – this is good advice for all students. When presenting written work, is it orderly, using good spelling, diction and layout of ideas and thoughts? These are reflections of order or chaos in the personality. In ancient times the technology to practice the teachings was architecture, medu neter (hieroglyphic test), the spiritual philosophy, devotional ritual and meditation as well as musical instruments, amulets, and spiritual artifacts. In the present day there are more tools that the avid aspirant can add to the arsenal of spiritual practice. These are necessary in order to help in handling the modern day stresses and economic pressures. The computer is the main one, which can be used for accelerated and more efficient studies, communications and creative work in the spiritual teachings.

Computer illiteracy and other forms of technological incapacities in the modern world will be detrimental to the advancement of an aspirant.

Good Company:
Who does the aspirant keep company with? Associations form a most powerful aspect influencing and coloring the mind. Therefore the teaching admonished that there is a necessity to keep company with wise ones and sages as well as other aspirants on the spiritual path and avoid contact with the unrighteous and the "hot bellied" people in order to purify the mind and develop a keen understanding of the teaching through a mind that is peaceful instead of agitated.

Faith:
A teacher of mystical spirituality should always remember that he or she cannot teach anyone who does not want to learn or who is not ready to learn any more that a person can force a tree to bear fruit before its time. Therefore, there should be no arrogance and no pride when students learn, and no pushing of students when they seem unwilling or unable to learn. The teacher can only show the way and should never try to live the way for the student. The student has to do that for him/her self. Otherwise the learning is not real and will not withstand the challenges of life. Does this person have faith in this path, or are they unable to concentrate on the path, looking at other traditions and unable to follow one? Are they frequently comparing this tradition to others, comparing the Preceptor(s)/priests/priestesses to other teachers? Are they naysayers or beset with faultfinding nature? Another aspect of faith is faith in self; does the person have faith in their own abilities, that they can succeed and overcome their failings and ignorance?

Sensitivity:
Is the person sensitive to the feelings of others, that their actions affect others? Is the person sensitive to his or her own deep feelings? Do they know when they are behaving in an non-maatian (unrighteous) way and if it is pointed out to them, do to they accept what is told to them? Do they follow advice or go their own way?

Self-Control:
Does the person control their temper or justify it? Does the person control the senses or are the senses controlling them? Can the person direct the body and is there perseverance or do they quit if an obstacle comes along or if they receive criticism?

Good Natured:
An important initiatic quality is good-naturedness. Is the person of negative disposition and do they remain so over time or is their anger, hatred, desire or greed diminishing with time? Do they have fault finding nature or are they looking for errors or faults in the teacher or the teaching constantly, not for answers but to put down the teaching so as to not follow it? Do they look for errors to put others down and make themselves feel good about themselves being better than others? Lack of humility is a strong obstacle to spiritual evolution and the proper running of a spiritual organization.

Maturity:
Why is it that the same people who have heard and agree with the spiritual teaching continue to *shems* (pursue) worldly illusions instead of applying themselves fully to the teaching? As stated elsewhere in this work, one of the obstacles to *shems Neter* (following the teaching) is *suga* 𓀀𓄿𓅓𓏺𓀁 – {"foolishness, helplessness, miserable, half-witted, immature nature"}. This word, *suga*, is derived from 𓀀𓄿𓅓 *sug-mes* – which means "suckling, baby, helpless child, etc.", and 𓀀𓄿𓅓 *sug-mit* – {"foolish, silly."}. Childishness prevents a person from giving up desires for worldly pleasures and worldly attainments, but also the egoistic childish notions remain as lingering complexes in the mind. This lack of humility prevents them from collaborating or cooperating with others on their same level or above, so they remain alone and living out

their delusion of self-importance. Being an aspirant means being awake to the importance of the spiritual teaching. Being awake implies wakefulness towards the teaching, that is, attentiveness, spending time, desire, etc. for spiritual pursuits. This means being mature enough to have grown beyond childish pursuits and interests, the worldly ideals of life. It is easy to think one is mature when one hears the Ancient Egyptian Proverb: *"Searching for one's self in the world is the pursuit of an illusion."* But until the action follows the thought, the thought is not being held as a reality or a priority. In such a person there is insufficient maturity to pursue the teaching in an intensive, effective and advanced way. Their choice of action reveals their lower state of maturity and aspiration. Such people should follow at the level of practice that includes devotional practices, rituals, and the study of myths and Maat 𓏠𓂓𓏏 teachings to develop purity or heart until a higher level of aspiration develops. The focus here is to develop 𓂋 𓏠𓂓𓏏 *arit maat* {"offering righteous actions, living life righteously"}.

Nehas means wakefulness and is opposite to 𓈖𓅓 *Nem* {"sleep, slumber, slothfulness, immaturity"}. A person who is immature cannot adopt the teaching properly and will thus not be able to follow it rightly. What is needed is wakefulness towards higher perspectives in life and slothfulness towards what is degraded. There should be 𓊃𓈖𓅓 *Snehas* {"Wakefulness, watchfulness, alertness, vigilance"}. There are many who follow spiritual teachings of all traditions who at times appear to have grown and at others seem to have fallen back to their old habits and degraded passions and desires *aba* 𓂝𓃀𓄿. In order to truly follow an ideal one must be steady on the path and watchful so that negative behaviors and patterns do not draw one back into earlier, lower states of consciousness.

Commitment:
Maturity, faith, good company, righteous living and all good qualities allow a person to have a true conviction about their path in life. When such a person is ready they do not have questions like: Is this the right path for me? What career should I pursue? Do I really need a spiritual preceptor? Am I a smart person? Can't I do this on my own? Etc. A mature, committed person is not a fanatic; they are driven by the fervor in their heart born of insight into the true essence of life. Even a spark of that knowledge leads to rectitude, peace, contentment and resoluteness in following the goal of life. This does not mean that every single choice in life is known beforehand. It means that there is a central guidance on the path that allows a person to be sure about the destination and the spiritual path they want to follow in life. A mature, committed person will check their messages frequently and take proper care in attending meetings on time and not schedule appointments during class times or services at the temple. They will not go on vacations during festival times. The teaching comes first and all other considerations may be considered when there are no programs ongoing, except for personal emergencies that may arise at any given time. This is even truer of those who would consider a full-time commitment to the Temple as priests and priestesses. Service to God comes before the family, job and personal considerations; the practical realities of life must be upheld, so one's job is to be done to pay the bills and the family is to be taken care of, but not doted[125] upon.

Those who are judged to be immature aspirants should be directed to
- Perform selfless service
- Perform devotional exercises, attend worship sessions and rituals
- Practice chanting and meditation
- Study the Neterian myths
- Study and practice maat philosophy

---

[125] To show excessive love or fondness, excessive attention and importance, sentimental attachment.

Chapter 8: The Sebait Curriculum- Education For the Clergy in Ancient Egypt

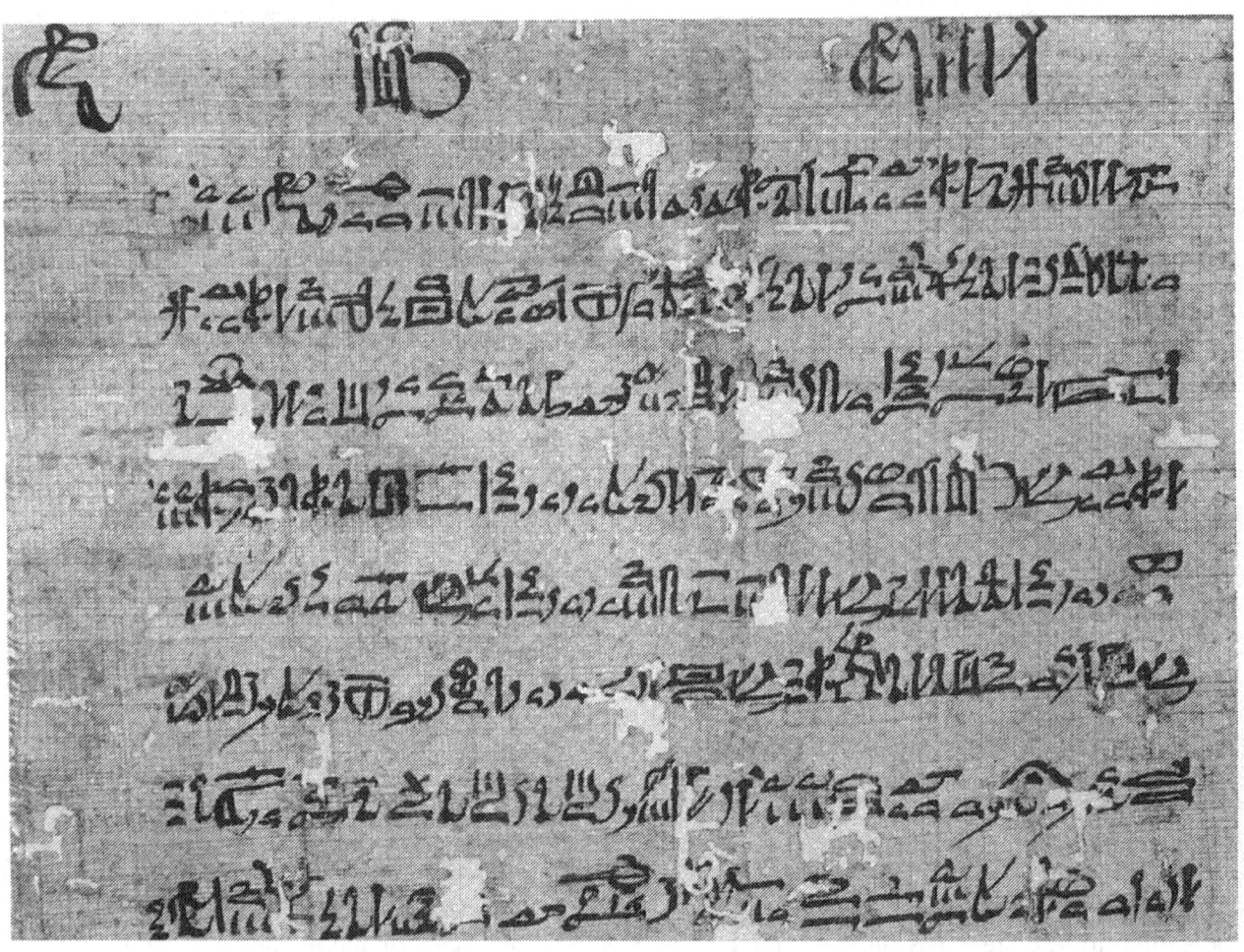

Above: Writing exercise of ancient Egyptian students learning the Medu Neter

The Clergy of Shetaut Neter study the disciplines and teachings of Shetaut Neter but also the disciplines necessary to function in the world of human experience. Therefore, both spiritual education and education for worldly endeavors are necessary for the efficient running of society, and are therefore integral to the Sebait Curriculum. Some clergy might specialize in the spiritual disciplines. Others might study the spiritual disciplines, but also develop some other useful skills as well.

Curriculum of the clergy in Ancient Egypt

In the time of Augustus (first century B.C.) Diodorus Siculus (Greek Historian) writes the following about the education of the sons of the priests.

> 81. "In the education of their sons the **Priests** teach them two kinds of writing, that which is called "sacred" (hieroglyphic) and that which is used in the more general instruction.(Demotic) Geometry and arithmetic are given special attention."

In the earlier periods, service in the varied occupations (professional positions) within the Ancient Egyptian society were filled by priests and priestesses of varying levels of apprenticeship or mastership. The professions were instructed at the Temples and the graduates went on to manage the varied aspects of the Kamitan society. Therefore, the heads of the various departments of the government, business and religious institutions were the priests and priestesses. The areas of instruction at the Ancient Egyptian Temple included:

Lower Mysteries	Professional Disciplines	Higher Mysteries

•Grammar,
•Arithmetic,
•Geometry,
•Music,
•History (social studies)
Geography
	•History
	   oAnthropology
	•Health (medical science),
	•Agriculture,
	•Geography,
	•Art,
	•Law,
	•Government (civics),
	   oManagement
	   oCensus taking
	•Sailing (ship building and navigation),
	   oMaritime trade
	•Economics,
	   oMacro- Economics
	   oMicro- Economics
	•Veterinary science
		•Philosophy (High Mysteries)
		   oMetaphysics
		      ▪Yoga sciences
		         • Meditation
		         • Wisdom
		         • Devotion
		         • Cosmic maatian action
		         • Tantrism
		o Scriptures
		o Ritual and cultural traditions - meaning
		o History – temple and religious traditions - meaning
		o Astronomy,
		o Architecture,
		   ▪Monuments
		o Embalming

Mentoring System

The Mentoring System of the Hm and Hmt consists in the older students helping the younger ones, tutoring them in the areas of academics and traditions, and also in the spiritual teachings that they have received. This dissemination of the newly received teachings allows these teaching to be reflected upon and better understood by the students, as they re-explain them for the second, third and even forth or more times. The nature of the mind in most humans is such that it is necessary to give it a teaching several times before the deeper understanding is truly revealed. By the time students are able to attend the higher philosophy classes, they will have a firmer basis to grasp the teachings.

The students would first be educated in the lower mysteries, and then in the higher mysteries. The lower mysteries include grammar, arithmetic, geometry, music, history, and geography. It is important to understand that lower mysteries education here also implies current events, politics, and technological advances. It is important to be well informed from a worldly point of view. Imparting the teachings sometimes occurs by referencing world events or arguments that require the listener to have a varied background or lucid intellectual capacity. The professional disciplines included accounting. This was one of the most important disciplines, as it was significant for the management of the Temple properties and the agricultural goods, and transferring the latter to people, and so on. It was important to make sure that people got sufficient food to eat. In the literary profession, the scribes were also very important, because their literacy and scriptural knowledge is what keeps the society culturally and spiritually alive. Secular knowledge is important because it supports the non-secular. An example of secular knowledge is knowledge of when the Nile flood is supposed to come so that planting can be done. Other examples are architecture, law, etc. Written records support all the knowledge. For example, lawyers (clergy of Maat) kept the listings of precedents.

On another level there are the higher mysteries, and that refers to philosophy, the yogic disciplines, the metaphysics, the mystical scriptures, and all of these had to be carefully inscribed for future generations. Also they had to be inscribed on Temples for spiritual instruction. Writing and mathematics were the basis that allowed the culture to develop a very large bureaucracy, not bureaucracy in the way that we think of today of a group of people who sit and manage government, collecting salaries and pensions regardless of the quality of service they provide, and who may act as obstructers to what people are trying to accomplish in the society. In ancient times the bureaucracy were managers of the society and facilitators of the culture.

The Higher and the Lower Mysteries

Where is the teaching to be found? It is important to understand that when we speak of the higher and lower mysteries, we are not talking about the inscriptions of the Temple. Many people think that they can get enlightened or resurrected by learning to read Medu Neter and going to Egypt and reading the Temple inscriptions. Furthermore, the higher teaching is not to be found in the papyri either, nor in this book for that matter. These texts contain allusions to the higher mysteries, but they themselves are not the higher mysteries. Why? The teaching cannot be fully conveyed in any form other than through a living preceptor. So even if you read texts that were written by enlightened teachers, you can only partake in a portion of the enlightening teaching. There is a portion that cannot be transmitted in that way. For that it is necessary to be in contact with real, living teachers. This point is most succinctly illustrated in the Ancient Egyptian story called ***The Book of Djehuti***[126](for details see the book *The Serpent Power* by Sebai Muata Ashby), containing the search of the book of Djehuti by Setna. The mythic story details the search for the book of Djehuti, written by the god himself, which bestows the great power of Self-knowledge and powers over nature to anyone who reads it. An excerpt of the story is presented below. It is included here especially for candidates to the clergy because it has important teachings in reference to the true spiritual research of the priests, and that of ordinary people or the ignorant, and where the true and higher knowledge is to be found.

1. *'We were the two children of the King Mer.neb.ptah, and he loved us very much, for he had no others: and Naneferkaptah was in his palace as heir over all the land.'*
2. *"And when my brother Na.nefenka.ptah went to the cemetery of Memphis, he did nothing on earth but read the writings that are in the catacombs of the kings, and the tablets of the*

---

[126] This tale of Setna only exists in one copy, a demotic papyrus in the Ghizeh Museum. The demotic was published in facsimile by Mariette in 1871, among "Les Papyrus du Musee de Boulaq" and it has been translated by Brugsch, Revillout, Maspero, and Hess. The last version-"Der Demotische Roman von Stne Ha-m-us, von J. J. Hess" -being a full study of the text with discussion and glossary, has been followed here; while the interpretation of Maspero has also been kept in view in the rendering of obscure passages. This presentation was edited by Sebai Muata Ashby. XIXTH DYNASTY, PTOLEMAIC PERIOD WRITING

'House of life,' and the inscriptions that are seen on the monuments, and he worked hard on the writings.

Naneferkaptah passes the time reading all the hieroglyphic inscriptions.

3. *And there was a priest there called Nesi-ptah; and as Na.nefer.ka.ptah went into a Temple to pray, it happened that he went behind this priest, and was reading the inscriptions that were on the chapels of the gods. And the priest mocked him and laughed. So Na.nefer.ka.ptah said to him:*

4. *"Why are you laughing at me?' And he replied, 'I was not laughing at you, or if I happened to do so, it was at your reading writings that are worthless. If you wish so much to read writings, come to me, and I will bring you to the place where the book is which Djehuti himself wrote with his own hand, and which will bring you to the gods. When you read but two pages in this you will enchant the heaven, the earth, the abyss, the mountains, and the sea; you shall know what the birds of the sky and the crawling things are saying; you shall see the fishes of the deep, for a divine power is there to bring them up out of the depth. And when you read the second page, if you are in the world of ghosts, YOU will become again in the shape you were in on earth. You will see the sun shining in the sky, with all the gods, and the full moon.'"*

Naneferkaptah pays the priest

5. *Then the priest said to Na.nefenka.ptah, 'This book is in the middle of the river at Koptos, in an iron box; in the iron box is a bronze box; in the bronze box is a sycamore box; in the sycamore box is an ivory and ebony. In the ivory and ebony box is a silver box in the silver box is a golden box, and in that is the book. It is twisted all round with snakes and scorpions and all the other crawling things around the box in which the book is; and there is a deathless snake by the box.'*

Gloss Naneferkaptah was immediately taken with the idea of pursuing the book regardless of the dangers. To summarize the ending, he did find the book and in the process he lost his family and his life. He was not ready to experience higher consciousness; that was his downfall. He was not virtuous. Also, he discovered that the book is not just a written text. He did find the scroll with special teachings and he did temporarily access Cosmic Consciousness, but in order to reach it he had to access the seven psycho-spiritual consciousness centers (*sefek-ba-ra*). So the wisdom teaching points the way, but God writes the true wisdom in the consciousness of the individual, in their spiritual energy consciousness centers. It is this teaching that a spiritual aspirant must learn how to read. It is that teaching which cannot be put into words or any form of writing. It is that teaching that the rituals and Temple disciplines are leading the priests and priestesses to understand, and that is why only they are qualified to be given higher instruction and to be initiated into the higher mysteries.

Education For the Clergy in Ancient Egypt; A Well-Planned and Long Proven System

The organization of the Temple and its ranks of clergy can be discerned from the following curriculum outline, drawn from the biography of the high priest Bekenchons who served and died under the Rameses II (New Kingdom). This provides an indication of the degrees as well as the years of training leading to the position of High Priest in his time. He received a military education in the stables, learning discipline, management and the trade of the stable from his fifth year to his fifteenth year. At the age of 16 he entered into the service of Amun as an Ab[127] priest, and held this position until the age of twenty, after which he officiated at the level of priesthood of a Divine Father for 12 years. Although he remained at this level (position) for 12 years, he was not yet a full priest. When he was 32, he entered the order of Prophets, the Hm Neter, the full priesthood. In this level of priesthood, there are different levels within one designation of the priesthood; you have the Third, the Second and the First Prophet. First Prophet is the position of High Priest. For 15 years he served as a Third Prophet. For 12 years he was the Second Prophet. Finally in his 59th year, the King raised him up to be First Prophet of Amun (High Priest).

This gives an idea of when the educational system began in Kamitan culture. Whether a person is going to the clergy tract or any other discipline, you start when you are five years old. This is an apprenticeship kind of period lasting for about ten years, where the student learns reading, writing, and so on. Bekenchons also went into primary school for four years. So by the time that he was 20 years old, he was ready to take his position in his trade, in his area of specialty for society. This was the standard for any other area of training for work in society also. Contrast that with the present day culture, by the time most people are 18 years old, they are still trying to find their way and are still floundering around, "hanging out." By the time they go to college, if they can qualify to get in, and if they can afford it, they often still don't know what they want to do in life, so they bounce around from one degree program to the next until they graduate in some area of education. But they are getting education only in their trade, and not a spiritual or an ethical basis for life. That is what society is producing here in the modern universities now, people who are perhaps good engineers or good lawyers, but don't have any ethical background or advanced spiritual foundation for life. Others may seem to know what they want in life, and may pursue a degree from the beginning, but later in life they become disillusioned and frustrated with their lives because they pursued it for the wrong reasons. Many times the lack of morals allows them to use their knowledge for doing things that are very degraded. The technologically advanced society can produce politicians who are powerful politically, economically and militarily, but possess no spiritual backbone, no integrity. In Kamitan culture, everybody had to be trained first and foremost, in the Maat philosophy. Since Maat was the foundation of society it surrounded everyone; you grow up in it and you go to the primary school that is in the Temple. The primary

---

[127] The lowest rank of the priesthood is the Ab; it is the entry point into priesthood.

school is in the Temple compound. It was a separate building called **Sba het** - schoolroom – school building.

So Bekenchons had 4 years of primary school, 11 years as an apprentice, 4 years as a novitiate priest, and then from there he went on in his career into his 50s, when he became a High Priest. This gives an idea of the life of a personality like Imhotep, who had achieved six academic degrees of which we have knowledge (medical doctor, lawyer, architect, sage, vizier). He was a government leader like a Vice-President. You can imagine how, if you start your career at 5 years of age, you will be highly trained by the time you are forty years old.

The Ab priest, the lowest rung priesthood was the most plentiful in numbers of priesthood. It may be thought of like a pyramid, where those with more experience and more expertise are fewer in number. The priesthood was based not based solely on seniority or nepotism, but on merit. Nepotism is family members giving each other jobs without merit. There are records that show priests and priestesses who are in the same family, brothers and sisters, working in different Temples. There were also instances where priests and priestesses would have children and raise them as novices, and they (children) would go to work in other Temples. Sometimes they work as clergy and sometimes not.

From the outline of the Temple organization the ranks of clergy can be discerned. The biography of the high priest Bekenchons, who served and died under Rameses II[128] provides an indication of the degrees as well as the years of training leading to the position of High Priest in his time. (Summary below)

1. From his fifth to his fifteenth year he received a military education in one of the royal stables;

2. At the age of sixteen he entered the service of Amun as *Uab*. He held this lower rank till the age of twenty.

3. He then officiated as *Divine Father* for twelve years.

4. When he was thirty-two he entered the order of *Prophets* (Hm Neter);

5. For fifteen years he served as Third Prophet,

6. For twelve years as Second Prophet.

7. Finally, in his fifty-ninth year, the king raised him to be " First Prophet of Amun and chief of the prophets of all the gods."

Therefore, the priestly ranks of Amun under the New Kingdom Period were five degrees.

A. First prophet,
B. Second prophet,
C. Third prophet,
D. The Devine Father,
E. The Uab; (who also function as reciter-priest in the Temple).

NOTE: The offices, ranks and number of clergy varied from one Temple to another and in different periods. Most priests and priestesses served in the lower ranks and no special dispensation was allowed even for the sons and daughters of the king or the high priests or priestesses. All had to begin at the lowest ranks, as

---

[128] On his statue in the Glyptothek at Munich

attested by the inscriptions of the high priests. The clergy is not hereditary, although it may have been treated as such in certain periods. Neither was it a "family business" wherein all family members gave each other positions at the same Temple. The same records show that members of the same family became priests and priestesses at different Temples, dedicated to different gods and goddesses.

Based on the system outlined above, it is clear that the educational system of a viable nation is a critical aspect of its survival. Well-trained, literate and moral people are needed to carry on the duties that allow a society to function so without these the nation will stagnate or collapse. The clergy formed the backbone of Kamitan culture as they were trained in all of the areas necessary to conduct the necessary functions of a well-ordered and prosperous society. In ancient times the training of a typical priest was as follows.

Primary School – 4 years

In Ancient Egypt the children were sent to primary school for 4 years to learn reading, writing and mathematics as well as music, speaking and ethics (Maat). This early education occurred within the precincts of the Temple in one of the adjunct rooms. This process was managed by the Basu priests, who were overseen by the Sba.

Apprenticeship – 11 years

Next the student would be enrolled in an apprenticeship program which would consist in working with one of the priests or priestesses of the Temple if the student was on a tract towards the career in the clergy, or working with one of the priests or priestesses of the trades or government service to learn a trade or government function. Priests and priestesses administered the Temples and government functions, thereby bringing to these duties a spiritual focus that was humanistic and ecumenical. The priests and priestesses of all the Temples worked in harmony to promote the well-balanced development of human beings in a peaceful and orderly environment.

Novitiate – 4 years

The young men and women enter into probationary positions as priests (Hm Uab) and priestesses (Hmt Uab) where they learn the basic aspects of their duties on a probationary basis. During this time they work closely with supervising priests.

Professional-Graduate Studies - Lifetime

Now as full priests and priestesses, the initiates enter into higher studies as they elevate themselves in successive levels of rank within the clergy. After 20 to 40 years they may attain a level of head supervisor priest and priestess (***Hem or Hemt Neter Tpy***).

In the earlier periods, the service in the varied occupations (professional non-Temple positions) within the Ancient Egyptian society were filled by priests and priestesses of varying levels of apprenticeship or mastership. The professions were instructed at the Temples and the graduates went on to manage the varied aspects of the Kamitan society. The heads of the various departments of the government, business and religious institutions in the earlier periods were the priests and priestesses. The areas of instruction at the Ancient Egyptian Temple included:

Lower Mysteries

- Grammar,
    - Learning through drill writing exercises (whole sentences at a time).
    - Speaking out loud while reading.
    - Copying down ancient traditional stories as exercises.
- Arithmetic,
- Geometry,
- Music,
- History (social studies)
    - Geography

Professional Disciplines

- History
    - Anthropology
- Health (medical science),
- Agriculture,
- Geography,
- Art,
- Law,
- Government (civics),
    - Management
    - Census taking
- Sailing (ship building and navigation),
    - Maritime trade
- Economics,
    - Macro- Economics - country
    - Micro- Economics - community
- Veterinary science

Higher Mysteries

- Philosophy (High Mysteries)
    - Metaphysics
        - The Mysteries
        - Sema (Yoga) sciences
            - Meditation
            - Wisdom
            - Devotion
            - Cosmic Maatian action
            - Tantrism
    - Scriptures
    - Ritual and cultural traditions - meaning
    - History – Temple and religious traditions - meaning
    - Astronomy,
    - Architecture,
        - Monuments
    - Embalming

The Priests and Priestesses of Ancient Egypt

Levels of Initiation of the Neterian Priests and Priestesses

Clergy Designation	Description, Training and Duties
Sba-t pupil student	The *Sbat* are students of the teaching, people who may or may not be formally attached to the Temple but who are interested in the teachings. In a broad sense all are Sbats, but here it refers to the uninitiated and uncommitted people. The people from this group come from the Rekhyt (masses of religious followers).
Unut - lay people, men and women, that serve part time	**Level - 1** The Unut are part-time priests and priestesses (ministers) who receive limited training to be informed of the basic tenets of the Neterian religion and how to facilitate the Neterian temple programs. They assist the full priests and priestesses.
uab or *uabt* – priest or priestess of purifications.	**Level 2** After years of service this is the entry-level (Apprentice) position for full priests and priestesses. The Uab take care of purifications, and all basic duties related to taking care of the temple.
Hm Neter – or *Hmt Neter* -servant or prophet of God – Priest– Priestess	**Level 3** After years and successful completion of their duties and apprenticeship period, the Uab are eligible to become Hm or full priests and priestesses. The Hm and Hmt in the various areas of specialty take on apprentices (Ab) to instruct as their mentors. They prepare the younger initiates as they were prepared to accept the duties and to purify themselves in order to become more proficient in the practice of the disciplines in order to be leaders for society and to better understand the teachings. The Hm and Hmt can present others who they have mentored as candidates for induction as ministers.
Hm Neter Tepy -head servant of god. Or *Hemut Neter Tpy*– High Priestess-wife of the god	**Level 4** After a period years of successful completion of their duties the Hm are eligible to become Tpy or supervisors in their respective areas of expertise. They supervise the Ab, Basu and Unut in their duties as they (the Tpy) continue to instruct in their own area of expertise.

The Priests and Priestesses of Ancient Egypt

Sbait kheria- assistant teacher instructor of Neterian philosophy	**Level 5** • The Sbait kheria are those on a tract to becoming Sebaiu. They also are preceptors. They work closely with the Sebaiu, assisting in the dissemination of the teachings and administration of the various programs of the Temple. Their task is to become proficient in all the specialized areas of theology and Yogic disciplines while becoming expert in one of each.
Sbaiu - wise ones, sages, instructor	**Level 6** The Sbai is a sage, spiritual preceptor or teacher of the High Mysteries who is well versed in the mystical traditions and practices.
Sba	∞ Infinity The Sba is an allusion to the supreme light that opens up consciousness, the light that is steady and does not flicker, i.e. imperishable (i.e. The Supreme Being). The Supreme Being is the enlightener and teacher of all, transcendental and infinite. The Sbau (preceptors) teach the wisdom of Sba, the divine star that means "illumination", i.e. Enlightenment that comes from Neter. The Sba use the Sba-ur -instrument -"Great Star" or "Mighty Star." This is an allusion to the supreme light that opens up consciousness, the light that is steady and does not flicker, i.e. imperishable (i.e. The Supreme Being).

Summary – main groups of clergy and leadership of the Temple

1. sebai(t)
2. Sbait kheria- assistant teacher instructor
3. seba(t)-philosophy teachers
4. Hm(t) {this level may have several sublevels-Ex. Fourth, Third, Second, First}
5. Ab(t) (Apprentice priests and priestesses)
6. Unut – (Ministers)

- Basu(t)-school teachers
- Rekhyt – (religious-devoted lay people)

Chapter 9: Cultural, Historical, Political and Social Concerns for the Neterian Clergy in the 21st Century

Shetaut Neter and other Spiritual Traditions

The Temple of Shetaut Neter is not affiliated with any other Kemetic studies group, Lodges, Rosicrucians, Masons, Freemason, Illuminati, or Greek Sororities or Fraternities. Those organizations are latecomers that seek to affiliate themselves with the glory and wisdom of the ancients. Those organizations were created in modern times, along lines other than Neterian Mystical spirituality, such as Christianity, Islam, or Judaism, and incorporate some teachings of Ancient Egyptian religion, but not the full mysteries of the mystic arts. Shetaut Neter is an indigenously originated religion of Africa that was practiced by the Ancient Egyptians and is not affiliated with Christianity, Judaism or Islam, Native American Religion, Bahaism, Hinduism, Taoism, Confucianism or Buddhism. Shetaut Neter African religion holds no animosity towards any spiritual tradition but recognizes that there are some fundamental differences, goals and objectives among the world religions. Consequently, their focus and agendas are different. Also, some have philosophies that are in complete disagreement with the Neterian culture and philosophy.

A religion turns its followers towards the culture and country of its origins even though it may be ecumenical in outlook. So even a practitioner of Buddhism looks to India, Tibet or China in the practice of Buddhism just as a Muslim looks to Arabia and Mecca. Shetaut Neter looks to Egypt and Africa. No one complains when a Christian talks about The "Holy Land" in Canaan (now called Israel), just as no one complains about a Muslim person praising Mecca and Arabia. So why is it that when a person praises some other "Holy Land" there is a commotion stirred? It is due to orthodoxy on the part of the disturbed groups but also an orthodoxy that has developed into intolerance, born of ignorance, cultivated by demigods and nurtured by fear. So while Neterians can coexist peacefully and work with those practitioners of ecumenical religion who have a perspective outside of Africa, Neterians can work more closely with those religions that have an African perspective or which acknowledge the right of African peoples or those non-Africans who follow the African religions to do so. However, Neterians should be weary when dealing with members of intolerant groups. Neterians also have other important issues to face in the modern world. How should those challenges be approached?

The Neterian System of Government

Ancient Egyptian government (Hekat) was set up politically as a theocracy (ruled by religious leaders). This form of government, if it is set up based on Maatian regulations, can be considered as a Humanist Theocracy, as opposed to a tyrannical theocracy in which the religious leaders rule over the population tyrannically, wielding power by force and imposing harsh punishments on all who do not obey. The Humanist Theocracy of Ancient Kamit was antithetical to the principles of Aristocracy, government by a privileged class, and Oligarchy, government wherein power is concentrated in the hands of a minority. While the priests and priestesses were the minority of the population, they were not a privileged minority in the sense that they amassed inordinate wealth and power to rule over people's lives tyrannically, as they languish in poverty. That kind of system is more closely related to the present day systems of government in many countries. Further, The Humanist Theocracy of Ancient Kamit was in contradiction to the modern concepts of Capitalism and Globalism. It was more akin to the philosophy of Buddhist Dharma and Chinese Confucianism.

The Priests and Priestesses of Ancient Egypt

Identity, Race, and the Neterian Clergy

The "race" of the Ancient Egyptians has been a contentious issue for many western scholars, contentious, that is, if one ignores the evidences. Also, it is important to note that the early European explorers who visited Egypt in the late 18th and early 19th centuries clearly expressed the obvious view that the Ancient Egyptians were not only Africans, but also "black" Africans.[129] This view was also expressed earlier by the German physician and traveler, Engelbert Kaempfer (1651-1716), who spent ten years, 1683-1693, traveling through Persia and Southeast Asia, including two years in Japan, 1690-92.[130] Though his writings clearly denote a condescending attitude towards the non-western religions (referring to them as heathens) and perhaps even a racist attitude based on his western upbringing, he emphatically acknowledges firstly that the early images of Buddha appear as Africans, and not Indians. He also states that the Indian religion has many commonalities with the Ancient Egyptian Religion, and that the Ancient Egyptian appears to be its original source. The pictorial evidences as to the appearance of the Ancient Egyptians still exist. The Ancient Egyptians exhibited dark skin tones like present day Africans, as well as their characteristic facial features, as well as lighter skin tones such as those of many people of African descent in the Diaspora who have mixed with Asiatics and Europeans of the present. That is history and that is evidence. We state that fact to set the record straight because that means that Africa and Africans contributed in a major way to world culture, religion and philosophy, and so are worthy of the respect accorded to any people. However, that fact does not mean that the Neterian teaching is for Africans alone or "blacks" alone. In fact, the ancient Neterian sages themselves said Neterian religion is universal and all human beings are brothers and sisters, having been created by the same Supreme Divinity. The concept of race was unknown in ancient times, and therefore modern day practitioners of Neterianism cannot and do not recognize such ignorant and destructive notions, just as geneticists do not, having proved that all human beings are members of one race. All human beings arose from Africa, and so all human beings are African, regardless of the country where they were born in recent times. Therefore, the Neterian clergy are required to accept and teach all those who wish to sincerely accept the oneness of all human beings and adopt the tenets, disciplines and culture of Shetaut Neter, regardless of their previous ethnicity. Sincerely accepting the Neterian tradition means renouncing racism, sexism, capitalism, religious orthodoxy and dogmatism as outlined above. It also means adopting the path of Maat, righteousness, non-violence, justice, truth, honor and peace. But beyond renouncing, they must act in accordance with Neterian principles so their actions must follow their speech. Otherwise they are unworthy of the service of the Neterian clergy. Those aspiring Neterian clergy who are unable or unwilling to extend this service due to animosity or prejudice towards other ethnic groups or those whom they perceive as having perpetrated some sinful or criminal act in the past cannot function as Neterian clergy.

---

[129] See the book *African Origins of Civilization* by Muata Ashby
[130] **The History of Japan by Engelbert Kaempfer (1651-1716) Reprint published in 1906**

Summary of the Neterian View on Race and Racism from the Ancient Egyptian Scriptures

• All Human Beings are Africans. The Sebait Curriculum espouses the universality of Humanity. Long before the science of genetics was developed, the Kamitan Culture of ancient Africa understood and acknowledged the fact that all human beings are created by the same God (Goddess) and therefore all human beings deserve respect and caring as do all creatures on earth and in the heavens.

• The concept of race was not acknowledged in ancient times and it is therefore rejected by the Sebait Curriculum.

Kamitan Proverbs on the nature of the soul:

"Souls, Horus, son, are of the self-same nature, since they came from the same place where the Creator modeled them; nor male nor female are they. Sex is a thing of bodies not of Souls."

Thou art The Supreme Being, who didst create beings endowed with reason;
thou makest the color of the skin of one race to be different from that of another,
but, however many may be the varieties of mankind, it is thou that makest them all to live.

I close this section with the following statement which summarizes the scientific findings related to the concept of race and racial differences.

"The concept of race has often been misapplied. One of the most telling arguments against classifying people into races is that persons in various cultures have often mistakenly acted as if one race were superior to another. Although, with social disadvantages eliminated, it is possible that one human group or another might have some genetic advantages in response to such factors as climate, altitude, and specific food availability, these differences are small. There are no differences in native intelligence or mental capacity that cannot be explained by environmental circumstances. Rather than using racial classifications to study human variability, anthropologists today define geographic or social groups by geographic or social criteria. They then study the nature of the genetic attributes of these groups and seek to understand the causes of changes in their genetic makeup. Contributed by: Gabriel W. Laser "Races, Classification of," Encarta." Copyright (c) 1994

The Struggle for Survival

The Neterian clergy in particular and the Neterian community in general must face certain realities of life, which exist due to the nature of humanity and the challenges of time and space reality at this point in history. Ignorance is an aspect of the human condition, and that ignorance always has the potential to turn towards violence. The key to peace and harmony in society or lack thereof is the government leadership. Does it appeal to the lowest aspects of the character or to the higher? Are the government leaders demagogs or are they wise shepherds? Just as in a righteous family, the father and mother set the tone and children know what their place is, what their duties are, and what they should and shouldn't do, so too in a righteous society the citizens act in accordance with what their leaders elicit. As the ancient Egyptian saying goes, "Morals are judged by deeds." So the Neterian cleric should listen to the speech of such people with whom he/she must interact, and then examine their actions and see where they are coming from, and thereby determine how to approach the interaction.

Realize that there have been several instances of breakdown and disorder in ancient Kamit, sometimes due to internal disintegration, but mostly due to outside invasions. What do you think was going through the minds of Ancient Egyptian priests and priestesses when the country was taken over by the Hyksos, and later the Persians, and even later on, the Greeks? We do not need to wonder. There is a special genre of Ancient Egyptian writings that provide us insights into what was going on and the means to realize how to raise culture again. The writings of Khakheperre-Sonb state: *"The events that occur throughout the land: Changes take place, it is not like last year, One year is more irksome than the other. The land breaks up, is destroyed, Becomes [a wasteland]. Order is cast out, Chaos is in the council hall; The ways of the gods are violated, Their provisions neglected. The land is in turmoil, There is mourning everywhere; Towns, districts are grieving, All alike are burdened by wrongs. One turns one's back on dignity... Unravel for me what goes on in the land, ... And turmoil will not cease tomorrow,? Everyone is mute about it. The whole land is in great distress, Nobody is free from crime; Hearts are greedy."* The distress of Khakheperre-Sonb could very well be the complaint of people today. Nevertheless, the priests and priestesses continued to uphold the traditions until a time when the government could be restored. Many people adopted the foreign ways, dress and spirituality. Yet the priests and priestesses kept the Neterian teaching alive. Even when the Christians closed the Temples the teachings survived. So too now is the time to keep the teaching alive and to perfect it within yourself, to prepare to pass it on for future generations, for one day it will be re-adopted. There will be a community that will adopt its principles and implement its philosophy on a cultural level. So therefore, we follow the teaching of Shetaut Neter for ourselves and for our descendants, because it is something of value for us and for humanity. The main differences between ancient times and the present is that in ancient times there were not so many distractions in life (now there is television, books, sports, proliferation of spiritual philosophies, etc.), and prior to the Jews, Christians and Muslims, the conquering forces did not seek to stop the practice of Neterianism.

The Egyptian culture and religion remained relatively intact under the Greeks as compared to the conditions imposed by the Hyksos and Assyrians. These conditions would not remain the same under the control by the Roman-Christians and the later Arab-Muslims who actively sought to stamp out the old religion (Ancient Egyptian religion- Shetaut Neter). Nubia was the last place to practice the Ancient Egyptian religion, and thus also the last to convert to Judaism, Christianity and Islam. Today, the Nubians living in southern Egypt consider themselves ethnically as Nubian, and at the same time nationally as Egyptian, and spiritually as Muslim. Beginning with the Roman-Catholics and then the Muslims, there has indeed been an active effort to stop any other religions, and thus, we are as if exiled from the land of Kamit. In any case, we can be exiled but not stopped, for this new generation of Neterian culture will carry on in the Diaspora. It will flourish in foreign lands as many individuals mature to see the errors of modern culture and orthodox religions, and at some point there will be a new nation based on Neterian principles that will bring light to a troubled world.

Culture, the Spiritual Practice and the Name

There are some difficult realities that the modern mystic must face in order to maintain purity in the spiritual teaching and the spiritual practice. Firstly, it must be understood that culture is related to spiritual practice. When one sees a Buddhist monk, regardless of the ethnicity of the monk (western or eastern), one is also seeing the Asiatic culture of the countries where Buddhism is/was established and practiced, and the customs associated not just with the spiritual tradition, but also those associated with the folklore and customs of the society. Even practitioners of Buddhism in the west who have never been to Asia adopt the clothing and customs of Buddhist culture (as it developed in Asia). Why should they do that? The culture from which a spiritual tradition comes contributes a psychological and psycho-spiritual component to the feeling of the spiritual teaching. Therefore, it is important to realize that in order to follow the Neterian path, it is vital to practice the Neterian culture as well. That involves the clothing, the customs and also the name. An advanced practitioner should have a Neterian name. It would sound strange to have a name like Muhammad Ali and then also be an "Egyptian Initiate" as much as it would sound odd to have a name like Muhammad Ali and be a Buddhist monk. It would be odd to see a devout Hindu wearing a suit and tie at a mystic Hindu ritual as much as it would be odd to have a turban at an Egyptian Mystery ritual. This would be like having a PC computer and trying to open a MAC file in it; that will not work. So, in this sense the spiritual teaching and the culture should fit; they should complement and not be discordant. That discordance leads to diffidence in the mind, and with that doubt comes ineffectiveness and ultimate failure. The name should denote something also of the character, and also the perspective of the personality, what it looks to, what it aspires to, and so on. So an aspiring Neterian initiate should have a Neterian name, and certainly a priest or priestess must have a Neterian name that is to be used generally and instead of the given name. (This is not the initiatic name received at initiation. We are here speaking of the cultural name, for interactions with society) An initiate should choose a name based on their highest Neterian ideals. A priest may assist in that choice.

Interactions Between Neterians and Orthodox Religions Practitioners

The Neterian clergy must have a clear understanding of the dynamics of religious interactions, such as interactions with peoples of other religions, especially the western religions. Many people come to the mysteries with varied delusions that they have learned in common society. Many people from orthodox religions would like to believe that their tradition is ecumenical and open. Often, members of western orthodox religions may come to a meeting of a non-western religious group. Someone may have invited them because they seemed open to an alternative insight into spirituality. Or perhaps they just happened by and decided to sit in. Nevertheless, often after the meeting they will express their solidarity with the participants and claim that there is no contradiction between them (practitioners of non-western religions) and the religion of the western practitioner. Since deep mystical philosophy is not discussed at open meetings, those people may sincerely believe that there is no difference, but sometimes they are merely comforting themselves so that they can avoid feeling at a loss because their own tradition seems lacking, especially in the face of highly evolved expositions of non-western religions. In the present day there are many orthodox practitioners of religion. Realize that there can be orthodox Hindus and Buddhists; the western religions are not the only traditions that suffer of the problem of orthodoxy. The practitioner of non-western religion needs to be watchful not to fall into the lower practice of religion that leads to dogma and fanaticism, and which foments orthodoxy and fundamentalism. However, the western religions are not just orthodox, but they also express an imperialistic agenda, to convert other people by force if necessary. Sometimes those people from the orthodox western religions (Judaism, Christianity, Islam) may claim that they have a mystical side of their tradition that is not widely known. Yet that side is never promoted or seen in practice, but the orthodox, exclusive and dogmatic side is always apparent. In the case of Kabbalah, which is touted to be a part of Judaism, the orthodox and dominant Jewish religious establishment does not officially recognize it. Sufism, which is promoted as a form of "Mystical Islam" is also not approved of by orthodox Islam. Also, Arab history records that Sufis were the ones who defaced the Great Sphinx, one of the most important monuments of non-western religion. How is that different from what Muslims such as the Taliban in Afghanistan have done around the world in modern times (destruction of non-western religious icons, monuments and practices)?

In the past and to the present day, orthodox religions used friendliness to approach practitioners of other religions but when the numbers of orthodox practitioners increases to the majority there is a turn towards open repudiation of other religions and violent acts of suppression and eradication of other religions. This is what Christians did in the Americas, stealing the land from Native Americans, destroying their holy sites and Temples and erecting churches on the same sites, and then forcing them to convert under pain of death. Muslims did the same to Africans in Africa and Hindus in India, and even to this day continue their destruction of relics and monuments of other religions. An example of the continued destruction of religious sites and artifacts is the demolition of Buddhist monuments in Afghanistan by the Taliban groups (orthodox Islamic). In Egypt, the destruction of Ancient Egyptian monuments was started by Christian zealots, and later on the Muslims took over and continued until the early 19th century. This was eventually stopped, for the most part, by the European conquest and the interest of scientists and secular leaders of the British Empire. Indeed there are stark differences between the two paths (mystical or orthodox) and students of the mysteries should not be duped into Pollyannaish ideas about living together in one happy family of ecumenical religions. If those from the orthodox western religion truly are sincere can they pass the following test? The following questions need to be faced by them and their actions will show their true convictions and allegiances.

QUESTIONS FOR PRACTITIONERS OF ORTHODOX WESTERN RELIGIONS: Do the practitioners of western orthodox religions accept responsibility for the atrocities and damages done by followers of their religion?

Do the practitioners of western orthodox religions accept that their scriptures contain contradictions and statements that promote violence and hatred towards other religions?

Further, if the practitioners of western orthodox religions accept responsibility, will they make amends (restitution) for the damages caused and the benefits that they are deriving today from the actions of their ancestors?

The following comes from the Jewish-Christian Bible:

Numbers 33:50-56

> 50 ¶ And the LORD spake unto Moses in the plains of Moab by Jordan near Jericho, saying,
> 51 Speak unto the children of Israel, and say unto them, When ye are passed over Jordan into the land of Canaan;
> 52 Then ye shall <u>drive out all the inhabitants of the land from before you, and destroy all their pictures, and destroy all their molten images, and quite pluck down all their high places</u>:
> 53 And ye shall <u>dispossess the inhabitants of the land, and dwell therein: for I have given you the land to possess it.</u>
> 54 And <u>ye shall divide the land by lot for an inheritance among your families</u>: and to the more ye shall give the more inheritance, and to the fewer ye shall give the less inheritance: every man's inheritance shall be in the place where his lot falleth; according to the tribes of your fathers ye shall inherit.
> 55 55 But if <u>ye will not drive out the inhabitants of the land from before you</u>; then it shall come to pass, <u>that those which ye let remain of them shall be pricks in your eyes, and thorns in your sides, and shall vex you in the land wherein ye dwell.</u>

In the passages above, "God" is giving permission to the Jews to usurp lands on which others currently live. The statements above expressly promote that violence should be used against those who are not followers of their faith to take their land, and destroy their Temples and icons.

QUESTION FOR PRACTITIONERS OF JUDEO-CHRISTIAN ORTHODOX WESTERN RELIGIONS: Do they (Jews and Christians) reject the statements above?

<u>Question for reflection for Neterian Aspirants:</u> How can orthodox Jew and Christians reject the above statements when they say that the Bible is the whole and perfect word of their God, who is the only true God, that must be accepted completely? Is there any wonder why the followers of Islam speak in such a derogatory manner about Jews and Christians? The following is what the Koran says about the Jews and Christians:

> 2:120 <u>Never will the Jews or the Christians be satisfied with thee unless thou follow their form of religion.</u>

3:118 O ye who believe! Take not into your intimacy those outside your ranks: <u>They will not fail to corrupt you.</u> They only desire your ruin: Rank hatred has already appeared from their mouths: What their hearts conceal is far worse. We have made plain to you the Signs, if ye have wisdom.

5:54 Section 8. O ye who believe! <u>Take not the Jews and the Christians for your friends and protectors: They are but friends and protectors to each other</u>. And he amongst you that turns to them (for friendship) is of them. Verily Allah guideth not a people unjust.

<u>Question for reflection for Neterian Aspirants:</u> If the Muslims (a western orthodox religion that has its basis in Judeo-Christian roots) are wary of the Jews and Christians, how much more vigilant should followers of non-western religions be?

An interesting argument often given by practitioners of western religions with respect of followers of their faith that commit unrighteous acts is that bad things are done by bad people who do not truly practice the teachings of the religion (Judaism, Christianity, Islam); this is an attempt to excuse the flaws and contradictions inherent in the orthodox western religions.

<u>Question for reflection for Neterian Aspirants:</u> Is it not in reality more the case that those people who do not repudiate others of other faiths violently are not following the exact teachings of their religions? In the Bible does it not say that those who do not believe in the God of Israel (such as the Ancient Egyptians in ancient times, the Hindus, the Buddhists, other Pagan religions, and the Palestinians in modern times) are unbelievers, and therefore God authorizes their eradication from the land so that the "chosen people" (Jews) may take it? While the Muslims seem to believe in the same "God" of Abraham the Jews and Christians see Islam as an aberration from the true path which is the "Bible." Therefore, in the final analysis Islam is seen by them as a "heathen" and blasphemous religion. Realize that individual Jews or Christians may not agree with this analysis but they are not the ones controlling and directing the religion. Those who do are supported by the masses of Jews and Christians and that is the driving force behind the acts of Jewish or Christian dominated governments.

QUESTION FOR PRACTITIONERS OF JUDEO-CHRISTIAN ORTHODOX WESTERN RELIGIONS: Will the Jews and Christians publicly renounce the statement that those who do not believe in the God of Israel are unbelievers, and that God authorizes their eradication from the land so that the "chosen people" (Jews) may take it, and make amends for the errors of the past and for the continuing benefits drawn from the errors of the past and restitution of the lands and pay for damages?

QUESTION FOR PRACTITIONERS OF ISLAMIC ORTHODOX WESTERN RELIGION: The Koran it says, *"For the Unbelievers are unto you open enemies."* 4:101 Section 15 (Koran). Specifically speaking about polytheists (Ancient Egyptians and Hindus) *"He (God) has cursed them and got Hell ready for them: and evil is it for a destination."* 48:6 (Koran) about the polytheists: *"Those who reject (Truth)"* 98:6 (Koran). Will the followers of Islam publicly renounce the statements contained in their own scriptures against those whom they consider infidels?

<u>Question for reflection for Neterian Aspirants:</u> How can Muslims renounce the statements contained in their own scriptures against those whom they consider infidels when they say that the Koran is the whole and perfect word of their one and only true God that must be accepted completely?

QUESTION FOR PRACTITIONERS OF ORTHODOX WESTERN RELIGIONS: Shetaut Neter, like monastic Buddhism and Vedanta of India and Taoism of China, is a mystic path. Mysticism is a spiritual path leading to oneness with God, to become "godlike." Such a statement is considered blasphemous to the followers of orthodox western religions. Do the practitioners of the western religions publicly accept this teaching?

Questions for reflection for Neterian Aspirants: How can the practitioners of the western religions publicly accept the mystical teachings of becoming one with God (godlike) when it is repudiated in their own teachings? So how can they say there is no contradiction between their religion and that of the Neterian Mysteries? Many people seek to do not highlight the seeds of violence contained within the orthodox western religious texts in order to give the appearance of promoting ecumenism and harmony, but is it not evident that that appeasement and acquiescence by non-westerners, by having practitioners of western religion in their midst and allowing themselves to be indoctrinated with western values, is a defunct social practice? Consider the current state of the world, which is religiously divided, ethnically segregated, economically enslaved and dominated by practitioners of the western religions or their secular counterparts. Doesn't this present the clearest evidence for the inadequacy and fallacy of western ecumenism and western social, political and economic order?

One last point is that many people like to advance the idea that since the early Jews were actually ancient Egyptian people and there are so many similarities (co-opted teachings) between Judeo-Christianity and Neterianism, that it is ok to follow Judaism or Christianity in the present, today. Of course the Jews in the Old Testament adopted many Neterian traditions, like the Creation Myth of the primeval ocean in the book of Genesis, the concept of Neter (Divinity) itself in the Jewish "Elohim," the wisdom of Solomon from the Ancient Egyptian teachings of Sage Amenemope, the three fold daily worship, and more.[131] The Christians adopted the resurrection, the Eucharist, the divine birth, the savior concept, the cross, and much more. However none of those adoptions signal either an understanding of or support for the ancient tradition. In fact, the ancient tradition is repudiated and shunned. In the Bible itself, Egypt is denigrated even though Egypt saved the so-called Jewish and Christian peoples on more than one occasion.[132] So those adoptions are co-optations. A cooptation is the taking of some preexisting element of culture and calling it one's own, to incorporate in one's own culture or tradition. So while there were many co-optations by the Jews and Christians, and while the ancient Jews and Christians were ancient Egyptian peoples, it cannot be said that they or the present day Jews and Christians are followers of the Ancient Egyptian religion. In fact the opposite is true. Therefore, what they are doing today cannot be considered to be in keeping or in harmony with the ancient tradition. To entertain such ideas is a delusion that the Neterian clergy must not allow in their midst, nor in the vicinity of their congregations. Such erroneous ideas are poisonous to a follower's ability to attain the depths of authentic spirituality.

Forced Conversion

The orthodox missionary movement has followed the Religious Conquest Pattern (RCP) of:

- 1st -Initially, western missionaries go to a country and promote peaceful introduction of their religion, living side by side with native, assisting natives with medical or financial aid (ironically to alleviate the ravages of poverty which were often caused by the countries from which the missionaries come).
- 2nd -Where conversion is slow, latent intolerance emerges. The conceitedness of the orthodox religion manifests as denigration of the other religions, condescendingly speaking of them as primitive and pagan, incorrect and hell-bound, along with admonishing converts to abandon their religion. They speak of their own religion as the only correct one, being truly divinely given, whereas other religions are given by human error, imagination or by the devil.
- 3rd –When the numbers of converts reaches a certain level, the orthodox religions' denigration turns to open hatred and statements inciting violence (hostility) and the illegitimacy of other

---

[131] See *The Mystical Journey From Jesus to Christ* by Muata Ashby
[132] See the books *African Origins of Civilization* and *Mystical Journey From Jesus to Christ* by Muata Ashby

religions, as well as active repudiation of those who choose to still follow the native (indigenous) religion.
- 4th -Then they move actively to violently close or destroy the native Temples or establishments of their religious rivals.
- 5th –Finally, if people do not convert after their Temple or place of worship is destroyed, then the edict is given to co-opt their symbols, rituals and traditions, forcing them to gradually believe they are worshipping the new divinity in some of the same ways they venerated the old (ancient). The people are to be compelled to practice the new religion. This is what was done by the Arab-Muslims in North and West Africa from 700 ACE to the present, and the Portuguese missionaries and traders in Western and Southern Africa in the 15th century A.C.E., which began the European slave trade of African peoples.[133] The Spanish followed this pattern in the treatment of Native Americans in the 16th century.

So, where outright destruction of Temples and murdering of priests and priestesses failed to convert people who persisted in carrying on the ancient religious traditions even when the priests and priestesses had been killed or forced to leave the Temple, the Christian zealots had an alternative plan. The evidences given by the Christian tradition itself and its own documents suggest that images such as the cross (Ancient Egyptian Ankh), the dove (Ancient Egyptian sundisk), the Black Mary or Madonna (Ancient Egyptian Aset), and the concepts of the resurrection, the eucharist, the birthday of the savior Jesus (Ancient Egyptian Heru), and many others[134] were taken directly from Ancient Egyptian religion, renamed (rededicated as it were) and used in Christian worship. This practice was consistent with the practice of inculturation, also known as co-optation,[135] the process of adopting symbols and rituals from other religions and calling them Christian, which were officially confirmed and endorsed as church policy by Pope St Gregory the Great, in a letter given to Priests written in 601 A.C.E.:

> "It is said that the men of this nation are accustomed to sacrificing oxen. It is necessary that this custom be converted into a Christian rite. On the day of the dedication of the [pagan] Temples thus changed into churches, and similarly for the festivals of the saints, whose relics will be placed there, you should allow them, as in the past, to build structures of foliage around these same churches. They shall bring to the churches their animals, and kill them, no longer as offerings to the devil, but for Christian banquets in name and honor of God, to whom after satiating themselves, they will give thanks. Only thus, by preserving for men some of the worldly joys, will you lead them thus more easily to relish the joys of the spirit."

The Bible appears to condone the killing of people even though one of the Ten Commandments of God to Moses seems to prohibit such an act. This is only one of many contradictions of the Judeo-Christian Bible. Therefore, it is not surprising to see people of the Judeo-Christian faith fighting in wars, engaging in acts of psychological violence, criminal behavior, etc., while professing to have a non-violent religion. In this aspect the first Muslims thought they were superior to the Jews and Christians in that they exhorted a stricter moral code. However, they too inflicted great pain and suffering on many people while at the same time converting them to Islam. It is ironic that the early Muslims derided the Christians and Jews for *"Never being satisfied with thee unless thou follow their form of religion."* (Koran 2:120) and yet beginning with Muhammad himself, and throughout Islamic history, Arabs who followed Islam conquered North and West Africa and Asia Minor, where previous to being conquered, the the people in those regions were practicing other religions. What happened to them and their religions?

---

[133] *African Religion: World Religion* by Aloysius M. Lugira
[134] See the book *The Mystical Journey From Jesus to Christ* by Muata Ashby
[135] To neutralize or win over (an independent minority, for example) through assimilation into an established group or culture.

Social and Political Perspectives for the 21st Century

The sections above have been included in this volume to illustrate some realities that must be faced by those practitioners who wish to practice and bring forth the tradition of Shetaut Neter as an authentic spiritual practice to be adopted by a society. In order for that to happen, the culture of Shetaut Neter must be protected from dilution and delusions. It must be protected from well meaning but ignorant and weak people who do not or cannot face the inadequacy and harm of their spiritual practices and beliefs. In ancient times Kamit, was ruled by a kingship system, but lest we forget that the king and queen were also High Priest and Priestess. This means that the Kamitan government is to be managed by those who are practitioners of the Neterian religious philosophy. It would be nice if peoples of different religions could live side by side without fear and pressure to convert. That is an adorable idea, but it is unrealistic and therefore not to be pursued until a period of high culture emerges in humanity, something we will not see in this age of human history. Only the highly elevated souls can live and express true ecumenism; that is because they have attained the heights of spirituality and so have no need to compete, or express arrogance or animosity towards any other spiritual tradition. That is the true test of a spiritual tradition, its tendency towards ecumenism and peace versus towards messianically demanding the conversion of others. The presence of hubris, arrogance, dogmatism and the promotion of suspended intellect all signal limitation and degradation in religious practice. Due to the realities of the lack of true ecumenism in this world, it is necessary to institute protectionist policies to prevent western and non-western religions from overrunning and destroying the Neterian faith and its practitioners.

Over a period of 1-3 generations of being deprived the opportunity to worship in the old fashion, in the old language and with the old understanding, the old religion is forgotten. Some of the rituals, symbols and traditions remain, but the original meaning is forgotten, and whatever prestige was due to the old religion is now ascribed to the new. Over time, a person is so conditioned and convinced of the new religion that even when evidences are presented to them that show what they are practicing is not the religion of their ancestors, they cannot even acknowledge that history or leave the superimposed religion. However, the negative conditioning can work in reverse also. By concentrating on the teaching, it can be readopted and if done properly, its descendants will be better practitioners than their parents, for by the second and third generations, such practitioners would lose the conditioning of the western culture and remain fully encompassed by the Neterian tradition. There is a saying: "Possession Is Nine Tenths Of The Law." Consider what happens when one parent kidnaps a child and the child is unable to grow up knowing the other parent. No matter what is done, after the child grows up there is no chance to undue the growing years. The experiences with the absent parent are impossible. Imagine now what has happened to whole cultures of people who have been taken away from their culture, language, religion, etc. (their parents). How can that be recaptured? The descendants cannot recapture the years lost, but they can re-adopt the religion, culture and traditions of their ancestors; and that is what must be done now. Those who want to build Neterian culture and community cannot allow their children to be possessed by the dominant culture or anyone else for that matter (sports, drugs, mindless entertainments, peer pressure, etc.).

If you seek economic freedom, it is difficult since we are increasingly all caught up in an interdependent web of globalism which is, by the way, supported by the extreme litigiousness of world culture. Even in the depths of the Amazon they cannot escape the reach of greed and those who would, because of economics, steal the land and use it for profit. Ultimately, due to modern technology and globalism, contact with other cultures is unavoidable at some point in life, but a well-established community can insulate itself to a great extent from the degraded values of the greater culture to promote an atmosphere of peace and altruistic inner research.

The answer is to associate with those who seek purity, to use economics and legality to promote peace; that is the closest one can come in present times, in this world of time and space, to a situation of autonomy and freedom. However, internally, through the practice of the spiritual philosophy and the disciplines of sema (yoga), one can become totally free from the world in a way that physical freedom is impossible.

In order for that to happen, the tools available to us, the resources and expertise of those who believe in the teaching, should be used wisely and managed properly; then our condition will be changed, but even that prosperity must be transcended through the teachings. That is the highest human culture, the greatest achievement. And that is what illumines the world with hope. That is the legacy of elevated personalities, the sages.

Providing love and support to the children in the form of time and caring is most important, but a requisite is sheltering them from the decadence of the wider culture, at the very least until their moral character is better developed and self-sustained. They should learn about other cultures, but not interact with them until young adulthood at the earliest. So just as spiritual aspirants should seek good associations, communities and cultures should also.

Thus, if it were possible, those serious and advanced practitioners should segregate their communities from the orthodox western religious practitioners, the secularists, and those of other traditions who do not understand or accept the existence of other religions besides their own. There can be interaction on the level of political contact and economic trade to the extent it is needed to support the Neterian community, but those followers of orthodox western traditions cannot be allowed to live in the Neterian communities or interact with the youth of the Neterian culture. They definitely may not hold political or social positions in the Neterian community or address the Neterian community, only its leaders. The community is to be governed by the precepts and teachings of Maat and the leaders are to be members of the religious order of Shetaut Neter. The mature and elder members of the Shetaut Neter community may interact with members of the culture at large as needed. They may travel and interact with other officials of other countries. But the youth may not do so until their moral character is well developed, and they are educated with the culture or Maat. That may take well into the early teen years. Non Neterian (contradictory to the principles of Maat) approved advertising, business enterprises and worldly pursuits of pleasure-seeking, greed, frivolous entertainments and the consumer culture are to be prohibited. Tourism is to be strictly controlled. Visitors should be kept to a low number and they should not be allowed to proselytize, propose "business" ventures, bring moral degradations or give tips, or gifts in exchange for services or even as "goodwill" gestures to the population of the Neterian community directly. Western religious monuments and icons are not to be displayed at large.

The country today known as Bhutan practices Buddhism at cultural, spiritual, economic and political levels of society, and exhibits many of the qualities that one would expect the Neterian culture to exhibit if it had survived intact from ancient times into the present. This is because in ancient times there was a close connection between Buddhism and Neterian religion. Therefore it is no surprise that the Buddhist culture would have developed similar teachings and forms of government to those of the Neterian culture. The history of government and social regulations in Bhutan is instructive for those who may in the future wish to create a Neterian community. The homeland of such a community should be located in the continent of Africa, in an African country not corrupted by western values or religions, and not within the territories controlled by the western religions and the western secular culture. The Neterian community should adopt the Kemetic language, clothing, and calendar, as well as the Neterian holidays and festivals. The Neterian community should adopt the Sebait curriculum supplemented by selected subjects covering modern technological advanced and political science, and should be learned by government leaders, priests and priestesses who may travel to foreign countries and serve as ministers in the government.

Challenges for Neterian Priests and Priestesses in the 21st Century

Above: The Challenges to African Religion: *Christianity, Islam, Marxism and Secularism*

Native African Religion has been challenged by Christianity and Islam for many years, but now also it is being challenged by at least two additional pressures, Marxism and secularism. The eminent Africologist Ali A. Mazrui[136] noted, on a visit to Ethiopia in the mid 1980's, that the country had adopted Marxism,[137] a philosophy of socialism or collectivism that requires, like its opposite extreme, capitalism – globalism (*Globalization*), the dropping of traditional customs and the adoption of a way of life that excludes spirituality, and even denies any validity to religion. Marxism repudiates religion altogether. Secularity is the turning away from religion and living with the conviction that one can direct one's life without divine guidance. Secularity is a degrading force in society, turning it towards pleasure seeking, un-tempered by the moral restraints or ethics which comes from religion. Thus, in due course of time, corruption and greed degrades the moral structure of the population. Individualism, high-living and self-gratification are facilitated by the secular viewpoint. This seduces people into engaging in capitalistic or despotic forms of government that promote certain segments of the population to become wealthy, while others languish in abject poverty. Globalism, the new term referring to opening up trade worldwide, really means giving up traditional values as well as individual rights to property and resources to be controlled by the few who become wealthy.

The important issues for the Neterian clergy are how to provide for a viable spiritual practice of the mysteries for themselves, and then also how to promote the Neterian culture for the wider community and for the betterment of the world? Those who feel the call of Neterian spirituality should come together to promote their common interest and to support the practice of the Neterian teachings by adopting the ancient tradition as it was given in the past, but with minor adjustments to accommodate the needs of our times. They must fiercely hold on to the Neterian principles, practicing them, teaching them to each other, and promoting peace and enlightenment for those who are ready to tread the path of Shedy. They should accumulate wealth and use that wealth to provide proper venues for the study of the Neterian teaching and the practice of the Neterian rituals, ceremonies and festivals. They should work tirelessly to attain the coveted goal of life, Nehast (Spiritual enlightenment) and leave a legacy for those who will come in the future so that they may be able to build on the glories of the past, and present, for the future. Then they will tap into the stream of cosmic forces from ancient times that are alive still today, which will carry them to heights of culture and illumination.

---

[136] *The Africans* by Ali Mazrui
[137] *The Africans* by Ali A. Mazrui

CONCLUSION

It needs to be clearly understood that those who claim to be "mystics" or ecumenical practitioners of the orthodox western religions are operating under a misconception since that is a contradiction in terms. Unable to fully separate from their religion of birth, they may seek to infuse certain ecumenical or esoteric principles into their practice of Judaism, Christianity or Islam. However, how can they reconcile the exclusivist and violent teachings in the orthodox scriptures? They cannot, so they act as if those statements do not apply or do not exist. They do not realize that supporting their religion even to the extent of calling themselves "Mystical Christians, Mystical Muslims or Mystical Jews actually means supporting the fundamental teachings of those religions which include religious imperialist exhortations and damnations towards all other traditions; even when Christians say that Christianity is for the "Jews and Gentiles alike" what is meant here is that the teaching is to be given to the Gentiles in an effort to convert them, and not just so that they may be benefited and left to practice religion in their own way as they see fit!.

The statements of the Judeo-Christian Bible and the Koran that speak of those religions as "the only true religion" and about themselves as the "chosen people," etc., lead to hubris, conceit and the condescending nature of practitioners of orthodox religion, which degrades to denigration and demonizing those who follow other traditions. That denigration and demonizing is what eventually allows a person to dehumanize others and then justify dispossessing them, killing them, and or treating them as less than human. That movement is diametrically opposed to the fundamental teachings of Neterian religion. Therefore, those denigration and demonizing movements are to be avoided by a Neterian community, and if necessary, confronted, opposed and held at bay. Evolved individuals can survive in such an atmosphere, but a community with lesser-evolved persons should be protected from such pressures. The community also needs to be protected from the consumer culture, the pleasure-seeking culture, the drug-culture, the secular culture, secular democracy, capitalism, etc.

The tension between Jews, Christians, Muslims and Arab Muslims is understandable since the teachings of their respective spiritual scriptures have been used to promote wars of conquest, one group trying to conquer the other. The wars of conquest led to apprehensions, and the western European countries set out to conquer and take the "Holy Lands" from the Islamist "heathens," but that was also an excuse to pillage and plunder, to conquer new lands and economic riches. However, the Muslims ultimately stopped the crusades. Later, during the Mogul Empire, the Muslims set out to conquer Europe and were stopped by the Christian Europeans. Is there any wonder why there is so much tension between Christians and Muslims? Both perceive the other as a conquering force. If they want to conquer each, other what can be said about other religions and cultures that are less prepared to meet this challenge? In order to survive and prosper, a religious society must be protected from infiltration by dogmatic and messianic forms of religion and dilution of the culture and values of the spiritual and cultural traditions.

How should practitioners of non-western religions, and especially the mystics, judge those with whom they interact who claim to be practitioners of western religions, and also at the same time claim to be ecumenical supporters of the mystical and non-western religions? Unless the followers of orthodox religion renounce the contradictory statements and make the necessary restitutions, they cannot be considered followers of ecumenical religion, which promotes peace and understanding among all religions. If they were to do so, by definition, they would not be practitioners of western orthodox religion. If they do not do so, they cannot be considered supporters of nonwestern religions nor can they be allowed (without being challenged) to make ecumenical sounding statements, thereby duping others of non-western religions into believing that they are friendly to practitioners of other religions, only to later cause discord and confusion among non-western religious groups who seek ecumenism and peace as well as the true practice of religion beyond dogmas, demagoguery and strife. Oftentimes there is a superficial harmony in the beginning but when it comes time to intermarry, share wealth, or control political power, there emerges, among the followers and leaders of orthodox western religion, repudiation, segregation from "nonbelievers" and open strife.

The true practice of religion entails three steps, myth, ritual and mysticism. The third level, mysticism, is not part of the orthodox western religious program. This renders those religions as limited, because their followers will only know about the myth and ritual aspects of religion, which are the folkloric level of culture and are different from culture to culture. Under these conditions, there will always develop competition and strife, leading to repudiation and violence. In fact, religions (western or non-western) that do not contain the full program to promote spiritual evolution cannot be considered religions, but rather limited spiritual practices. Mysticism promotes Cosmic Consciousness and transcendental union with God(dess). Another aspect of contention is the western repudiation of the Goddess principle. The orthodox western religions are based on a patriarchal system of culture that rejects the female principle as a leader, and so those religions that promote the goddess are and will be repudiated by them. The western traditions also are in part affected by racism, so they also reject non-Europeans as spiritual leaders or as originators or religion. Orthodox dogmatic religions actively repudiate mysticism, meditation and yoga as "black" arts or "occultism" and admonish their followers to turn away from those practices. As for those followers of the western religions who say they are in harmony with the mystical religion, do they practice meditation, yoga or the mysteries? How can they when their traditions actively repudiate that? While it is true that the western religions seem to have turned out authentic mystics such as St. Francis of Assisi, Teresa de Avila and Rumi, it is important to understand that those practitioners engaged in practices such as meditation, mystical philosophy and actively renounced violence and promoted universal love for all human beings and not just for Jews, Christians or Muslims, and they also adopted the mystic vision of becoming one with God. So they are not seen as models of western religion by the western religious authorities, but rather are seen by them as outsiders. However, those outsiders are the real friends to practitioners of non-western religions and the mysteries. Nevertheless, the western traditions do not have a well organized and supported program for mystics, so those practitioners mentioned above are aberrations from the norm of western religion who practiced outside of the traditional western religious model and cannot be considered as representative of the western religions or the capacity of the western religions to lead a human being to a mystical spiritual realization.

Neterians should face those of other religions with peace and humility, but also with a forthright nature. Neterians should not try to convert anyone, nor should they go around proselytizing or arguing with those who are part of orthodox religious traditions or who do not have an ecumenical outlook on spiritual life. On the other hand, Neterians should not allow themselves to be proselytized to or duped into believing the dogmatic nonsense of orthodox traditions. Neterians should not allow themselves to be disturbed by the teachings followed by others. As a Neterian, you should confront your own ignorant but powerful indoctrinations you may have received in your youth. These issues are overcome by study of the teachings under qualified preceptorship. Neterians should deeply study the history of religions and dispel the hold of their ignorant upbringing, and then they will be able to respond intelligently to those who blindly follow religious traditions if such a response is necessary. Responses to dogmatists, fanatics and cult followers will fall on deaf ears, but sometimes responses need to be made, such as in situations when one is invited to make a presentation and ignorant statements are made as commentary by attendees, or if ignorant statements or questions are presented in a Neterian spiritual venue. However, it is proper to, as the ancient Egyptian proverb says, "Speak to those who understand you;" this means holding conversations, talks, presentations, etc., for those who are interested, but only to the level of their spiritual evolution. Neophytes should receive introductory teachings and not high philosophy, mystical wisdom or advanced meditation techniques. A person needs to be properly initiated, and they must practice the teachings of Maat for a time first before they can be admitted to higher knowledge. Otherwise they will receive "too much information," too soon, and either develop a mundane opinion of it and drop it, thinking it is much ado about nothing, thinking it is nothing much except imaginations and rantings of kooks , or they will progress into advanced experiences they are not ready for yet and cause themselves harm, and thereby repudiate the teaching.

In order to be effective, the teaching must be received by a person who has faith in it, and not a person who has faith in other systems or is distracted by other philosophies and or worldly desires. Also, the person needs to be pure of heart, that is, virtuous. The person needs to be physically and mentally healthy, and not agitated, deranged or egoistic. The scriptures prohibit teaching those who are not qualified or who are not serious about the teachings. This would be an ill use of time that should be spent teaching those who are ready to listen to the teachings with a mature countenance, realizing that the world and life are fleeting and that life has a greater and more sublime purpose than mere pleasure-seeking, procreation or the accumulation of wealth. And there must be willingness to pursue the teachings with sincerity and tenacity, and not whimsically or in a juvenile fashion. The person to be taught needs to be devoted to God(dess), not fanatically, but intelligently, using the intellect for critical thinking, not with a fault finding nature, but with a sharp, inquisitive mind that seeks for truth. And finally, the ideal aspirant needs to have strength of will to apply herself/himself to practice the teachings for an extended period of time, to give the teaching a real possibility for success.

Chapter 10: Pledging One's Life to The Temple

Arit Ankh – "to take an oath of life"

Pledging One's Life to The Temple: The Creed of the Rekhyt

 Rekhyt bird - common folk (congregation)

Ancient Egyptian records show that it was not uncommon in the late period for some common men and women (rekhyt) to pledge themselves to the service of a particular deity; in doing so they served the Temple and in exchange received sanctuary and spiritual upliftment. An example of such a pledge was that of Tanebtunis, who devoted herself to a Temple using the following words:

> *"I am your servant, along with my children and my children's children; I will not be able to leave your enclosure, ever. You will guard me and you will protect me, safe and sound, you will defend me against any evil spirit, male or female, any sleepwalker, any epileptic, any incubus, any dead person, any drowned person, any hostile spirit".*[138]

Some aspirants do a lot of research, a lot of reading of books on other spiritual traditions, trying to elevate themselves. But to do the research, there must be what the sages admonished, an unobstructed ability to concentrate on the teaching; this means that the aspirant must do research in one teaching, in one path, and with one teacher. This one teacher does not include the aspirant. Specifically, some aspirants want to "co-teach" themselves. They want to approve of whatever the teacher says and choose to adopt it or not, or choose whatever suits them and leave the rest. All human beings have a choice to follow or not. However, those who recognize the true teaching should relinquish that right and give themselves to that teaching, submitting to the authority of that teaching. Otherwise the aspirant will be distracted, and there will be conflict with his or her own misconceptions or between one teacher who teaches one way and another teacher who teaches another way. In the Neterian traditions, there was the same kind of understanding. If an aspirant was admitted to the ancient Temple of Aset, even though there was a recognition of the relationship of all the Temples and all the divinities, the aspirant would follow the teaching of that particular Temple and its supervising priest or priestess; thus, their mentor would be from the Aset Temple, not the Khnum Temple, Djehuti Temple or some other Temple.. So one's serious studies have to be guided, and there has to be a concerted effort in one path, with full devotion and dedication with obedience and respect.

The aspirant must be following a single path and other paths can be ancillary. This idea of surrendering oneself to the Temple, surrendering the egoism, and surrendering one's life is enjoined in this pledge. One should resolve to be, as it were, in the fold of the teaching of the Temple. You give your life to that teaching and that Temple supports you in your life. In this particular example of the *Tanebtunis'* pledge, *Tanebtunis* is also pledging her children, but of course the children will be trained as they grow up and will have their own choice to make. When a person is brought up in a system, they are likely to adopt it

---

[138] H. Thompson, 'Two Demotic Self-Dedications," *Journal of Egyptian Archaeology* 26 (1940), pl. XII; see also his translation, ibid., 70.

automatically. This is especially so when the mother culture is not taught and the children are allowed to be exposed to another culture which is dominant. This is how entire nations have lost their culture and heritage. When conquering nations raise children from the conquered nation and teach them the language and culture of the conquering nation, the children automatically grow up to believe the new, dominant culture is their own. This is one of the big problems of present day aspirants. They have grown up in cultures where they have been indoctrinated with the western religious concepts, the secular culture of individuality and pleasure-seeking. Consequently, it is very hard for them to throw off these influences and adopt a new path, especially when they are being bombarded by these influences pressuring them constantly, day by day. It would be a lot easier to take a person from scratch, as an infant, rather than one who has been indoctrinated into their adolescent years. This is perhaps the most important challenge that faces modern day aspirants.

Commitment to Serve God

Being a "Servant of God" means giving one's life to service of the world and humanity, to act as a conduit for divine love and compassion to the world, to become a divine instrument to bring healing and peace to the world. This service is not confined to the Temple, but it is to be exercised in every aspect of the life of a priest or priestess. Treading the path of the Neterian Clergy demands this kind of dedication and concentration, and none should aspire to be Neterian priests or priestesses who are not willing to pledge this oath to the Neterian Path.

"Searching for one's self in the world is the pursuit of an illusion."
-Ancient Egyptian Proverb

There are many ways that the mind can fool itself into believing it can maintain the status quo and still also enter into the nether regions of Cosmic Consciousness. Some people seek the priesthood for social status or because it boosts their ego to feel important or special. Those personalities who hold onto their worldly ideals, possessions, and desires, couching these in the guise of worldly responsibility, the search for peace, warmongering, cultural survival, etc., are deluding themselves. Any excuse can be used to not face the things that contradict the desires of the ego to allow the ego to remain unchanged. An aspirant may say he/she believes in the non-violent teachings of Maat and yet justify hitting someone by saying they had to do it to protect honor, when in reality they did it because they enjoyed the strife. There is only one way to be truly free from the bonds of ignorance, illusion and the sorrows of life; the worldly ego consciousness must die, just as Asar died in the Asarian Resurrection Myth. This is the ultimate quest of the priesthood, to die and be reborn as Asar, a divine being. Those who are not on that quest should not pursue the path of the Neterian clergy. They should remain as the rekhyt, the devout common folk, until they are through searching for happiness in the world and are ready to follow the course of advanced spirituality. In the Asarian Resurrection Myth, the divinity Asar, who symbolizes the soul in a human being, is dismembered by his brother Set who represents egoism, and put back together (re-membered) and resurrected by his wife, goddess Aset. The true meaning of the dismemberment of Asar is the disintegration of the ego consciousness. When Aset reconstitutes (reintegrates-resurrects) the dismembered soul (Asar), it is reintegrated with new wisdom, the enlightening teachings of Aset. Thus, the ego must be deconstructed and reconstructed. This cannot happen as long as there has not been a real experience of Transcendental Consciousness. If that deconstruction and reconstruction were to happen, the ego as it was in the past would be no more and a new personality would emerge, one aligned with the Higher Self.

There is only one way to attain the goal of life and that is by righteousness. Any actions that are not righteous, but rationalized as such, constitute a grave act of unrighteousness, born of miseducation or willful ignorance, and will lead to the opposite of spiritual Enlightenment, peace and harmony. In the inner life a person can rationalize lying, cheating, stealing, not practicing meditation, not studying a teaching, not protecting the right of all human beings, etc., and there may seem to be prosperity in their land, and in their bank account. However, that apparent wealth will become the source of great sorrow for those people and their families. The surest way to attain personal integrity and purity is to follow the injunctions of Maat, and that should be the primary responsibility of all aspirants and clergy alike. Recall the important teaching in Chapter 33 of the *Book of the Dead*, it states that a righteous aspirant should be able to utter the following declarations:

Excerpts of Chapter 33(18) of the Pert M Heru [139]

1. I have lived by righteousness and truth while on earth. I live in righteousness and truth; I feed upon right and truth in my heart. I have done what is required to live in harmony in society and the gods and goddesses are also satisfied that I have worshipped rightly.
2. I have done God's will. I have given bread to the hungry, water to the thirsty, clothes to the clotheless and a boat to those who were shipwrecked (home to the homeless). I made the prescribed offerings to the gods and goddesses and I also made offerings in the Temple to the glorious spirits.

The Concept of Guru and The Concept of Seba

Left: The Guru Vasistha teaches Lord Rama. Right: Lord Heru leads the initiate to the mysteries.

This section is included here for those who are considering treading the path of Neterian priesthood and for those who may have been exposed to the Indian system of teacher-disciple relationships so that they may understand the similarities and contrasts of the Ancient Egyptian-African path and the Hindu-Indian path of the priesthood. There are many similarities in the traditional roles of spiritual preceptors in Ancient Egypt and India, but also some fundamental differences. In Ancient Egypt the priests and priestesses were revered as enlightened councilors and spiritual leaders or sages. There are few cases where they are canonized or considered as gods and goddesses as such. Imhotep is one such example. However, they were charged with becoming one with the tutelary divinity of their Temple during rituals, in order to bring forth the glory of that divinity. The priesthood in India developed into a highly revered caste of society due to the emphasis amongst spiritualists on a particular form of Yoga, the path of Bhakti, as well as the discipline of upanishad (following a spiritual preceptor and revering him/her as possessor of God consciousness). Bhakti means "Devotion," specifically developing the capacity of divine love as a means to achieve spiritual Enlightenment. In the path of Bhakti, one must develop love for God, a process that is made easier for the

---

[139] For the full text see the *Book of the Dead* by Sebai Muata Ashby

spiritually immature by developing love for the Guru, who is revered as a personification of God. This is the same idea that is behind the used of statues of the divinities in both the Kamitan and Indian traditions, that it is easier for the human mind to focus on, accept and love something that has a name and form, as opposed to the formless Transcendental Self. Thus, icons and spiritual preceptors serve as alternative foci for the mind to facilitate it in shifting from its egoistic interaction with the gross world of names and forms to still embracing names and forms, but now with a shift from the worldly to the Divine (spiritual icons, spiritual preceptor), and finally, when one has become sufficiently immersed in the teachings and have received a glimpse of Cosmic Consciousness, transcending even the attachment to these spiritual names and forms (the spiritual preceptor and the icons).

Ancient Egyptian Proverbs:

> "It is very hard, to leave the things we have grown used to, which meet our gaze on every side. Appearances delight us, whereas things, which appear, not, make their believing hard. Evils are the more apparent things, whereas the Good can never show Itself unto the eyes, for It hath neither form nor figure."

> "Of all marvels, that which most wins our wonder is that man has been able to find out the nature of the Gods and bring it into play. Since then, our earliest progenitors were in great error- seeing they had no rational faith about the Gods, and that they paid no heed unto their cult and holy worship- they chanced upon an art whereby they made Gods. To this invention they conjoined a power that suited it derived from cosmic nature; and blending these together, since souls they could not make, they evoked daimon's souls or those of angels; and attached them to their sacred images and holy mysteries,
> so that the statues should, by means of these, possess the powers of doing good and the reverse."

Quote from Dionysus the Areopagite:

> "If anyone suggests that it is disgraceful to fashion base images of the Divine and most Holy orders, it is sufficient to answer that the most holy Mysteries are set forth in two modes: one by means of similar and sacred representations akin to their nature, and the other to unlike forms designed with every possible discordance ... Discordant symbols are more appropriate representations of the Divine because the human mind tends to cling to the physical form of representation believing for example that the Divine are "golden beings or shining men flashing like lightning." But lest this error befall us, the wisdom of the venerable sages leads us through disharmonious dissimilitudes, not allowing our irrational nature to become attached to those unseemly images ... Divine things may not be easily accessible to the unworthy, nor may those who earnestly contemplate the Divine symbols dwell upon the forms themselves as final truth."

The Upanishadic tradition of India highlighted the importance of being close to and listening to the teachings of a spiritual preceptor, in order to gain the necessary instruction, guidance and insight to understand the mystical teachings. All of this led to a developing reverence towards spiritual personalities, and the highest being the guru. The guru is treated as God incarnate because that person is seen as a walking, talking conduit of divine awareness, which can at will bestow wisdom and Enlightenment directly from the source. However, the danger here is that if the Yoga of Devotion is practiced improperly, as can easily occur with the practice of spiritually immature aspirants, this can prove to be a hindrance on the spiritual path, leading to stagnation instead of a movement towards God and transcendence. This is because the aspirant, instead of relating to the personality of the guru as an instrument for the flow of Divine consciousness and developing attachment to the Divine through the Guru, becomes attached to the personality (name and form) of the Guru, sometimes so much so that if their guru dies, they cannot allow themselves to become associated with another preceptor. The personality of the Guru may be a receptacle for the Divine, but it is nevertheless a worldly image and reminder of time and space, thus making devotion to the personality of the sage worldly attachment. This is what Dionysus the Areopagite was pointing out in the above quote as the reason that the Kamitan sages configured zoomorphic (animal) or composite (part human – part nonhuman) images as divinities, because they recognized that non-human representations of the Divine will still give the mind a name and form to focus on, but will make it less likely for the mind to develop blind attachment, and therefore, the mind will more easily be able to focus on the principle behind the image, and transcend the image itself.

This kind of reverence towards priests and priestesses was unknown in Ancient Egypt. Rather, the mysteries were kept closely amongst the initiates within the Temple system, and the public was only allowed to participate during holidays, traditions and public festivals. The teaching was disseminated within the Temple system, and it was the Divine and the teaching that were the primary focus and not the spiritual preceptor. It was perhaps in their wisdom that the Kamitan priests and priestesses sought to avoid the situation that has developed in modern India, where the teachings are so proliferated that there are many charlatans throughout the country conning the common folk. Also, there is no central authority to control the dissemination of the teachings, and consequently there are many people saying many things, which perhaps even they believe are correct, and yet are based on their own imaginations or fabrications. Further, one world renowned Guru remarked that while the Bhagavad-Gita, considered as the Hindu Bible, is revered in many Indian homes, common people hardly ever study its text, but remain only uttering mantras (verses-chants) from its text. In Ancient Egypt the Sebai was a teacher of the highest mysteries, and he or she led the initiate to understand these.

For more insight into the term, Seba means star. It means an illuminating force, a shining object. Seba also means teacher of the philosophy. Sebai is the mystical spiritual preceptor. Therefore the reason why teachers are called Seba is because they illumine. Now, what do they illumine? They illumine the 'sebat' (seba with the 't' at the end of it). In Kamitan literature, when you add a 't' to a word it makes if female. What all this means is that all of you as students are females, whether you are physically a male or female, and the preceptor is male, whether the preceptor is physically male or female. This means the illuminator is shining on you, just like the sun shines on the moon, and just as the moon, a symbol of mind, receives illumination from the sun, the student receives illumination from the teacher. That illumination is an emanation of seed from Spirit, which is received in the mind of the aspirant, which is the womb, just as in an ordinary sexual relationship, the male is emits (ejaculates) and the female is receives the seed (sperm). The female receives and with that creates a fertilized egg and brings forth life. In the same way the student is to allow their mind to become pregnant with the teachings, and through the teachings, eventually give birth to Enlightened Consciousness. That is the deep tantric philosophy behind the term 'Seba'.

Similarly in India, the term 'guru' symbolizes illuminator, one who illumines the cave of the heart or shines a light on there to see what is in there, the Divine. In the deep mysticism of the Kamitan Culture and there is an artifact that is called Seba-ur; ur means great, therefore, it is 'the great illuminator.'

Priestess is Mother, Priest is Father

The term *Hemut Neter* – High Priestess-wife of the God is derived from *Hmt* –woman. These words are related to *mut*, which means "mother." All mothers are originated from the Mother Goddess: *Mut*. With respect to father, we have *atf Her* - Divine Father.

In mystical philosophy, the mother gives life. Thus, woman is the principle of what is, what exists. The man protects and disciplines the child. The father provides authority and gives approval. The father therefore, is the principle of dominion. It is the father who trains the child and tests him or her, and just as the sage tests the initiate and finally, grants authority to the initiate to become a teacher, to lead others on the path. These are mythic principles. However, a man or woman can fill either role, as either contains within them the capacity to mother or discipline. Recall the teaching of the sage Lady Aset to her son Heru from the Asarian Resurrection text:

> "Souls, Horus, son, are of the self-same nature, since they came from the same place where the Creator modeled them; nor male nor female are they. Sex is a thing of bodies not of Souls."[140]

Anyone who wants to grow to adulthood must obtain the teaching of the mother and the approval of father just as anyone who aspires to the priesthood must be approved by the overseer (parent) priests and priestesses. When this approval is given, the father symbolically dies and the child assumes the role of teacher and protector of the faith and the society. In the Asarian Resurrection Myth, this is one meaning of the death of Asar, his ascension to the Netherworld, and the coronation of Heru.[141] In a greater sense, women come from Creation and Men come from Spirit. Creation gives physical life to all creatures and the Spirit infuses them with the spark of consciousness that makes them live.

The Ritual of Initiation

besintu- "induction, initiation"

The Hieroglyphs of the Initiation Rites

The priesthood is an initiatic science and there is a special initiation that occurs at different levels of the priesthood. In a sense the priestly initiations are like rites of passage and recognition of spiritual attainment, but also pathways to greater illumination. Many people have heard of the term "initiation" and numerous misconceptions have been developed around it. The Ancient Egyptian term for initiation or induction is *Bes* or *Bez* – meaning to *induct* - initiate a priest or priestess. This term is related to *Besu* – fire and *Besy* - advance in the study of books, i.e. the scriptures. Also very importantly it is related to the term *Bess* - rise up – elevate – pass though - go up, advance. In other words *bes* relates to initiation into the spiritual philosophy, which is the fire of wisdom that allows one to elevate in spiritual consciousness, i.e. to burn away the ego personality.

The ritual of initiation has certain basic components. The following writings by Ancient Egyptian initiates give insight into the events that took place, as well as the process of spiritual elevation which constituted their initiatic program. A demotic papyri provides one of the details of initiation.

> *They went to seek Ptahnefer, the new prophet of Amun, they conducted him to the Temple, and they anointed his hands to initiate him into the service of Amun.*[142]

---
[140] see the book *Resurrection of Osiris* by Sebai Muata Ashby
[141] ibid
[142] P. Rylands IX; see F. Ll Griffith, *Catalogue of the Demotic Papyri in the John Rylands Library Manchester* (Manchester), 1909)

The anointing is a very important ritual act as it relates to the overflowing expansion of consciousness that occurs when the mind expands. The ritual of the anointing is a symbol of the act of transcending and opening up to Cosmic Consciousness and immortality. That experience is a blissful feeling not unlike the sexual orgasm, but purer and more profound. The following image from the Temple of Seti I at Abdu shows the ritual of the anointing.

A text on a statue in the Cairo Museum provides more details of the initiation ritual as a new priest states:

> *"I was presented before the god, being an excellent young man, while I was introduced into the horizon of heaven. . . . I emerged from Nun (the primordial waters), and I was purified of what ill had been in me; I removed my clothing and ointments, as Heru and Seth were purified. I advanced before the god in the holy of holies, filled with fear before his power."*[143]

Thus, the first aspect of the initiation ritual itself is the washing or dunking in the Temple pool. Nun is actually the primordial waters from which Ra-Atum arose in the beginning to engender Creation. The Temples in ancient times were constructed with artificial lakes or pools, which symbolized the Nun. Accordingly, the new initiate would have been taken to the divine lake and completely submerged there, and arise anew to discover the mystery of life. This is the purification by Nun, the Primeval Waters of Creation, i.e. Creation as it was/is without differentiation, without form, or conditioning. When the mind takes on that undifferentiated form it reverts back to its pure state, transcending time and space and the opposites of Creation. This is the goal of the work of the priests and priestesses.

The initiate is thus purified and cleansed of all worldly attachments as Heru and Set were purified in ancient times. The legendary conflict between Heru and Set is the quintessential battle between the ego (vice) and the soul (virtue) for control of the personality. When these opposing forces are purified, there emerges *Hetep* or Supreme Peace in the personality; this leads to elevation of consciousness, i.e. transcendence of the opposites in creation, the discovery of non-duality. This is what it means to advance (*Bes*) or be initiated into the knowledge of the Higher Self, which is symbolized by the image itself. Only the high priests and the new initiates are allowed to go into the inner shrine, the Holy of Holies, to behold the divine image, a statue that displays the special form of the Divine that is being worshipped. The images of the Divine are carved into the Temple walls for all initiates to see, but the image that was kept in the *Khem* - Holy of Holies - inner shrine - sanctuary, was the special image. This special image of the Divinity was also referred to as *Khem* - the Divinity of Power - generative force. It was made of gold and jewel ornaments, bedecked with special clothing and was to be handled only by the special priest or priestess designated to take care of the needs of the Divinity. Offerings to the Divinity were to be brought into the inner shrine only by the special clergy. So the image was kept in a special place for the eyes of the initiates exclusively. At festival time the image would be taken out of the Temple in a special container, but would remain unseen by the uninitiated masses. So if this special image was of a male divinity it was called *Khem n ren f*- he whose name is not known - i.e. God. These terms are phonetically related to *Qamit* - Ancient Egypt *Qamit* - blackness – black. Thus, the priesthood retains the secrecy as well as the special urgency to know the divine image, for when too much information given to the masses, it becomes mundane and uninteresting to them. Therefore, the mystery and the mystique of the inner shrine was a well-refined art in Ancient Egypt. The later Greek initiates such as Plutarch and Apuleius (initiates into the Temple of Aset {Isis}) revealed many teachings about the procedures of the mysteries, but explained that they were told secrets that they could not repeat for the uninitiated.

---

[143] Cairo Catalogue General 42230; for a translation of the text see K. Jansen-Winkeln, *Agyptische Biographien der 22. und 23. Dynastie*, Agypten und Altes Testament 8 (Wiesbaden, 1985), 172.

The initiation of Lucius into the cult of Aset (Isis) at Rome was reported by Apuleius in his writings called *Metamorphoses:* Book II. Using hieroglyphic scrolls, the priest, explained the rites of the initiation. Next Lucius was purified in "the nearest public baths" and was

> "sprinkled ... with holy water.... After this, he (the priest) brought me back to the Temple and placed me at the very feet of the Goddess. He gave me certain orders too holy to be spoken above a whisper."

This was the introductory stage of the initiation; Lucius was obliged to ten days of fasting, which was followed by the entry into the Holy of Holies and the reception of the secret knowledge. Lucius continues as he explains that the priest then

> "invested me in a new linen garment and led me by the hand into the inner recesses of the sanctuary itself." "I approached the very gates of death and set one foot on Prosperpine's threshold, yet was permitted to return, rapt through all the elements. At midnight I saw the sun shining as if it were noon; I entered the presence of the gods of the under-world and the gods of the upper-world, stood near and worshipped them."

Picture of a priest dressed in the form of the god Heru leading the initiate (Nefertari) to the inner shrine.

Fasting is a way to promote a condition in which the body is least obstructive to the clear vision of the transcendental worlds. However, there is a line between fasting for spiritual insight, guided by spiritual preceptorship, and fasting for attaining altered states of consciousness. The spiritual vision that is sought by initiates requires purity of body, mind and soul. This means a rigorous training in philosophy and control of the mind in order to discern reality from unreality or hallucinations from divine visions. So while modern day religions use limited forms of fasting at religious festivities or observances, the initiates use it to reduce the pull of the physical aspect of the personality so that the mind may soar free to explore the higher realms of expanded consciousness. Fasting can be dangerous for the uninitiated, both physically and mentally. If the body is unprepared it may be plunged into a health crisis. If the mind is untrained, it may be pushed into a world that it is ill equipped to understand and integrate, and thus develop insanity. For more on fasting see the book *Kamitan Diet* by Sebai Muata Ashby.

On the next page: Heru leads Ani in the Temple Ritual (Papyrus Ani)

Summary of the steps of the initiation ritual:

- ➢ Study of the Philosophy
- ➢ Preparation through virtue
- ➢ Practice of the worship rituals
- ➢ Preparation through vegetarianism
- ➢ Fasting
- ➢ Anointing
- ➢ Cleansing
- ➢ Presentation of the initiate before the Divine image.
- ➢ Receiving secret knowledge in reference to the nature of the Divine.
- ➢ Emerging with new clothes and new identity

After days of fasting and meditation, the initiate was led by a priest or priestess, who wore the garments and headdress of the particular divinity which served that function at the specific Temple, in a procession leading to the sanctuary (the inner shrine) which is the highest point of the floor of the entire Temple, symbolizing the primeval mound which God elevated out of the primordial waters and upon which God stood in the beginning of time. (See the book *Egyptian Mysteries Vol. 1*)

The change of clothing is evident also in the *Prt m Hru* or *Book of the Dead*. In the scene above, the initiate, Ani, enters the hall of Maati for summary judgment. Here he is depicted entering with his wife and both wear completely white clothing. However, upon successfully passing through the hall and being found to be righteous, he alone is led and his clothing is changed to white and gold. The symbolism of the change of clothing is the metaphor of a change of bodies, somewhat like a snake that sheds the skin in order to expand into a new life. No longer is the aspirant aware of only the physical, mortal existence, but also the Transcendental Reality. In the scene below, initiate Ani displays a change of clothing in the middle register from what he originally wore as he began the approach to the sanctuary to behold the Divine image, in this case, Asar. At the far left register (A) the priest, dressed as Heru, leads the initiate Ani by the hand. In register B, Ani is anointed as he kneels before the Divine image (C).

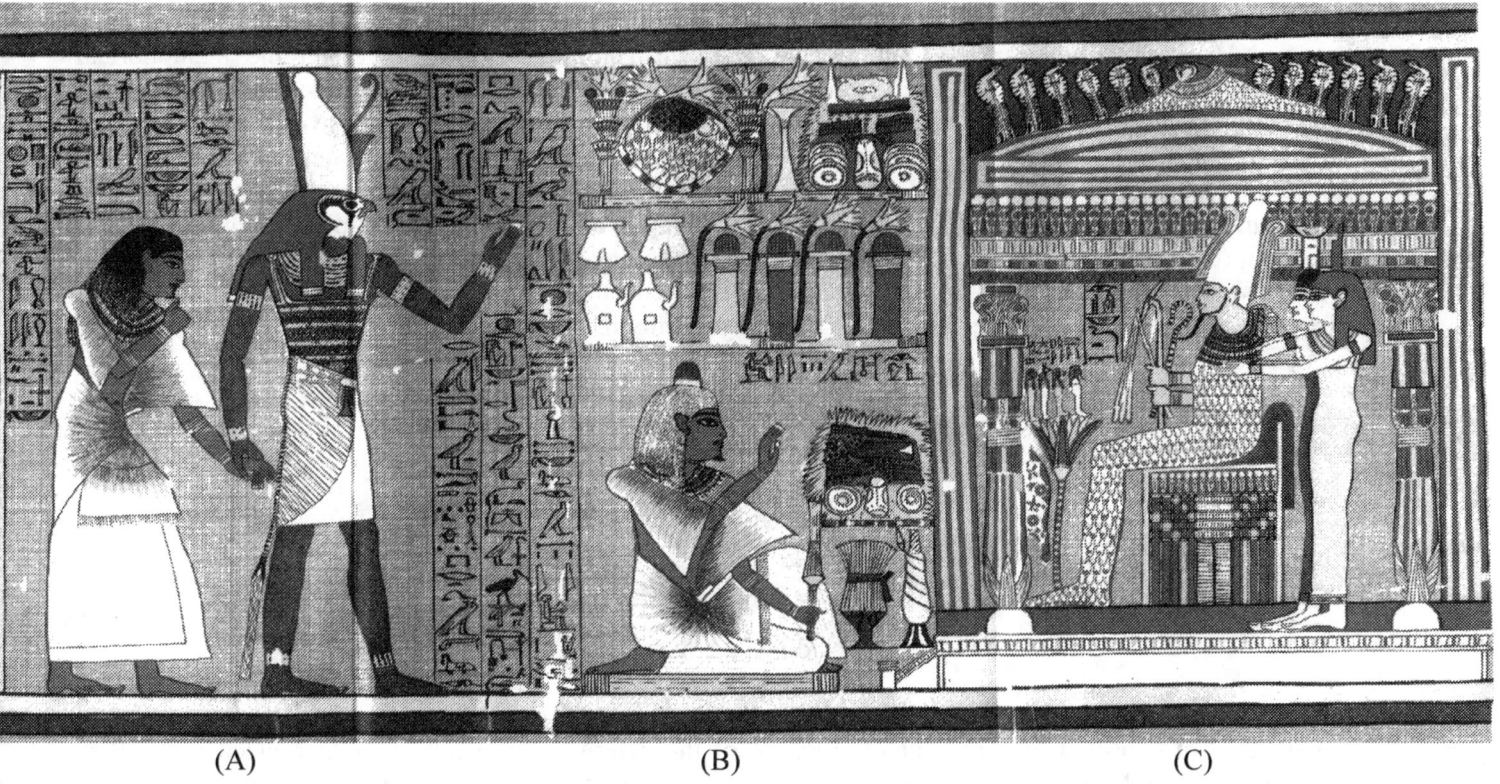

(A) (B) (C)

The Power of the Initiation Ritual

Rituals are a powerful process that can lead the mind toward spiritual thoughts and aspirations, or toward pain and sorrow in life. People cling to ignorance by constantly seeking for pleasure and fulfillment in the world of time and space through human relationships, wealth, possessions, etc. Examples of negative rituals are: going to the video store, watching television, gossiping, partying or going to the movie theater in search of excitement and happiness. In the course of ordinary life one may experience activities and entertainments, but if they are relied upon as sources of pleasure and happiness, one is bound for disappointments. All of life's activities are ritualistic to some degree. Every day we repeat many actions such as eating, sleeping, going to work or school, and watching television. Other activities are less frequent but just as ritualistic; these include marriage, childbearing, etc. The basis of society's rituals is custom and habit. Society teaches and socializes young individuals into the activities it deems acceptable, and thereby societal rituals develop. Rituals can be bad or good according to the level of spiritual realization within the individual, as well as the society as a whole. If a society allows exploitation of some of its members, then rituals and customs develop which affirm that belief system. When society developed the materialistic view of life and discounted the spiritual values, material values became part of the general culture. Thus, pursuing material wealth and the experience of sensual pleasures have become the most commonly practiced rituals in modern day society. This is reflected in business, government and in the family way of life at all levels of society. These rituals are all performed toward perishable goals and thus can never satisfy the inner need of the soul. This movement constitutes a movement in ignorance that leads to further ignorance. While religious rituals are also in the realm of human activity, if performed with growing levels of understanding and devotion toward the Divine, they will lead to greater and greater peace and self-knowledge. Therefore, the Sages and Saints have enjoined several rituals, prayers and words of power to help spiritual aspirants turn the mind toward spiritual realization rather than toward perishable worldly attainments that will inevitably lead to disappointments, pain and sorrow.

The avid aspirant should seek to discover the mysteries of life. The initiation ritual is a means to promote that discovery. Only the superficial details of the secret initiation have been discussed here. As for the ritual of initiation in ancient times, the ceremony included the reading of certain mystical hekau, the rite of submerging into the Temple pool, the unveiling of the initiate and the formal induction into the ranks of Hem and Hemt practitioner priests and priestesses. The Temple pool was in effect the metaphorical representation of the primeval ocean. This ritual was preceded by days (3 to 10) of fasting, cleansing and Hesi (chants). Also, there was the ritual anointing of the initiate as a metaphor of the overflowing nectar of Divine Consciousness that emerges from the crown of the head as Divine Consciousness is raised through the agency of the Serpent Power. Depending on the period and the particular Temple wherein the aspirant was initiated, the ritual might have included an extended stay in a coffin or burial chamber for the purpose of meditating (experiencing) on the mystery of death and engaging in the ritual identification with Asar, who died but was resurrected. Further, the ritual involved reenactments of the most important myths, most importantly, the Asarian Resurrection myth, the Creation myth, the myth of Hetheru and Djehuti, and the myth of Aset and Ra.

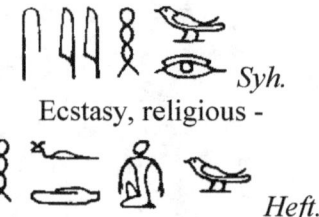

Syh.
Ecstasy, religious -

Heft.
Swoon or subsiding during religious ecstasy -

Through the initiatory experience the initiate is to experience *Syh*. The objective is to be transported to another level of consciousness in which the nature of the neteru is to be felt and experienced rather than theorized and pondered; that is called *Syh* (seeh). The initiate may even experience *Heft*, swooning. Henceforth, the glimpse attained acts as an encourager, allowing the initiate to have some little proof of the existence of the beyond. Then through further work the initiate becomes established in that transcendental state of consciousness. This stage is called illumination, Akhu, and resurrection, Nehast. This is the ultimate goal of the Neterian priesthood.

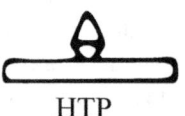

HTP

Sebai Maa

INDEX

Aahs, 183
Ab, 110, 116, 117, 138, 201, 208, 209, 212, 213
Abdu, 9, 14, 23, 47, 85, 117, 147, 237
Abraham, 70, 221
Absolute, 11, 52, 77, 106, 134, 254
Abu Simbel, 21, 50, 80
Acts, 64
Afghanistan, 219
Africa, 7, 9, 10, 12, 15, 16, 19, 20, 21, 22, 31, 37, 51, 52, 67, 69, 70, 74, 76, 90, 92, 165, 184, 185, 215, 216, 217, 219, 223, 225
African Religion, 99, 110, 134, 184, 200, 223, 226
Akhenaton, 11, 183
Akhnaton, 9, 86
Akhus, 87
Alexander the Great, 52
Alexandria, 24, 111
Allah, 65, 69, 70, 221
Amasis, 24, 25, 57
Amen, 24, 54, 63
Amenhotep III, 180, 181
Amenta, 256
Amentet, 257
Americas, 219
Ammit, 157
Amun, 9, 11, 24, 50, 53, 54, 67, 68, 80, 83, 99, 101, 114, 120, 122, 123, 127, 131, 153, 163, 175, 190, 200, 208, 209, 236, 254

Amun-Ra-Ptah, 99, 254
Anat, 189
Ancestors, 113
Ancient Egypt, 1, 2, 7, 9, 10, 11, 12, 13, 14, 15, 16, 17, 18, 19, 20, 21, 22, 23, 24, 25, 26, 27, 31, 39, 42, 43, 45, 46, 48, 50, 51, 52, 53, 54, 55, 57, 61, 63, 64, 65, 66, 67, 69, 70, 71, 72, 73, 74, 76, 77, 78, 80, 88, 90, 91, 92, 95, 101, 106, 108, 110, 111, 112, 114, 119, 120, 123, 124, 126, 127, 128, 131, 132, 134, 135, 139, 143, 147, 151, 152, 153, 155, 156, 157, 160, 161, 162, 163, 164, 165, 166, 169, 171, 173, 180, 181, 182, 183, 184, 185, 186, 188, 189, 191, 197, 203, 204, 205, 206, 208, 210, 215, 216, 217, 218, 219, 221, 222, 223, 231, 232, 233, 234, 235, 236, 237, 252, 253, 254, 255, 256, 257, 258, 259, 260
Ancient Egyptian Pyramid Texts, 173
Ancient Egyptian Wisdom Texts, 184, 186
Ancient Greek religion, 25
Ani, 11, 54, 87, 109, 137, 153, 167, 238, 240

Ankh, 66, 73, 91, 168, 223, 230
Anpu, 46, 106, 109, 157, 166, 167
Anu, 9, 23, 24, 26, 80, 94, 120, 200, 256
Anu (Greek Heliopolis), 9, 23, 24, 26, 80, 94, 120, 200, 256
Anunian Theology, 11, 22, 79, 80, 112, 153
Apep serpent, 124
Aquarian Gospel, 70, 215
Arabia, 70, 215
Arabs, 70, 183, 223
Architecture, 13, 151, 211
Ari, 184, 185
Aristotle, 48
Aryan, 70, 72, 254
Aryans, 72
Asar, 9, 11, 16, 17, 24, 27, 30, 31, 32, 46, 63, 70, 73, 80, 85, 87, 91, 92, 101, 106, 109, 112, 117, 123, 126, 131, 136, 138, 139, 141, 153, 157, 161, 162, 163, 165, 166, 167, 173, 183, 189, 190, 196, 198, 232, 236, 241, 242, 255, 256, 257, 258, 260
Asarian Myth, 89
Asarian Resurrection, 11, 92, 117, 153, 165, 232, 236, 242, 255, 257, 258
Asclepius, 162
Aset, 7, 9, 30, 31, 63, 66, 80, 84,

85, 91, 92, 99, 101, 117, 122, 126, 131, 139, 153, 157, 164, 166, 170, 183, 189, 196, 197, 198, 223, 231, 232, 236, 238, 242, 255, 256, 257, 258, 260, 262
Aset (Isis), 7, 9, 30, 31, 63, 66, 80, 84, 85, 91, 92, 99, 101, 117, 122, 126, 131, 139, 153, 157, 164, 166, 170, 183, 189, 196, 197, 223, 231, 232, 236, 238, 242, 255, 256, 257, 258, 260, 262
Ashoka, 52
Asia, 50, 51, 52, 55, 70, 73, 218, 223
Asia Minor, 50, 51, 52, 55, 70, 73, 223
Asiatic, 45, 50, 70, 71, 164, 218
Assisi, Francis of, 228
Assyrian, 63
Assyrians, 51, 55, 73, 183, 218
Astral, 106, 189, 256
Astral Plane, 106, 189, 256
Aten, see also Aton, 260
Aton, 9, 86, 112
Atonism, 86
Attitude, 179
Atum, 153, 237
Augustus, 17, 188, 205
Ba (also see Soul), 94
Balance, 201
Basu, 115, 116, 210, 212, 213
Beatitudes, 186

Being, 11, 12, 29, 66, 75, 77, 78, 79, 80, 82, 83, 85, 86, 88, 96, 101, 104, 134, 139, 156, 163, 170, 171, 172, 181, 190, 198, 203, 213, 232, 254, 257
Benben, 29
Benin, 184
Bernal, Martin, 27
Bhagavad Gita, 88, 235
Bible, 22, 63, 64, 65, 69, 185, 186, 220, 221, 222, 223, 227, 235, 257
Bishops, 184
Black, 27, 66, 189, 223
Black Athena, 27
Blackness, 10, 17
Book of Coming Forth By Day, 11, 190, 256
Book of Enlightenment, 10, 124
Book of the Dead, see also Rau Nu Prt M Hru, 10, 11, 52, 53, 79, 145, 153, 155, 156, 184, 185, 196, 233, 240, 256
British Empire, 219
Brooklyn Museum, 101, 164, 173, 175
Buddha, 52, 72, 216
Buddhism, 7, 23, 51, 52, 53, 72, 200, 215, 218, 221, 225
Buddhist, 20, 23, 52, 60, 72, 189, 215, 218, 219, 225
Bull, 140
Byzantine, 63
Cairo, 71, 106, 145, 177, 237
Canaan, 50, 215, 220
Canonized, 64
Capitalism, 215
Caribbean, 7
Catholic, 57, 64, 120, 184, 257
Causal Plane, 106
Celibacy, 191, 192, 196
Chakras, 53
Chakras (see energy centers of the body), 53
Chanting, 94, 146
Cheops, see also Khufu, 15
Child, 15
China, 22, 51, 64, 72, 90, 185, 215, 221
Christ, 21, 22, 27, 63, 64, 65, 66, 70, 123, 222, 223, 256
Christian Church, 63, 64, 67
Christian Zealots, 65
Christianity, 22, 24, 35, 37, 52, 63, 64, 65, 67, 69, 70, 71, 111, 184, 186, 197, 215, 218, 219, 221, 222, 226, 227, 253, 257
Chronology, 11
Church, 57, 63, 64, 65, 184, 257
Civilization, 11, 14, 16, 19, 20, 21, 22, 23, 26, 27, 51, 73, 90, 184, 216, 222
Coffin Texts, 11, 153, 155, 156
Colossi of Memnon, 181
Company of gods and goddesses, 29
Confucianism, 51, 52, 185, 215
Consciousness, 74, 89, 90, 134, 136, 137, 168, 173, 179, 208, 228, 232, 234, 235, 237, 242, 255
Contentment (see also Hetep), 76
Co-optation, 73
Coptic, 77, 155, 256
Cosmic consciousness, 88
Counseling, 112
Cow, 84
Creation, 11, 28, 29, 76, 78, 79, 80, 82, 83, 84, 85, 86, 131, 133, 147, 153, 222, 236, 237, 242, 254, 255, 256
Crusades, 63, 64
Culture, 16, 19, 20, 21, 22, 23, 28, 45, 72, 76, 92, 102, 113, 120, 154, 165, 184, 217, 218, 235, 254, 255
Cymbals, 259, 260
Dance, 163
December, 22, 73, 257
Delphi, 24
Demotic, 17, 155, 205, 206, 231, 236
Denderah, 9, 23, 62, 149, 151, 256
Dharma, 185, 215
Diaspora, 216, 218
Diet, 7, 140, 198, 238, 253
Diodorus, 16, 17, 26, 57, 188, 205
Dionysius, 64
Dionysius the Areopagite, 64
Dionysius, Pseudo, 64
Dionysus the Areopagite, 234, 235
Diop, Cheikh Anta, 16, 26, 27, 51
Discipline, 7, 52, 94, 126, 141, 151, 171
Divine Consciousness, 174, 242
Djed Pillar, see also Pillar of Asar, 109, 117
Djehuti, 11, 30, 31, 91, 106, 108, 117, 121, 128, 147, 156, 157, 162, 182, 206, 207, 231, 242
Dogon, 22
Drum, 259, 260
Duat, 123, 127, 172, 189, 190, 256
Dynastic period, 11
Dynastic Period, 11, 154, 165, 197
Ecstasy, 99, 242
Edfu, 8, 9, 23, 85, 94, 97, 105, 146, 147, 181, 256
Egyptian Book of Coming Forth By Day, 11, 190, 256
Egyptian civilization, 72, 183
Egyptian Mysteries, 11, 20, 60, 80, 117, 123, 135, 162, 171, 240, 253, 258
Egyptian Physics, 257
Egyptian proverbs, 91, 254
Egyptian religion, 11, 20, 22, 23, 31, 51, 66, 71, 74, 120, 156, 218, 222, 223
Egyptian Yoga, 7, 27, 52, 60, 74, 83, 88, 90, 91, 92, 95, 99, 164, 252, 253, 254, 255, 256, 259, 260
Egyptian Yoga Book Series, 7

244

Egyptian Yoga see also Kamitan Yoga, 7, 27, 52, 60, 74, 83, 88, 90, 91, 92, 95, 99, 164, 252, 253, 254, 255, 256, 259, 260
Egyptologists, 12, 13, 46, 65, 67, 71, 74, 92, 186
Elohim, 22, 222
Enlightenment, 7, 10, 19, 21, 23, 27, 31, 39, 41, 72, 74, 76, 79, 80, 82, 83, 85, 86, 87, 89, 92, 95, 108, 112, 117, 119, 123, 127, 128, 134, 136, 137, 140, 147, 165, 178, 185, 190, 191, 213, 232, 233, 234, 253, 254, 255, 256, 257, 258
Ethics, 11, 21, 22, 23, 27, 73, 94, 184
Ethiopia, 16, 17, 51, 65, 226
Ethiopian priests, 17, 188
Eucharist, 22, 73, 174, 222, 256
Eudoxus, 23, 25, 26
Eurasia, 51
European explorers, 216
Evil, 65, 70
Exercise, 7, 255
Eye of Heru, 174
Eye of Ra, 124
Faith, 202
Fasting, 238, 240
Female, 123
Folklore, 24, 218
Form, 262
Fundamentalism, 64, 65
Geb, 28, 30, 80, 92, 255
Geography, 26, 211
Giza, 12, 13, 15
Globalism, 215, 226
Globalization, 226
Gnostic, 63, 64, 111
Gnostic Christianity, 64
Gnostic Christians, 63
God, 1, 8, 22, 28, 31, 38, 40, 42, 46, 63, 64, 65, 66, 67, 69, 70, 71, 72, 76, 77, 88, 91, 92, 94, 96, 97, 99, 100, 105, 106, 107, 108, 116, 119, 120, 122, 123, 126, 128, 130, 131, 135, 139, 145, 147, 157, 160, 175, 177, 181, 182, 185, 186, 187, 188, 190, 191, 199, 203, 208, 212, 217, 220, 221, 222, 223, 228, 229, 232, 233, 234, 235, 237, 240, 254, 256, 257, 260
Goddess, 11, 52, 77, 84, 92, 124, 131, 153, 170, 185, 187, 189, 217, 228, 235, 238, 257, 259, 260, 261
Goddesses, 22, 75, 77, 80, 83, 84, 95, 123, 134, 135, 252, 255
Gods, 17, 22, 71, 75, 77, 80, 83, 95, 108, 123, 134, 135, 159, 234, 252, 255
Good, 108, 202, 234
Good Association, 108
Gospel of John, 64
Gospels, 257
Great Pyramid, 14, 15
Great Truths, 71, 74, 76, 96
Greece, 16, 23, 24, 25, 27, 51, 52, 90, 115, 160, 161, 164, 165, 186, 253
Greed, 54
Greek classical writers, 16, 23
Greek philosophers, 20, 24, 27, 160, 161, 185
Greek philosophy, 24, 253
Greek Philosophy, 24
Greeks, 20, 23, 24, 25, 26, 27, 51, 57, 61, 66, 132, 160, 161, 162, 164, 165, 180, 183, 185, 186, 189, 196, 218
Green, 101
Gregory, 66, 223
Gregory the Great, 66, 223
Guru, 128, 137, 233, 234, 235
Haari, 260
Hapi, 10, 63, 123
Harmony, 183
Hatha Yoga, 7, 53
Hathor, 11, 121, 255, 256, 257, 258
Health, 7, 95, 211, 253
Heart, 258
Heart (also see Ab, mind, conscience), 258
Heaven, 65, 257
Hebrew, 22, 42, 71, 156, 186
Hebrews, 71, 185
Hekau, 52, 94, 156, 260
Heliopolis, 9, 23, 24, 25, 26
Hell, 65, 70, 221
Hermes, 111
Hermes (see also Djehuti, Thoth), 111
Herodotus, 16, 20, 22, 24, 51, 196, 197
Heru, 8, 9, 10, 11, 13, 22, 23, 30, 31, 32, 66, 70, 73, 79, 80, 85, 90, 91, 94, 97, 101, 105, 108, 117, 126, 131, 141, 146, 147, 149, 153, 157, 165, 173, 174, 183, 187, 196, 223, 233, 236, 237, 238, 241, 256, 257, 258, 260
Heru (see Horus), 8, 9, 10, 11, 13, 22, 23, 30, 31, 32, 66, 70, 73, 79, 80, 85, 90, 91, 94, 97, 101, 105, 108, 117, 126, 131, 141, 146, 147, 149, 153, 157, 165, 173, 174, 183, 187, 196, 223, 233, 236, 237, 238, 241, 256, 257, 258, 260
Hetep, 46, 91, 136, 160, 170, 173, 174, 182, 237
Hetep Slab, 173
Hetheru, 9, 30, 31, 46, 62, 79, 84, 91, 95, 117, 120, 121, 124, 149, 151, 153, 163, 165, 189, 242, 258, 259
Hetheru (Hetheru, Hathor), 9, 30, 31, 46, 62, 79, 84, 91, 95, 117, 120, 121, 124, 149, 151, 153, 163, 165, 189, 242, 258, 259
Hetkaptah see also Menefer, Memphite, 9
Het-Ka-Ptah, see also Men-nefer, Memphis, 79, 82
Hieratic, 155
Hieroglyphic, 13
Hieroglyphic Writing, language, 13, 53, 126, 155, 156, 255
Hieroglyphs, 236

Hindu, 20, 23, 66, 67, 69, 70, 72, 94, 218, 233, 235
Hindu religion, 66, 69, 70
Hinduism, 23, 52, 71, 72, 154, 197, 200, 215
Hindus, 20, 23, 69, 219, 221
Holy Land, 215, 227
Holy of Holies, 98, 99, 106, 143, 144, 168, 237, 238
Homer, 57
Honesty, 201
Horus, 11, 50, 85, 90, 105, 145, 153, 157, 177, 178, 200, 217, 236, 260
Hyksos, 50, 51, 55, 73, 217, 218
Hymns of Amun, 186
Iamblichus, 25, 26, 158, 159, 160, 171, 172
Ibis, 30
Identification, 89
Ignorance, 217
Imhotep, 119, 189, 209, 233
Inculturation, 66, 223
India, 7, 16, 23, 51, 52, 53, 55, 67, 69, 72, 88, 90, 115, 162, 163, 185, 215, 219, 221, 233, 234, 235, 253, 254, 255, 260
Indian Yoga, 7, 88, 252, 254, 260
Indra, 72
Indus, 13, 90, 254
Indus Valley, 90, 254
Initiate, 33, 190, 218, 253
Intellect, 171, 172
Intelligence, 201
Isfet, 184

Isha Upanishad, 72
Isis, 11, 53, 63, 65, 84, 85, 99, 112, 139, 153, 161, 179, 196, 197, 198, 237, 238, 255, 256, 257, 260
Isis, See also Aset, 11, 53, 63, 84, 85, 99, 112, 139, 161, 179, 196, 197, 198, 237, 238, 255, 256, 257
Islam, 35, 37, 52, 65, 67, 69, 70, 71, 131, 156, 186, 197, 215, 218, 219, 220, 221, 223, 226, 227, 253
Israel, 69, 215, 220, 221
Jainism, 51, 52
Jerusalem, 21, 186
Jesus, 21, 22, 27, 31, 37, 63, 64, 65, 66, 70, 73, 111, 186, 222, 223, 256, 257
Jesus Christ, 256
Jewish, 11, 21, 22, 41, 65, 69, 70, 71, 72, 156, 186, 219, 220, 221, 222
Jewish Bible, 71
Jewish religion, 71, 156
Jews, 20, 22, 42, 65, 69, 70, 71, 186, 218, 220, 221, 222, 223, 227, 228
Joshua, 186
Joy, 76, 105
Judaism, 21, 22, 35, 37, 52, 65, 69, 70, 71, 154, 186, 197, 215, 218, 219, 221, 222, 227, 253
Judeo-Christian-Islamic, 20, 153
Justice, 185
Ka, 79, 123
Kabbalah, 219, 253

Kamit, 8, 9, 10, 11, 14, 20, 23, 30, 32, 48, 50, 52, 54, 57, 67, 72, 73, 75, 76, 78, 84, 85, 91, 94, 95, 97, 134, 147, 156, 165, 184, 185, 215, 217, 218, 224
Kamit (Egypt), 8, 9, 10, 11, 14, 20, 23, 30, 32, 48, 50, 52, 54, 57, 67, 72, 73, 75, 76, 78, 84, 85, 91, 94, 95, 97, 134, 147, 156, 165, 184, 185, 215, 217, 218, 224
Kamitan, 7, 10, 11, 16, 19, 20, 21, 23, 38, 46, 48, 52, 57, 61, 63, 70, 73, 75, 77, 79, 87, 89, 92, 101, 105, 111, 115, 119, 123, 128, 132, 133, 140, 145, 146, 153, 157, 162, 164, 166, 169, 185, 186, 188, 191, 197, 198, 201, 205, 208, 210, 217, 224, 234, 235, 238, 253, 257, 259, 260
Karma, 7, 89, 255
Karnak, 45
Kemetic, 7, 11, 21, 128, 188, 215, 225, 235, 259, 260
Khepri, 28, 29, 30, 32, 157
Khonsu, 83, 175
King, 11
King David, 186
King Solomon, 186
Kingdom, 16, 46, 47, 50, 55, 73, 83, 86, 119, 189, 257
Kingdom of Heaven, 257

KMT (Ancient Egypt). See also Kamit, 17
Know thyself, 87
Know Thyself, 24, 91, 117
Knowledge, 140
Koran, 69, 70, 220, 221, 223, 227
Krishna, 23, 31, 72, 257
Kundalini, 7, 52, 53, 89
Kundalini XE "Kundalini" Yoga see also Serpent Power, 7
Kush, 10, 11
Latin, 77
Learning, 43, 211
Libyans, 183
Life Force, 61, 91, 94, 135, 149, 198, 255
Listening, 94, 99, 140
Lord of the Perfect Black, 189
Lotus, 91
Love, 50, 88, 89, 94, 255
Lower Egypt, 11, 53, 90, 91, 189
Luxor, 67, 68
Maakheru, 75, 156, 157
Maat, 11, 13, 20, 22, 30, 35, 36, 40, 42, 50, 54, 72, 75, 89, 92, 94, 107, 112, 133, 151, 153, 157, 162, 163, 164, 169, 172, 173, 175, 177, 178, 180, 182, 183, 184, 185, 187, 192, 193, 203, 206, 208, 210, 216, 225, 228, 232, 233, 255, 257, 258
MAAT, 11, 36, 183, 185, 254, 255
Maati, 35, 163, 184, 240
MAATI, 255

Madonna, 22, 223
Mafdet, leopard goddess, 124
Magic, 52
Mahabharata, 72, 88
Male, 123
Manetho, 14
Manetho, see also History of Manetho, 14
Mantras, 94
Mars, 64
Marxism, 226
Masters, 21
Mathematics, 151
Matter, 257
Matthew, 63, 64, 186
Mecca, 215
Meditation, 30, 84, 88, 89, 92, 94, 96, 99, 112, 133, 140, 141, 171, 211, 253, 254, 255, 260
Mediterranean, 10
Medu Neter, 30, 91, 108, 153, 154, 156, 157, 163, 204, 206
Mehurt, 84
Memnon, 179, 180, 181
Memphis, 9, 23, 24, 25, 52, 179, 206
Memphite Theology, 11, 23, 82, 84, 112, 153
Men-nefer, see also Het-Ka-Ptah, Memphis, 9
Mer, 206
Merikara, 181
Mesopotamia, 50
Metaphysics, 48, 99, 211, 257
Middle East, 16, 51, 70, 123, 164, 165, 253
Middle Kingdom, 46, 48, 55, 119, 120, 155, 181
Min, 49, 92, 255
Mind, 7, 112
Moon, 10, 17, 141
Morals, 23, 39, 217
Mortals, 99, 100, 168
Moses, 21, 69, 71, 185, 186, 220, 223
Muhammad, 42, 70, 218, 223
Mundaka Upanishad, 72
Music, 7, 20, 27, 39, 126, 131, 147, 161, 162, 163, 164, 165, 169, 206, 210, 260
Muslims, 42, 63, 67, 68, 69, 70, 71, 165, 186, 218, 219, 221, 223, 227, 228
Mut, 11, 54, 83, 84, 92, 235
Mysteries, 11, 20, 21, 30, 31, 35, 52, 53, 64, 84, 99, 112, 134, 135, 136, 139, 158, 159, 160, 162, 165, 166, 171, 206, 211, 213, 222, 234, 252, 253, 257, 258
Mystical religion, 66
Mysticism, 2, 7, 27, 64, 92, 99, 221, 228, 254, 256, 257, 258
Mythology, 27, 74, 92, 161
Nat, 189
Native African Religion, 226
Native American, 64, 67, 215, 219, 223
Nature, 77, 179
Neberdjer, 30, 75, 254
Nebethet, 117, 260
Nebthet, 80, 122, 126, 157, 164, 166, 189
Nefer, 91, 182, 259, 260
Nefertari, Queen, 238
Nefertem, 82
Nefertum, 82
Nehast, 31, 87, 226, 242
Nekhen (Hierakonpolis), 14
Neolithic, 11, 13, 72
Neo-Platonism, 64
Nephthys, 131
Net, 189
Net, goddess, 9, 11, 84, 121, 153, 189, 261
Neter, 7, 11, 20, 22, 28, 30, 31, 33, 46, 74, 75, 76, 77, 78, 79, 86, 87, 88, 91, 92, 97, 99, 111, 114, 115, 116, 119, 120, 122, 123, 126, 127, 153, 154, 156, 157, 163, 173, 192, 202, 205, 208, 209, 210, 212, 213, 215, 222, 224, 225, 235, 252, 256
Neterian, 1, 11, 14, 19, 22, 23, 28, 30, 32, 34, 35, 39, 41, 43, 44, 57, 60, 61, 64, 69, 72, 74, 79, 84, 87, 93, 95, 96, 97, 98, 99, 100, 101, 102, 105, 106, 107, 114, 116, 117, 119, 120, 123, 128, 130, 131, 132, 133, 134, 136, 140, 141, 147, 152, 153, 154, 156, 158, 161, 168, 169, 172, 173, 175, 178, 182, 183, 186, 187, 188, 191, 192, 193, 196, 200, 201, 203, 212, 213, 214, 215, 216, 217, 218, 219, 220, 221, 222, 224, 225, 226, 227, 228, 231, 232, 233, 242
Neterianism, 19, 23, 28, 40, 74, 76, 77, 78, 136, 153, 159, 216, 218, 222
Neters, 92, 157
Neteru, 7, 75, 77, 78, 79, 87, 92, 95, 96, 134, 255, 259, 260
Netherworld, 236
New Kingdom, 46, 48, 50, 52, 55, 61, 73, 83, 86, 119, 143, 164, 208, 209
New Testament, 64
Nile River, 10, 76
Nine, 224
Nirvana, 60
Nomes, 57
North East Africa. See also Egypt
Ethiopia
Cush, 9
North East Africa. See also Egypt
Ethiopia
Cush, 9
Nubia, 10, 11, 16, 51, 73, 115, 218
Nubian, 10, 11, 71, 120, 155, 218
Nubians, 10, 22, 51, 76, 120, 218
Nun, 28, 29, 79, 141, 237
Nun (primeval waters-unformed matter), 28, 29, 79, 141, 237
Nun (See also Nu), 28, 29, 79, 141, 237
Nut, 28, 30, 80, 92, 189, 255
Nutrition, 7
Obelisk, 21, 29
Ogdoad, 106
Old Kingdom, 45, 46, 119, 121, 155, 189

Old Testament, 21, 22, 156, 185, 222
Om, 260
Opening of the Mouth Ceremony, 124, 127, 136, 138
Opposites, 11
Orion Star Constellation, 257
Orpheus, 57, 160
Orthodox, 13, 15, 35, 37, 41, 42, 63, 64, 67, 69, 71, 192, 218, 219, 220, 221, 222, 225, 227, 228
Orthodox religions, 37, 42, 64, 69, 218, 219, 220, 222
Osiris, 9, 24, 27, 70, 84, 85, 106, 112, 117, 139, 140, 153, 161, 162, 165, 198, 236, 255, 256, 260
Pa Neter, 75
Paleoanthropology, 51
Palermo Stone, 13
Palestine, 53, 65, 71, 186
Palestinians, 221
Papyrus of Any, 153
Papyrus of Turin, 14
Patanjali, 88
Paul, 42, 64, 184
Paul, St., 64
Paut, 7, 133
Peace (see also Hetep), 7, 76, 173, 190, 237
Pentateuch, 185
Pepi II, 49
Per-Aah, 183
Peristyle Hall, 99, 100, 143, 161
Persia, 50, 51, 52, 73, 115, 216
Persians, 51, 55, 183, 218
Pert Em Heru, See also Book of the Dead, 91, 165, 196, 256
phallus, 27, 161
Pharaoh, 13, 15, 48, 50, 53, 54, 57, 101, 114, 115, 180, 183
Philae, 9, 23, 65, 256
Philosophy, 2, 7, 11, 14, 16, 18, 20, 21, 22, 23, 24, 27, 33, 40, 54, 72, 74, 90, 91, 95, 96, 100, 119, 128, 153, 163, 166, 184, 188, 211, 240, 253, 254, 256, 258
Philosophy of Nothingness, 188
Phoenix, 21
Physical body, 106
Pillar of Asar, 117
Plato, 20, 23, 25, 26, 64, 132, 162, 164, 171, 183, 185, 186
Plutarch, 20, 23, 25, 93, 131, 139, 140, 196, 197, 237
Priests and Priestesses, 1, 2, 36, 46, 51, 78, 94, 104, 105, 107, 111, 119, 128, 133, 136, 139, 147, 168, 171, 176, 177, 178, 188, 191, 201, 212, 223, 226, 252, 253
Primeval Waters, 24, 237
Protestant, 65
Protestantism, 65
Ptah, 9, 11, 24, 79, 82, 121, 140, 153, 189, 254, 257
PTAH, 257
Ptahotep, 11, 153
Ptolemaic period, 61, 181
Puerto Rico, 7
Pyramid, 9, 11, 14, 15, 29, 145, 153, 154, 155, 156
Pyramid texts, 155, 156
Pyramid Texts, 9, 11, 145, 153, 154, 156
Pyramids, 12, 52
Pythagoras, 20, 23, 24, 25, 26, 57, 132, 160, 162, 171, 183
Qamit, 10, 237
Ra, 8, 9, 11, 21, 24, 28, 29, 31, 54, 80, 83, 92, 94, 105, 121, 124, 127, 128, 141, 153, 175, 177, 200, 237, 242, 254, 255, 259, 260
Race, 216, 217
Racism, 217
Ram, 54, 101
Rama, 72, 233
Ramayana, 72
Rameses II, 16, 21, 54, 208, 209
Rastau, 190
Reality, 134, 240
Realization, 96
Realm of Light, 11
Reflection, 94, 99
Religion, 2, 7, 9, 11, 14, 18, 20, 21, 22, 23, 27, 52, 70, 71, 72, 73, 74, 76, 77, 87, 91, 92, 99, 112, 168, 179, 184, 215, 216, 223, 226, 256, 257, 260
Resurrection, 11, 31, 141, 153, 165, 232, 236, 255, 256, 257, 258
Righteousness, 112
Ritual, 89, 92, 94, 95, 99, 113, 123, 136, 138, 141, 145, 147, 149, 153, 158, 211, 236, 238, 241
Rituals, 100, 141, 143, 241, 257
Roman, 26, 46, 50, 52, 53, 57, 63, 64, 65, 66, 111, 119, 153, 206, 218
Roman Catholic, 52, 63, 64
Roman Empire, 52, 63
Romans, 183
Rome, 63, 165, 184, 238
Rosicrucians, 215
S, 203
Sages, 24, 160, 162, 164, 190, 241, 254, 256, 258
Saints, 182, 190, 241, 256
Sais, 9, 23, 186
Sakkara, 9, 154, 164
Sakshin, 23
Salvation, 92, 157
Salvation, See also resurrection, 92, 157
Sanskrit, 88, 90
Satan, 22
Schwaller de Lubicz, 12
Scribe, 152
Sebai, 7, 11, 20, 43, 57, 64, 65, 66, 71, 73, 79, 80, 82, 83, 84, 85, 86, 95, 99, 115, 116, 117, 118, 140, 146, 152, 160, 166, 171, 184, 185, 193, 198, 206, 233, 235, 236, 238, 242, 252, 259, 260
Second Intermediate Period, 51
Secularism, 226
See also Egyptian Yoga, 7, 92, 166
See also Ra-Hrakti, 8, 9, 11, 21, 24, 28,

29, 31, 54, 80, 83, 92, 94, 105, 121, 124, 127, 128, 141, 153, 175, 177, 200, 237, 242, 254, 255, 259, 260
See Nat, 9, 11, 84, 121, 153, 189, 261
See Nefertum, 82
Sekhem, 52, 61, 92, 117, 124, 172
Sekhmet, 11, 106, 124
Self (see Ba, soul, Spirit, Universal, Ba, Neter, Heru)., 10, 19, 30, 35, 38, 40, 41, 89, 90, 91, 92, 94, 105, 108, 117, 135, 139, 163, 164, 170, 172, 173, 179, 187, 196, 202, 206, 231, 232, 237, 254, 255, 256
Self (seeBasoulSpiritUniversal BaNeterHorus)., 10, 89, 91, 94, 139, 163, 187
Selfless service, 187
Sema, 2, 7, 10, 27, 42, 52, 75, 88, 90, 91, 92, 93, 94, 95, 99, 102, 108, 134, 136, 141, 160, 178, 201, 211, 252, 262
Sema XE "Sema" Paut, see also Egyptian Yoga, 7, 52, 92, 95, 134
Sema Tawi, 7, 42, 93, 99, 108, 178
Semitic, 71
Serpent, 12, 13, 52, 88, 89, 92, 94, 117, 172, 206, 242

Serpent Power, 52, 88, 89, 92, 94, 117, 172, 206, 242
Serpent Power (see also Kundalini and Buto), 52, 88, 89, 92, 94, 117, 172, 206, 242
Serpent Power see also Kundalini Yoga, 52, 88, 89, 92, 94, 117, 172, 206, 242
Set, 10, 22, 32, 75, 80, 90, 91, 131, 139, 141, 182, 198, 232, 237
Seti I, 94, 183, 237, 255, 260
Seven, 121
Sex, 217, 236, 255
Sexuality, 134, 191, 198
Sheps, 31, 108
Shetaut Neter, 1, 11, 14, 20, 28, 30, 31, 33, 38, 42, 43, 52, 60, 71, 74, 76, 87, 88, 92, 102, 108, 109, 110, 111, 112, 116, 134, 136, 139, 141, 146, 153, 156, 157, 162, 164, 166, 170, 171, 172, 178, 205, 215, 216, 218, 221, 224, 225, 252, 256
Shetaut Neter See also Egyptian Religion, 1, 11, 14, 20, 28, 30, 31, 33, 38, 42, 43, 52, 60, 71, 74, 76, 87, 88, 92, 102, 108, 109, 110, 111, 112, 116, 134, 136, 139, 141, 146, 153, 156, 157, 162, 164, 166, 170, 171, 172, 178, 205, 215, 216, 218, 221, 224, 225, 252, 256

Shu (air and space), 28, 30, 80
Shunya, 189
Sirius, 11, 257
Sky, 11, 12, 13
Sma, 90, 92, 126, 166
Smai, 7, 10, 75, 88, 90, 91, 92, 99
Smai Tawi, 88, 90, 92
Society, 53, 112, 188, 241
Socrates, 164
Solon, 23, 57, 186
Soul, 7, 91
Southeast Asia, 52, 216
Sphinx, 11, 12, 13, 14, 15, 219
Spirit, 11, 12, 28, 35, 75, 79, 91, 94, 100, 110, 135, 162, 170, 173, 187, 235, 236
Spiritual discipline, 92, 253
St. Augustine, 63
Storytelling, 99
Strabo, 23, 26, 161, 162
Study, 23, 203, 240
Sublimation, 255
Sudan, 9, 10
Sufi, 131
Sufi, see also Sufism, 131
Sufism, 219
Sufism, see also Sufi, 219
Sumer, 13, 73, 90, 141
Sundisk, 94
Supreme Being, 12, 29, 30, 66, 75, 77, 78, 79, 80, 82, 83, 84, 85, 86, 88, 96, 156, 190, 213, 217, 254, 257
Supreme Divinity, 216
Survival, 217
Syria, 51

Tantra, 53, 193, 198, 255
Tantra Yoga, 193, 198, 255
Tantric Yoga, 88, 89
Tanzania, 10
Taoism, 51, 52, 215, 221, 253
Tawi, 7, 10, 75, 88, 90, 99, 166
Tefnut, 28, 30, 80
Tefnut (moisture), 28, 30, 80
Tem, 147
Temple of Aset, 7, 9, 31, 53, 65, 85, 92, 94, 99, 101, 131, 139, 140, 170, 196, 197, 231, 237, 256, 262
Temple of Delphi, 24
Ten Commandments, 22, 42, 69, 71, 185, 186, 223
Thales, 20, 23, 24, 25, 160
the , Dionysius Aropagite, 64
The Absolute, 254
The God, 11, 22, 80, 84, 107, 112, 185, 187, 189, 255
The Gods, 11, 80, 255
The way, 107
Theban Theology, 11, 112, 153
Thebes, 9, 23, 24, 25, 175, 254, 255
Theodosius, 53
Third Intermediate Period, 120
Thoughts (see also Mind), 94
Tomb, 16, 94, 121, 184, 255, 260
Tomb of Seti I, 255, 260
Tradition, 19, 67, 72, 80, 82, 83, 84, 85, 86, 92, 112, 200

Transcendental Self, 234
Triad, 254
Trinity, 9, 11, 20, 22, 23, 24, 65, 82, 83, 85, 99, 112, 254, 256, 260
Truth, 70, 96, 221
Tutankhamun, 166
Tutankhamun, Pharaoh, 166
Tutu, Desmond (Archbishop), 185
Ubuntu, 22, 184, 185
Uganda, 10
Understanding, 38, 54, 134
United States of America, 65
Universal Consciousness, 255
Upanishads, 72, 256
Upper Egypt, 90, 91
Ur, 74, 80, 120, 127
Uraeus, 89
Vaishnava, 72
Vatican, 184
Vedanta, 72, 221
Vedas, 72
Vedic, 72, 254
Vegetarianism, 196
Vishnu, 72
Waset, 9, 23, 24, 67, 68, 175, 254
West Africa, 51, 223
West, John Anthony, 12, 13, 67
Western civilization, 24
Western Culture, 20, 184
Western religions, 184, 200
Will, 221
Wisdom, 11, 22, 38, 88, 89, 92, 94, 96, 112, 151, 153, 163, 164, 169, 184, 185, 186, 211, 254, 255
Wisdom (also see Djehuti), 11, 54, 89, 96, 112, 153, 163, 164
Wisdom (also see Djehuti, Aset), 11, 22, 38, 88, 89, 92, 94, 96, 112, 151, 153, 163, 164, 169, 184, 185, 186, 211, 254, 255
Words of power, 94
Yahweh, 186
Yellow, 101
Yoga, 2, 7, 11, 14, 21, 22, 23, 27, 72, 73, 74, 83, 88, 89, 90, 91, 92, 94, 95, 99, 126, 141, 162, 166, 184, 211, 233, 234, 252, 253, 254, 255, 256, 257, 258, 259, 260, 262
Yoga Exercise, 7
Yoga of Action, 89
Yoga of Devotion (see Yoga of Divine Love), 88, 89, 94, 234
Yoga of Divine Love (see Yoga of Devotion), 89
Yoga of Meditation, 88, 89
Yoga of Selfless Action. See also Yoga of Righteous, 88, 89
Yoga of Wisdom (see also Jnana Yoga), 88, 89
Yoga Sutra, 88
Yogic, 88, 94, 95, 213
Yoruba, 22, 43, 66, 154, 184
Zealots, 65
Zeus, 24, 27, 161
Zoroastrianism, 22, 51, 52

The Priests and Priestesses of Ancient Egypt

SEMA UNIVERSITY

Teacher of Kamitan Culture Certificate
2004 CORRESPONDENCE (DISTANCE LEARNING)
ASSOCIATE DEGREE PROGRAM CLASSES –SCHEDULED ON TRIMESTER BASIS:
Register to begin January, May or September

Associate Degree   15 Credits $225 PER CORSE (curriculum subject to change)

Associate of Arts in SEMA (Yoga) and Neterian Spirituality Studies COURSES:

INTRODUCTION TO SEMA-YOGA AND NETERIAN THEOLOGY and METAPHYSICS
AS102 Class subject: Introduction to Neterian Spirituality and Philosophy – Text Egyptian Mysteries Vol 1

KEMETIC DIET – INTRODUCTION TO NETERIANISM AND SEMA PHILOSOPHY, NATURAL LIVING AND SELF HEALING FOR ASPIRANTS
AS101 Class Subject: Kemetic Diet Level 1: Natural Living – Text Kemetic Diet

INTRODUCTION TO SEMA-YOGA DISCIPLINES and METAPHYSICS
AS103 Class Subject: Initiation into Shetaut Neter And Sema Tawi – Text Initiation into Egyptian Yoga

INTRODUCTION TO MAAT PHILOSOPHY
AS104 Class subject: Introduction to Maat Philosophy and Metaphysics –Text Wisdom of Maati

AFRICAN ORIGINS & HISTORY OF RELIGION, YOGA AND PHILOSOPHY LEVEL 1
AS105 Class Subject: Level 1: *African Origins of African Civilization*-Text African Origins Vol. 1

****

Neterian Minister Certificate
SEMA UNIVERSITY
BACHELOR DEGREE PROGRAM

DEGREE PROGRAM CLASSES ARE SCHEDULED ON TRIMESTER BASIS:
Register to begin January, May or September
Prerequisite: Complete the AA Degree.

Unut Minister Certificate & Ordination 8 Credits
Assignments: 4 book reports, 4 oral examinations, 1 presentation, 1 ritual performance.

INTRODUCTION TO THE PHYLOSOPHY OF HEMU (UN 101 Class text: Egyptian Mysteries Vol. 3 The Priests and Priestesses of Ancient Egypt) (2 Credits) Course fee $125
INTRODUCTION TO THE PHYLOSOPHY OF NETERU (UN 103 Class text: Egyptian Mysteries Vol. 2 The Gods and Goddesses of Ancient Egypt) (2 Credits) Course fee $125
AFRICAN ORIGINS & HISTORY OF RELIGION, YOGA AND PHILOSOPHY LEVEL 2 & 3 (UN102 Class Subject: Texts: *African Origins of African Civilization* Vol 2 & Vol 3) (2 Credits) Course fee $125
INTRODUCTION TO MEDU NETER (UN 103 Class text: TBA) (2 Credits) Course fee $125

Evaluation of Academic work: A-Candidates will be required to write a term paper on the selected texts in accordance with guidelines that will be provided. B- Book report will be evaluated on a pass fail basis and Candidates will be administered an oral test for proficiency in the knowledge base, history, and philosophy or Shetaut Neter and Sema Tawi. C- Candidates will conduct 1 presentation at Annual Meeting (INTRO TO SHETAUT NETER), D- Ritual test: To be administered at the Unut conference. Candidates will conduct 1 complete ritual worship program under the supervision of senior priests of Shetaut Neter.

Other Series Books by Sebai Muata Ashby

P.O.Box 570459
Miami, Florida, 33257
(305) 378-6253 Fax: (305) 378-6253

This book is part of a series on the study and practice of Ancient Egyptian Yoga and Mystical Spirituality based on the writings of Dr. Muata Abhaya Ashby. They are also part of the Egyptian Yoga Course provided by the Sema Institute of Yoga. Below you will find a listing of the other books in this series. For more information send for the Egyptian Yoga Book-Audio-Video Catalog or the Egyptian Yoga Course Catalog.

Now you can study the teachings of Egyptian and Indian Yoga wisdom and Spirituality with the Egyptian Yoga Mystical Spirituality Series. The Egyptian Yoga Series takes you through the Initiation process and lead you to understand the mysteries of the soul and the Divine and to attain the highest goal of life: ENLIGHTENMENT. The *Egyptian Yoga Series*, takes you on an in depth study of Ancient Egyptian mythology and their inner mystical meaning. Each Book is prepared for the serious student of the mystical sciences and provides a study of the teachings along with exercises, assignments and projects to make the teachings understood and effective in real life. The Series is part of the Egyptian Yoga course but may be purchased even if you are not taking the course. The series is ideal for study groups.

THE EGYPTIAN MYSTIERIES BOOK SERIES

Available Now

EGYPTIAN MYSTERIES VOLUME 1: Shetaut Neter- The Mysteries of Ancient Egypt
EGYPTIAN MYSTERIES VOLUME 2: Shetaut Neteru - The Mysteries of the Gods and Goddesses

Other Books by Sebai Muata Ashby

P.O.Box 570459
Miami, Florida, 33257
(305) 378-6253 Fax: (305) 378-6253

This book is part of a series on the study and practice of Ancient Egyptian Yoga and Mystical Spirituality based on the writings of Dr. Muata Abhaya Ashby. They are also part of the Egyptian Yoga Course provided by the Sema Institute of Yoga. Below you will find a listing of the other books in this series. For more information send for the Egyptian Yoga Book-Audio-Video Catalog or the Egyptian Yoga Course Catalog.

Now you can study the teachings of Egyptian and Indian Yoga wisdom and Spirituality with the Egyptian Yoga Mystical Spirituality Series. The Egyptian Yoga Series takes you through the Initiation process and lead you to understand the mysteries of the soul and the Divine and to attain the highest goal of life: ENLIGHTENMENT. The *Egyptian Yoga Series*, takes you on an in depth study of Ancient Egyptian mythology and their inner mystical meaning. Each Book is prepared for the serious student of the mystical sciences and provides a study of the teachings along with exercises, assignments and projects to make the teachings understood and effective in real life. The Series is part of the Egyptian Yoga course but may be purchased even if you are not taking the course. The series is ideal for study groups.

Prices subject to change.

1. EGYPTIAN YOGA: THE PHILOSOPHY OF ENLIGHTENMENT An original, fully illustrated work, including hieroglyphs, detailing the meaning of the Egyptian mysteries, tantric yoga, psycho-spiritual and physical exercises. Egyptian Yoga is a guide to the practice of the highest spiritual philosophy which leads to absolute freedom from human misery and to immortality. It is well known by scholars that Egyptian philosophy is the basis of Western and Middle Eastern religious philosophies such as *Christianity, Islam, Judaism,* the *Kabala,* and Greek philosophy, but what about Indian philosophy, Yoga and Taoism? What were the original teachings? How can they be practiced today? What is the source of pain and suffering in the world and what is the solution? Discover the deepest mysteries of the mind and universe within and outside of your self. 8.5" X 11" ISBN: 1-884564-01-1 Soft $19.95

2. EGYPTIAN YOGA II: The Supreme Wisdom of Enlightenment by Dr. Muata Ashby ISBN 1-884564-39-9 $23.95 U.S. In this long awaited sequel to *Egyptian Yoga: The Philosophy of Enlightenment* you will take a fascinating and enlightening journey back in time and discover the teachings which constituted the epitome of Ancient Egyptian spiritual wisdom. What are the disciplines which lead to the fulfillment of all desires? Delve into the three states of consciousness (waking, dream and deep sleep) and the fourth state which transcends them all, Neberdjer, "The Absolute." These teachings of the city of Waset (Thebes) were the crowning achievement of the Sages of Ancient Egypt. They establish the standard mystical keys for understanding the profound mystical symbolism of the Triad of human consciousness.

3. THE KEMETIC DIET: GUIDE TO HEALTH, DIET AND FASTING Health issues have always been important to human beings since the beginning of time. The earliest records of history show that the art of healing was held in high esteem since the time of Ancient Egypt. In the early 20th century, medical doctors had almost attained the status of sainthood by the promotion of the idea that they alone were "scientists" while other healing modalities and traditional healers who did not follow the "scientific method' were

nothing but superstitious, ignorant charlatans who at best would take the money of their clients and at worst kill them with the unscientific "snake oils" and "irrational theories". In the late 20th century, the failure of the modern medical establishment's ability to lead the general public to good health, promoted the move by many in society towards "alternative medicine". Alternative medicine disciplines are those healing modalities which do not adhere to the philosophy of allopathic medicine. Allopathic medicine is what medical doctors practice by an large. It is the theory that disease is caused by agencies outside the body such as bacteria, viruses or physical means which affect the body. These can therefore be treated by medicines and therapies The natural healing method began in the absence of extensive technologies with the idea that all the answers for health may be found in nature or rather, the deviation from nature. Therefore, the health of the body can be restored by correcting the aberration and thereby restoring balance. This is the area that will be covered in this volume. Allopathic techniques have their place in the art of healing. However, we should not forget that the body is a grand achievement of the spirit and built into it is the capacity to maintain itself and heal itself. Ashby, Muata ISBN: 1-884564-49-6 $28.95

4. INITIATION INTO EGYPTIAN YOGA Shedy: Spiritual discipline or program, to go deeply into the mysteries, to study the mystery teachings and literature profoundly, to penetrate the mysteries. You will learn about the mysteries of initiation into the teachings and practice of Yoga and how to become an Initiate of the mystical sciences. This insightful manual is the first in a series which introduces you to the goals of daily spiritual and yoga practices: Meditation, Diet, Words of Power and the ancient wisdom teachings. 8.5" X 11" ISBN 1-884564-02-X   Soft Cover $24.95 U.S.

5. *THE AFRICAN ORIGINS OF CIVILIZATION, MYSTICAL RELIGION AND YOGA PHILOSOPHY* HARD COVER EDITION ISBN: 1-884564-50-X $80.00 U.S.   81/2" X 11"   Part 1, Part 2, Part 3 in one volume 683 Pages Hard Cover First Edition Three volumes in one. Over the past several years I have been asked to put together in one volume the most important evidences showing the correlations and common teachings between Kamitan (Ancient Egyptian) culture and religion and that of India. The questions of the history of Ancient Egypt, and the latest archeological evidences showing civilization and culture in Ancient Egypt and its spread to other countries, has intrigued many scholars as well as mystics over the years. Also, the possibility that Ancient Egyptian Priests and Priestesses migrated to Greece, India and other countries to carry on the traditions of the Ancient Egyptian Mysteries, has been speculated over the years as well. In chapter 1 of the book *Egyptian Yoga The Philosophy of Enlightenment,* 1995, I first introduced the deepest comparison between Ancient Egypt and India that had been brought forth up to that time. Now, in the year 2001 this new book, *THE AFRICAN ORIGINS OF CIVILIZATION, MYSTICAL RELIGION AND YOGA PHILOSOPHY,* more fully explores the motifs, symbols and philosophical correlations between Ancient Egyptian and Indian mysticism and clearly shows not only that Ancient Egypt and India were connected culturally but also spiritually. How does this knowledge help the spiritual aspirant? This discovery has great importance for the Yogis and mystics who follow the philosophy of Ancient Egypt and the mysticism of India. It means that India has a longer history and heritage than was previously understood. It shows that the mysteries of Ancient Egypt were essentially a yoga tradition which did not die but rather developed into the modern day systems of Yoga technology of India. It further shows that African culture developed Yoga Mysticism earlier than any other civilization in history. All of this expands our understanding of the unity of culture and the deep legacy of Yoga, which stretches into the distant past, beyond the Indus Valley civilization, the earliest known high culture in India as well as the Vedic tradition of Aryan culture. Therefore, Yoga culture and mysticism is the oldest known tradition of spiritual development and Indian mysticism is an extension of the Ancient Egyptian mysticism. By understanding the legacy which Ancient Egypt gave to India the mysticism of India is better understood and by comprehending the heritage of Indian Yoga, which is rooted in Ancient Egypt the Mysticism of Ancient Egypt is also better understood. This expanded understanding allows us to prove the underlying kinship of humanity, through the common symbols, motifs and philosophies which are not disparate and confusing teachings but in reality expressions of the same study of truth through metaphysics and mystical realization of Self. (HARD COVER)

6. AFRICAN ORIGINS BOOK 1 PART 1 African Origins of African Civilization, Religion, Yoga Mysticism and Ethics Philosophy-Soft Cover $24.95 ISBN: 1-884564-55-0

7. AFRICAN ORIGINS BOOK 2 PART 2 African Origins of Western Civilization, Religion and Philosophy(Soft) -Soft Cover $24.95 ISBN: 1-884564-56-9

8. EGYPT AND INDIA (AFRICAN ORIGINS BOOK 3 PART 3) African Origins of Eastern Civilization, Religion, Yoga Mysticism and Philosophy-Soft Cover $29.95 (Soft) ISBN: 1-884564-57-7

9. THE MYSTERIES OF ISIS: The Path of Wisdom, Immortality and Enlightenment   Through the study of ancient myth and the illumination of initiatic understanding the idea of God is expanded from the mythological comprehension to the metaphysical. Then this metaphysical understanding is related to you, the student, so as to begin understanding your true divine nature. ISBN 1-884564-24-0 $24.99

10. EGYPTIAN PROVERBS: TEMT TCHAAS *Temt Tchaas* means: collection of ——Ancient Egyptian Proverbs How to live according to MAAT Philosophy. Beginning Meditation. All proverbs are indexed for easy searches. For the first time in one volume, ——Ancient Egyptian Proverbs, wisdom teachings and meditations, fully illustrated with hieroglyphic text and symbols. EGYPTIAN PROVERBS is a unique collection of knowledge and wisdom which you can put into practice today and transform your life. 5.5"x 8.5" $14.95 U.S   ISBN: 1-884564-00-3

11. THE PATH OF DIVINE LOVE The Process of Mystical Transformation and The Path of Divine Love This Volume will focus on the ancient wisdom teachings and how to use them in a scientific process for self-transformation. Also, this volume will detail the process of transformation from ordinary consciousness to cosmic consciousness through the integrated practice of the teachings and the path of Devotional Love toward the Divine. 5.5"x 8.5" ISBN 1-884564-11-9 $22.99

12. INTRODUCTION TO MAAT PHILOSOPHY: Spiritual Enlightenment Through the Path of Virtue Known as Karma Yoga in India, the teachings of MAAT for living virtuously and with orderly wisdom are explained and the student is to begin practicing the precepts of Maat in daily life so as to promote the process of purification of the heart in preparation for the judgment of the soul. This judgment will be understood not as an event that will occur at the time of death but as an event that occurs continuously, at every moment in the life of the individual. The student will learn how to become allied with the forces of the Higher Self and to thereby begin cleansing the mind (heart) of impurities so as to attain a higher vision of reality. ISBN 1-884564-20-8 $22.99

13. MEDITATION The Ancient Egyptian Path to Enlightenment   Many people do not know about the rich history of meditation practice in Ancient Egypt. This volume outlines the theory of meditation and presents the Ancient Egyptian Hieroglyphic text which give instruction as to the nature of the mind and its three modes of expression. It also presents the texts which give instruction on the practice of meditation for spiritual Enlightenment and unity with the Divine. This volume allows the reader to begin practicing meditation by explaining, in easy to understand terms, the simplest form of meditation and working up to the most advanced form which was practiced in ancient times and which is still practiced by yogis around the world in modern times. ISBN 1-884564-27-7 $24.99

14. THE GLORIOUS LIGHT MEDITATION TECHNIQUE OF ANCIENT EGYPT ISBN: 1-884564-15-1$14.95 (PB) New for the year 2000. This volume is based on the earliest known instruction in history given for the practice of formal meditation. Discovered by Dr. Muata Ashby, it is inscribed on the walls of the Tomb of Seti I in Thebes Egypt. This volume details the philosophy and practice of this unique system of meditation originated in Ancient Egypt and the earliest practice of meditation known in the world which occurred in the most advanced African Culture.

15. THE SERPENT POWER: The Ancient Egyptian Mystical Wisdom of the Inner Life Force.   This Volume specifically deals with the latent life Force energy of the universe and in the human body, its control and sublimation. How to develop the Life Force energy of the subtle body. This Volume will introduce the esoteric wisdom of the science of how virtuous living acts in a subtle and mysterious way to cleanse the latent psychic energy conduits and vortices of the spiritual body.   ISBN 1-884564-19-4 $22.95

16. EGYPTIAN YOGA MEDITATION IN MOTION Thef Neteru: *The Movement of The Gods and Goddesses* Discover the physical postures and exercises practiced thousands of years ago in Ancient Egypt

which are today known as Yoga exercises. This work is based on the pictures and teachings from the Creation story of Ra, The Asarian Resurrection Myth and the carvings and reliefs from various Temples in Ancient Egypt 8.5" X 11" ISBN 1-884564-10-0 Soft Cover $18.99   Exercise video $21.99

17. EGYPTIAN TANTRA YOGA: The Art of Sex Sublimation and Universal Consciousness This Volume will expand on the male and female principles within the human body and in the universe and further detail the sublimation of sexual energy into spiritual energy. The student will study the deities Min and Hathor, Asar and Aset, Geb and Nut and discover the mystical implications for a practical spiritual discipline. This Volume will also focus on the Tantric aspects of Ancient Egyptian and Indian mysticism, the purpose of sex and the mystical teachings of sexual sublimation which lead to self-knowledge and Enlightenment. 5.5"x 8.5"   ISBN 1-884564-03-8 $24.95

18. ASARIAN RELIGION: RESURRECTING OSIRIS The path of Mystical Awakening and the Keys to Immortality NEW REVISED AND EXPANDED EDITION!   The Ancient Sages created stories based on human and superhuman beings whose struggles, aspirations, needs and desires ultimately lead them to discover their true Self. The myth of Aset, Asar and Heru is no exception in this area. While there is no one source where the entire story may be found, pieces of it are inscribed in various ancient Temples walls, tombs, steles and papyri. For the first time available, the complete myth of Asar, Aset and Heru has been compiled from original Ancient Egyptian, Greek and Coptic Texts. This epic myth has been richly illustrated with reliefs from the Temple of Heru at Edfu, the Temple of Aset at Philae, the Temple of Asar at Abydos, the Temple of Hathor at Denderah and various papyri, inscriptions and reliefs.   Discover the myth which inspired the teachings of the *Shetaut Neter* (Egyptian Mystery System - Egyptian Yoga) and the Egyptian Book of Coming Forth By Day. Also, discover the three levels of Ancient Egyptian Religion, how to understand the mysteries of the Duat or Astral World and how to discover the abode of the Supreme in the Amenta, *The Other World*   The ancient religion of Asar, Aset and Heru, if properly understood, contains all of the elements necessary to lead the sincere aspirant to attain immortality through inner self-discovery.   This volume presents the entire myth and explores the main mystical themes and rituals associated with the myth for understating human existence, creation and the way to achieve spiritual emancipation - *Resurrection*. The Asarian myth is so powerful that it influenced and is still having an effect on the major world religions. Discover the origins and mystical meaning of the Christian Trinity, the Eucharist ritual and the ancient origin of the birthday of Jesus Christ. Soft Cover ISBN: 1-884564-27-5 $24.95

19. THE EGYPTIAN BOOK OF THE DEAD MYSTICISM OF THE PERT EM HERU $26.95   ISBN# 1-884564-28-3 Size: 8½" X 11" I Know myself, I know myself, I am One With God!–From the Pert Em Heru "The Ru Pert em Heru" or "Ancient Egyptian Book of The Dead," or "Book of Coming Forth By Day" as it is more popularly known, has fascinated the world since the successful translation of Ancient Egyptian hieroglyphic scripture over 150 years ago. The astonishing writings in it reveal that the Ancient Egyptians believed in life after death and in an ultimate destiny to discover the Divine. The elegance and aesthetic beauty of the hieroglyphic text itself has inspired many see it as an art form in and of itself. But is there more to it than that? Did the Ancient Egyptian wisdom contain more than just aphorisms and hopes of eternal life beyond death? In this volume Dr. Muata Ashby, the author of over 25 books on Ancient Egyptian Yoga Philosophy has produced a new translation of the original texts which uncovers a mystical teaching underlying the sayings and rituals instituted by the Ancient Egyptian Sages and Saints. "Once the philosophy of Ancient Egypt is understood as a mystical tradition instead of as a religion or primitive mythology, it reveals its secrets which if practiced today will lead anyone to discover the glory of spiritual self-discovery. The Pert em Heru is in every way comparable to the Indian Upanishads or the Tibetan Book of the Dead." Muata Abhaya Ashby

20. ANUNIAN THEOLOGY THE MYSTERIES OF RA The Philosophy of Anu and The Mystical Teachings of The Ancient Egyptian Creation Myth Discover the mystical teachings contained in the Creation Myth and the gods and goddesses who brought creation and human beings into existence. The Creation Myth holds the key to understanding the universe and for attaining spiritual Enlightenment. ISBN: 1-884564-38-0 40 pages $14.95

21. MYSTERIES OF MIND AND MEMPHITE THEOLOGY Mysticism of Ptah, Egyptian Physics and Yoga Metaphysics and the Hidden properties of Matter   This Volume will go deeper into the philosophy of God as creation and will explore the concepts of modern science and how they correlate with ancient teachings. This Volume will lay the ground work for the understanding of the philosophy of universal consciousness and the initiatic/yogic insight into who or what is God? ISBN 1-884564-07-0 $21.95

22. THE GODDESS AND THE EGYPTIAN MYSTERIESTHE PATH OF THE GODDESS THE GODDESS PATH The Secret Forms of the Goddess and the Rituals of Resurrection The Supreme Being may be worshipped as father or as mother. *Ushet Rekhat* or *Mother Worship*, is the spiritual process of worshipping the Divine in the form of the Divine Goddess. It celebrates the most important forms of the Goddess including *Nathor, Maat, Aset, Arat, Amentet and Hathor* and explores their mystical meaning as well as the rising of *Sirius,* the star of Aset (Aset) and the new birth of Hor (Heru). The end of the year is a time of reckoning, reflection and engendering a new or renewed positive movement toward attaining spiritual Enlightenment. The Mother Worship devotional meditation ritual, performed on five days during the month of December and on New Year's Eve, is based on the Ushet Rekhit. During the ceremony, the cosmic forces, symbolized by Sirius - and the constellation of Orion ---, are harnessed through the understanding and devotional attitude of the participant. This propitiation draws the light of wisdom and health to all those who share in the ritual, leading to prosperity and wisdom. $14.95 ISBN 1-884564-18-6

23. *THE MYSTICAL JOURNEY FROM JESUS TO CHRIST* $24.95   ISBN# 1-884564-05-4 size: 8½" X 11" Discover the ancient Egyptian origins of Christianity before the Catholic Church and learn the mystical teachings given by Jesus to assist all humanity in becoming Christlike. Discover the secret meaning of the Gospels that were discovered in Egypt. Also discover how and why so many Christian churches came into being. Discover that the Bible still holds the keys to mystical realization even though its original writings were changed by the church. Discover how to practice the original teachings of Christianity which leads to the Kingdom of Heaven.

24. THE STORY OF ASAR, ASET AND HERU: An Ancient Egyptian Legend (For Children)   Now for the first time, the most ancient myth of Ancient Egypt comes alive for children. Inspired by the books *The Asarian Resurrection: The Ancient Egyptian Bible* and *The Mystical Teachings of The Asarian Resurrection, The Story of Asar, Aset and Heru* is an easy to understand and thrilling tale which inspired the children of Ancient Egypt to aspire to greatness and righteousness.   If you and your child have enjoyed stories like *The Lion King* and *Star Wars you will love The Story of Asar, Aset and Heru.* Also, if you know the story of Jesus and Krishna you will discover than Ancient Egypt had a similar myth and that this myth carries important spiritual teachings for living a fruitful and fulfilling life. This book may be used along with *The Parents Guide To The Asarian Resurrection Myth: How to Teach Yourself and Your Child the Principles of Universal Mystical Religion.* The guide provides some background to the Asarian Resurrection myth and it also gives insight into the mystical teachings contained in it which you may introduce to your child. It is designed for parents who wish to grow spiritually with their children and it serves as an introduction for those who would like to study the Asarian Resurrection Myth in depth and to practice its teachings. 41 pages 8.5" X 11"   ISBN: 1-884564-31-3 $12.95

25. THE PARENTS GUIDE TO THE AUSARIAN RESURRECTION MYTH: How to Teach Yourself and Your Child the Principles of Universal Mystical Religion.   This insightful manual brings for the timeless wisdom of the ancient through the Ancient Egyptian myth of Asar, Aset and Heru and the mystical teachings contained in it for parents who want to guide their children to understand and practice the teachings of mystical spirituality. This manual may be used with the children's storybook *The Story of Asar, Aset and Heru* by Dr. Muata Abhaya Ashby. 5.5"x 8.5"   ISBN: 1-884564-30-5 $14.95

26. HEALING THE CRIMINAL HEART BOOK 1 Introduction to Maat Philosophy, Yoga and Spiritual Redemption Through the Path of Virtue   Who is a criminal? Is there such a thing as a criminal heart? What is the source of evil and sinfulness and is there any way to rise above it? Is there redemption for those who have committed sins, even the worst crimes?   Ancient Egyptian mystical psychology holds important answers to these questions. Over ten thousand years ago mystical psychologists, the Sages of Ancient Egypt, studied and charted the human mind and spirit and laid out a path which will lead to spiritual redemption, prosperity and Enlightenment.   This introductory volume brings forth the teachings

of the Asarian Resurrection, the most important myth of Ancient Egypt, with relation to the faults of human existence: anger, hatred, greed, lust, animosity, discontent, ignorance, egoism jealousy, bitterness, and a myriad of psycho-spiritual ailments which keep a human being in a state of negativity and adversity. 5.5"x 8.5"   ISBN: 1-884564-17-8 $15.95

27. THEATER & DRAMA OF THE ANCIENT EGYPTIAN MYSTERIES: Featuring the Ancient Egyptian stage play-"The Enlightenment of Hathor' Based on an Ancient Egyptian Drama, The original Theater - Mysticism of the Temple of Hetheru $14.95   By Dr. Muata Ashby

28. GUIDE TO PRINT ON DEMAND: SELF-PUBLISH FOR PROFIT, SPIRITUAL FULFILLMENT AND SERVICE TO HUMANITY Everyone asks us how we produced so many books in such a short time. Here are the secrets to writing and producing books that uplift humanity and how to get them printed for a fraction of the regular cost. Anyone can become an author even if they have limited funds. All that is necessary is the willingness to learn how the printing and book business work and the desire to follow the special instructions given here for preparing your manuscript format. Then you take your work directly to the non-traditional companies who can produce your books for less than the traditional book printer can. ISBN: 1-884564-40-2 $16.95 U. S.

29. Egyptian Mysteries: Vol. 1, Shetaut Neter ISBN: 1-884564-41-0 $19.99 What are the Mysteries? For thousands of years the spiritual tradition of Ancient Egypt, S*hetaut Neter,* "The Egyptian Mysteries," "The Secret Teachings," have fascinated, tantalized and amazed the world. At one time exalted and recognized as the highest culture of the world, by Africans, Europeans, Asiatics, Hindus, Buddhists and other cultures of the ancient world, in time it was shunned by the emerging orthodox world religions. Its temples desecrated, its philosophy maligned, its tradition spurned, its philosophy dormant in the mystical *Medu Neter*, the mysterious hieroglyphic texts which hold the secret symbolic meaning that has scarcely been discerned up to now.   What are the secrets of *Nehast* {spiritual awakening and emancipation, resurrection}. More than just a literal translation, this volume is for awakening to the secret code *Shetitu* of the teaching which was not deciphered by Egyptologists, nor could be understood by ordinary spiritualists. This book is a reinstatement of the original science made available for our times, to the reincarnated followers of Ancient Egyptian culture and the prospect of spiritual freedom to break the bonds of *Khemn,* "ignorance," and slavery to evil forces: *Såaa* .

30. EGYPTIAN MYSTERIES VOL 2: Dictionary of Gods and Goddesses ISBN: 1-884564-23-2 $21.95 This book is about the mystery of neteru, the gods and goddesses of Ancient Egypt (Kamit, Kemet). Neteru means "Gods and Goddesses." But the Neterian teaching of Neteru represents more than the usual limited modern day concept of "divinities" or "spirits." The Neteru of Kamit are also metaphors, cosmic principles and vehicles for the enlightening teachings of Shetaut Neter (Ancient Egyptian-African Religion). Actually they are the elements for one of the most advanced systems of spirituality ever conceived in human history. Understanding the concept of neteru provides a firm basis for spiritual evolution and the pathway for viable culture, peace on earth and a healthy human society.   Why is it important to have gods and goddesses in our lives? In order for spiritual evolution to be possible, once a human being has accepted that there is existence after death and there is a transcendental being who exists beyond time and space knowledge, human beings need a connection to that which transcends the ordinary experience of human life in time and space and a means to understand the transcendental reality beyond the mundane reality.

31. EGYPTIAN MYSTERIES VOL. 3 The Priests and Priestesses of Ancient Egypt ISBN: 1-884564-53-4 $22.95 This volume details the path of Neterian priesthood, the joys, challenges and rewards of advanced Neterian life, the teachings that allowed the priests and priestesses to manage the most long lived civilization in human history and how that path can be adopted today; for those who want to tread the path of the Clergy of Shetaut Neter.

32. THE KING OF EGYPT: The Struggle of Good and Evil for Control of the World and The Human Soul ISBN 1-8840564-44-5 $18.95   Have you seen movies like The Lion King, Hamlet, The Odyssey, or The Little Buddha? These have been some of the most popular movies in modern times. The Sema Institute of

Yoga is dedicated to researching and presenting the wisdom and culture of ancient Africa. The Script is designed to be produced as a motion picture but may be addapted for the theater as well. 160 pages bound or unbound (specify with your order) $19.95   copyright 1998 By Dr. Muata Ashby

33. FROM EGYPT TO GREECE: The Kamitan Origins of Greek Culture and Religion ISBN: 1-884564-47-X $22.95 U.S. FROM EGYPT TO GREECE This insightful manual is a quick reference to Ancient Egyptian mythology and philosophy and its correlation to what later became known as Greek and Rome mythology and philosophy. It outlines the basic tenets of the mythologies and shoes the ancient origins of Greek culture in Ancient Egypt. This volume also acts as a resource for Colleges students who would like to set up fraternities and sororities based on the original Ancient Egyptian principles of Sheti and Maat philosophy. ISBN: 1-884564-47-X $22.95 U.S.

34. THE FORTY TWO PRECEPTS OF MAAT, THE PHILOSOPHY OF RIGHTEOUS ACTION AND THE ANCIENT EGYPTIAN WISDOM TEXTS <u>ADVANCED STUDIES</u> This manual is designed for use with the 1998 Maat Philosophy Class conducted by Dr. Muata Ashby. This is a detailed study of Maat Philosophy. It contains a compilation of the 42 laws or precepts of Maat and the corresponding principles which they represent along with the teachings of the ancient Egyptian Sages relating to each. Maat philosophy was the basis of Ancient Egyptian society and government as well as the heart of Ancient Egyptian myth and spirituality. Maat is at once a goddess, a cosmic force and a living social doctrine, which promotes social harmony and thereby paves the way for spiritual evolution in all levels of society. ISBN: 1-884564-48-8 $16.95 U.S.

The Priests and Priestesses of Ancient Egypt

Music Based on the Prt M Hru and other Kemetic Texts

Available on Compact Disc $14.99 and Audio Cassette $9.99

Adorations to the Goddess

Music for Worship of the Goddess

**NEW Egyptian Yoga Music CD
by Sehu Maa
Ancient Egyptian Music CD**
Instrumental Music played on reproductions of Ancient Egyptian Instruments– Ideal for meditation and reflection on the Divine and for the practice of spiritual programs and Yoga exercise sessions.

©1999 By Muata Ashby
CD $14.99 –

MERIT'S INSPIRATION
**NEW Egyptian Yoga Music CD
by Sehu Maa
Ancient Egyptian Music CD**
Instrumental Music played on reproductions of Ancient Egyptian Instruments– Ideal for meditation and reflection on the Divine and for the practice of spiritual programs and Yoga exercise sessions.
©1999 By
Muata Ashby
CD $14.99 –
UPC# 761527100429

ANORATIONS TO RA AND HETHERU
**NEW Egyptian Yoga Music CD
By Sehu Maa (Muata Ashby)
Based on the Words of Power of Ra and HetHeru**
played on reproductions of Ancient Egyptian Instruments **Ancient Egyptian Instruments used: Voice, Clapping, Nefer Lute, Tar Drum, Sistrums, Cymbals** – The Chants, Devotions, Rhythms and Festive Songs Of the Neteru – Ideal for meditation, and devotional singing and dancing.

©1999 By Muata Ashby
CD $14.99 –
UPC# 761527100221

SONGS TO ASAR ASET AND HERU
NEW
Egyptian Yoga Music CD
By Sehu Maa

played on reproductions of Ancient Egyptian Instruments– The Chants, Devotions, Rhythms and Festive Songs Of the Neteru - Ideal for meditation, and devotional singing and dancing.
Based on the Words of Power of Asar (Asar), Aset (Aset) and Heru (Heru) Om Asar Aset Heru is the third in a series of musical explorations of the Kemetic (Ancient Egyptian) tradition of music. Its ideas are based on the Ancient Egyptian Religion of Asar, Aset and Heru and it is designed for listening, meditation and worship. ©1999 By Muata Ashby
CD $14.99 –
UPC# 761527100122

HAARI OM: ANCIENT EGYPT MEETS INDIA IN MUSIC
NEW Music CD
By Sehu Maa

The Chants, Devotions, Rhythms and Festive Songs Of the Ancient Egypt and India, harmonized and played on reproductions of ancient instruments along with modern instruments and beats. Ideal for meditation, and devotional singing and dancing.

Haari Om is the fourth in a series of musical explorations of the Kemetic (Ancient Egyptian) and Indian traditions of music, chanting and devotional spiritual practice. Its ideas are based on the Ancient Egyptian Yoga spirituality and Indian Yoga spirituality.
©1999 By Muata Ashby
CD $14.99 –
UPC# 761527100528

RA AKHU: THE GLORIOUS LIGHT
NEW
Egyptian Yoga Music CD
By Sehu Maa

The fifth collection of original music compositions based on the Teachings and Words of The Trinity, the God Asar and the Goddess Nebethet, the Divinity Aten, the God Heru, and the Special Meditation Hekau or Words of Power of Ra from the Ancient Egyptian Tomb of Seti I and more... played on reproductions of Ancient Egyptian Instruments and modern instruments - Ancient Egyptian Instruments used: **Voice, Clapping, Nefer Lute, Tar Drum, Sistrums, Cymbals**
— The Chants, Devotions, Rhythms and Festive Songs Of the Neteru – Ideal for meditation, and devotional singing and dancing.
©1999 By Muata Ashby
CD $14.99 –
UPC# 761527100825

GLORIES OF THE DIVINE MOTHER
Based on the hieroglyphic text of the worship of Goddess Net.
The Glories of The Great Mother
©2000 Muata Ashby
CD $14.99 UPC# 761527101129`

Order Form

Telephone orders: Call Toll Free: 1(305) 378-6253. Have your AMEX, Optima, Visa or MasterCard ready.

Fax orders: 1-(305) 378-6253   E-MAIL ADDRESS: Semayoga@aol.com

Postal Orders: Sema Institute of Yoga, P.O. Box 570459, Miami, Fl. 33257. USA.

Please send the following books and / or tapes.

ITEM

_____Cost $_____
_____Cost $_____
_____Cost $_____
_____Cost $_____
_____Cost $_____

Total $_____

Name:_____

Physical Address:_____

City:_____ State:_____ Zip:_____

Sales tax: Please add 6.5% for books shipped to Florida addresses

_____Shipping: $6.50 for first book and .50¢ for each additional

_____Shipping: Outside US $5.00 for first book and $3.00 for each additional

_____Payment:_____

_____Check -Include Driver License #:

    _____

_____Credit card: _____ Visa, _____ MasterCard, _____ Optima,
_____ AMEX.

Card number:_____

Name on card:_____ Exp. date:_____/_____

Copyright 1995-2005 Dr. R. Muata Abhaya Ashby
Sema Institute of Yoga
P.O.Box 570459, Miami, Florida, 33257
(305) 378-6253 Fax: (305) 378-6253

www.ingramcontent.com/pod-product-compliance
Lightning Source LLC
Chambersburg PA
CBHW081106080526
44587CB00021B/3466